COMIC FAITH

ROBERT M. POLHEMUS

COMIC FAITH

The Great Tradition from Austen to Joyce

The University of Chicago Press · Chicago and London

The University of Chicago Press, Chicago 60637
The University of Chicago Press, Ltd., London

©1980 by the University of Chicago
All rights reserved. Published 1980
Printed in the United States of America
84 83 82 81 80   9 8 7 6 5 4 3 2 1

ROBERT M. POLHEMUS is Professor of English
at Stanford University.
He is the author of *The Changing World
of Anthony Trollope* and several journal articles.

Library of Congress Cataloging in Publication Data

Polhemus, Robert M.
Comic faith.

Bibliography: p.
Includes index.
1. English fiction—19th century—History and
criticism.   2. Comic, The.   3. Religion in literature.
4. Joyce, James, 1882–1941—Criticism and interpretation.   I. Title.
PR868.C63P6   823'.03   79–24856
ISBN 0–226–67320–0

FOR MARY

CONTENTS

CONTENTS

ACKNOWLEDGMENTS

Many people have helped me in making this book. I want to express my deep gratitude to Ian Watt, Wilfred Stone, Thomas C. Moser, W. Bliss Carnochan, John Henry Raleigh, George Levine, and John A. Miles, Jr., for reading the entire manuscript and giving me useful, wise, and generous criticism. I have also benefited greatly from the sensitive reading of particular chapters and from the suggestions and encouragement I have received from Elizabeth Hamilton Polhemus, Rebecca Reynolds, David Riggs, John Bishop, Nicholas Bromell, William Chace, Karen Chase, Vincent Cheng, Barbara Charlesworth Gelpi, Susan Lowell Humphreys, Anne K. Mellor, and Susan Morgan.

The good sense, patience, and editorial exactitude of Linda Jo Bartholomew also aided me greatly in preparing the manuscript for publication, and I owe thanks, too, to Polly Tooker for her outstanding typing and decoding skills and her general wisdom; to Sue Riggs for her skill in preparing the index; to Pat Hishiki, Judi Friedlander, and Mary Loeffelholz for their bibliographical work; and to Denise D'Aunno and Paul Angelchik for their time and general assistance.

I also wish to acknowledge my gratitude to my students and friends at Stanford for the contributions they have made to my thinking over the past decade; to the Stanford English Department for its generous support, particularly to George Dekker and Carolyn Fetler; and to the National Endowment for the Humanities, whose award of a Junior Fellowship allowed me to begin the study that finds its completion here.

Finally, I am indebted to my father, J. A. Polhemus, Jr., for my first lessons in understanding the value and importance of comedy, and to my children, Camilla, Mack, Joe, and Andra, for sustaining and proving my own comic faith. My greatest debt is to Mary Munter, whose practical help, generosity, and love enabled me to complete this book.

COMIC FAITH

Comedy is an escape not from truth, but from despair:
a narrow escape into faith.

Christopher Fry

1

INTRODUCTION

Worlds Without End

But comedy has had no history because it was not at first treated
seriously.

Aristotle[1]

PURPOSE

At the end of Joyce Cary's *The Horse's Mouth,* the artist Gulley
Jimson is dying, but he tells the nun attending him he feels like
laughing. "'How don't you enjoy life, mother. I should laugh all
round my neck at this minute if my shirt wasn't a bit on the tight
side.' 'It would be better for you to pray.' 'Same thing,
mother.'" That union of prayer and laughter asserts in a flash
the existence in modern life and literature of what I call *comic
faith:* a tacit belief that the world is both funny and potentially
good; a pattern of expressing or finding religious impulse, motive, and meaning in the forms of comedy; and an implicit assumption that a basis for believing in the value of life can be
found in the fact of comic expression itself.

Cary's dialogue suggests the underlying, original ties between
religious and comic celebration. It also points up the uneasy
relationship that has historically existed between comedy and
religion. It even compresses in a few words the gist of the
tension and conflict between Christian orthodoxy and comic
imagination that was crucial in generating the major British
comic fictions of the nineteenth century and, in the first part of
the twentieth century, the later writings of James Joyce. Gulley's equation of the will to laughter with an act of faith—and all

that his identification implies, culturally and aesthetically—comes directly out of the comic tradition in English prose fiction that is my subject.

I have three broad aims:

1. I want to make clear the accomplishment and significance of eight comic works of English prose by eight novelists: Austen, Peacock, Dickens, Thackeray, Trollope, Meredith, Carroll, and Joyce. These specific comic visions, which appear in a period spanning a little more than a century, running roughly from the end of the Napoleonic wars to the aftermath of World War I, constitute a profoundly consequential and distinctive literary achievement. And if we care to look for a "great tradition" in literature that promotes important "human awareness . . . of the possibilities of life,"[2] we will surely find one in these books and authors.

2. I want to stress the connection in these works between their comic intentions and religious concerns. I mean also to show how this relationship between comedy and religion develops, culminating with Joyce, who explicitly sought to make religious text out of comic writing. The best nineteenth-century comic novels express a deepening social need to supplement, broaden, mock, attack, revise, and transmute orthodox faith and the moral order established by traditional theological institutions.

Much of the essential quality of British fiction—in particular of the writings I am going to discuss—grows out of the novelists' wishes and efforts to augment, modify, or replace the Christian "divine comedy," the "scheme of redemption and resurrection to which Dante gave the name of *commedia*."[3] That universal "comic" vision had offered the hope of immortality through union with God; but for many in the nineteenth century, faith in this orthodox supernatural agency came to seem inadequate, constricting, or impossible. George Eliot, for example, bemoans the lack of a "coherent social faith and order which could perform the function of knowledge for the ardently willing soul."[4] The need for some kind of faith, however, is a human constant, and the best comic writers try to imagine new patterns, strategies, and kinds of humor for dealing with life's pressures and depredations.

Their fictions perform, in secular and hypothetical fashion, many of the conventional religious functions of the old "divine comedy." Think of what the main purposes and uses of religion are: to honor creation; to provide hope; to reconcile people to their harsh fates; to smooth over social enmity and to defend culture by authoritative moral sanction against selfish and destructive behavior; to organize and discipline the energies and emotions of people; to make people feel that they are important and part of a "chosen" group; to institutionalize ways of getting rid of guilt; to allow people to identify with righteousness and let loose wrathful indignation and hostility in good conscience; to assure them of the possibility of future well-being; to lift them out of themselves and free the spirit. Consciously or not, these novelists are trying, by means of wit, humor, and satire, to fulfill at one time or another all of these missions of religious faith. For Meredith near the end of the nineteenth century and Joyce in the early twentieth century, belief in the power of comic insight and the inclusiveness of comic form becomes itself an explicit faith. The emergence of such comic faith deserves attention.

3. I want to make a case for the centrality of comic imagination and the "sense of humor" in life by shedding light on some of their most important modern manifestations. If we can now recognize, to some extent, the validity of equating prayer and laughter—or even if we can only grasp intuitively that there is some sort of basis for the analogy—we can surmise that our culture has come to pay more conscious attention to the sense of humor and its social role than it did two hundred years ago. (It is now, in fact, considered shameful not to have a sense of humor.) No doubt, blatantly comparing prayer and laughter would have seemed shocking or incomprehensible to most thoughtful Britons in the nineteenth century, including several of the comic writers whose fiction has helped to make the analogy both enlightening and true.

What people laugh at and why, and what moves them to formalize their will to mirth in jokes or comedy, show the direction of their lives, the obsessions of their souls, and the course of their world. Comedy, of course, evolves, and we need a history of laughter—as we need, for instance, a history of love, of death, of fear of failure—to illuminate the evolution of humanity. This book is only a small part of such a record; it is highly selective; I do not intend it to be a history of Victorian humor or of comic theory in the nineteenth century or in any other time. It is, however, an inquiry into the comic form of eight documents whose implications, singly and together, about the range and nature of life ought to shatter any lingering notions that comedy is trivial or in any sense "a minor form."[5] And I mean it to show, both explicitly and implicitly, how much each comic piece can reveal about humanity's developing, cumulative, and enduring sense of humor.

Our comic sense—like our linguistic capability, our habits of reflection, our emotionally complicated love life, and our preparation of food—seems to be one of those elementary characteristics of our species that define us as human. When we discover the comic motive and understanding in great works of art, we go straight to the heart of civilization.[6]

BACKGROUND

This study, I repeat, is of particular comic fictions and writers. Its value, I hope, lies in its detailed analysis of this literature, its contribution to a greater understanding and appreciation of each of the eight authors, its careful attention to the specific significance of their comic visions, its revelation of how the complex processes of humor actually work, and its focus on the development of an integral comic tradition. I want, however, to state some of my premises about comic imagination and to speculate briefly on the comic tradition of the West, on some of its major figures, and on the background that existed for the emergence of distinguished comic fiction in the nineteenth century.

I

Comedy has had a relatively low status in the hierarchy of literary forms. Why? Why, for example, has more not been made of the achievement of British comic fiction? It may be that no English or Irish novelist has the scope of Tolstoy, the passion of Dostoyevsky, the psychological penetration of Proust, or the questing metaphysical spirit of Melville, but the European and the American novel cannot collectively match the brilliant comic performance and rich comic interpretations of life that we find in the British novel. Yet there has been a certain reluctance in influential critical circles about asserting this mastery, as if there were something a bit frivolous about this penchant for comic form. What exactly is it about the comic that has made it seem, to many, a lesser mode?

There are many answers, but a primary one is that laughter and comic revelry have been tinged with an aura of blasphemy; the comic has traditionally had to bear the stigma of sacrilege. The heritage of Greek idealism and Judeo-Christian monotheism taught men that the comic sense delights in the physical, the common, and the ephemeral and ignores or insults the spiritual and the everlasting. Plato, who lauds hierarchy and aristocracy, says that "the actions performed in comedy are a frivolous and giddy experience, demoralizing to the spirit of serious citizenship."[7] In the view of institutionalized religious and political orthodoxy, an active sense of humor has an unsafe quality about it. It is potentially destructive of order and authority because it can make them seem ludicrous; the comic, with its convulsions of mirth and its exaltations of pleasure and immediate sensual gratification, may seduce people, to their great peril, from the paths of truth, duty, and religion—from, that is, the paths that authorities wish them to take.

Those who look down on comedy do so because they believe in higher forms of truth, and the ultimate source for that hierarchical mindset is, historically, the authority of God. In Ecclesiastes we read: "I said of laughter, It is mad: and of mirth, What doeth it" (2:2), and also, "The heart of the wise is in the house of mourning; but the heart of fools is in the house of mirth" (7:4). We are steeped in this tradition, and it has meant that the comic impulse and the comic form have had to misrepresent and downplay themselves in order to gain any kind of a hearing.

I suggest, however, that we consider whether the exercise of the comic sense may not itself be a mode of religious consciousness, odd as that may seem to those who have learned to think that the words "comic" and "serious" are opposites and that religion is strictly a dignified matter of church, formalized creed, and "higher" spiritualities. The comic imagination deals in miraculous transformations and the instantaneous casting-off of burdens and sufferings. It releases sudden floods of feelings and allows the purging of enmity in play. The comic sense can cause a sensation of wholeness and integrity of being, though one that is almost always brief and passing. When we are in a festive mood and laughing, we seem to go out of our normally anxious, reflective selves into a different phase of being, and the comic flow within us dissolves our sense of limitation. Time stands still, and we feel ourselves to be the center of life. Mirth so intensifies the moment that it could be described as sanctifying life by the sheer unself-conscious vitality that it stimulates within us. No wonder, then, that the act of laughter and the surge of comic joy in a death-haunted, misery-prone creature could be, and sometimes has been, seen and felt as a natural intrusion of the miraculous into the self—as, that is, a religious experience.

If we compare comic euphoria with religious ecstasy, we readily see the ties between mirth and religious emotion: both often manifest themselves in states of rapt bliss in which people become oblivious of the ordinary circumstances and concerns of passing life. Orthodox religion has sought to preserve and immortalize life by locating the source of joy and being in a god or gods external to the mutable self and world and by organizing religious experience in churches and forms of worship that give mankind a sense of permanence and continuity. It has tried to make the life-force and faith spiritual, eternal, and accessible only through devotion and awe-inspiring ritual. It therefore must tend to deny or belittle the genuineness and value of other kinds of experience—such as a Bacchic orgy or a joke—that perform religious functions and locate the life-force and faith in the flesh.

When we turn again to Ecclesiastes, we find a prominent passage that contradicts the orthodox view of mirth I previously quoted: "Then I commended mirth, because a man hath no better thing under the sun, than to eat, and to drink, and to be merry" (8:15). That is the nub of a comic faith deeply implanted in human nature and history, and its context here in the Bible shows its religious implication. It may be, as the contradictory words of Ecclesiastes indicate, that comic mirth and orthodox faith exist in such tension and conflict with each other because they are closely intertwined psychologically and show alternate forms of the impulse to religious expression. The statement, by itself, is unequivocal, though Christianity directly contradicts it: mirth, says the preacher, is *the way;* there is nothing better than material well-being, the will to pleasure, and the rousing of the comic spirit. The overall purpose of my book is nothing more, really, than to show precisely how the import of this succinct expression of a dialectical, religious hedonism, "I commended mirth," took root and grew in the creative imaginations of some of the finest novelists of modern times.

II

I assume, conventionally, that comic modes, like tragic modes, grew out of rituals, revels, feasts, or kindred practices of an essentially religious character (most probably connected with fertility and harvest celebrations).[8] It follows that some sort of religious homage offered to the physical world was inherent in early comic form, and it is in the innate reverence for material being in comedy that I want to insist on. The comic mode is historically, psychologically, and metaphorically grounded in the physical experiences of laughter, sex, and eating.

The traditional comic form not only imitates or represents thematic variations on the regeneration of life; it also seeks to abstract and convey the emotional quality of a moment of mirth. That is what connects comic form to comic laughter and permits us, with some logic, to give the name *comedy* both to an art work and to anything that we laugh at. When people are experiencing the hilarity of the comic moment, they feel free of restraint; it is that sense of freedom and vitality that the makers of comic forms often strive to capture.

But developing religious and cultural authority sought to suppress or to control and channel the ridicule in mirth and its celebration of physical pleasure. Ridicule can threaten elites, can be disruptive, and the pursuit of pleasure can upset the principle of deferred gratification upon which developing societies depend in order to grow strong. The material world is unpredictable, and physical being decays; that, no doubt, is why the mystery religions—culminating in Christianity—succeeded so well in establishing themselves. They could promise a reality beyond the reality of unstable matter—a surety and salvation that supposedly did not rely on the caprice of nature or the unreliable agencies of men.

To understand the history and development of comic form in the West, we must keep in mind the uneasy, often hostile, but continuing and determining relationship between Christian faith and comedy. And we must consider briefly particular authors who reflect significantly on vital aspects of this connection. Influential Christians often tried to expunge from the beatific vision of their faith both tendentious mirth and the power of the sexual libido. Christ is born of a virgin and lives without carnal knowledge of woman; the Apostle Paul, himself single, counsels celibacy, and centuries later the Church mandates celibacy for the clergy. John Chrysostom proclaims that laughter and jokes come from the devil. Dante usurps the word "comedy" for the outstanding rendering in literature of Christian faith—save the Bible—and he purges it of laughter. The goal of Christianity is to transcend the world and the flesh.

Paul himself employs the comic technique of reversal as a weapon for Christian faith: "it pleased God by the foolishness of preaching to save them that believe" (1 Cor. 1:22). "If any man among you seemeth to be wise in this world, let him become a fool, that he may be wise. For wisdom of this world is foolishness with God" (1 Cor. 3:18–19). The way to truth, in other words, lies in what conventional wisdom calls folly, and that is often an unstated premise in mirth and an implicit claim of comic form. Actually, Paul is rhetorically condemning the world, calling it foolish, and using "foolishness" to mean "wisdom." Wisdom, virtue, salvation, and real life do not lie in the realm of the senses but with the Holy Spirit. To be a "fool" is the very opposite here of commending mirth and merrymaking.

In the British tradition, Chaucer, at the end of the fourteenth century, offers us, in his retraction of *The Canterbury Tales,* as striking an example as could be of orthodox Christian hostility to worldly mirth.[9] Abjectly renouncing his glorious comic gifts and accomplishment, he leaves little doubt about institutionalized, hierarchical religion's propensity to condemn comedy—here, the whole human comedy. The retraction, however, ironically echoes the sense of one of Chaucer's most famous passages: Troilus looks down from the heavens and laughs in contempt at the utter folly and worthlessness of terrestrial life and human experience. This laughter, completely subservient to authoritarian religion, ridicules all experience that does not focus on heaven and God.

III

There are, however, as Chaucer proves, signs of a vigorous comic tradition that orthodoxy had somehow to accommodate lest it alienate people by denying them any sort of comic release. The area of formal comic activity in the Christian Middle Ages is like a red-light district in a morally orthodox city, grudgingly tolerated for the public good because it dissipates dangerous tensions.[10] One example appears in the vulgar farce that enters into the miracle-play cycles, those popular dramas of the divine comedy. Another is the Latin parody, both written and oral, of Scripture and liturgy—a kind of academic humor in which clerics mock modes of their vocation and the discipline of the Church. Still others occur in the existence of licensed fools, the topsy-turvy customs of the Lord of Misrule, the Boy Bishop, and the Feast of the Ass that temporarily overthrow the normal order, and in, as Northrop Frye says, "all the dramatic activity that punctuated the Christian calendar with the rituals of an immemorial paganism," which he calls "the drama of the green world."[11]

The comedies of Shakespeare give the best evidence of an almost holy comic impulse asserting itself beyond the orthodox vision of Christian dogma.[12] Shakespearean comedy blends comic and religious experience, but the religion is not pure Christianity by any stretch of the imagination. The fairies, the magic, the wizard figures, the miracles and festivities of the fertile green setting suggest the ritual practices of suppressed religions as well as a heterodox comic imagination. Out of his comedy emerges a lovely reverence for the renewal of virtue and love in mirth. The comic resolutions in these plays depend on supernatural means, and metaphorically they do still fit into a broadly Christian framework. Shakespeare's comedies, however, stress mysterious and wonderful forces of natural regeneration operating in *this* world.

Heterodox by nature, comedy blossoms in the theological controversy and multiplicity of the Renaissance and Reformation, but ethically it is still on the defensive and must rationalize itself. Ben Jonson professes that the purpose of his *comedy of humors* is to flail the follies of his times; ridicule, the enemy of vice, serves morality. He appeals to classical authority and, implicitly, to Christian ethics in order to gain respect for comedy,

11

and he argues that he who rejects his satire rejects moral truth. For Jonson, a person's humor, or his affectation of a humor, is what makes him ludicrous, and "humor" is based on physiology. According to the medieval and ancient medical theory that he adapts, the content and flow of body fluids give people their particular dispositions, or humors. As a source of individualism, humor causes heterodoxy and strife. The influence of a dominant humor, actually or metaphorically, tends to lead one away from the moral norm and into foolish eccentricity and ethical deformity. "Humor," which later comes to mean "the thing that causes merriment," arises and moves in the body. It is of the flesh, fleshy. Theoretically, Jonsonian comedy is therefore very much in the orthodox Christian tradition: the comic playwright is a satirical scourge of God, lashing with mockery the obstreperous physicality of humorous human nature.

Actually—as is so often the case with comic art—the effect of Jonson's comedy is much more various than his professed intention. It seethes with volatile energy. Plays like *The Alchemist* and *Volpone* dramatize the eruption of physical humor on the world's stage that was the Renaissance, and they express such marvelous opportunities for revel in the foolishness and corruption of the earth that by comparison the call of heavenly wisdom can seem muffled and pallid.

Part of the deep and abiding conflict between Christian authority and comic impulse shows through in the history of the English theater. The mockery of Puritans and their ilk, and, more important, the natural comic stress on physical love and mating that we see in Shakespeare and Jonson, continued and developed in the seventeenth-century stage comedy until the theaters were closed by the religious. The sexual intrigue of Restoration comedy and its heritage provoked great and successful pressure from religious authority to censor and sometimes to suppress comic drama. The steady war of orthodoxy on sexual content in comic forms has had a very great influence on the shape of comic fiction, and, since the beginning of the eighteenth century, the comic artist who openly breaks from the religious tradition of sexual repression has always risked quick and firm censorship. One of the main reasons why the comic masters of the eighteenth century, like Fielding, Sterne, and Smollett, turned to prose fiction and helped make the novel rise was that they could get the comedy of physical life into print if not onto the stage. Even in the later, more censorious, Victorian age, the comedy of irrepressible sex life burst out, though in sublimated ways.

IV

The fact that four of the men whose work is central to the development of comic prose fiction—Erasmus, Rabelais, Swift, and Sterne—were ordained clerics and professional churchmen shows a massive change taking place in cultural sensibility. As their respective contributions indicate, a comic tradition in literature was steadily gathering life and strength, and each of them put his stamp on it. In their own ways they all tried to reconcile their comic and satirical impulses with a Christian vocation, and in each case comic expression and a sense of humor gave them a way of rationalizing their faith.

By the end of *The Praise of Folly,* Erasmus sanctifies folly and unifies it with the spirit of Christianity. At first folly is the benighted agent of shortsighted worldliness, but he then transforms her into the "foolish" spirit, from a worldly point of view, of self-sacrifice and charity. Erasmus's little book in Latin, reflecting the Pauline text, imbues comic folly with moral authority and thus sets a precedent for putting comedy on a respectable footing. Erasmus shows that comic folly can be rehabilitated and used to put life in proper perspective. He uses folly, for example, to criticize and ridicule the sinful pride of the Church.

Rabelais, from within the Church, launches an exuberant satire on the abstraction and silly remoteness of scholasticism and makes a gigantic joke—literally—out of its attempt to stifle the senses. But what has been branded as the monstrousness of the flesh turns out in *Gargantua and Pantagruel* to be full of mirth. Rabelais gives to the prose comic tradition a license to indulge in an outpouring of hyperbolic language and gross physical humor that conveys the wild energy of God's material creation.

Swift uses his satirical humor as a deadly moral weapon to condemn the world. His satire plays on the ugliness of the flesh and the moral repulsiveness of unredeemed human nature. Much of his art of savage indignation and black humor comes out of the old *memento mori, danse macabre* Christian tradition, but his subtle, scathing irony is new and very important in the history of comic prose fiction. His irony creates a community of

13

ridicule between the author and reader, and it becomes a mode of comic conspiracy between them against various scapegoats. Thackeray's pose in the Victorian period, for instance, as a weekday preacher writing comic satire for the moral edification of his reading public, would be unthinkable had not Swift created a congregation for satire.

Sterne, in contrast, coming later, makes a sort of religion of good humor. He was, as Ian Watt says, "at one with the affirmative, and indeed somewhat complacent, latitudinarian Christianity of his age,"[13] as were Fielding and Goldsmith. The ridicule of the flesh, by which comedy had appeased an earlier and fiercer Christian orthodoxy and won its grudging imprimatur, becomes in Sterne the verbal farce of sexual innuendo. It mocks the pride of those who would deny the physical basis of life. Despite the superficial chaos and freakishness of life in *Tristram Shandy,* it contains a moral order and good humor that seem to come ultimately from the benevolence of divine providence. Though the characters ride private hobby-horses and can't communicate well, they at least share a commonality of having their own quirkish humors and a community, too, of sympathy and sentiment. In Sterne, humor, once the proof of man's sinful and corrupt material nature, now forms a blessed part of God's creation. His casual attitude about sex has offended devotees of the religious or of high seriousness, but, as Stuart Tave has shown, he was instrumental in the process by which a sense of humor became considered a virtue.[14]

v

Long before Sterne parodied the novelistic form, Cervantes—the most important figure in establishing a great comic tradition in the novel—had made parody of literary conventions a staple of comic prose. Chivalric romance was his specific target, but there was even bigger game. *Don Quixote* begins, as comedy so often does, in the desire to ridicule and expose some unrealistic, incongruous form of behavior—in this case, mad knight-errantry in a mundane world—but the satire reflects on any form of spiritual faith. Also, setting Don Quixote's blind idealism against Sancho Panza's peasant materialism allows readers to infer a potentially subversive message about living by blind faith in the supposed word of God. Structurally, Cervantes shows how to make a fictional world resonate by bringing together two vivid characters who, apprehending reality in entirely different ways, reflect upon each other in an extended comic dialectic.

By the end of *Don Quixote* Cervantes has transcended his original intentions and shown that the ridiculous can be sublime: the comic imagination can change reality. He makes us respect the pluralism of life and the shifting nature of appearance and reality; most originally, he manages to give readers an option of respecting and loving a truly ridiculous and eccentric character—that is, an option of *embracing the humorous.* He contradicts himself, and he also chastises the unorthodox and the fanciful, but he opens up a whole new range of possibilities for the comic imagination. Whether or not it was his intention, his book undermines the ingrained idea that a comic work must deal with "the low," that is, with people relatively inconsequential or morally inferior.

Henry Fielding, very much a disciple of Cervantes, ostensibly set out in *Joseph Andrews* to parody the romantic nonsense and hypocritical morality of Richardson's *Pamela,* but the center of his novel becomes the quixotic knight-cleric of Christianity, Parson Adams. In the figure of Adams he uses comedy to humanize Christian faith, and Adam's benevolence and charity make the humor "amiable."[15] Fielding works to fuse Christian and comic vision by making Adams at once ridiculous and an admirable defender of a sacred and humane faith. He is trying with Adams to relax tension between the will to Christian belief and the impulse to ridicule. (Trollope would do the same thing a hundred years later.) Fielding's fusion of Christian assumptions and a sense of humor became a model for the less sanguine novelists of the nineteenth century.

In the preface to *Joseph Andrews,* Fielding calls his work a "comic epic-poem in prose."[16] The actions proper to comic prose, he says, are "light and ridiculous," the characters inferior in rank and manners. He wants to give the sanction of classical tradition to a form that, he admits, does not yet exist in the language. The novel as a genre and comic fiction were both still suspect, and his practice is therefore often at odds with his comic theory. Notice that Fielding breaks down the categorical structure for comic characters in the figure of Parson Adams even while he is trying to set it up in theory. What matters most in his preface is that ambition to write a comic epic in prose. The desire to achieve epic quality and significance in comic fiction would be shared by novelists as diverse as Dickens, Thackeray, Meredith, and Joyce.

VI

John Bunyan's *The Pilgrim's Progress* (1675), the Protestant prose allegory of divine comedy that for two centuries nearly every literate English-speaking person read, begins with a remarkably powerful image. Christian starts off on his journey to salvation, and when his family tries to make him come back home, Bunyan writes: "the man put his fingers in his ears, and ran on, crying Life! life! eternal life!" That cry, screaming out the motive of one Protestant's faith, also articulates the motive of comic impulse; it too, in its way, turns a deaf ear to everything but the call of life. Institutional religion seeks immortality by offering an afterlife; the comic sense works by momentarily purging the mind of unpleasant contents—such as the consciousness that "I am a creature who must die." Comic laughter produces within us a surge of pure life uncontaminated by thanatos. That intense comic pleasure, however, cannot be sustained, and a system able to convince people that it has the key to "eternal life," even if it requires the regulation of conduct and pleasure—including comic pleasure—will obscure the life-enhancing role of comedy.

And yet people must live in this world and do not, for the most part, perceive themselves or others living in afterlife or spiritual worlds. The revival of, and comparatively tolerant attitude toward, comic art in the British Reformation, Renaissance, and Restoration eras signifies the widespread ideological turning-back-to-the-world. Bunyan allegorizes in the freshly developing form of prose fiction the gospel of redemption and depicts worldly life as a dangerous but successful adventure story, with salvation as the happy ending. The very fact that he would do so shows the tremendous resurgent pull of the world and the growing pressure to remodel and reinterpret mythic patterns of regeneration.

The history of the seventeenth and eighteenth centuries shows man's increasing ability to control nature and to exploit the riches of the earth. More was constantly being discovered about the world and its workings; the rudiments of modern science were appearing; capitalism was taking shape. For writers like Defoe and Richardson, as we see in the plots of *Robinson Crusoe, Moll Flanders,* and *Pamela,* the world offers fine new opportunities for enrichment. This very growth of success in mastering the world would eventually sap credence in the divine comedy of eternal life. According to Lawrence Stone, "the concept of rationality developed in the West in the eighteenth century concurrently with the concept of individualism. In consequence the probability of personal extinction became at the same time more logically compelling and more emotionally unacceptable." And he adds, "The intellectual and psychological tension has actually intensified in the last 200 years."[17]

The basic plot of comic form, I have surmised, grew out of the process and hope of regeneration. For nearly two millennia Christianity had spiritualized the process and, with its powers of consolation, had expropriated and almost completely controlled the pattern of comic vision, suppressing or drastically minimizing the cultural importance of other variations on comic plot and form. It had officially monopolized the narrative content and structure of the human comedy. With an ebbing of deep faith in the Christian comedy of afterlife, people would naturally be looking for ways in which they could plausibly relate themselves to the whole regenerative process of life—looking, that is, for ways of supplementing the divine comic vision. The purpose of comedy is to strengthen our hold on life. Sterne, for example, states one of the principal ideas behind the representation of humor and the ludicrous in the eighteenth century: "True *Shandeism,* think what you will against it, opens the heart and lungs, and like all those affections which partake of its nature, it forces the blood and other vital fluids of the body to run freely thro' its channels, and makes the wheel of life run long and chearfully round."[18]

The comic could not command wide and official respect as long as there were subjects of high importance it was forbidden to treat. Fielding's Parson Adams, Goldsmith's Vicar of Wakefield, Smollett's satire of Humphry Clinker's preaching, and Sterne's mockery of Dr. Slop's Catholicism all show that by the start of the nineteenth century, comic fiction has a history of touching upon religious matters and characters. Everywhere in eighteenth-century fiction we find both humor and the comic dream of earthly abundance and rising social status being used to bolster the Christian vision of regeneration. But the intrusion of broad comedy and farce into latitudinarian Christian theology shows that for many people the power of Christian doctrine to awe was beginning to weaken.

Even so, I believe that the eighteenth-century comic fiction of Fielding, Smollett, Sterne, Goldsmith, and Fanny Burney is still, in fact as well as in name, orthodoxly Christian and that their visions of creation are comprehended by Christian faith and a Christian God. In the great nineteenth-century comic fictions, whose authors often show more deference to organized religion—to what Matthew Arnold calls the Hebraism of their age—and proclaim their orthodoxy, that is not generally so. These later comic writers reject the supernaturalism on which most previous comedy is based. The orthodox Christian view of creation is no longer sufficient by itself, in their comic fiction, to sustain or provide faith in the goodness or the continuity of life. That view must be overcome or transmuted, even while the loss of its efficacy and solace is regretted, mourned, and even denied.

I suggest that the existence of strong puritanical strains of Christianity in post-Renaissance Britain—present, for example, in the faith of the various seventeenth-century nonconformist Protestants, the Irish Catholics, the eighteenth-century Methodists, and the nineteenth-century evangelicals—has much to do historically with the flourishing of comedy in Victorian and modern British fiction. Puritanical religion's repressiveness, its rigidities, its hostility to various kinds of artistic expression, its distrust of levity, its very success in coercing people to accept certain codes of moral behavior, and its sometimes unintentional assault on the Established Church's role in guarding truth and faith all helped to arouse longings for the vision, release, and ridicule of comedy. And, since the Puritan side of religion did not hold a totalitarian power of censorship in the relatively latitudinarian British world, it not only provoked a desire for comic literature, it could not stop comic writers from reaching the public.

With the cataclysmic social upheavals and the release of new energies and forces in the nineteenth century, the opportunity and even the necessity grew for the makers of comic fiction to compose secular visions able to convince people imaginatively of the possibilities of attaching themselves to large processes of regeneration. Potentially the greatest effects available in comic

18

art would seem to be attainable by combining the intensity of the comic moment—the mood of laughter and release—with the promise of some form of enduring life in which we have a part, and that is what the best modern comic fiction achieves. It asserts, as we shall see, the power of the mind and body over the universe of death. To the sudden flow of mirth, it adds comic structure.

VII

One more fact of literary and social history has the utmost importance for nineteenth-century comic fiction: the emergence and prominence of women as subjects, authors, and readers of eighteenth-century novels. In the culture of male supremacy, comedy, relatively speaking, has a built-in feminist bias. It deals with generational matters and the relations of the sexes; and, in matters of the heart, to say nothing of reproduction, the sexes are equally concerned. Comedy is strongest just where religion had been weakest: in opening up the great subject of sexual identity and examining the always difficult and fascinating relationships between men and women. Christianity, with its hope for the meek and the oppressed in a future state and its stress on personal salvation, had offered women much solace, but a religion of spirituality run on earth by and for men had not much concerned itself with feminine points of view. Comic art, relegated to treating the "low," had usually done a better job than other literary forms of holding the mirror up to the nature of women's lives, but by 1800 the potential for portraying women in comic fiction had barely been touched. Even the work of Fanny Burney, the first English female comic novelist of any consequence, hardly intimates that comic fiction could become a chief means for exploring the individualization of women's lives and the sexual revolution that were well under way at the beginning of the nineteenth century.

PROCEDURE

I

Following Ecclesiastes, I consider comedy a commendation of mirth, and following Dr. Johnson I define comedy as a *"repre-*

19

sentation of human life, as may excite mirth."[19] Furthermore, for the purposes of this study, I stipulate that a comic work of literature must (1) seek or tend to be funny and (2) have a happy ending. By "happy" I mean simply an ending to which the normal audience response is "This should be."[20] (A happy ending thus could be the death of Hitler as well as the birth of twins; it could even be the birth of twin Hitlers, if the story could convince us that that fate is what the world in this fiction deserves.) A happy ending represents the successful conclusion of a given segment of time and stands as a metaphor for the success, through all time, of human life and will.

We can properly apply the terms "comic" and "comedy" to prose fiction as well as drama when novelists explicitly intend their books to be funny and end happily. I have chosen to discuss only fictions that were consciously meant to be comic in form and effect, and to focus closely on just one work by each author. Each of these novels offers a distinctive comic vision but one that relates significantly to those of the other writers. By the term *comic vision* I mean the novelist's particular insight and sense of the world that allow him or her to find or "excite" mirth, to justify life, and to imagine the means of its benevolent regeneration in the future.

I have selected what I think are the major comic visions of British prose fiction that come out of nineteenth-century experience. Their creators wrote with serious moral purpose, even if that purpose was to ridicule existing moral conventions and to show where lay the hope for joy in life. Whether or not others agree with all my choices, I believe that few who read the language of these fictions carefully would deny that, individually and together, they reflect with extraordinary percipience upon modern human conditions.

My method is to identify and define the kind of comedy each of the authors wrote, to describe, in the divisions and subsections of my chapters, the comic structure and components of each work, to analyze its comic effects and the means by which it "may excite mirth," and, while doing so, to meditate upon the larger meanings and implications that the comedy reveals. Each book, I reiterate, offers us something crucially important for understanding what modern comedy is and how it typically works. I have made use of much social and psychological theory of comedy, humor, and wit, but I have scrupulously tried to avoid imposing comic theory reductively on these texts. From each work there emerges, upon close reading, a clear organizing pattern of human nature and procedure that illuminates its comic vision. It can often be summed up in one word. For Dickens, for example, it is "expression"; for Thackeray, "perspective"; for Carroll, "regression"; for Meredith, "egoism." But we can also see that all of these structuring concepts overlap and blend. Each comic vision, we will find, partakes of all, and later writers learn directly or indirectly from earlier ones; it is hard, for example, to conceive of Trollope's comedy without Austen's, Meredith's without Peacock's, Joyce's without Dickens's and Carroll's. I will proceed inductively and chronologically, except that I will take up Meredith's *The Egoist* (1879) before Carroll's *Through the Looking-Glass* (1871), since Carroll bears more directly on historical modernism, on twentieth-century modes of comedy, and, in particular, on Joyce.

I am going to quote liberally from the books and discuss particular prose in detail. I have chosen, however, to analyze and speculate on only that which helps to illustrate the strategies and motives of our collective comic processes. Passage after passage will reveal shrewd and entertaining attempts to understand, render, and make fun of the mystery of things. Since key passages may epitomize the significance of a whole novel or telling parts of it, I will identify and refer to excerpts that show the structuring principle of the comedy. Moreover, I believe that, more than ever, we need to be reminded of, and to confront personally, the transforming power of what we still, conventionally, may call imaginative literature and to understand its reverberating quality.

One of the greatest problems in literary studies is that the prose of a long novel can be as dense and highly charged as the language of poetry. Ten pages of *Vanity Fair* or *Martin Chuzzlewit* may have as much import and human consequence as, let us say, T. S. Eliot's *The Waste Land,* sacrilege though it be to say so. Because we cannot give the language of huge novels the intense scrutiny we give to a few lines of verse, our study of fiction—particularly comic fiction—has been comparatively spotty and superficial.

My focus is on the comic texts themselves. My general arguments and ideas grow out of my readings of these particular novels, and, in organizing my discussions and dividing them into parts, I try to reflect the organic quality of each work's comedy and to avoid squeezing it into any reductive critical system. Though I obviously owe great debts to other readers and critics—debts that I seek to acknowledge in my notes and bibliography, no doubt with very imperfect success—I deem it essential that my discourse not get bogged down in other commentators and secondary material. Direct confrontation with the specific language of these comic fictions is always my burden and my goal.

The truth of literary criticism is tentative. I am fully aware of—and I emphasize—the hypothetical nature of my speculation on these books and the evolving connection between comedy and religious function that I find in them; but I hope that, by the end of this inquiry, the existence of this tie and of a dynamic comic tradition embodying a quest for comic faith will impress itself upon most readers.

II

"Subjects have their fates," says Louis Cazamian in *The Development of English Humor*,[21] and he goes on to state that it is often the fate of disquisitions on the comic to seem grim and dreary because thinking about laughter reminds us of the pleasures of humor without being able to arouse it. If that is the fate of this book, I am sorry, but so be it. The subject is serious. It is important that we see the force of comic language and that we try to understand what comic faith is and how it came into being. People crave mirth and comic vision, and we can perhaps see why, and what it is they hope to get, by looking patiently at examples of the art that generates comedy and in which it radiates.

Hannah Arendt quotes Berthold Brecht's remark, "One may say that tragedy deals with the sufferings of mankind in a less serious way than comedy." She adds, "This of course is a shocking statement; I think that at the same time it is entirely true."[22] They mean, I think, that comic vision does not give to suffering and to evil a dangerous romantic grandeur or an inevitable dominance. Instead, it makes suffering mean and seeks to transcend it. Comic vision is also very serious about the *joys,* as well as the sufferings, of mankind, more serious in one way than organized religions have often been: growing out of a transitory pleasure, comedy does not disparage or devalue the passing joys and victories in the world. Comic faith seeks something less grandiose and more reasonable than infinite or permanent happiness and blessed immortality: it seeks more joyful life in a lasting world. The comic fictions that I am going to discuss give us openings to the future and show the noble and ludicrous human struggle to create worlds without end.

2

AUSTEN'S *EMMA* (1816)

The Comedy of Union

What . . . is inseparable from the comic is an infinite geniality and
confidence capable of rising superior to its own contradiction . . . .
G. W. F. Hegel[1]

. . . it was all in unison; words, conduct, discretion, and indiscre-
tion, told the same story.
Jane Austen, *Emma*[2]

Jane Austen was the first woman to write great comic fiction in
the English language. Nothing about her is more important or
more original than the comic vision and the sense of humor that
Emma shows, and no word signifies more in the novel than the
last one, "union." The comedy works to raise and resolve tensions and conflicts between self and society, inner and outer
life, imagination and truth, gaiety and seriousness, wit and decorum; it brings together a sense of the good and a sense of the
ridiculous. From the opening, "Emma Woodhouse, handsome,
clever, and rich, with a comfortable home and happy disposition, *seemed to unite* some of the best blessings of existence," to
the end, "the wishes, the hopes, the confidence, the predictions
of the small band of true friends who witnessed the ceremony,
were fully answered in the perfect happiness of the *union*"
(italics mine), the book moves dialectically to a joyous state of
fusion and balance. What makes life good in *Emma* is the blend
of comic perception and ethical sensibility.[3]

The happy ending, for Austen, lies in the necessary union of
the moral and the comic imagination, and by that I mean
something more than the platitude, "her comedy is moral." I am
saying that, in the logic of *Emma,* morality includes a comic
understanding of things and that life without the resources of a
sense of humor has little value. Comedy itself becomes indispensable to Austen in finding and showing the goodness of

24

being, and that seems to me new in *Emma* and different from Austen's predecessors in comic fiction.

I

Anyone who reads Jane Austen's letters and fiction carefully can sense the tension between her urge to be funny and her will to uphold moral orthodoxy. Commenting on *Emma,* she indirectly tells us about the contradiction she felt: "I am very strongly haunted with the idea that to those readers who have preferred *Pride and Prejudice* it will appear inferior in wit, and to those who have preferred *Mansfield Park* inferior in good sense."[4] To appreciate the drama and achievement of *Emma,* we must realize how deep were her passions for both reverence and ridicule and how hard it was to reconcile them. *Mansfield Park* shows them in conflict. Wit may turn wicked, but complete acquiescence to all received moral proprieties may pall and stifle the verve of personality. In this novel, however, a well-developed sense of humor goes with frivolity and immorality. Austen dramatizes the blasphemous potential of humor to rock religious convention in the exchange of remarks between witty, bad Mary Crawford and pious Edmund and Fanny as they tour the Rushworth Chapel and grounds. I quote this passage because it shows so clearly the conflict in its author: she was disposed to utter—through comic license—daring satirical thoughts and to ridicule the false façade of society's moral structure; but she was also genuinely inspired to support and honor traditional institutionalized Christianity.

> Mrs. Rushworth began her relation. . . . "Prayers were always read . . . by the domestic chaplain, within the memory of many. But the late Mr. Rushworth left it off."
>
> "Every generation has its improvements," said Miss Crawford, with a smile, to Edmund. . . .
>
> "It is a pity," cried Fanny, "that the custom should have been discontinued. It was a valuable part of former times. . . ."
>
> "Very fine indeed!" said Miss Crawford, laughing. "It must do the heads of the family a great deal of good to force all the poor housemaids and footmen to leave business and pleasure, and say their prayers here twice a day,

25

while they are inventing excuses themselves for staying away."...

For a few moments she was unanswered. Fanny coloured and looked at Edmund, but felt too angry for speech; and *he* needed a little recollection before he could say, "Your lively mind can hardly be serious even on serious subjects." [*MP,* 86–87]

We are getting in this scene a split between orthodox religious views and the insights of comedy, and that makes it qualitatively different from the humor of earlier prose writers—such as Swift, Fielding, and Sterne—who make fun of religious people but not of true piety. Austen here mocks, implicitly at least, the genuinely pious and the limitations of their faith. Shortly after viewing the chapel, the three characters walk outside, and Mary learns that Edmund is to be ordained:

" . . . So you are to be a clergyman, Mr. Bertram . . . . But why . . . ?"

"Do you think the church itself never chosen then?"

"*Never* is a black word. But yes, in the *never* of conversation which means *not very often,* I do think it. For what is to be done in the church? . . . A clergyman is nothing."

"The *nothing* of conversation has its gradation, I hope, as well as the *never.* . . . But I cannot call that situation nothing, which has the charge of all that is of the first importance to mankind, individually or collectively considered, temporally and eternally—which has the guardianship of religion and morals, and consequently of the manners which result from their influence. No one here can call the *office* nothing. . . ."

"Certainly," said Fanny with gentle earnestness.

"There," cried Miss Crawford, "you have quite convinced Miss Price already."

"I wish I could convince Miss Crawford too."

"I do not think you ever will," said she with an arch smile; "I am just as much surprised now as I was at first that you should intend to take orders. You really are fit for something better. Come, do change your mind. It is not too late. . . ."

[H]e was not yet so much in love as to measure distance, or reckon time, with feminine lawlessness. [*MP,* 91–94]

The author of this dialogue loved both wit and piety, but they sometimes clashed. The different voices of Mary Crawford, Fanny Price, and Edmund Bertram *all* spoke in her mind, and though *Mansfield Park* suppresses Mary and her disruptive irresponsibility, Austen's idea of the full potential of personality includes a radiant sense of humor and brings her to create Emma, the character, and *Emma,* the novel.

II

"Feminine lawlessness": that ironic and interesting phrase sheds light on the comedy in *Emma*. I want to argue that the inadequacies and the constraints of her patriarchal society could not help but stir rebellious impulses—deflected and sublimated though they might be—in a woman of genius and relative leisure like Austen and that her comedy was a way of both expressing and controlling her critical spirit. Her father and her brother, whom she admired, were clergymen, and she had both a brilliant intellect and a deep pastoral concern for the moral well-being of people. But of course, in the Anglican Church there could be no vocation for her, no outlet for her ethical imagination or talents. In her feminine life, she felt that the moral order of conventional faith, even though she might love and respect it as much as she did her father and embrace it with all her conscious mind, was lacking something essential. To reconcile her intelligence to the world and to preserve orthodox allegiances, she needed a transforming comic imagination. Life without a highly developed sense of the ridiculous would not do, because the solemn, serious law—the set of mores that was in the keeping of men—was, in a fundamental way, oppressive and insufficient. In her art, therefore, a justified "feminine lawlessness" takes the shape of comic vision and unites with the world to broaden and change the possibilities of life.

We can see a union of feminine independence, commitment to comedy, and implied criticism of the male-dominated, parochial moral order developing in Austen's correspondence with J. S. Clarke, domestic chaplain to the Prince Regent. He had asked her "to delineate in some future Work the Habits of Life and Character and enthusiasm of a Clergyman," and she answered: "I am quite honoured by your thinking me capable of drawing such a clergyman as you gave the sketch of in your note of Nov. 16th. But I assure you I am *not*. The comic part of the character I might be equal to, but not the good, the enthusiastic, the literary."

Why not? Her self-deprecating reasons carry the ironic undertone of an indictment of a system that kept her in comparative ignorance:

> Such a man's conversation must at times be on subjects of science and philosophy, of which I know nothing; or at least be occasionally abundant in quotations and allusions which a woman who, like me, knows only her own mother tongue, and has read very little in that, would be totally without the power of giving. A classical education, or at any rate a very extensive acquaintance with English literature, ancient and modern, appears to me quite indispensable for the person who would do any justice to your clergyman; and I think I may boast myself to be, with all possible vanity, the most unlearned and uninformed female who ever dared to be an authoress.

When Clarke again asked that she write about "an English clergyman" and suggested that she dedicate "to Prince Leopold: any historical romance, illustrative of the history of the august House of Cobourg," she replied: "I could not sit seriously down to write a serious romance under any other motive than to save my life; and if it were indispensable for me to keep it up and never relax into laughing at myself or other people, I am sure I should be hung before I had finished the first chapter."[5]

John Henry Newman, after praising Austen's *Emma,* remarked, "What vile creatures her parsons are!"[6] One reason why they might seem so becomes clear if we substitute "woman" for "man" in the following excerpt from Shaftesbury's essay "The Freedom of Wit and Humour" (1709): "The natural free spirits of ingenious man, if imprisoned or controlled, will find out other ways of motion to relieve themselves in their constraint; and whether it be in burlesque, mimicry or buffoonery, they will be glad at any rate to vent themselves, and be revenged on their constrainers. . . . 'Tis the persecuting spirit has raised the bantering one."[7] That, of course, has profound implications, not only for the development of Austen's comedy, but for the relationship between nineteenth-century comic fiction and institutionalized Christianity with its powers of so-

28

cial "constraint." A century and a half after Shaftesbury wrote, the Victorian novelist Margaret Oliphant would discuss Austen with great sympathy for her plight and, though wrong in some details, would illuminate beautifully both the matrix of her comic art and the quiet revolution of feeling that that comedy signifies:

> Mr Austen Leigh...throws out...a passing gleam of light upon the fine vein of feminine cynicism which pervades his aunt's mind. It is something altogether different from the rude and brutal male quality that bears the same name. It is the soft and silent disbelief of a spectator who has to look at a great many things without showing any outward discomposure, and who has learned to give up any moral classification of social sins, and to place them instead on the level of absurdities.... the feminine cynicism which we attribute to Miss Austen...includes a great deal that is amiable, and is full of toleration and patience, and that habit of making allowance for others which lies at the bottom of all human charity. But yet it is not charity, and its toleration has none of the sweetness which proceeds from that highest of Christian graces. It is not absolute contempt either, but only a softened tone of general disbelief—amusement, nay enjoyment, of all those humours of humanity.... [N]o power has constituted her her brother's keeper. She has but the faculty of seeing her brother clearly all round as if he were a statue, identifying all his absurdities.[8]

What Mrs. Oliphant ascribes to Austen is in fact a way of seeing and dealing with social life that has within it not only the potential for apostasy from orthodoxy but the seeds of an alternative faith as well. A sense of humor playing over existence could become a way of finding self-confidence and transforming the meaning of life.

The comic motive that Thomas Hobbes identified in his notorious explanation of laughter moves Austen and animates *Emma: "Sudden Glory,* is the passion which maketh those *Grimaces* called LAUGHTER; and is caused either by some sudden act of their own, that pleaseth them; or by the apprehension of some deformed thing in another, in comparison whereof they suddenly applaud themselves."[9] Notice that the comic, in this definition, is a kind of instant election, a surge of well-being that resembles a religious conviction of salvation, except that it is transitory: *Emma* renders the elective, self-esteeming powers of the comic, but Austen also claims for it more positive and socially responsible functions. I think she wanted to use comedy as a means of reconciling herself to traditional faith by releasing doubts and resentments harmlessly. Poised between the decorous rationalization of eighteenth-century society's conformist religion and the restless energy and ambition of nineteenth-century individualism, she was striving for a form and a creation that would preserve the best of the past, including Christian ethics, but would allow for the change and development her expanding feminine soul craved.

Kant, shortly before *Emma* was written, said, in discussing the comic, "Laughter is an affection arising from the sudden transformation of a strained expectation into nothing."[10] Austen's comedy transcends this idea by its power to turn "nothing" into something: "A mind lively and at ease, can do with seeing nothing, and can see nothing that does not answer" (233), she says of Emma in a crucial sentence. It is a comic understanding that creates such a mind and infuses nothingness with worth and gaiety. Says King Lear, the accursed father-hero of the most piteous and terrible of all tragedies, proclaiming the failure of human generation and creativity: "Nothing will come of nothing." But for Emma, the blessed daughter-heroine, the comic imagination plays with her "nothing" and, dispelling the threat of nihilism, makes from it meaning and pleasure. One comic union of the novel is the marriage of comedy itself with the world; the ability to see what is ridiculous and to devise happy endings on earth becomes the very basis for faith.

VALUES

the best blessings of existence [5]

Jane Austen's values, as they emerge in *Emma,* are utilitarian, secular, intellectual, moral, and material. She is continually evaluating her characters and their behavior, and the world she creates is a hierarchy in which status depends on uniting intelligence, morality, wealth, social standing, health, and physical attractiveness: people rank according to how great a sum of these parts they possess *in toto*. She does not pretend that a rich, full life is possible if one does not have both enough money and a benevolent, intelligent mind. She defines morality pragmatically: ultimately, what causes worthwhile people pain is immoral, what brings them joy is moral. No great novel is freer of canting idealism; want is bad, plenty is good. Happiness depends on having a lively, candid perception of things and an imagination that can play over reality and find attainable aims that will help achieve connection and harmony between the self and the world. Nothing in *Emma* indicates that the worth and meaning of life are to be found anywhere but in the actual processes of living. Austen values personal success, and, for Emma, success means using her gifts to find value in love.

In *Emma,* as Mark Schorer says, "we are in a world of peculiarly material value," and he notes that Austen's language is loaded with commercial diction and metaphor. She gives us a secular vision in which there is no help and no appeal beyond this world. It is misleading, however, to suggest that her intention was to satirize the society for its "lack of spiritual awareness or emotional fullness."[11] Few characters have the fullness or the awareness of Emma, and the economic and business idiom seems mainly to show the fusion of material, moral, and emotional concerns. Austen's commercial vocabulary tends to represent morality and virtue as having as real a material existence and as much worldly significance as money and property.

It is true that in *Emma* Austen, unlike her most distinguished predecessors in British fiction—Swift, Defoe, Fielding, Richardson, Sterne, and Goldsmith—never directly offers Christian consolation, and the absence of Christian "spiritual awareness" is significant. I have already speculated that keeping Christian concerns and spiritual matters out of her novel was a way of dealing with the shortcomings of spiritual orthodoxy and of building a new faith in the world. There is a telltale sentence near the end of the book that shows the state of Austen's mind as well as Emma's. In a moment of frustration Emma thinks to herself, "Was it new for anything in this world to be unequal, inconsistent, incongruous—or for chance and circumstance *(as second causes)* to direct the human fate?" (413; italics mine). That little parenthesis, barely a halfhearted nod to orthodoxy, is the only serious direct reference to Christian Providence in the novel. Emma doesn't deny Providence; if she thinks of it, she'll make a small mental genuflection to it, but her passion is for the world.

Historically, *Emma* is clearly a comedy about and for a confident middle-class audience, expanding in numbers, power, and riches. Austen shows nearly all the characters—e.g., the Westons, the Eltons, and Jane Fairfax—"rising," i.e., gaining, in measurable ways, money and social standing. With this general "rise" as a background, Emma gains in self-knowledge, sympathy, virtue, and joy.

Material and moral values are complementary in this book, not antithetical. We have folly and error, but the burden of social and class guilt is missing. There is no bad conscience about being rich, little idea that wealth and leisure might rest on exploitation, no indication that materialism inevitably corrupts—none of that later *Angst* about money and the scramble for it that would become a staple of the nineteenth-century novel. Though no one at times can be more caustic about human failing or exploitation than Austen, problems and troubles are still felt here as personal, not social or political. One ought, of course, to work to remedy one's own failings and the troubles of the world that one can reach, but one need not feel responsible for what lies beyond the private ken.

Emma succeeds in getting what she wants. The novel has the optimistic tone of a buoyant individualism in which personal success, comprehending intellectual, ethical, and physical well-being, can be a praiseworthy and possible goal.

COMIC HEROINE

The child of good fortune! [448]

Emma is a comic heroine in three different ways: she is the central figure of the romantic plot; she has a fine, irrepressible sense of humor; and she herself is often ridiculous. That particular union, as Austen renders it, makes her a character whose literary largeness and consequence rival or surpass such great comic creations as the Wife of Bath, Don Quixote, Sancho

Panza, Falstaff, Rosalind, Tartuffe, Millamant, and the Blooms. *Emma,* the only one of Austen's novels to be named for a single character, makes a woman the center of the world and celebrates self-fulfillment. She finds her comic vision in the flourishing whole life of Emma rather than in the state of the community or the world. By focusing arbitrarily on one young woman, Austen can make the dream of success and happiness seem convincing and plausible; but by making Emma sometimes ridiculous and laughable, she shows also how comedy can be used to control the egocentric excesses of individualism.

I

Emma has something of a tough Calvinist assessment of life about it, and Austen in this is closer to Bunyan and Richardson, for example, than to Dickens or Trollope. The heroine is one of the elect, "handsome, clever, and rich" (5); however, the god who chooses the elect is the god of comedy, Fortune, who distributes, to favorites, rewards right here on earth. Just as proof of the excellence of divine Providence was once thought to lie in the personal salvation of the righteous, who were predestined for glory, and not in the state of human nature generally, so the glory of earthly life in Austen's vision depends on the flourishing of the single self, Emma.

Northrop Frye, noting that comedy has been tenacious of its structural principles and character types, says, "the movement of comedy is usually . . . from one kind of society to another. At the beginning . . . the obstructing characters are in charge of the . . . society. . . . At the end . . . the device in the plot that brings hero and heroine together causes a new society to crystallize, . . . and the moment when this crystallization occurs is the point of resolution in the action, the comic discovery." The fundamental principle of comedy, he says, is its tendency "to include rather than exclude."[12] When we apply this to *Emma,* we see that by internalizing the traditional comic world in a single self, Austen has given to her heroine an almost unparalleled inclusiveness. The conventional "blocking" characters of comedy—the boaster, the self-deceiver, the buffoon—are all to be found in Emma herself. But she performs the functions and roles of comedy's sympathetic characters too. She is romantic lead, her own helpful confidante in her bouts of reflection, the plain dealer who speaks the truth when no one

33

else will, and the shrewd commentator as well; and her unconscious mind, plotting her ultimate success with Knightley, even
works at times like the facilitating go-between servant of stage
comedy.

The comprehensiveness of Emma's humanity is astonishing
because Austen has given her specific traits and characteristics of
nearly all the other figures in the novel. Not only is she inclu-
sive, but our view of her is also; we see her from inside and
outside. Wylie Sypher's phrase describing the effect of great
comedy, "human blunders . . . seen from a godlike distance, and
also from within the blundering self,"[13] fits exactly, except that
we see human effort, charm, humor, and intelligence as well.

Emma has faults as serious as a character can have without
being malevolent. In fact her two main flaws—manipulating
other people for her own advantage, and misperception—do
cause most of the man-made evil in the world. In her famous
remark about Emma, " a heroine whom no one but myself will
much like,"[14] Austen foresaw the difficulty in holding sympathy
for someone who behaves at times foolishly and even callously.
But the insecurity of that self-effacing judgment also betrays, I
think, her awareness that she was trying to do something original that might easily be misunderstood. She would take the
traits of a comic character, traditionally "low," and give them to
a real heroine. That was a very novel thing to do. Even Congreve's Millamant—perhaps the most consequential comic
heroine between Shakespeare's Rosalind and Emma—though
she has wit and imagination, like Emma, is herself rarely, if ever,
ridiculous. By making Emma very often silly, Austen gambled
that her readers would see that not just "fools" are ridiculous;
the best and brightest, like themselves, are ridiculous too.

Knightley's response to Emma seems the proper one: fault
the sin but love the sinner; judge the whole and not the part.
Emma's mistreatment of Harriet, her unfairness to Jane Fairfax,
her rudeness to Miss Bates, and her mistakes about Frank
Churchill, Robert Martin, and others do not have evil results.
Emma is lucky, but she is also deserving, and she grows morally.
She learns that she must love and be loved by Knightley to be
happy. She uses her conscience and admits her folly. Her
understanding and imagination finally work to improve herself
and her world; looking always to the future, she doesn't get

bogged down in the mistakes of the past. Thus, in her, we have Austen's comic affirmation.

II

I want to look at some representative passages featuring Emma to show, in detail, the range and depth of personality she has and to show also Austen's development of the comedy of her heroine. Early in the novel, Emma, using her power over simple Harriet to discourage Robert Martin's suit, says to her:

> "A young farmer, whether on horseback or on foot, is the very last sort of person to raise my curiosity. The yeomanry are precisely the order of people with whom I feel I can have nothing to do. A degree or two lower, and a creditable appearance might interest me; I might hope to be useful to their families in some way or other. But a farmer can need none of my help, and is therefore in one sense as much above my notice as in every other he is below it." [29]

And she continues,

> "You understand the force of influence pretty well, Harriet; but I would have you so firmly established in good society, as to be independent even of Hartfield and Miss Woodhouse . . . ; therefore, I say that if you should still be in this country when Mr. Martin marries, I wish you may not be drawn in, by your intimacy with the sisters, to be acquainted with the wife, who will probably be some mere farmer's daughter, without education." [31]

That is Emma at her worst, a potentially dangerous snob and a manipulative, presumptuous egoist. She shows a will to power and a recklessness that must be curbed and exposed if she is to be contained by comic vision. She plays on a weak intellect in an especially nasty way. The cool precision of her speech conveys intelligence, but her love of sweeping generalization, which has no experience to support it, sounds silly. (What can Emma know of "the yeomanry"?) The kind of thing Emma is voicing is very important; no matter how deluded she is, the class attitudes her speech displays have social and political implications of high significance. This young woman is talking the perilous nonsense of rampant egoism and irresponsible privilege.

A little later Emma again uses Harriet as a sounding board as they go on a charity mission. One reason she keeps her simpleminded friend around is so that she can experiment with ideas and try on poses, as bright young people must, without worrying about being censored; she needs to hear what she is thinking and feeling even if it turns out to be half-baked:

> ... "And I am not only, not going to be married, at present, but have very little intention of ever marrying at all. . . .
>
> "I have none of the usual inducements of women to marry. Were I to fall in love, indeed, it would be a different thing! but I never have been in love; it is not my way, or my nature; and I do not think I ever shall. . . .
>
> "Never mind, Harriet, I shall not be a poor old maid; and it is poverty only which makes celibacy contemptible to a generous public! A single woman, with a very narrow income, must be a ridiculous, disagreeable, old maid! . . . but a single woman, of good fortune, is always respectable, and may be as sensible and pleasant as anybody else. And the distinction is not quite so much against the candour and common sense of the world as appears at first; for a very narrow income has a tendency to contract the mind, and sour the temper. Those who can barely live, and who live perforce in a very small, and generally very inferior, society, may well be illiberal and cross. . . .
>
> "If I know myself, Harriet, mine is an active, busy mind, with a great many independent resources; and I do not perceive why I should be more in want of employment at forty or fifty than one-and-twenty. Woman's usual occupations of eye and hand and mind will be as open to me then, as they are now; or with no important variation. If I draw less, I shall read more; if I give up music, I shall take to carpet-work." . . .

They were now approaching the cottage, and all idle topics were superseded. Emma was very compassionate; and the distresses of the poor were as sure of relief from her personal attention and kindness, her counsel and her patience, as from her purse. She understood their ways, could allow for their ignorance and their temptations, had no romantic expectations of extraordinary virtue from those, for whom education had done so little; entered into their troubles with ready sympathy, and always gave her assistance with as much intelligence as good-will. . . .

"These are the sights, Harriet, to do one good. How trifling they make every thing else appear!—I feel now as if I could think of nothing but these poor creatures all the rest of the day; and yet, who can say how soon it may all vanish from my mind?"

. . . Mr. Elton was immediately in sight; and so near as to give Emma time only to say farther,

"Ah! Harriet, here comes a very sudden trial of our stability in good thoughts. Well, (smiling,) I hope it may be allowed that if compassion has produced exertion and re-lief to the sufferers, it has done all that is truly important. If we feel for the wretched, enough to do all we can for them, the rest is empty sympathy, only distressing to our-selves." [84–87]

It would be hard to conceive of a more varied and suggestive comic passage. Besides smugness, self-deception, naïve pre-tensions, and self-importance, Emma shows here self-mockery, competence, benevolence, incipient feminist humor, and a bril-liant perception of various ways of the world. The dramatic irony of her disdain for marriage and love reminds us of how life makes our sureties look foolish, but her remarks on the power and sweetening effects of income prove to us how in-telligent she really is. "Carpet-work" shows her making fun of herself and of the fate of women generally, but the bantering tone carries with it a tinge of rebelliousness. The paragraph in which the narrator describes Emma's visit to the poor is crucial because it flatly states that, far from being merely an error-prone exploiter, Emma is actually a morally superior person, kinder and more efficient in her good deeds than most people. Notice that Austen chooses to portray the heroine of the com-edy ministering to the poor and not Mr. Elton the parson, whose Christian duty it is. This description of her virtue means that when, in its aftermath, we see the tricks of her mind—finding self-congratulatory pleasure in helping the unfortunate and, in the face of titillating intrigues of personal life, forgetting her social concern— we cannot distance outselves from Emma's vanity, since few readers, if any, could possibly do better than she in helping the needy.[15] We are meant to see, not just Emma's foibles, but the foibles of even the best human nature.

In her last remark, we ought to recognize Emma's genius. No other character in the novel, not even Knightley, has the free mind and frank good humor to face so squarely and utter so unsentimentally such a hard truth: "If we feel for the wretched enough to do all we can for them, the rest is empty sympathy, only distressing to ourselves." Nearly all comedy and all religions are based on her insight here: that people need to observe a cutoff point in feeling sympathy. So, too, are such civilized endeavors as the effective practice of medicine, statesmanship, social work, and—sometimes—education.

Why is it, therefore, that when we read those words we are likely to laugh at or resent them? One reason is that Emma the comic heroine—like the comic mode itself—often cuts through sentiment and illusions to say things people want to ignore; but another is Emma's coldness. No one, we feel, should be able to face pain and painful facts quite so easily and directly.

Emma, in the first part of the book, lacks the emotional vulnerability and self-doubt that would humanize her. She has a static quality; it seems as if nothing can touch her. Her ideas and her life seem cool, fixed, closed, almost inanimate. Only by being open and vulnerable to life can one be touched by love, and love must reach and warm Emma if she is to grow and change and enrich her life and world.

Here is a passage from late in the book, after Emma, indulging in the comic repartee of disunion, has insulted poor Miss Bates at Box Hill and Knightley has sternly reprimanded her:

> How could she have been so brutal, so cruel to Miss Bates!—How could she have exposed herself to such ill opinion in any one she valued! And how suffer him to leave her without saying one word of gratitude, of concurrence, of common kindness! . . .
>
> The wretchedness of a scheme to Box Hill was in Emma's thoughts. . . . [I]n her view it was a morning more completely misspent, more totally bare of rational satisfaction at the time, and more to be abhorred in recollection, than any she had ever passed. A whole evening of

back-gammon with her father, was felicity to it. . . . In the warmth of true contrition, she would call upon her [Miss Bates] the very next morning, and it should be the beginning, on her side, of a regular, equal, kindly intercourse.

She was just as determined when the morrow came, and went early, that nothing might prevent her. It was not unlikely, she thought, that she might see Mr. Knightley in her way; or, perhaps, he might come in while she were paying her visit. She had no objection. She would not be ashamed of the appearance of the penitence, so justly and truly hers. [376–78]

Austen gives us a new, humble Emma, mortified by the living memory of her past behavior, vulnerable in the extreme to the criticism of Knightley, whom we see that she loves—though she does not quite know it yet—trying to be good and unselfish, and vowing to change her conduct (which she does). But we also see that her true contrition has self-interest as a motive; it will help her gain the regard and love of Knightley (which it does). It is a beautiful comic moment, for Austen, without denying or denigrating the reality of conscience and the moral struggle to do better, shows how they are tied to self-seeking. The will to virtue is real, but so is the self-serving quality of good deeds. Moreover, we see in Emma's devotion to her demanding father the nuance of self-justification and also of the provocation to outburst and resentment that this petty world gives to Emma.

We must not mistake this ironical passage for cynicism. Emma's anguish is real, her repentance is sincere, and she does, from now on, act more kindly toward others. But how nice that it should be so and that, in being good, we might meet the object of our desire. When Jane Austen, every bit as much a comic "imaginist" as her heroine, shows Emma successfully uniting, in her consciousness, virtue and libido, she gives form to a vision that haunts the modern imagination: the dream of individual integrity in which self-interest and morality coincide. That is the hope that the best modern comic fictions, like traditional religions, try to make vivid for people.

The final conversation between Emma and Knightley and the description of Emma in its wake make clear the irreducible largeness and complexity of her character. Knightley has just told her that Harriet has accepted Martin's proposal:

... "But, Mr. Knightley, are you perfectly sure that she has absolutely and downright *accepted* him. . . . Did not you misunderstand him?—You were both talking of other things. . . . It was not Harriet's hand that he was certain of—it was the dimensions of some famous ox." . . .

"Do you dare say this?" cried Mr. Knightley. "Do you dare to suppose me so great a blockhead, as not to know what a man is talking of?—What do you deserve?"

"Oh! I always deserve the best treatment, because I never put up with any other; and, therefore, you must give me a plain, direct answer." . . .

"I am quite sure," he replied, speaking very distinctly, "that he told me she had accepted him. . . ."

"I am perfectly satisfied," replied Emma, with the brightest smiles, "and most sincerely wish them happy."

"You are materially changed since we talked on this subject before."

"I hope so—for at the time I was a fool." . . .

. . . She was in dancing, singing, exclaiming spirits; and till she had moved about, and talked to herself, and laughed and reflected, she could be fit for nothing rational. . . . What had she to wish for? Nothing, but to grow more worthy of him, whose intentions and judgment had been ever so superior to her own. . . .

Serious she was, very serious in her thankfulness, and in her resolutions; and yet there was no preventing a laugh, sometimes in the very midst of them. She must laugh at such a close! Such an end of the doleful disappointment of five weeks back! Such a heart—such a Harriet! [473–75]

That passage can bring home both the full range of life accessible to a single human being and the richness of Emma's personality. In linking herself firmly to another, with love, she has become even more individualistic. Her bold humor is as daringly original as ever; "dimensions of some famous ox" and "I always deserve the best treatment" are examples of the way Emma uses repartee to dazzle and charm Knightley, but her wit makes a claim for psychological independence and freedom too. Her spontaneity and her playfulness shine through, but she joins them now with frank humility ("I was a fool") and genuine concern for others. We see also that she is jealous of her right to

40

privacy and her inner life, where the flux of events takes on meaning. There is a marvelous, almost manic, energy about Emma's inner experience, and Austen wants to revel in the exuberance of consciousness (hence her performing-art metaphors, "dancing, singing, exclaiming," for her emotions), but there is self-knowledge too. Emma knows that she needs control, needs fostering, and now realizes how easy it is to err. Yet what stands out most in Emma's reflections is that, at a point of seriousness, Austen lets her comic sense burst out. That laugh, the imperative of laughter ("she *must* laugh") at a time when we are witnessing, in her meditations, the flowering of her education in moral responsibility, represents the triumph and the power of humor in Austen's imagination and art. Emma is laughing at her old self as well as Harriet's nature and rising above both. The will to find comic delight in the surprise and the resiliency of human behavior unites with the comic heroine's ultimate seriousness. High seriousness must not prevent a laugh, and laughter must not exclude moral seriousness.

III

Both Emma and her author assert their individuality and distinction as women through comedy. Austen's contemporary, Fourier, declared that "in any given society the degree of woman's emancipation is the natural measure of the general emancipation."[16] Women are badly constrained in the Highbury world, as the genteelly impoverished Miss Bates; Jane Fairfax, who nearly falls into the governess "slave-market"; the illegitimate Harriet; Isabel Knightley, drudge to her husband and children; and even Mrs. Weston, married to a man beneath her in intelligence, all go to show. In this society, Emma is the closest thing there can yet be to an emancipated woman. Nevertheless, compared to the men, she is cramped and confined. In nearly all the passages I have cited, she is pushing directly or indirectly against the limits that her womanhood imposes. Even when her humor goes wrong, as in her morally indefensible but funny joke against Miss Bates, Emma is using it to try to distinguish herself from the mediocrity and trivialization that threaten women's lives. As a woman, Emma has the interest and significance of the great heroines of nineteenth-century fiction—e.g., Becky Sharp, Emma Bovary, Jane Eyre,

41

Dorothea Brooke, Glencora Palliser, Anna Karenina, Gwendolyn Harleth, and Isabel Archer—and she has a finer mind, a better sense of humor, and a richer imagination than any of them.

Most of the problems and questions about women that later became the glory and obsession of the novel hover about the horizons of Austen's art and are prefigured in Emma's life: How will middle-class women imbue their increasing leisure time and freedom with meaning and value? How can a woman keep her emotions from starving and her sex from withering when, in a commercial age, she herself is an item of commerce and knows it? Should there be narrow limits on a woman's liberty? Must a woman marry to fulfill herself? But these issues, some of which carry heartbreaking overtones of inevitable tragedy, do not spoil the comic tone and optimistic mood of the book because Jane Austen so clearly is celebrating the potential and relative freedom of Emma's life and giving her audience and herself an image of hope.

Like nearly all of Austen's young women, Emma is an orphan. Not only has she lost her mother; metaphorically she has almost no kinship with her father. The lack of consistency in heredity in Austen (e.g., intelligent Elizabeth Bennet has a stupid mother, and Emma has a doltish father) points up the fact that, except in rare cases, a woman inherits rank and destiny from the man she marries rather than directly from her own past. Something in Austen's imagination suggests that in a society of male privilege and primogeniture, all women are orphans. The curious search for father-like qualities in suitors that her heroines, including Emma, engage in seems natural once we realize that orphans need approval and the security of a guardian. Emma finds in Knightley what many bright women have sought in older men: not just a lover but a mentor who can inspire her creative and moral life.

As a heroine, Emma has sometimes been called sexually cold and repressed.[17] Her whole relationship with Knightley, the warmth and depth of her feeling for him, her regard for his physical person (326), and her desire to touch him (385–86) belie the charge. But more to the point, such criticism ignores the reality of Austen's world, where, for a woman, outer reserve is necessary. Sexual caution and cool calculation may mean the difference between leveling poverty and the opportunity for a distinguished life—distinguished, that is, in the literal sense that one has leisure and means to develop an inner life and form a unique and active consciousness. Before a woman can discover the meaning of her femininity, she must be able to achieve an inner independence and a contemplative self. Emma does.

MIND

animated contemplation [480]

Emma's mind is a maker, an actor, and a scene of the comedy. It often misinterprets things, but it also moves Emma toward self-gratification and love. It mediates between past and future, reason and fancy, conscious thought and unconscious intention, and it creates identity. Austen filters most of her narrative through Emma's point of view, and she makes us see into the mind of another. We watch as it registers, meditates, invents, moves, learns, goes right and goes wrong. We witness and judge subjectivity, but we become implicated by it too. It undermines the idea of an absolute, objective reality because it points up the shifting and always personal nature of perception and the continuous impact of individual psychology on the world. This dialectical interplay between Emma's mind and her world changes the nature of each.

I

One paragraph epitomizes the role and workings of Emma's mind and also the pattern of the whole comedy:

> Harriet, tempted by every thing and swayed by half a word, was always very long at a purchase; and while she was still hanging over muslins and changing her mind, Emma went to the door for amusement.—Much could not be hoped from the traffic of even the busiest part of Highbury;—Mr. Perry walking hastily by, Mr. William Cox letting himself in at the office door, Mr. Cole's carriage horses returning from exercise, or a stray letter-boy on an obstinate mule, were the liveliest objects she could presume to expect; and when her eyes fell only on the

43

butcher with his tray, a tidy old woman travelling home-wards from shop with her full basket, two curs quarrelling over a dirty bone, and a string of dawdling children round the baker's little bow-window eyeing the gingerbread, she knew she had no reason to complain, and was amused enough; quite enough still to stand at the door. A mind lively and at ease, can do with seeing nothing, and can see nothing that does not answer. [233]

There is no better example of the transforming power or the subtlety of Austen's comedy. Typically, Harriet's ditherings and the boredom of Highbury spur Emma's imagination. Her mind begins to play with the dullness of her surroundings, and, making fun of her own situation, she pretends, for example, that the most lively and entertaining thing she could see would be "a stray letter-boy on an obstinate mule." She projects comic images out of a need to amuse herself and make things interesting. She ironically realizes that here the most diverting sight she can imagine ("Mr. Perry walking hastily by") differs only slightly from such tedious fare as Harriet dawdling over muslins or Miss Bates blabbing endlessly. But when, instead of imagining, she actually looks and sees "only the butcher," etc., she can place herself in the field of her perception and take a good look at herself in perspective. Austen shows Emma understanding how much better her lot is than most and how lucky she is to have the means to enjoy life. Moreover, she comes to recognize that, to some extent, one must give meaning and value to the perceived phenomena of reality. Boredom—or rapt interest—lies in the mind, and Emma discovers in herself the capacity to find pleasure and wonder in what others might consider banal. "A mind lively and at ease" is, for the most part, the gift of fortune, but setting a mind at ease may depend on individual effort and on a well-developed comic sense that acts to make laughter out of unpleasantness.

The last sentence of the paragraph speaks volumes and says, among other things, that the unperturbed mind is quickest; that intelligence and security go together; that the agile, self-satisfied mind may, however, make up some of what it sees and therefore be prone to error.

The movement of Emma's mind in the Highbury Street is the exact movement of her mind during the course of the novel: out of trying circumstances, she uses her imaginative bent to please herself, find the ridiculous around and in herself, correct her fancy with actual perception, come to understand her privilege and good luck, and become happier and more responsible.

II

Austen draws much of her comedy from the incongruity between what Emma thinks is in her mind and what we actually see there. She loves Knightley long before she knows it, and the force of her unconscious mind is moving her toward him, directly opposing her rationalizations against marriage. Near the end, we read that the thought "darted through her, with the speed of an arrow, that Mr. Knightley must marry no one but herself" (408), but much earlier we find her betraying the truth, after she meets Mrs. Elton, in this reflection:

> "Insufferable woman! . . . Knightley!—never seen him in her life before, and call him Knightley!—and discover that he is a gentleman! . . . And Mrs. Weston!—Astonished that the person who had brought me up should be a gentlewoman! Worse and worse. I never met with her equal. Much beyond my hopes. Harriet is disgraced by any comparison. Oh! what would Frank Churchill say to her, if he were here? . . . Ah! there I am—thinking of him directly. Always the first person to be thought of!" [279]

Knightley, obviously, is first—not Frank, who is a distant fourth—but not until much later does she consciously realize it. When she thinks she might lose Knightley, she decides that loving him does her credit, and "Every other part of her mind was disgusting" (412). Ironically, however, "Every other part of her mind" has often been a part of an unconscious drive to win Knightley. Emma's fanciful matchmaking, for instance—Elton and then Frank Churchill with Harriet, Jane Fairfax with Mr. Dixon—looks very much like an unconscious way of trying to get rid of eligible mates who might block the eventual union of Knightley and herself.

In *Emma* the unconscious works to render silly ideas and failings of the intellect relatively harmless and pushes Emma toward Knightley without making her risk openly or prematurely the wound of unrequited love. It allows her spontaneity to flow and directs her in her own best interest without

45

making her undergo a possibly inhibiting trial by conscience in the delicate early stages of love. In the end, however, an unconscious wish must become conscious so that it can be tested by reason and fulfilled. For Austen, "understanding and gratification" finally come together.

Emma must learn to see the infirmities of her mind, but it would be wrong to say that only weakness and folly reside in "that very dear part of Emma, her fancy" (214). To do so would dissipate the powerful tensions of the novel and much of its significance. Though her fancy does real mischief and even shows clearly the terrible human propensity to treat others as if they were one's own creations, it provides the vitality and interest that make Knightley love her; her fancy also gives her a comic strategy for survival in a constraining milieu. It is, for example, imaginative fancy that lets Emma respond to the outrageous vulgarity of Mrs. Elton by thinking "Much beyond my hopes." Comic fancy can stand "reality" on its head. The mind can make comedy of gracelessness and an amusement park of Highbury provincialism. The fanciful trick of humor, by which what is bad can be converted into a source of delight and what is wrong can fill one with pleasure at one's own superiority, is, for Austen, one of "the best blessings of existence."

Significantly, Austen internalizes and humanizes the process and the power that lead to the happy ending and the final comic vision. She makes the spirit of comic affirmation the disposition of Emma's whole mind. In nearly all previous comedy, the agent of comic salvation had been an external force, such as a *deus ex machina,* divine grace, an imposed solution, miraculous revelations, and the like. The great comic fact about Emma's mind is that, as broker and point of union between inner and outer life, between imagination and reality, between what has happened and what might come, it sets a pattern for beneficial change without limit. Emma goes forward, adapts, and changes. We must see Emma's mind, in this novel, as Austen's model of dialectical progress. In the interaction between the self and the world, we have an image of the healthy human mind, capable, despite its flaws and contradictions, of infinite growth and discovery in the seeking of its own good.

TIME

all in happy enjoyment of the future [256]

Time in *Emma* is future-oriented and generative. Austen's time moves from reflection to anticipation. It is a time of hope, of looking-forward-to, and that makes it seem full of promise. Much of the life of the novel is spent in waiting—waiting for visitors, dances, proposals, and events to happen. Jane Fairfax waits for Frank Churchill to return to Randalls; Mrs. Weston waits for her baby to come; Emma waits for Elton to ask for Harriet's hand and later for her father to get used to the idea of her marriage, and so on. Time lacks the breathless urgency of the death-haunted time of Sterne, the dated specificity of Richardson, Smollett, and Fanny Burney, with their letter headings, and the packed immediacy of crisis and farce of Defoe, Fielding, Goldsmith, and the Gothic novelists. The rush of violence, adventure, and sudden changes of fortune that we often find in eighteenth-century fiction is missing in Austen. Her time is the time of a leisured class and also of women, who, historically, have had to wait for the great events of their lives.

Such time may nourish a self-conscious and full psychological life. Since waiting and leisure can lead to ennui, the bored mind will usually seek to make life more interesting. It will create expectations and give meaning and drama to what it perceives and awaits. To fill the time and to compensate for a relatively passive existence, Emma shapes for herself a vital inner life.

Human progress is real in Austen, and time is benevolent. The existence of an active inner life makes even the past a part of a person's present and future. Every new experience means that the reflecting consciousness may give a new form and meaning to what has come before. For example, Emma's rude joke on Miss Bates causes Knightley to speak to her, and her contrition brings her closer to him; her "blindness" leads her to acknowledge her love for Knightley. Consciousness, in other words, renews time and life, and nothing that can be recalled to mind is ever over and done with: "Time," Knightley says to Emma, "will make one or the other of us think differently" (471).

Time always has the potential, then, to turn blunders into joys. Thus, the fiction of Austen and *Emma,* seemingly so unpretentious, relates directly to the positivist, optimist fiction of

Hegel and Scott, to name two of her most illustrious contemporaries. (The philosopher gives us the dialectical progress
of history, and the novelist offers us, in what we might almost
call the comedy of commonwealth, his vision of a strong and
unified nation and people emerging from historical conflict and
bloodshed.) Austen has little to say about conventional history
per se. The pattern of progress that she sees in *Emma*'s kind of
time and the pattern of the narrative in which events of the past
and future can be reinterpreted in terms of present and future
goals, however, are very much like the patterns of nineteenth-
and twentieth-century historical interpretation, which allows
people to replace the Christian fiction of a divine comedy with
the fiction of a progressive history of humanity—with, in other
words, an anthropomorphic god of history.

The calendar time of *Emma* is exactly one year. Austen carefully opens her book in October, with Mrs. Weston's marriage,
and ends it with Emma's marriage in the following October.
Though she doesn't stress this symmetry, her time span has the
same kind of tidy neatness that a fiscal year has in accounting: it
is an arbitrary but convenient period for measuring accurately
and taking stock. Just as the results of the fiscal year may be
profit and accruing interest—a happy outcome—so a year of a
person's life may have a happy result that we can show without
falsifying reality, as we acknowledge when we say we have had
"a good year." An individual life ends in the tragedy of death,
but the results of a day, a week, or a year may end comically. By
setting such a stipulative time limit, the novelist can give both
finality and verisimilitude to her comedy and avoid the sentimentality of an "and they lived happily ever after" ending.

Subjective, goal-seeking, future-centered time and calendar
time fuse in *Emma,* and that is significant. In traditional
theological thought they were kept separate (that is, salvation
and gratification would not occur in the time of this world), and
previous comic fiction rarely had the expectant quality of this
novel. Again, what matters here is the resonance of the pattern
Austen creates. Emma's mode of thought—waiting and working
for a change in her father's attitude toward her marriage to
Knightley, which she knows will inevitably take place in a few
months—and the mode of thought of people who anticipate and
work for what they know will happen in a few decades (for

example, the triumph of empire, capitalism, democracy, or communism) differ only in degree, not in kind.

SPACE

neither geography nor tranquillity [189]

Space is confining in *Emma*; distances are great. Relative immobility characterizes this world, and the narrow physical range creates a drive to enlarge the inner space of the mind. Images of confinement and hampered movement abound: for example, "Her father never went beyond the shrubbery" (26); "Her sister . . . only sixteen miles off, was much beyond her daily reach" (7). One of the most telling paragraphs occurs just after Mr. Elton has proposed to Emma and not to Harriet, as he was supposed to: "Their being fixed, so absolutely fixed, in the same place, was bad for each, for all three. Not one of them had the power of removal. . . . They must encounter each other, and make the best of it" (143). There is no exit in this novel.

Just as leisure time stimulates the interior life, so fixed place creates a need for attention to personal relationships, for sensitivity to the feelings of others, for manners, which make it possible to live together for long periods, and for predictable behavior. All this takes its toll and necessarily limits personal freedom. *Emma* has something claustrophobic about it, and it shows in Mr. Woodhouse's mania for keeping things shut.

As time is women's time in *Emma,* so space is women's space—different from the space of men. The embarrassed Elton, though he must eventually live in Highbury, can run off to Bath to find a wife there, but Harriet must remain at home. Frank Churchill can go to London in a day to get a haircut and buy a piano, but if Jane goes wandering about in the meadows near town, it causes a sensation. At a time of tension, Knightley can hike off to the city, but Emma must stay and pamper her father. The confinement, the restricted movement, of women has been a staple theme of narrative from the *Iliad* and the Bible, through Jack the Giant-Killer and Rapunzel, to Lolita and John Fowles's *The Collector*—a fact that shows the anxiety of the race about the exploitation of women. Mobility has always been equated with freedom.[18]

The setting in *Emma* is most often indoors—in a drawing room, a parlor, a ballroom, or a dining room—and that reinforces the confined nature of its life. But if space presses, it is still remarkably uncrowded with physical objects. Austen uses less visual detail than almost any novelist of high reputation. No one, for example, could be further from the sensuousness of Richardson, the graphic sights of Smollett, the overwhelming clutter of Dickens, or the fascination with material surfaces of Thackeray. The one physical detail that we know a good deal about in *Emma* is the weather, but Austen uses it almost always to point up the difficulty of movement and communication in her world or to reflect the emotional weather of the characters.

Her interests are psychological and moral. Consider her one famous description of landscape. Emma is looking out over the country from Knightley's Donwell: "It was a sweet view—sweet to the eye and the mind. English verdure, English culture, English comfort, seen under a sun bright, without being oppressive.... Abbey-Mill Farm...might be safely viewed with all its appendages of prosperity and beauty, its rich pastures, spreading flocks, orchard in blossom, and light column of smoke ascending" (360). That is more an intellectual view and value judgment than a physical description, more a view of the mind than of the eye. Even this is not aimed at making us see, literally; it helps, however, to make clear the moral stakes and the social import behind the life of the novel.

Though she is the least metaphysical of authors and recognizes firmly and steadily the material basis of culture, physical surface does not matter to her. Privileged status, in fact, means expanding consciousness and getting free of the tyranny of objects and physical annoyance. When Mrs. Elton remarks on Emma's wedding, "Very little white satin, very few lace veils; a most pitiful business!" (484), Austen is showing how obsession with material objects and petty acquisitiveness can enslave people and make them ridiculous.

The most important setting of the novel exists in Emma's mind, and that is large enough. One advantage of the space that envelops and immobilizes Emma is that, while it keeps her more or less in one place, it also keeps what is new and shocking at a distance. It gives her time to prepare a face or plan for meeting the unfamiliar. Enforced provinciality also carries with it a limited liability of conscience. Problems remain personal and amenable to individual solutions. For what goes wrong outside one's circle, one need not feel responsible or guilty. According to Austen, however, restricted space forces one to live life carefully and to try to avoid, or else remedy, intellectual and moral sloppiness. Since one is fixed, without "the power of removal," one must learn to obey the ethical no-littering signs, because one must live with the consequences of one's thoughts and actions. In a sense, the confined space of *Emma* represents all mental space: we are all the life-long provincials of our own minds and share with Emma that limited and narrow focus. Even if Emma could fly to the moon, she still could not escape herself.

SPEECH

conversation, rational or playful [7]

Speech in *Emma* defines character, reflects quality of mind, and does much to create the comic mood. Austen makes conversation the means and opportunity for her intelligent figures to touch and move one another, often, in the process, displaying their wit and sense of the laughable. Proper speech in some way brings about change for the better, and wit, which discovers unsuspected connections, generates new awareness, lets loose hostilities in civilized fashion, and leads to moral and mental progress. Wit is, therefore, a positive virtue in *Emma* (that is not true in all of Austen's novels) and an indicator of potential merit in a character. Emma, Knightley, Mrs. Weston, Jane Fairfax (when she speaks), and even Frank have it. The talk of the unintelligent, however, reveals their ridiculousness, the humor of one-track minds that cannot properly connect. They betray their trivial obsessions and their ignorance of both themselves and others. Expression should inform, join, please, alter, and clarify minds, as talk between Emma and Knightley almost always does. Here is an example of excellent Austen dialogue:

"I shall not scold you. I leave you to your own reflections.
"Can you trust me with such flatterers?—Does my vain spirit ever tell me I am wrong?"
"Not your vain spirit, but your serious spirit.—If

51

one leads you wrong, I am sure the other tells you of it."

"I do own myself to have been completely mistaken in Mr. Elton. There is a littleness about him which you discovered, and which I did not: and I was fully convinced of his being in love with Harriet. It was through a series of strange blunders!"

"And, in return for your acknowledging so much, I will do you the justice to say, that you would have chosen for him better than he has chosen for himself. . . ."

"Whom are you going to dance with?" asked Mr. Knightley.

She hesitated a moment, and then replied, "With you, if you will ask me."

"Will you?" said he, offering his hand.

"Indeed I will. You have shown that you can dance, and you know we are not really so much brother and sister as to make it at all improper."

"Brother and sister! no, indeed." [330–31]

Emma and Knightley are accomplishing a great deal in this interchange. They are testing each other, drawing each other out, and coming together with grace and charm. Compare that playful but consequential talk with the following monologue:

> . . . Mrs. Elton . . . was very ready to lead the way in gathering, accepting or talking—strawberries, and only strawberries, could now be thought or spoken of.—"The best fruit in England—every body's favourite—always wholesome.—These the finest beds and finest sorts. . . . Morning decidedly the best time—never tired—every sort good—hautboy infinitely superior—no comparison—the others hardly eatable—hautboys very scarce—Chili preferred—white wood finest flavour of all—price of strawberries in London—abundance about Bristol—Maple Grove—cultivation—beds when to be renewed—gardeners thinking exactly different—no general rule—gardeners never to be put out of their way—delicious fruit—only too rich to be eaten much of—inferior to cherries . . . only objection to gathering strawberries the stooping—glaring sun—tired to death—could bear it no longer—must go and sit in the shade." [358–59]

Mrs. Elton's speech—disjointed, crude, contradictory, and going nowhere—reflects her character perfectly. Mired down in meaningless chatter, learning and teaching nothing, sinking back on her tiresome standbys, "Maple Grove" and "price," she is stuck in a mind that can't progress toward others and expand. Monologue in *Emma* often signals folly and limitation. Miss Bates talks and talks, but Emma can mimic and sum her up in a single phrase, "So very kind and obliging!" (225). Silly talk stagnates and is, quite literally, of no consequence, except that it shows the obstacles that keep people apart and provides wry pleasure to the wise.

Austen seems to revel in composing foolish speeches, and they show something essential about her comic imagination. "You divert me against my conscience," says Mrs. Weston, laughing, to Emma, who is mimicking Miss Bates (225). But, of course, Austen, in composing Miss Bates's talk, is doing exactly the same kind of thing as Emma and mocking the intellectual limitations of her world. Austen uses the eccentricities of her foolish characters, as these emerge in their speech, to flatter her readers; the subliminal message they reiterate is "You are not like this, you are superior, you are one of the elect." The comic artist can take the banal speech of others and make an audience feel just what Emma feels when she makes a game out of the banalities of her world: "she knew she had no reason to complain and was amused enough."

Austen recognizes that everyone is to some extent guilty of improper speech: "Seldom, very seldom, does complete truth belong to any human disclosure; seldom can it happen that something is not a little disguised, or a little mistaken" (431). But Knightley and Emma are least at fault. They are the best speakers in a novel in which the function of language is always to open up, in one way or another, the comic possibilities for happiness in the future.

COMIC IRONY

It depends upon the character of those who handle it. [212]

Irony depends upon its audience to detect and complete meanings extending beyond the literal sense of the language.

Austen's habitual irony distances her from appearances and behavior in her society, but it unites her with her readers by drawing us into a conspiracy of intellect. Whoever does not perceive it becomes its target. Irony is her mind's bridge between what is and what may be or ought to be, and at times it spans and supports alternative interpretations of reality, none of which she is ready to discard. It emphasizes her willingness to question social surface and conventional assumptions, and it stresses her moral pragmatism, together with her belief in the tentative nature of perception. It mocks the presumptions and pretensions of others by accepting them at face value in order to make clear their foolishness. It protects by performing a nearly miraculous psychological reversal, turning incongruous misfunctioning and the inconsistencies of the world into a positive source of delight for the mind. This verbal irony liberates by suggesting different options in assessing life and different strategies for coping with it. It is not surprising that readers disagree about *Emma;* the ironical prose suggests and suspends several meanings, and it demands participation and ingenuity on the part of the audience.

Here are five typical examples of irony in *Emma:*

> (1) Miss Bates . . . had no intellectual superiority to make atonement to herself, or frighten those who might hate her, into outward respect. [21]

That statement, ostensibly about Miss Bates, discriminates "between convention and essence" and points out, in the shock words "hate" and "frighten," the discrepancy between the society's façade of polite decorum and the selfish and hostile passions of its members.[19] It presupposes that we, like the author, have the sense and courage to face unpleasant facts about humanity and to see its dark realities, but it also assumes that we have the imagination to object and hope for better. The prose actually tells us more about Emma, who does have the "intellectual superiority" to make atonement to herself, and about Jane Austen, who finds irony a prime means by which people can "make atonement" to themselves for unpleasantness, than about Miss Bates, whom no one, after all, does "hate." Typically, the irony contains social criticism and suddenly strips away affectation. It implies that the individual mind can and must work out its own form of salvation or "atonement," and the use of the word "might" leaves open the possibility that "hate" may not always be inevitable. Austen's irony, above all else, works to expand our intellectual awareness by quick changes of perspective.

(2)   She [Emma] felt for Harriet, with pain and with contrition; but no flight of generosity run mad, opposing all that could be probable or reasonable, entered her brain. She had led her friend astray, and it would be a reproach to her for ever; but her judgment was as strong as her feelings, and as strong as it had ever been before, in reprobating any such alliance for him [Knightley], as most unequal and degrading. [431]

That is a good instance of Austen's multileveled irony. The point of view is both within and outside Emma's mind; she thinks she is deciding rationally that Harriet would be an unfit wife for Knightley, but we know that her judgment follows her feeling and that her rationalization coincides with selfish desire. Emma has injured Harriet several times and has repeatedly recovered from moments of self-reproach. The idea that she will ever sacrifice her own interests to Harriet or that her guilt will stay with her "for ever" is laughable. As usual, there is a selfish motive behind Emma's thought process, and the irony calls into question the sincerity of Emma's contrition and also of any rational pretense that is self-serving. People do mean well, but they find it very easy to think they are acting ethically when they are serving their own ends.

But, ironically, Emma is right: Harriet is unfit for Knightley. Out of selfishness may come what is "probable or reasonable," the union of Emma and Knightley. This second irony questions sentimental ideas of poetic justice and shows the dangers of flights "of generosity run mad"—not dangers to Emma but to sentimental readers. Life may be unfair in favoring Emma, but the very unfairness of fortune and the rationalizing power of the ego, which can rise phoenix-like from past mistakes and ignore contradictions, may sometimes work to the advantage of the whole community, as they do in this novel.

(3)   The hair was curled, and the maid sent away, and Emma sat down to think and be miserable. [134]

Though Emma may be "miserable," she is lucky enough to have a maid to serve her and to take her servant for granted, and she is not unhappy enough to forgo having her hair done. Here we have Austen's multiple perspective at work. The words describe Emma's own mortified view of her plight and also the external view of her from within the society, which enables us to see, by the way in which normal life continues, that Emma overestimates her misery. But the irony gives us an even more detached, distancing point of view, one that lays open to question the normal practices and assumptions of the society itself: the state of things in which, as the logic and balance of the ironical prose make clear, one's maid, like one's hair, is a kind of appendage to oneself. Austen often uses passive construction ironically, as she does here, to give the action a sense of the impersonal and mechanical. This ironical claim of inevitability for what is not inevitable calls attention to the arbitrariness of the social arrangement and to Emma's luck. Others may simply be instruments for a rich young woman in this world, but Austen knows that life might very well be otherwise. Her irony allows us to question the society, as well as Emma, for its blindness toward classes of people.

(4)   It may be possible to do without dancing entirely. Instances have been known of young people passing many, many months successively, without being at any ball of any description, and no material injury accrue either to body or mind;—but when a beginning is made—when the felicities of rapid motion have once been, though slightly, felt—it must be a very heavy set that does not ask for more. [247]

At first this appears to be just a piece of rather obvious irony directed against the tendency of young people and others to make much of little. Of course it is "possible to do without dancing." But on second thought there is a deeper irony. Humanity may be able to do without dances, but we can't be very sure, since the race seems seldom to have tried. Dancing is as permanent and as old as warfare. And that precise, yet generalizing, elegant, typically Austenian phrase, "the felicities of rapid motion," extends the irony further. All dances are essentially mating dances, and the end, as well as the means, of dancing is the felicity of rapid motion. Through such prose and such manifold strands of irony Austen brings home the importance of the "little things" she writes about and of the whole tenor of women's belittled lives. A conventional ironist might find balls trivial, much ado about nothing, but the ironist of genius may discover that dancing is even more significant than anxious dancers can imagine and that, just as a dance may be much more important to a particular woman than a Napoleonic war, so might the fact of dancing be just as significant to the human race as the fact of battle. And if we were to carry this kind of logic further, we might even imagine and see how the prose of ironic comedy could be as important an instrument of revelation as—say—scripture.

(5)   Goldsmith tells us, that when lovely woman stoops to folly, she has nothing to do but to die; and when she stoops to be disagreeable, it is equally to be recommended as a clearer of ill fame. Mrs. Churchill, after being disliked at least twenty-five years, was now spoken of with compassionate allowances. In one point she was fully justified. She had never been admitted before to be seriously ill. The event acquitted her of all the fancifulness, and all the selfishness of imaginary complaints. [387]

The irony here jokes and plays with the murderous impulse of aggression, with the conventional response to death, and with death itself. As in another sudden intrusion of death in *Emma*, "a young person, who either marries or dies, is sure of being kindly spoken of" (181), the subtle effect is to turn the focus back on the living and make death a part of the process of life. The last sentence of the paragraph even hints at a parody of Last Judgment ideas, satirizing the notion that to be justified in the eyes and gossip of the living could possibly matter to the dead. Austen has little patience with misplaced sympathy or sentiment, and the cold penetration of this passage brings home again that *sauve-qui-peut*, Protestant strain in her comic vision.

Throughout *Emma*, Austen's irony exposes the folly and blindness of social habit. It also creates a kind of uncertainty principle, whose effect liberates. It implies that the mind is free to proceed hypothetically in its practical search for understanding and gratification as long as it recognizes its own fallibility and the inherent confusion between seeming and being; it must retain its flexibility toward the future. For Austen, life itself is the principal ironist, whose meanings can and do change with the passing of time and the flux of perception.

MARRIAGE: THE HAPPY ENDING

My liveliness and your solidity would produce perfection."[457]

" . . . the perfect happiness of the union." [484]

Marriage, promising generation and new life, has often been to comedy what death is to tragedy: the fundamental human event that supports, in the thoughts and feelings it arouses, the validity of the mode. As *King Lear* makes us better sense the awfulness of death, so *Emma* makes us better imagine the wonder of marriage and the species that invented it. Marriage has been the traditional point of fusion between personal and social life. It is the most private kind of relationship, and yet it is the outstanding evidence that proves one's obligation to the community and one's need of its sanction. Marriage institutionalizes sex and the means of regenerating the race. It has been a comic compromise between self-gratification and social responsibility. In it, biology, psychology, theology, anthropology, and economics are wed.

Austen makes marriage the aim and end of her fiction, and perhaps that fact has been taken too much for granted. To believe in the goodness and central importance of marriage is to have faith in the goodness of this world, and that may be one reason why Christianity and some other god-centered religions have regarded marriage problematically and have shown ambivalent and sometimes belittling attitudes toward it. Seeing marriage as the climactic event of moral life means placing more stress on the harmony of the sexes and, implicitly, on the importance of women than institutionalized religious ethics had tended to do. *Emma* also offers marriage as the hope of intimacy and a potential remedy for the incompleteness of personality in an individualistic age. That people long for it to work that way explains why, in the face of much evidence to the contrary, it is the conventional happy ending of so much fiction of the past two hundred years.

Austen, however, takes more care than most comic writers

do in matching the qualities of her romantic leads and in show-ing exactly the kind of union that ends her plot. Emma, of course, needs to learn to love, but so does Knightley. It is not enough to be right, proper, and truly moral; one must also be capable of loving another person. "I could not think about you so much without doating on you, faults and all," says Knightley to Emma, "and by dint of fancying so many errors, have been in love with you ever since you were thirteen at least" (462). From the point of view of moral orthodoxy, that might be suspect, but surely there is nothing more appealing about this character than his love for Emma. The unspoken ideology behind Austen's comedy is that the community must love and cherish the individual—the comic creature the single human being is—or the culture will be sterile. Knightley has his personal quirks—his bluntness, for instance, and his jealous prejudice against Frank Churchill—but for the most part he is the society's ideal, ethical man. Austen insists that morality must be married to comic particularity if either is to have any worthwhile effect on the future. It may seem ironic that Austen never married, but, when she was writing this novel, the Emma and Knightley within her *did*. Emma, the striving, kinetic, lucky, ironic, ridiculous, subjective comic heroine weds Knightley, who speaks with the rational voice of moral conscience and acts forcefully in the name of social and personal responsibility. The desire and imagination of the intelligent, self-seeking soul are joined with the best and the wisest of her community. The union, we are told, promises a happy future.

Through "union," a word connoting physical intimacy, human solidarity, and contractual association, the self, in *Emma,* makes a commitment to the future. In Austen's fiction, comic concern for one individual woman includes comic concern for the society. Her comedy of union turns out to be the witty celebration of potent individualism embracing the world.

3

PEACOCK'S *NIGHTMARE ABBEY* (1818)

Comic Communion

When he sings the wild songs of Bacchus, man loses his personal
identity....
Wylie Sypher[1]

A change in mood is the most precious thing that alcohol achieves
for mankind.... A cheerful mood ... reduces the inhibiting
forces, criticism among them, and makes accessible once again
sources of pleasure which were under the weight of suppression.
Sigmund Freud[2]

Not "individualism embracing the world," but egotism swal-
lowing it, would have better described what many in the Re-
gency period thought of their new nineteenth-century world.
For them, living close to Jacobin, Napoleonic, and Romantic
upheavals, things seemed to be falling apart. Pessimism was
fashionable. The center (as usual) did not seem able to hold;
subjectivity, anarchy, even a blood-dimmed tide threatened.
But Thomas Love Peacock, in his masterpiece of equanimity
Nightmare Abbey, imagines an underlying commonality of life
and a *wine*-dimmed tide instead. He sees the *fraternité* of mankind, though not the one that political progressives saw. In
prehistoric times, some resourceful tribal revelers invented in-
toxicating liquors and, performing their rituals of life and death,
presumably decided that they could and would substitute wine
for blood: they inaugurated a ceremony of innocence, thus
opting for communal pleasure, drunkenness, delusion, play,
folly, charity, and civilization. It does not matter whether that
sense of the development of human nature is literal or symbolic: the greatest truth for Peacock is that humanity survives, is
bound together and renewed in a foolish, beautiful comic mystery.[3]

Northrop Frye calls Peacock a "great writer," as "exquisite
and precise an artist in his medium as Jane Austen is in hers";[4]
but the usual critical estimate is much more patronizing. Even

many of his admirers find him only a clever but eccentric minor talent. Yet *Nightmare Abbey,* his best fiction, fully justifies Frye's verdict. It is one of the most thought-provoking and original works of the English Romantic period, and, if no one has said this as emphatically before, it may well be because of deep prejudices not only against Peacock's comic insight and assessment of life but against comedy itself. Of excellent British comic writers, he has become a chief victim of the doctrine of high seriousness and its many avatars. These excerpts from three critics well disposed to him show what I mean:

If one judges Peacock by the highest qualities of literature, loftiness to inspire, wisdom to instruct, nobility to incite, or beauty to enchant, one will simply depreciate him.[5]

He is not a "seminal mind," a creative thinker. Nor is it appropriate to call him a great creative artist. For, even in a successful imaginative work like *Nightmare Abbey,* he strikes us primarily as a keenly intelligent mind responding to and offering us insight into outstanding men who rank above him in his age.[6]

He had little understanding of which questions were really worth asking, or of which kinds of enquiry might lead towards truth.[7]

An ugly duckling among the Romantic swans, Peacock nevertheless succeeded, as surely as Coleridge, Wordsworth, Shelley, or any of those questing poets whom he parodies, in finding and rendering what Frank Kermode calls the Romantic Image, "the Image as a radiant truth out of space and time."[8] It is as an image of the reality of human communion, symbolized by the wine its figures consume, that *Nightmare Abbey* makes its impact.

Its subject is not, as in *Emma,* the development and integrity of an individual person but rather the continuity of human nature itself. Beneath Peacock's geniality there is a greater fear of the excesses of egoism and the disintegrating process at work in the world than we find in Austen. He saw and felt in himself, as well as his friends and contemporaries, a principled but selfish alienation and a brave but warped individualism. He knew at first hand how the Industrial Revolution, the politics of the postrevolutionary era, the elevation of economic competition into an ideology, the influence of French nationalism and German idealism, the ebbing of Christian supernaturalism, and a score of other historical facts could feed a sense of social and personal fragmentation and create a vacuum of faith. He looked for unity and happiness in life, and he found them in comic communion. The urge to parody inspired *Nightmare Abbey,* but the result is a fiction that tries "to make sense of our lives"[9] through a genuinely religious sense of humor.

HUMORS

We are most of us like Don Quixote, to whom a windmill was a
giant, . . . all more or less the dupes of our own imagination.
Peacock, *Nightmare Abbey*[10]

"Oh! it's your only fine humour, sir!"
Ben Jonson[11]

In Peacock's book we see what he imagined were the divisive and the unifying forces in his world. His figures are *humors:* those rituals of ego expressing habitual states of mind, mental qualities, predilections, moods, and patterns of behavior that show forth in speech, action, or writing. These characters are not individuals but aspects of people; taken as a whole, however, they give us a vision of human commonality. Peacock's comedy assumes that human nature can be known and understood. It works to make the unexpected predictable, and it shows that there is something essential about a figure that communicates itself through public behavior. The comedy of humors may seem to rest on the freaks of aberrant personality, but it really depends on implicit social norms and the social nature of life. It takes for granted the fact that we can agree about what is freakish and obsessive. Watching people in their humors, we see what makes them tick, and we infer that we can know what we need to know about others in order to get along. The comedy of humors strengthens faith in community by making clear the lopsidedness of individual personality. Balance and harmony can come about only in a communion of humors. Peacock moves to fuse *humors* into *humor:* he animates, that is, the change from the old meaning of the word—that particular blend of fluids in one's makeup that determines one's temper and personality—to a newer meaning: *the amusing and essential comicality of being.* (Every act of humor, in a sense, repeats the etymological history of the word: what is grounded in physical being or natural conditions is transformed to the "high spirits" of comic mood and perspective.) His method is to collect the eccentricities of modes of thinking and particular people and bring them together until they appear as tics and gestures of communal being and cumulatively produce a joyous impression of mankind. His humors are rooted in time, place, and personalities, but he tries to reconcile what is changing and inconstant about humanity to what is constant. For him, "the crazy fabric of human nature" (364) is everlasting and all of a piece.

Peacock makes me want to add a corollary to Marx's dictum that all important facts and personages in history occur twice, the first time as tragedy, the second as farce: the most important currents of nineteenth-century intellectual history run together first in the humor of his fiction; later they appear in the real world to change and shake it. In *Crotchet Castle* (1831) a party discusses ways of regenerating society:

MR. MAC QUEDY. Build lecture rooms and schools for all.

MR. TRILLO. Revive the Athenian theatre: regenerate the lyrical drama.

MR. TOOGOOD. Build a grand co-operative parallelogram, with a steam-engine in the middle for a maid of all work.

MR. FIREDAMP. Drain the country, and get rid of *malaria,* by abolishing duck-ponds.

MR. MORBIFIC. Found a philanthropic college of anti-contagionists, where all the members shall be inoculated with the virus of all known diseases. Try the experiment on a grand scale.

MR. CHAINMAIL. Build a great dining-hall: endow it with beef and ale, and hang the hall round with arms to defend the provisions.

MR. HENBANE. Found a toxicological institution for trying all poisons and antidotes. . . .

MR. PHILPOT. Surely in no way so beneficially as in exploring rivers. Send a fleet of steamboats down the Niger, and another up the Nile. So shall you civilise Africa, and establish stocking factories in Abyssinia and Bambo. . . .

SEVERAL VOICES. That is my scheme. I have not heard a scheme but my own that has a grain of common sense. . . .

The schemes for the world's regeneration evaporated in a tumult of voices. [*CC,* 689–94]

Peacock creates a symposium of intellectual farce, but nothing could dramatize more clearly the urgent need, and custom, of the nineteenth century to prop up, modify, or replace a tottering faith in Christianity with some new kind of faith in the possibilities of human "regeneration."

Nightmare Abbey makes fun of several early-nineteenth-century intellectual humors that would become very influential, among them cultivation of the emotional self (Scythrop), popular transcendentalism (Flosky), pessimism, nostalgia, and degeneration-of-the-world theories (Mr. Toobad, Cypress), natural science (Asterias), privileged-class feminism (Celinda), bourgeois pseudo-revolutionary fervor (Scythrop), reactionary passion (Mr. Glowry, Flosky). The great humor of the age that Peacock dramatizes—primarily in Scythrop, Glowry, and Flosky—is the tendency to disassociate thought and feeling from material reality.

I

Peacock got the idea for Scythrop and Flosky from the lives of Shelley and Coleridge; for his parodies of them, he has been severely criticized. Peacock's failure to do justice to Coleridge's ideas "is a serious failure," says Humphry House. "He did not really understand or care about philosophy; he never dealt with the deeper and more exacting struggles of thought but only with thought as it emerged into opinion or emotional attitude."[12] Comedy *is* notoriously hostile, at times, to abstract thought (because abstract thought and intellectual system sometimes dangerously ignore sensual reality), and comic writers like Peacock are often charged with various forms of anti-intellectualism. But these charges, like House's, are usually antiintellectual themselves. They imply that the free play of the scoffing, skeptical mind is somehow impious. They seem to assume the absolute ethical value of systematizing philosophies, traditional schools of idealistic thought, transcendental aspirations and cosmologies, isms and ologies of all kinds—the very assumption, in other words, that comedy, in criticizing the fruit of such thinking, so frequently ridicules.

It is at least moot whether the formulations of philosophical schools can ever be more than elaborate, disciplined, sometimes lovely, sometimes terrible, games of opinionated minds rationalizing their emotions and fantasizing intellectual omnipotence. Peacock is right to show in his fiction that any philosophy, ideology, or theology, no matter what it is, will inevitably result in pretentious posing and faddish humors that can divide and mislead people. *Nightmare Abbey,* like many of his other books, desanctifies intellectual systems and their makers. It reminds us that Shelley, Coleridge, and, by extension, Kant, Plato, Freud, Marx, and Augustine, for example, were all a part of collective humanity and quirky, like other people—not mythic figures to be revered like gods, set apart and exempted from the play of criticism. A. E. Dyson asks rhetorically, "Did Peacock realise, in fact, that Shelley really was an exceptional man, for all his absurdities, and that Coleridge (to use Mill's tribute) was one of the two great seminal minds of his age?"[13] The point is that it is just because Peacock found these men "seminal" that he imagined and satirized the possible harvest from the seeds of their ideas and conduct. Critics and readers of *Nightmare Abbey* have spent too much time on the figures who stimulated the parody and too little on the humors figures themselves.

II

Scythrop Glowry, the center of the plot, is neither Shelley nor Shelley's thought but a kind of modern young Everyman in His Humor. Rousseau sent forth that tremendous assertion of self and Romantic sensibility that has reverberated ever since: *"I may not be better than other men, but I am different."* Peacock treats this sentiment as the major humor of his times and denies it. "Not so different as you think," he says, in effect, through the figure of Scythrop; "fundamentally, not different at all."

Scythrop fancies himself unique, but he turns out to be like other people. He is the very humor of self-dramatizing youth. Thinking himself motivated by unselfish idealism, he hopes to be a leader of progress and reform; he wants women and idyllic, unconventional free love; he apes *avant-garde* life-styles; he insists that he would rather die than live without his love or his nonconformist integrity; and when his schemes don't work out and he believes that failure dooms him forever, he plans suicide and an apocalyptic end. *Nightmare Abbey* shows, however, that self-interest guides him; that he can't be a leader; that reform is a doubtful proposition, since the world, like some weak-willed, oblivious drunk, doesn't seem to care much about mending its ways; that he loses women to convention; that there seems to be no such thing as free love; and that, even though there's no having life on one's own terms, still, for youth, there is continuing hope and pleasure rather than disaster and suicide. The old morality play to the contrary, Everyman does not die; he lives. Beneath the fashionable morbidities in Scythrop and in *Nightmare Abbey,* there lurks the fatal life-wish.

Peacock keeps connecting Scythrop's experience to a general fate. In the first paragraph he writes of old Mr. Glowry: "He had been deceived in an early friendship: he had been crossed in love" (355); and, by the end, the history of private life repeats itself and the exact same thing has happened to the son. Throughout the book such phrases as "neither new . . . nothing strange," "as usual," "as most lovers would do in similar circumstances" occur, showing that Scythrop is like other men; his behavior follows a pattern. Despite his philosophizing, his poses and gestures, he is a slave to external reality and physical stimulus. A pretty song and a smile from a lovely woman can bring him out of the blackest melancholy in a moment, and climate tyrannizes over his temperament as it does over almost everyone's.

When Scythrop, chasing after a girl to make up a lovers' quarrel, bumps into Mr. Toobad and falls sprawling, he lets loose a Manichean tirade that must surely be one of the most eloquent utterances decrying the human condition in all comedy. Toobad claims they collided because "the devil is supreme," and Scythrop takes up the theme:

> Evil, and mischief, and misery, and confusion, and vanity, and vexation of spirit, and death, and disease, and assassination, and war, and poverty, and pestilence, and famine, and avarice, and selfishness, and rancour, and jealousy, and spleen, and malevolence, and the disappointments of philanthropy, and the faithlessness of friendship, and the

crosses of love—all prove the accuracy of your views, and the truth of your system; and it is not impossible that the infernal interruption of this fall downstairs may throw a colour of evil on the whole of my future existence. [369]

Having tripped, a man deduces the Fall of Man. It is bruised bones and feelings that bring Scythrop's generalizing powers into play. Mr. Toobad spouts his Manichean credo, "the devil is come among you, having great wrath," each time his unlucky body blunders into slop, mire, and misfortune. In context, Scythrop's catalogue is ridiculous. We expect yelps of frustration and get, instead, a conjunctive inventory of all the ills that flesh is heir to. Yet there is something comic and wonderful in that articulation of endless suffering; out of petty pain and common trouble Scythrop becomes man, the crazy improviser, turning to verbal abstraction and fancy. By the end, the silly, resourceful being takes on near mythic proportions as a figure who, despite losing his dignity and botching his plans, goes on living.

Scythrop is Peacock's agent for turning humors into humor; that is, Peacock creates in him a figure whose destiny is the sum meaning of all the other characters: the persistence of communal life, which is inevitably renewed in particular folly. I see him as a humor of essential human *being* rather than a humor of talk and opinion, like the others; and, as such, he gives *Nightmare Abbey* a greater unity and consequence than Peacock's other novels have. The last chapter transcends its parody of Goethe's *Werther* and turns into a comic vision of humanity's fate: regeneration, in spite of itself. Scythrop appoints a precise time to kill himself if by then his father has not returned with one of his loves. When the fatal hour approaches with no sign of his father, he rings for his servant, Raven:

"Raven, . . . the clock is too fast."
"No, indeed," said Raven . . .; "if any thing, it is too slow."
"Villain!" said Scythrop, pointing the pistol at him; "it is too fast."
"Yes—yes—too fast, I meant," said Raven, in manifest fear.
"How much too fast?" said Scythrop.

"As much as you please," said Raven.

"How much, I say?" said Scythrop, pointing the pistol again.

"An hour, a full hour, sir," said the terrified butler.

"Put back my watch," said Scythrop. [431]

Afterwards, his father, having come back late and empty-handed, easily convinces Scythrop that there's no point in killing himself, since the appointed time for it is long past. Scythrop—having had a stay of execution and a kind of comic resurrection—feigns anger at Raven for deceiving him but decides to live anyway. He even finds cheer in the dashing of his plans: "I have just reflected that these repeated crosses in love qualify me to take a very advanced degree in misanthropy; and there is, therefore, good hope that I may make a figure in the world" (432). He ends the book with the words, "Bring some Madeira." Scythrop finally becomes the comic emblem of what he seeks to be: the true regenerator of the world. The self-dramatizing, bumbling cheater of time and death, the self-deluding, egotistical, crotchety, well-meaning, risible hunter of silver linings, becomes the quintessential comic man in his diverting humor of staying alive.

III

Most of the other characters are figures in a comic symposium. Of these, Flosky is most important. If Scythrop, like Don Quixote, finally transcends time and place, Flosky best epitomizes the historical situation out of which the text and the comedy of communion grew. In his person and his talk, Peacock defines some of the most significant divisive forces at work in both the society and the individual psychology of the Romantic era (in whose aftermath we still live). In the very first chapter we read:

> Mr. Flosky [was] a very lachrymose and morbid gentle-man, of some note in the literary world. . . . Mystery was his mental element. He lived in the midst of that visionary world in which nothing is but what is not. He dreamed with his eyes open, and saw ghosts dancing round him at noontide. He had been in his youth an enthusiast for liberty, and had hailed the dawn of the French Revolution as the promise of a day that was to banish war and slavery,

68

and every form of vice and misery, from the face of the earth. Because all this was not done, he deduced that nothing was done; and from his deduction, according to his system of logic, he drew a conclusion that worse than nothing was done; that the overthrow of the feudal fortresses of tyranny and superstition was the greatest calamity that had ever befallen mankind; and that their only hope now was to rake the rubbish together, and rebuild it without any of those loopholes by which the light had originally crept in. To qualify himself for a coadjutor in this laudable task, he plunged into the central opacity of Kantian metaphysics, and lay *perdu* several years in transcendental darkness, till the common daylight of common sense became intolerable to his eyes. He called the sun an *ignis fatuus;* . . . [359–60]

As Howard Mills says, "this is . . . a History of Ideas, and of Coleridge's ideas,"[14] but we have much more here than a witty satire on one man or even on a typical reactionary. The passage sets the terms, so to speak, for Peacock's symposium and the issues he raises. Radical dissatisfaction with contemporary times and disillusionment with politics were prevailing humors in his intellectual milieu. Since the end of the eighteenth century, vast numbers of thinkers and idealists have had to live in the wake of failed or betrayed revolutions, with only the dimmest hopes of ever seeing their political aims achieved. They have had to learn hard and sometimes heartbreaking lessons of their own political impotence. That kind of experience and knowledge can set off all sorts of rationalizing and sublimating processes, e.g., the world is bad, there is a higher reality that only special intelligences can reach and appreciate, certain delicate spirits are too good for this earth, and poets and intellectuals are the *unacknowledged* legislators of the world.

Compare what Sartre has to say about Flaubert's mid-nineteenth-century intellectual audience with the characters' modish pessimism and the Floskyan mysticism in *Nightmare Abbey:* "These young readers are *defeatists:* they demand that their writers show that action is impossible in order to blot out their shame at having failed in their attempt at Revolution. For them realism is the condemnation of reality: life is absolute disaster. . . . *pessimism* has its positive counterpart (aesthetic mysticism), which is found everywhere in *Madame Bovary*."[15] Again intellectual history seems to have put a serious face on Peacockian farce; but whether or not we accept Sartre's speculation, it at least helps us to see that the principal targets of Peacockian satire are not Coleridge, not Byron, not Shelley's youth, not passing literary fads, but the devaluation of life and elitist, mystical idealism. Coleridge and the rest were the means, not the ends, of *Nightmare Abbey*'s ridicule, and the proper question is not whether Peacock was unfair to Coleridge but how and why Flosky functions in the book.

Jean-Jacques Mayoux, Peacock's best critic, makes an excellent point: "Coleridge, dans *Nightmare Abbey*, est surtout l'homme qui ne voit pas clair en lui-même, qui refuse de voir la suite de ses idées et le but où tendent ses principes."[16] (Coleridge, in *Nightmare Abbey*, is, above all, the man who lacks self-knowledge, who refuses to see the connection between his ideas and the end result of his principles.) We see the result of these "ideas" in the scene in which Marionetta asks Flosky if he knows why Scythrop is behaving so strangely. Flosky has lost touch with normal humanity; there is a complete breakdown in communication:

> MARIONETTA. . . . I am not conversant with Metaphysical subtleties, but—
> MR. FLOSKY. Subtleties! my dear Miss O'Carroll. I am sorry to find you participating in the vulgar error of the *reading public*, to whom an unusual collection of words, involving a juxtaposition of antiperistatical ideas, immediately suggests the notion of hyperoxysophistical paradoxology. . . .
> MARIONETTA. Will you oblige me, Mr. Flosky, by giving me a plain answer to a plain question?
> MR. FLOSKY. It is impossible, my dear Miss O'Carroll. [394–97]

Obscurantism results in obscurity and, unfortunately, in the loss of any hope that philosophical and ethical reasoning may influence common life. "[Flosky] exhorted all who would listen to his friendly voice, which were about as many as called 'God save King Richard'" (360). Peacock sees the failure to communicate as a predominant humor of modern intellectual life, and a glance at a few of our own "learned" journals will show how right he is.

But in Flosky's idealistic principles there is potentially an even more dangerous tendency than opacity. A priori idealism calls real, good, and most important that which many—the brightest as well as the dullest—cannot perceive through their senses. Ultimately, it makes the transcendent experience within the single mind, rather than shared empirical knowledge, the measure of all things. It thus puts a frightful distance between people.

Before we condemn Peacock for antiintellectual philistinism, we need to ponder the results of intellectual idealism. As Flosky's words often imply, idealism is fully capable of liquidating any particularity (such as other people) that does not fit its tenets of how things ought to be. It easily leads to mysticism and violence. Peacock, for example, mocking Flosky, seizes on some ghastly historical results of the idealizing, faithful, religious mind at work: "The good old times were always on his lips; meaning the days when polemic theology was in its prime, and rival prelates beat the drum ecclesiastic with Herculean vigour, till the one wound up his series of syllogisms with the very orthodox conclusion of roasting the other" (360). To eliminate facts and the real world is to eliminate the focus and substance of shared human feeling and communion. "Ideal beauty," says Mr. Hilary to Flosky and the rest, "is not the mind's creation: it is real beauty, refined and purified in the mind's alembic" (412). In his travesty of Flosky, Peacock insists on the materiality of life and makes a joke out of the mind/body split, which has so often allowed people, for idealistic reasons, to mortify the flesh of others. For him, only what exists beyond the limits of a particular mind can unite different minds in harmony.

IV

Three other characters—Cypress, Listless, and Toobad—almost seem to be the offspring of Flosky's ideology. Each shows a form of discontent with the present, together with the lack of human sympathy that his philosophy implies. Cypress, the Byronic humor, speaks for the insatiability of egotism that ends in nihilism. Since the world can never meet the ego's swollen

71

demands, it is therefore worthless: "There is no worth nor beauty but in the mind's idea," Cypress says (412), and he sings, "The soul is its own monument" (414). There is no human community for him: "The sum of our social destiny," he says, "is to inflict or to endure" (412). Peacock saw what is now clear: Byronism, which seemed revolutionary to so many in the nineteenth century, was simply, in its popularized forms at least, a disguised form of reaction.

Listless, the charming parasite, personifies the phrase *As for living, our servants will do that for us:* "Fatout!" he shouts to his man, "Did I ever see a mermaid?", "Fatout! Did I ever see a ghost?" He reverences Flosky and finds support for his apathetic luxury and world-weariness in the message of the Floskyan school: "But I must say, modern books are very consolatory . . . to my feelings. There is, as it were, a delightful north-east wind, an intellectual blight breathing through them; a delicious misanthropy and discontent, that demonstrates the nullity of virtue and energy, and puts me in good humour with myself and my sofa" (377). Idealism can provide a good rationale for inaction because it can always make the results of human effort look shoddy by comparing them to what might be. It, like ennui, often finds reality uninteresting.

Toobad, the Manichean millenarian, beats everyone at condemning life outright. He takes the apocalyptic seer's perverse joy in broadcasting the present bad state of affairs and predicting worse to come. In practice, professors of apocalyptic thought, a desperate but very common form of idealism, often turn out to be, like Toobad, praisers of the past and devotees of universal-degeneration theories. Peacock gives Toobad one of the most entertaining pieces of rhetoric in the book:

> "We see a hundred men hanged, where they saw one. We see five hundred transported, where they saw one. We see five thousand in the workhouse, where they saw one. We see scores of Bible Societies, where they saw none. We see paper, where they saw gold. We see men in stays, where they saw men in armour. We see painted faces, where they saw healthy ones. We see children perishing in manufactories, where they saw them flourishing in the fields. We see prisons, where they saw castles. We see masters, where they saw representatives. In short, they saw true men,

where we see false knaves. They saw Milton, and we see Mr. Sackbut." [411–12]

This attack on an alienating industrialism, utilitarian thought, and positivism has a stirring plausibility, and, coming a generation later, it could be straight Carlyle, Ruskin, or even Peacock himself (cf. *Gryll Grange* [1860]). Here Peacock sets it forth in context as both a wonderfully engaging humor of his times and a fragmenting attitude in itself. The trouble, of course, is that it isn't true; the past wasn't like that, and shouting about the good old days nearly always masks woolly thinking. Apocalyptic rant leads to idealizing the past or the future and, from that, to easy condemnation and lack of sympathy for living people. Toobad's opinions—like those of Flosky, Cypress, and Listless—disdain real life; they are, finally, literal nonsense. How ironic it is that a writer who exposes so many forms of nineteenth-century reaction—e.g., bourgeois idealism, ideological pessimism, fatalism, ennui, and intellectual snobbism—should himself be branded as a reactionary.

V

Peacock makes that balmy walking humor of natural science, Asterias, into a much more ambivalent figure than most of the other characters. Though ridiculously obsessed with tritons and mermaids, he is far from being simply the butt of a satire on science. In fact, he makes an excellent spokesman for science. Peacock has him say to Listless:

"I have known many evils, but I have never known the worst of all . . . those which are comprehended in the inexhaustible varieties of *ennui* . . . which have alike infected society, and the literature of society; and which would make an arctic ocean of the human mind, if the more humane pursuits of philosophy and science did not keep alive the better feelings and more valuable energies of our nature." [390]

Asterias continues with a paean to his vocation:

" . . . while science moves on in the calm dignity of its course, affording to youth delights equally pure and vivid—to maturity, calm and grateful occupation—to old

73

age, the most pleasing recollections and inexhaustible materials of agreeable and salutary reflection; and, while its votary enjoys the disinterested pleasure of enlarging the intellect and increasing the comforts of society, he is himself independent of the caprices of human intercourse and the accidents of human fortune. Nature is his great and inexhaustible treasure." [390–91][17]

The gists of the most serious rationales of science, which have been repeated and expanded *ad nauseam,* show up in this concise oration. Asterias indicates science's place in progressive, positivistic thought, its utility, its communal nature, the common faith in its fairness and objectivity, and the appeal of the scientific method as a moral end in itself. Because Asterias's own hypothesis about mermaids is crazy, Peacock has been attacked: "Would Peacock have seen a Mr Asterias in Darwin? It is virtually certain that he would. . . . he makes his cranks representative of the men who shape destiny, as cosy reactionaries always do."[18] Peacock's answer is implicit in the text: cranks, and those who are called cranks, *do* shape destiny; the crank may be part genius, and the genius is certainly part crank; there *was* an Asterias in Darwin; at the very least, even if we were to grant science an impersonality and exactitude that few scientists would claim, modern science depends on the work of men who were part crank, and the drawing of rigid lines between geniuses and cranks would have prevented science from ever developing. To a godlike observer of all human history, it might well appear that science was the prevailing intellectual humor of the nineteenth and twentieth centuries, as totemism might have been ten thousand years ago or Christian supernaturalism in the thirteenth century. For such a witness, these "humors" might all contain elements of foolishness and incongruity, but they might also appear as structures of communal organization attempting to link people. Regarding science irreverently as a humor of humanity that leads people into as much affectation and folly as any other historical humor and whose ultimate value may still be up in the air, as it were, is of course intellectually respectable and needs no apology.

VI

The case of Asterias, a silly quester who nevertheless speaks plausibly and behaves aimiably, typifies the genial and open nature of *Nightmare Abbey*. All the characters are part of a social congregation, even against their will. In this fictional world, any and all mental hobbyhorses will be ridden, any and all opinions advocated. Moreover, they ought to be. Peacock relishes intellectual ferment—even if particular ideas are absurd—and he makes from it part of the vintage of human communion. Even Flosky, Toobad, and Cypress sometimes speak sensibly and put forth challenging views. Intellectual contentiousness is healthy, and diverting too, provided that we see it in a proper framework: truth is not a matter of individual expression but of collective process and experience.

Peacock himself rarely makes a judgment among competing ideas in his own voice; he prefers to withdraw his narrator and let his characters speak for themselves, as in the text of a drama. Mayoux shows him as a man incapable of holding a position without seeing the force of the opposite position, and his dialogue and dramatized debate reflect that kind of mind. Negative capability of a sort informs his symposium. In *Nightmare Abbey* there is no "irritable reaching after fact and reason," little intellectual bullying or disguised proselytizing for some moral creed, no self-righteousness. It is true that we sometimes find Mr. Hilary expressing Peacock's own humor of thoughtful epicureanism:

> "To expect too much is a disease in the expectant, for which human nature is not responsible; and, in the common name of humanity, I protest against these false and mischievous ravings. To rail against humanity for not being abstract perfection, and against human love for not realizing all the splendid visions of the poets of chivalry, is to rail at the summer for not being all sunshine, and at the rose for not being always in bloom. . . ." [412][19]

In *Nightmare Abbey,* however, it is not by the strength of any intellectual argument that the communion of men and women shall be saved. Since Everyman does not consciously seem to choose the humor he is in, Everyman is not to be reasoned out of his humor. In their egoism, people think and imagine differently from other people. But for Peacock, there are impulses anterior to articulate thought and personal imagination, things even deeper in human nature; one is the biological urge to life, and another is the desire for pleasure and fellowship—a desire that binds a person to others and makes him remarkably like them, no matter what he professes.

IMAGES

the only symbol of perfect life [409]

Peacock has a "religious feeling for the real, material world."[20] A nonbeliever in Christian dogma, he finds an inseparable oneness in body and spirit, but, like a Christian, he longs for everlasting life. Reversing orthodoxy, he finds immortality in the permanence of the body and its senses rather than in eternal spirit, and in the human species rather than in the individual soul's salvation through the grace of God. His comedy is mundane, not divine, but it is reverent. Those country houses whose names become the titles of his novels—*Headlong Hall, Melincourt, Nightmare Abbey, Crotchet Castle,* and *Gryll Grange*—are really neo-Bacchic temples of communion. Nightmare Abbey, no longer "a stronghold of the ancient church militant," is still a religious hostel. Like a church, it serves as both a sanctuary from the urgencies of the world and a gathering place for the world. These fictional structures, like Nightmare Abbey and Crotchet Castle, contain and represent disparate men and women meeting, talking, and living foolishly by individual patterns that turn out to be alike, and they are surely images that Peacock formed out of a catholic sensibility that felt the communion of human life.

I

In his fiction, as in Bacchic rites or the Eucharist, wine is the controlling image—especially in *Nightmare Abbey*. This wine is not the cause of inebriation and hangovers but a symbol of enduring, festive being. The most important moments come when his characters drink, almost ritually, celebrating a comic

76

mass in which they are at one with each other and with all humanity. In nearly every chapter the wine flows freely, and we become more and more conscious of its central role. Here are the beginning and the end of the great incantatory drinking scene of chapter 11:

The conversation that took place when the wine was in circulation, and the ladies were withdrawn, we shall report with our usual scrupulous fidelity.

MR. GLOWRY: You are leaving England, Mr. Cypress .... A smiling bumper to a sad parting, and let us all be unhappy together.

MR. CYPRESS (*filling a bumper*): This is the only social habit that the disappointed spirit never unlearns.

THE REVEREND MR. LARYNX (*filling*): It is the only piece of academical learning that the finished educatee retains.

MR. FLOSKY (*filling*): It is the only objective fact which the sceptic can realise.

SCYTHROP (*filling*): It is the only styptic for a bleeding heart.

THE HONOURABLE MR. LISTLESS (*filling*): It is the only trouble that is very well worth taking.

MR. ASTERIAS (*filling*): It is the only key of conversational truth.

MR. TOOBAD (*filling*): It is the only antidote to the great wrath of the devil.

MR. HILARY (*filling*): It is the only symbol of perfect life. The inscription 'HIC NON BIBITUR' will suit nothing but a tombstone.... [408–9]

MR. GLOWRY: ... Let us all be unhappy together.

MR. HILARY: Now, I say again, a catch.

THE REVEREND MR. LARYNX: I am for you....

MR. HILARY AND THE REVEREND MR. LARYNX: ...

> The bowl goes trim. The moon doth shine.
> And our ballast is old wine;
> And your ballast is old wine....

This catch was so well executed by the spirit and science of Mr. Hilary, and the deep tri-une voice of the reverend gentleman, that the whole party, *in spite of themselves* [italics mine], caught the contagion, and joined in chorus at the conclusion, each raising a bumper to his lips:

> The bowl goes trim: the moon doth shine:
> And our ballast is old wine.

[414–15]

Such writing renders and helps to explain the seemingly odd but persistent attraction of alcohol, drugs, and their cults. They appeal to tribal instincts and longings for an end to separateness. The self is drowned in wine and, with it, for the moment, one vulnerability of the self: its nagging knowledge that "I" must die. Drinking, one is momentarily consumed by the rest of the human company and, indeed, by the outside world; our language puts it starkly: one is "drunk."

In the chanting, the singing, and the transformation of gloom and dispute into play and exhilaration, Peacock shows the magical properties of wine to create solidarity. For him, as for Hilary, it symbolizes perfect life. It is, as Flosky says, an "objective fact," connoting pleasure, companionship, the continuity of human culture through the ages, and—not least—the metaphorical power of the race. Says Mayoux:

> Le Vin crée la joie. . . . La même bouteille fait le tour de la table; elle est la source visible, tangible, commune, de sensations personnelles non seulement heureuses mais quasi-fraternelles. Ainsi le vin—joignez-y la bonne chère—n'est pas seulement le symbole de tous les plaisirs, vifs sans être extrêmes, de la vie du corps; c'est aussi l'espèce d'une communion en ces plaisirs; opposant à la solitude des esprit [*sic*] la sociabilité des corps. [And he adds wittily:] La bouteille, même si chacun la voit double, fait encore figure de réalité objective au milieu des convives; plus réelle que les élucubrations de moments plus tempérants, mais solitaires—n'oublions pas qu'il s'agit de symboles.[21]

> [Wine creates joy. . . . The same bottle goes round the table; that bottle is the visible, tangible, communal source of well-being—more, of near-brotherhood. Thus wine— not to mention good food—symbolizes not only all the keen yet moderate pleasures linked to corporeal exis-

tence, it also exemplifies the way that human nature seeks out society as a means of escaping spiritual solitude. (And he adds wittily:) The bottle, even if the company sees it double, is nevertheless the emblem of objective reality amidst the guests: it has in fact more reality than the lucubrations of our more temperate but solitary moments. But let us not forget that we are speaking of symbols.]

I would add that the wine stands also for the existence and potency of symbols themselves.

I want to stress that the wine is a symbol of the human ability to make one thing stand for something else. The drinking bout of chapter 11 makes clear the involuntary changes in drinkers' consciousness, the release from inhibition and thought, and the unpretentious but satisfying nature of the communion that flows from the wine. Peacock's wine reminds us that people can and do use substances and objects to call up emotions that bind them to beings and experiences beyond their immediate knowledge. "I am the true vine," said Christ, and, passing the wine cup, proclaimed, "This is the blood of the new testament which is shed for many." Christ's blood may no longer be present in the bowl for Peacock as it would be for a faithful Christian, but the cup does hold the symbol for him of lasting human nature, a pledge to life, and the renewal of one's bond to others. Wine is a primary communal image and medium of physical and metaphorical transubstantiation by which distinctions are dissolved, external life is internalized, and the past is regenerated into the present.

The huge joke and comic mystery of all this is that people carousing in their cups, in their least serious moments, commune most freely with each other and liberate themselves most effectively from the bondage of time and death. When they indulge their senses, drop their tragic mien, forget their noble ideas and credos, and live for the pleasure of the present, they become part of timeless humanity and participate in its primordial, indestructible existence. Peacock does not dignify man, but he does immortalize him. Scythrop talks to Marionetta of drinking blood, pretends to his father that he will drink poison from a skull, but he always drinks wine instead. Shelley may cry that he falls upon the thorns of life and bleeds, but Scythrop shouts that wine is the only "styptic for a bleeding heart."

The great comic image works cumulatively. The last words in *Nightmare Abbey,* Scythrop's "Bring some Madeira," give us man the undying pleasure-seeker, calling for another round, taking on ballast for eternity. The molecules of humanity may change; the image remains.

II

Like wine, *women* and *song,* the rest of the old hedonistic trio, serve as images of communion. The two girls in the novel function in part as humors characters: Celinda as a Romantic blue-stocking and Marionetta as coquette. Their casting-off of Scythrop and their betrothals to Flosky and Listless, respectively, again help form the pattern of humors blending into humor. Sooner or later even cloudheads and layabouts, feminists and flirts, usually join the human flow of couples.

Though they are presented sympathetically—especially Marionetta—Peacock's women are primarily symbolic objects representing the substance of femininity, objects whose lovely qualities make the joy and beauty of life possible. He adores women, but he is a sexist—mildly and benevolently, but a sexist nonetheless. A casual phrase from chapter 11 characterizes his culture and his outlook: "the wine was in circulation, and the ladies were withdrawn." (We shall see how Peacock's son-in-law, George Meredith, would expose and satirize the social meaning of this juxtaposition of wine and women.) He is more interested in what attractive women symbolize and what effect they have on men than in their own particularities or opinions. He wants to show by the magnetism of his feminine images that, no matter what sort of ideology men profess or what sort of idiosyncratic styles they adopt, they still live by, and are united by, conventions that overpower private will. Marionetta is not so much an individual or even a humor as a beautiful and mysterious womanly image that for Peacock inspires love and not only makes the world go round but justifies it. "Her life was all music and sunshine," he says, and he conceives of her—like them—as an entity naturally pleasing and delightful to the senses of nearly everyone. Like wine, and like the music with which she surrounds herself, Marionetta radiates the joy of life.

Peacock loved music passionately, and in *Nightmare Abbey* he imagines that it draws the dissonant company together and provides a paradigm for human harmony. (See chap. 11.) In *Homo Ludens,* Johan Huizinga seems to catch the spirit of music as Peacock understands it: "We moderns have lost the sense for ritual and sacred play. . . . But nothing helps us to regain that sense so much as musical sensibility. In feeling music we feel ritual. In the enjoyment of music . . . the distinction between play and seriousness is overwhelmed."[22] Songs, like wine, bring comic communion. When Hilary wants to prove objectively the goodness in life, he reminds the melancholy misanthropes that "there are such things as music and sunshine in the world." Marionetta, playing and singing, can still arguments and lift spirits as no speeches or appeals to reason can. Music, like liquor and sexuality, changes moods and stirs the emotions. P. J. Salz has shown how important music was in influencing the style and structure of Peacock's novels. (Both she and Edmund Wilson point out his kinship with Mozart.)[23] He almost seems to score *Nightmare Abbey,* using his figures the way different voices or instruments are used in a musical piece to make one overall impression. Of course we hear no music when we read the text, but music becomes another controlling image of the human comedy.

These major images of the book fuse together to show how much people have in common, and in their fusion they reveal that shared experience has far more power over people than that which is private and unique. Peacock's communion of man is sensual, extrarational, and inevitably full of beauty, crazy nonsense, insouciant truth, latent sexual tension, drinking, and laughter—like some fabulous party that never ends, though people may come and go.

STYLE

a whisper becomes a peal of thunder in the focus of reverberation
[422]

"Nothing superfluous and nothing wanting" was the comment of
India House on the papers that won Peacock his job there.
Edmund Wilson[24]

Peacock's distinctive prose style works organically with the story of Scythrop's survival, the large organizing images, and the grouping of the figures to create and convey his comic vision. Let us look briefly at three representative passages—a piece of narrative exposition, a conversation between Scythrop and his father on the match made for the son, and a *profession de foi* by Mr. Hilary—to see how the details of the language contribute to our sense of *Nightmare Abbey* as a whole:

(1)   This only son and heir Mr. Glowry had christened Scythrop, from the name of a maternal ancestor, who had hanged himself one rainy day in a fit of *taedium vitae,* and had been eulogized by a coroner's jury in the comprehensive phrase of *felo de se;* on which account, Mr. Glowry held his memory in high honour, and made a punchbowl of his skull.

    When Scythrop grew up, he was sent, as usual, to a public school, where a little learning was painfully beaten into him, and from thence to the university, where it was carefully taken out of him; and he was sent home like a well-threshed ear of corn, with nothing in his head. . . .

    His fellow-students . . . who drove tandem and random in great perfection, and were connoisseurs in good inns, had taught him to drink deep ere he departed. He had passed much of his time with these choice spirits, and had seen the rays of the midnight lamp tremble on many a lengthening file of empty bottles. [356–57]

(2)   "Sir, I have pledged my honour to the contract—the honour of the Glowries of Nightmare Abbey: and now, sir, what is to be done?"

    "Indeed, sir, I cannot say. I claim, on this occasion, that liberty of action which is the co-natal prerogative of every rational being."

    "Liberty of action, sir? there is no such thing as liberty of action. We are all slaves and puppets of a blind and unpathetic necessity."

    "Very true, sir; but liberty of action, between individuals, consists in their being differently influenced, or modified, by the same universal necessity; so that the results are unconsentaneous, and their respective necessitated volitions clash and fly off in a tangent."

"Your logic is good, sir: but you are aware, too, that one individual may be a medium of adhibiting to another a mode or form of necessity, which may have more or less influence in the production of consentaneity; and, therefore, sir, if you do not comply with my wishes in this instance (you have had your own way in every thing else), I shall be under the necessity of disinheriting you, though I shall do it with tears in my eyes." [370–71]

(3)   MR. HILARY: It is very true; a happy disposition finds materials of enjoyment every where. In the city, or the country—in society, or in solitude—in the theatre, or the forest—in the hum of the multitude, or in the silence of the mountains, are alike materials of reflection and elements of pleasure. It is one mode of pleasure to listen to the music of "Don Giovanni," in a theatre glittering with light, and crowded with elegance and beauty: it is another to glide at sunset over the bosom of a lonely lake, where no sound disturbs the silence but the motion of the boat through the waters. A happy disposition derives pleasure from both, a discontented temper from neither, but is always busy in detecting deficiencies, and feeding dissatisfaction with comparisons. The one gathers all the flowers, the other all the nettles, in its path. The one has the faculty of enjoying every thing, the other of enjoying nothing. The one realises all the pleasure of the present good; the other converts it into pain, by pining after something better, which is only better because it is not present, and which, if it were present, would not be enjoyed. [392]

Peacock's love of antithetical phrasing stands out ("The one gathers all the flowers, the other all the nettles," "where ...learning was painfully beaten into him...where it was carefully taken out of him"). The succession of opposed clauses, with their incremental repetitions, raises a tension and conflict that are resolved in the neat symmetry of the whole sentence. The play of contradictory forces and tendencies ends in a balance of contrasts, and exactly the same thing may be said of the book in general. The conversation shows Peacock using elaborate, pedantic diction for comic effect. Queer, antiquated, and latinate words like "consentaneous" and "adhibiting" keep turning up, and usually, as here, they mock presumption. He is satirizing the way glib intellectuals can and do mask a selfish will to power in their discourse and learned jargon. The very precision of the characters' language and the rhythm of their phrases show a spirit of mockery. As in the dialogue between father and son, Peacock sometimes seems to give people the kind of command of words that everyone would want and then shows that full powers of articulation just make the pretentiousness and inadequacy of the single intellect that much clearer.

Also, he can and does use such precise pedanticisms as "comprehensive phrase of *felo de se*" to neutralize sympathy and create the emotional distance on which comedy depends. The particular suicide gives way to the formal description by which society can order and classify it, thereby turning private suffering and death into an official term of the ongoing process of public life. The stilted, formalistic prose makes death academic and impersonal.

As we might expect, the exposition and the soliloquy stress what is general in human experience. No numbering of tulip streaks for Peacock. Scythrop's education repeats the history of others; Hilary talks of characteristics of human nature (e.g., "a happy disposition"), not of individuals. In *Crotchet Castle,* Peacock has Dr. Folliot denounce Sir Walter Scott for never having written "any sentence worth remembering" (*CC,* 711): "his works contain nothing worth quoting; and a book that furnishes no quotations, is, *me judice,* no book—it is a plaything" (*CC,* 713). That criticism implies that prose style should be able to locate and fix what we have in common. Properly composed language ought to have a pithiness that causes a reader to remember some of it and apply it to his own life. Like Mr. Hilary, Peacock tends to express himself epigrammatically, and only an imagination that finds and concentrates on constant patterns in human nature produces epigrams.

Along with his generalizing powers, he shows care and economy in choosing his particular images. "A theatre glittering with light," for example, and "the rays of the midnight lamp" that "tremble on many a lengthening file of empty bottles" evoke immediately the bright mood of convivial gaiety that

Peacock wants to give to his whole novel. And the phrase telling us that, to honor his suicide relative, Mr. Glowry "made a punchbowl of his skull" is a marvel of precise imagery and diction: it epitomizes the absurd humor of gothicism, which sentimentalizes terror and domesticates horror to give a pleasing *frisson* to the comfortable or bored; but, more importantly, it sums up, with concise symbolic wisdom, the whole history, fate, and reveling immortality of mankind as Peacock sees it.

He is much given to simile and metaphor ("like a well-threshed ear of corn," "all flowers...all nettles"), and this habitual discovery of likenesses points toward the unity of being. Also, all those allusions and quotations that he uses ("drink deep ere he departed," "liberty of action," "Don Giovanni"), because they draw connections between different works and characters and assume the reader's learning as a communal possession, tend to create a general and unified impression of human nature.

Peacock's style calls attention to itself and focuses on the artifice of language. It gives *Nightmare Abbey* a playful tone. Like wine, language appears in *Nightmare Abbey* as a medium of communal pleasure for both the author and mankind. His credo appears to be talk for talk's sake. Hilary may express gracefully a truth about human nature, but his elegant speech will not change anything. It signifies instead that expression *is* human nature.

CONDENSATION

As Prince Hamlet says: "Thrift, Horatio, thrift." It seems to be all a matter of economy.

Sigmund Freud[25]

One of the most striking things about *Nightmare Abbey* is that it is so short—barely a hundred pages. Peacock's prose operates like a refinery for distilling the crude diversity of reality. Exceptional among nineteenth-century novelists, he is deliberately brief, and some lines of parody describing Scythrop after his farcical downfall show why he believed in compressing his material.

The whole party followed, with the exception of Scythrop, who threw himself into his arm-chair, crossed his left foot over his right knee, placed the hollow of his left hand on the interior ancle of his left leg, rested his right elbow on the elbow of the chair, placed the ball of his right thumb against his right temple, curved the forefinger along the upper part of his forehead, rested the point of the middle finger on the bridge of his nose, and the points of the two others on the lower part of the palm, fixed his eyes intently on the veins in the back of his left hand, and sat in this position like the immoveable Theseus. . . . We hope the admirers of the *minutiae* in poetry and romance will appreciate this accurate description of a pensive attitude. [426]

An infinity of minutiae distinguishes one person from another, and a writer, if he chooses, can describe a character as long as he can hold a pen or push the typewriter keys. As authors like Robbe-Grillet or Joyce in the "Ithaca" section of *Ulysses* prove, there is no end to the amount of particularizing detail that can be set down; but in doing so, they run the risk of burying what is genuinely significant. For Peacock, detail for the sake of minute realism is literary self-indulgence. A novelist should select only what counts, and, to Peacock, what counts about a character is what matters to others, what joins him in some way to a community. Peacock excludes realistic proper names, the ephemeral data of the registering individual psyche, extensive physical descriptions of people and place, and anything else that does not contribute to the comedy of common experience. Condensing humanity and eliminating redundancy, he concentrates on a few fundamental points of human union: the race's endurance, the absurd fascination and fear of death, the inevitability of egoism and distorting subjectivity, the permanence of faddishness, the power of history, comic affectation, the rule of sensuality, and the existence of beauty and metaphor. Theorizing about reduction in art, Claude Lévi-Strauss sheds light on *Nightmare Abbey*'s comic treatment of romantic individualism, on Peacock's comic art, and on all comedy:

What is the virtue of reduction either of scale or in the number of properties? It seems to result from a sort of reversal in the process of understanding. . . . The resistance

86

it offers us is overcome by dividing it. Reduction in scale reverses this situation. Being smaller, the object as a whole seems less formidable. By being quantitatively diminished, it seems to us qualitatively simplified. More exactly, this quantitative transposition extends and diversifies our power over a homologue of the thing, and by means of it the latter can be grasped, assessed and apprehended at a glance. A child's doll is no longer an enemy, a rival or even an interlocutor. In it and through it a person is made into a subject. . . .

In other words, the intrinsic value of a small-scale model is that it compensates for the renunciation of sensible dimensions by the acquisition of intelligible dimensions.[26]

In the crucible of his humor, Peacock purges the limitless diversity of individualistic realism and shrinks complexity into a comprehensive form. When Scythrop reproaches the Byronic Cypress for leaving England and not trying to make it better, Cypress answers, "Sir, I have quarrelled with my wife; and a man who has quarrelled with his wife is absolved from all duty to his country" (410). It would take paragraphs to do justice to the liberating ideas and feelings these words suggest about marriage, patriotism, Romantic egoism, and logic. According to Freudian theory, condensation is the heart of the comic process, and comedy reduces the disturbing tensions of inhibition, thought, and emotion by dissolving them in a new and playful perspective.

I said that Peacock has a genuinely religious sense of humor, and by that I mean that his comedy, like religion, tries to convey a sense of well-being and immortal life by changing the perspective in which we see ourselves. He is one of the few "amiable humorists" who manage to avoid sentimentality; he does not make moral claims for the goodness of man and does not base his vision of communion on conscious human sympathy. In his view, much of what we take the most personal pride in reveals our affectation and, like us, passes away. But so-called frivolity lives on, and that must mean something very important. We are part of something larger, more permanent, less exalted than our doomed and agonizing selves. Happiness, language, the need for companionship, and survival of the species are real. In *Nightmare Abbey,* we are all condensed into the same unsinkable bowl, which sails crazily on.

4

DICKENS'S *MARTIN CHUZZLEWIT* (1843–44)

The Comedy of Expression

... man's world is, above all, intricate and puzzling. The powers of language and imagination have set it utterly apart from that of other creatures.

Susanne K. Langer[1]

" ... a Werb is a word as signifies to be, to do, or to suffer (which is all the grammar, and enough too, as ever I wos taught); and if there's a Werb alive, I'm it. For I'm always a-bein', sometimes a-doin', and continually a-sufferin'."[2] So says Mark Tapley, the apostle and embodiment of "jollity" in *Martin Chuzzlewit*. These words proclaim the essence of what I call Dickens's comedy of expression, and they show how completely his imagination could identify language with life. They show also the range and density of meaning in his own comic language and invention. Dickens plays on the incarnation of the Logos that begins the Gospel of John: "In the beginning was the Word, and the Word was with God, and the Word was God"; and his joking logic says that articulate "jollity"—i.e., the comic Word, *comedy*—is his Christ and Savior.

Mark's parody of syllogisms, *verbs suffer, I suffer, therefore I am a verb*—implying also *Christ is a word, I am a word, therefore I am Christ*—has more than a tinge of blasphemy about it. The comedy, as usual in Dickens, is making fun of confining authority and working to liberate and raise his readers' spirits. It mocks not only the academic logic of a constricting rationalism but the inhibitory awe of Christian dogma and institutional power that separates God from man. Since Mark's description fits all of us so well, we too can identify for the moment with the Incarnate Word.

88

By the time Dickens was writing, the zeal and success of organized religion in preserving and extending its social power and influence in nineteenth-century British life was clear. *Martin Chuzzlewit* explicitly upholds Christian values, but the comedy often undermines religion as it appears in the world. Tapley, throughout the novel, does personify a happy, selfless nature and, like Tom Pinch, embodies a kind of Christian charity. Much of the book's finest comedy, however, grows out of the oppressive religiosity of the age and feeds off its biblical language—the dinning moralizing and the evangelical tone that permeated public and private life. Mark's burlesque incarnation epitomizes perfectly the tendency of Dickens's comic fiction in particular, and much of the great Victorian comic fiction in general, to ridicule covertly or directly the moral affectation of the religious and, beyond that, to usurp the role of institutional Christianity in showing the way to truth, freedom, and transcendence.

Enough meanings and motives cluster in Mark's brief outburst for a chapter of explication: the image of a printed word on a page as a living person is ridiculous, and yet it may give us a new way of seeing ourselves and our language. A verb doesn't really "suffer," but, on the other hand, we do abuse words all the time. Maybe, if language is what makes us human, we are, in some literal sense, parts of speech. As there are classes of words, such as verbs, so there are classes of society, as the pronunciation "werb" for "verb" tells us. Greek rationality and philosophy (the syllogism) and Christian mysticism (the Logos) come together explosively in Dickens's comic language as, some scholars have said, they do in John's Gospel.[3] The point I want to make is that the comic prose of *Martin Chuzzlewit* must awe any sensible reader. It can set off trains of thought and emotional effects the way Proust's *madeleine* sets off memories, and there are nearly two hundred pages of comedy in the book that have the same sort of signifying intensity that this short speech of Tapley's has.

I can think of no other novel in the language before Joyce's *Ulysses* that has so much fantastic, suggestive, and astonishingly original comic language as *Chuzzlewit*. It has been called, in passing, "the greatest work of comic genius in the whole of English literature."[4] Yet until recently it has had relatively little critical attention,[5] and, apart from the notoriety of Pecksniff,

Mrs. Gamp, and the American satire, it remains comparatively obscure. The contradictions in the novel itself have kept it from being recognized as a masterpiece.

Martin Chuzzlewit lacks wholeness and order. It does not have the unified and relatively optimistic vision that we find in both *Emma* and *Nightmare Abbey*. The real interests of people clash with the good of society, as they do not in Austen; Dickens is much less certain about the possibilities of human communion and the goodness of life than Peacock. He sees the consciousness of human nature and experience as being formed in language, and language cannot be an objective reporter of reality. Individuals, as well as nations, live under the curse of Babel, and no one's speech or verbal understanding quite coincides with anyone else's. What makes the book a hodgepodge, however, is that Dickens cannot stick to a comic form for this fiction. He mixes his modes, and the force of comedy wrecks the moral fable and the sentimental, pathetic, and melodramatic parts of *Chuzzlewit,* reducing pages and pages to what Barbara Hardy calls "unintentional self-parody."

Pointing out the disintegrated form and failure of much of the novel, she is surely right in concluding that "The farce, the brilliant linguistic incongruity, parody, and zany oddity . . . and the harsh, unfair, splendid American satire, show a sure handling and an expansiveness which other parts of an ineffectual action sorely need."[6] And yet, though undoubtedly true, to sum up *Martin Chuzzlewit* this way is like saying that Chartres has lots of ugly buildings in it and that the whole town could use the magnificent architecture and beauty that the cathedral shows. She ends where we begin: by recognizing the comic brilliance.

Chuzzlewit may not cohere, but Dickens's comic expression in it does. As V. S. Pritchett says, "It is above all in the comic Dickens that we find the artist who has resolved, for a moment, the violent conflicts in his disorderly genius";[7] and that is because the "comic Dickens" mocks whatever opposes him. The basic comic strategy and the basic schism in Dickens's mind show most fully in *Martin Chuzzlewit,* but there is a passage in *Great Expectations* that tells us how his comic imagination works and why it is problematic. Pumblechook and Mrs. Joe send Pip to play at Satis House, where he learns the horror of class exploitation and shame. After being mentally tortured by Miss Havisham and Estella, he returns home to be badgered and interrogated by Mrs. Joe and Pumblechook. Browbeaten, depressed, not really understanding the meaning of what has happened to him or the formative experience he has had, he defiantly launches into a wonderful series of lies and fantasies about what went on at Satis House. He creates a funny and marvelous vision in his speech that astounds his listeners and pleases himself. It is a moment that renders the indefatigability of the human spirit and the power of imagination. But when Pip confesses shortly afterwards to Joe Gargery that he made up the whole account, Joe, a truly good man and the epitome of virtue in the book, tells him that "lies is lies" and come from the devil. There is no reconciling, in the structure of the novel, the pleasure that Pip's invention brings us—and the victory for the free and creative human soul that it seems—with the conflicting sense that it is a deplorable sin.

Dickens's comic sense and his moral sense are often at odds in this way. If we are to understand the full significance of his comic expression, we need to see that this kind of split is something more than a personal conflict that might have grown, for example, out of the private experience of a boy, traumatized by the blacking factory, who to survive needs both to defy the world and adapt to its conventions. The contradiction is cultural as well as individual. Comic expression in the nineteenth century tends to elude the control of fixed moral convention and religious orthodoxy, which Dickens perceives as insufficient unto his world. Turning on them, it asserts its own priorities. In *Chuzzlewit,* it overwhelms everything else.

I will take, as my starting and reference points in discussing *Chuzzlewit* and arguing for the imaginative force and importance of its comic expression, Mark's incarnated "werb" speech and the following oration by the con man, Montague Tigg:

> "I wish I may die, if this isn't the queerest state of existence that we find ourselves forced into, without knowing why or wherefore, Mr. Pecksniff! Well, never mind! Moralise as we will, the world goes on. As Hamlet says, Hercules may lay about him with his club in every possible direction, but he can't prevent the cats from making a most intolerable row on the roofs of the houses, or the dogs from being shot in the hot weather if they run about the

91

streets unmuzzled. Life's a riddle: a most infernally hard riddle to guess, Mr. Pecksniff. My own opinion is, that like that celebrated conundrum, 'Why's a man in jail like a man out of jail?' there's no answer to it. Upon my soul and body, it's the queerest sort of thing altogether—but there's no use in talking about it. Ha! ha!" [48–49]

This wild flight of speech gives us a précis of Dickens's comic interpretation of the world, which makes of life an exuberant, never-ending play of language. And fittingly, Tigg ends with Dickens's own answer to life's mystery: comic expression itself, "Ha! ha!"

LANGUAGE: NAMES, WORDS, VOICES

...every word uttered by his characters was distinctly *heard* by him.

George Henry Lewes[8]

"Life's a riddle," says Tigg, speaking a truth for Dickens. A riddle is a linguistic puzzle, a playing with words; and what is life in the aural and vocal world of *Martin Chuzzlewit* but a puzzling play in and on words? Personal identity, character, history, and circumstances cannot be separated from the power and vagaries of language. Words are the means of joy and selfishness for Dickens. They live, behave capriciously, and sometimes break free of definition into fresh life. They often betray and shift meaning. They use, define, and control people, as people use, define, and control them. Characters articulate words, but words articulate characters too. Dickens's famous animation of things depends first of all on the animation of language. Objects and animals, as well as people, are perceived to be fit entities to address and are sometimes capable of speaking. Even signs, letters, newspaper items, epitaphs, and other forms of writing seem to have voices in Dickens.

Language itself is a recurrent subject, and distinct voices are everywhere in *Martin Chuzzlewit*. Everything in the world seems to proclaim itself and be proclaimed. Like the whole nineteenth century, an age of mass conversion to literacy, when the number of authors, presses, journals, books, and libraries was multiplying phenomenally, to swamp the public with printed words, *Martin Chuzzlewit* gives us a world where words proliferate into a deluge of rhetorical voices, competing for attention and striving to enunciate and preserve individual voices and wills.

I

The novel opens with the most subjective kind of word, the proper (or improper) name "Chuzzlewit." Dickens chose the name, according to his biographer Forster, "after much hesitation and discussion." It had varied from "Sweezleden, Sweezleback, and Sweezlewag, to . . . Chuzzletoe, Chuzzleboy, Chubblewig, and Chuzzlewig."[9] No one can miss Dickens's fascination with strange and funny names, but it is worth noting how much his having fun with names tells us about his comic imagination. Play with words is an early stage of joking, according to Freud, and part of his hypothesis on the genesis of pleasure in wordplay sheds light on Dickens's names.

> During the period in which a child is learning how to handle the . . . mother-tongue, it gives him obvious pleasure to . . . "experiment with it in play." . . . Little by little he is forbidden this enjoyment, till all that remains permitted to him are significant combinations of words. But when he is older, attempts still emerge at disregarding the restrictions that have been learnt on the use of words. . . . *Play* with words and thoughts . . . would thus be the first stage of jokes.[10]

Comic naming, by mocking the constraints imposed by the world, is thus a way of asserting personal authority and freedom.

In the prefatory first chapter, Dickens makes the Chuzzlewit family stand for the family of man. His comic Genesis asserts "Here are your common ancestors." With the pun and *double-entendre,* he describes the Chuzzlewit pride in "chiselled feature" and "chiselling" ("chizzle" was a common spelling for "chisel" in the eighteen-forties); through the satirical name "Chuzzlewit," Dickens means us to understand that the foolish human family employs its brains in chiseling itself. Man is a selfish cheater who even takes pride in the silly word that announces what he is. Moreover, in this first chapter, in the great fourth chapter featuring the greedy reunion of the Chuzzlewits and their relations and friends (the Pecksniffs, Slyme, Spottletoes, and Tigg), and in the book as a whole, Dickens actually represents humanity as *a gathering of funny words.*

"Chuzzlewit," the name, is the beginning of Dickens's wordplay, his comedy, and his typical word magic. He fuses, according to Taylor Stoehr, the "name" and "the thing named,"[11] and he tries to create, by uttered sound and unconscious connotations of names, certain emotional responses in his audience. Stoehr says that Dickens's names—like dreams—condense many meanings, concealing and revealing at the same time, and that is true also of the language most of the characters speak.[12] Chuzzlewit, Pecksniff, Gamp, Pinch, Tigg, Chuffey, Sweedlepipe, Young Bailey, Elijah Pogram, and scores of other marvelous, silly names work in metonymical and metaphorical fashion to hint at the qualities and functions of these characters and to set a comic tone.

Names were once intended, say anthropologists, both to describe certain facts about a person (for example, one's trade: Cooper; one's paternity: Robinson) and to induce, through word magic, desired qualities and pleasant associations into the nominee (e.g., Ruby, Rose, Strong). Anyone who has ever named a child—or even characters in a story or play—knows the strong and generally pleasurable feelings that the act of naming brings. Something godlike adheres to the giving of names, but so, too, does something Adam-like and childlike: a sense of the freshness of new life and of the joy at being able to distinguish and comprehend people and things by manipulating language. Dickens not only fulfills the original intentions of name-giving, he also taps that unconscious source of exhilaration in the act and conveys comic pleasure. He seldom settles for common names or even for allegorical, "humor" names like Pandar, Mr. Wordly-wiseman, Backbite, or Toobad. He creates names, inventing new combinations of sounds and syllables, or he uses old ones in surprising ways. His naming thus has the self-contained nature of sheer play and the rational content of tendentious comedy as well. And what is true of Dickens's names is true of his language as a whole in *Martin Chuzzlewit:* it is filled with pointed satire and the joy of self-expression.

I dwell on names because, as words which by definition belong to individuals and assert subjectivity and yet still function as common agents of communication, they provide a good insight into the whole nature of speech in the novel. It is personal and communal, at once selfish and social. Dickens creates distinct, recognizable speech patterns for scores of his characters; but, though their talk has tag mannerisms, it would be wrong to call figures like Pecksniff, Gamp, or Tigg simply linguistic humors. The unpredictability of what they say and their amazing range of reference convey a sense of liberty within the prison of language patterns. To paraphrase Tigg, they're like beings in jail and out of jail at the same time.

II

To understand the comedy of expression in *Chuzzlewit,* we must be very clear about the animistic qualities and innate contradictions in the nature of language as Dickens imagined it. It is imposed on one, but it is the means of imposing oneself on the world. People may memorize words by rote, but they must invent the combinations of words they speak. In the first lines of *Great Expectations,* Dickens portrays the beginnings of consciousness: "My father's family name being Pirrip, and my christian name Philip, my infant tongue could make of both names nothing longer or more explicit than Pip. So, I called myself Pip, and came to be called Pip."[13] Identity, for him, depends on language and a dialectic between what is heard and what can be said. A person begins by articulating his own being, and he must keep on. Dickens, through image, takes pains to render the subjective properties of language, both spoken and written. Pip tells us that he gained "his first fancies regarding what [his parents] were like from the writing on their tombstones." In *David Copperfield,* Dickens writes: "I can faintly remember learning the alphabet. . . . To this day, when I look upon the fat black letters in the primer, the puzzling novelty of their shapes and the easy good-nature of O and Q and S, seem to present themselves again before me as they used to do." Letters and words have various personalities and histories for Dickens that reach back even beyond memory and will. Something in his mind found writing and speech sentient, as his imagery continually shows.

In the time that an infant moves from squalling beast to speaking person, he sometimes indulges in a happy private babble and enjoys a kind of verbal freedom that, say some psychologists, his later self longs for. Learning words and hearing his own voice, he begins to distinguish himself from his surroundings and form his identity. Also, in an almost magical way, he finds that he can make his desires known and satisfy more of them. Word formulas fulfill certain needs. But all the while that he has the pleasure of mastering and using sound, he is also discovering how ubiquitous is the other, the not-self. He hears and learns to recognize other voices too, which tell him that he must conform to patterns of speech and behavior. Standardization of utterance—language—with all the advantages it brings him, means bowing to the will of others. Imperatives and prohibitions make up a good part of what is said to a child. That may be why those extravagant, soaring speeches in unique style that Dickens invents for Pecksniff, Mrs. Gamp, and Tigg, for example, delight us, even though the speakers may be immoral. A pleasure principle, a kind of primitive comic drive that disdains conventional reality, animates their language, and their original tongues can sound like assertions of a lost individual freedom.

"Moralise as we will," says Tigg, and morality is first of all the will of others set forth in language. With the learning of words comes the knowledge of good and evil, of guilt and sin, which do not exist before words. From the earliest time, then, language means power, individuality, alienation, subjectivity, subjugation, and the conflict between one's own voice and the voices and wills of others.

In *Martin Chuzzlewit,* the action proper begins with Pecksniff, identified as "that voice," intruding on the beauty and harmonies of nature. Falling suddenly into the scene, like the burlesque Satan that he is, he recovers and "speaks again," thus bringing consciousness, fraud, the spoken word, and entertaining mockery into the novel's world. The linguistic jokes of the prefatory first chapter show, as Steven Marcus says, the essentially deceiving nature of language,[14] but they show much more. Its nature is also comic, full of possibility, selfish, and imperfect. The Chuzzlewits, i.e., *all people,* receive knowledge in words that they interpret, modify, distort, and play on in order to aggrandize their little selves. They take the language in which the past is presented to them and out of it construct new self-serving versions of history and "truth." "Toby Chuzzlewit, who was your grandfather?" "The Lord No Zoo," he answers (4), but the transcription of the sound allows his relatives to assert their noble ancestry. Making fun of class presumption, Dickens also shows the almost infinite flexibility of words; for mankind is the lord of creation, whose linguistic consciousness puts him above other animals (the Lord No Zoo), and yet his antecedents remain obscure in a mysterious past (the lord knows who!).

Announced in the opening, and present throughout *Chuzzlewit,* is a Bergsonian comic principle of language (the comic, Bergson says, is *"Something mechanical encrusted on the living"*).[15] Despite the huge variety and freedom of utterance, and no matter how good humanity is at fooling itself, speech has something mechanical about it. People are doomed to try to make words, as the instruments of their egos, mean what they want them to while they disguise this fact from others—and usually from themselves as well. Since, however, they must depend on words for all their information, they have to listen to or read others doing the same. Men and women exist, therefore, in a kind of comic ritual bondage to language, which is both personal and social, and their recurrent affectations that it is either the disinterested servant of communication and knowledge or their own private possession to do with what they will must be continually ridiculed. But, as their only means of liberty and identity, their linguistic inventiveness must also be celebrated.

III

The world of *Martin Chuzzlewit* is a huge rhetorical sounding board—half battlefield, half playground—for colliding, interacting verbal fictions all clamoring for attention. Such a vision inevitably works to weaken the foundations of absolutist thought and authoritarian structures. The nature of humanity and of language as *Chuzzlewit* reveals it makes the idea of Absolute Truth highly suspect, but what we can have faith in is the constant ingenuity of self-expression.

Tigg, himself an amoral dog having his day, spouts in his marvelously creative parody of Shakespeare, "As Hamlet says, Hercules may lay about him . . . ." People construct magnificent word configurations like Hamlet and Hercules, which then become, in a sense, as real as yowling cats and a part of the lives, the expression, and the humor of others. "Rich folks may ride on camels, but it ain't so easy for them to see out of a needle's eye," says Sairey Gamp, and she talks of a "witness for the persecution" and the "torters of the imposition." She blends, imaginatively, old sayings, biblical saws, Christian teaching, church history, and tags and phrases from literature into her life, but, unlike Mrs. Malaprop, she ingeniously shifts and transforms their meanings into something rich and strange. That virtuoso moralist and parodist Pecksniff adapts the words from the Agony of the Cross, "Forgive them, father, for they know not what they do" to his own ends and fiction:

> "If you find yourself approaching to the silent tomb, sir, think of me. If you should wish to have anything inscribed upon your silent tomb, sir, let it be, that I—ah, my re-morseful sir! that I—the humble individual who has now the honour of reproaching you, forgave you. That I forgave you when my injuries were fresh, and when my bosom was newly wrung. It may be bitterness to you to hear it now, sir, but you will live to seek a consolation in it. May you find a consolation in it." [812]

People live by linguistic fictions in which they try to find authority and authenticity for themselves, but sometimes these can turn out to be ridiculously inappropriate. Dickens himself, in order to revitalize the values of Golden Rule Christianity, takes the story of Eden and the Fall and adapts it, making Pecksniff a comic devil figure, Tom Pinch a Christ-like holy fool, Eden an antiparadise, and young Martin Chuzzlewit a new Adam who undergoes a moral elevation rather than a fall in Eden. "Such," as Mrs. Gamp says scornfully, in words that express the proper skepticism toward Dickens's attempts to appear orthodox, "was his Bible language."

The crying need in *Martin Chuzzlewit* is to give voice to one's being and create reality out of one's words. A Dickens version of Descartes holds true for much of its population: *I speak; therefore I am.* Monologue figures as the means of relating the external world to the self and trying to abolish the distinction between the two. Dozens of characters on both sides of the Atlantic talk as if a rush of words could control circumstance—as if language, the original messenger of self-consciousness and alienation, could unite the universe and the single human being. They literally seek to recreate the world in their own images.

The most powerful and funniest voices in the novel belong to Pecksniff and Mrs. Gamp. They express, in their manic verbal lives, certain essential realities in the nature of the Victorian world and in their author that moral convention and an internal censor sought to stifle but that Dickens was driven to voice somehow. Through Pecksniff, Dickens articulates the all-encompassing energized hypocrisy and the fabulous sophistical talent of a civilization and a self doomed to live under the moral imperative of professing and honoring self-sacrificing altruism while practicing enlightened and enriching selfishness—to be, that is, both Christian and capitalist. Through Mrs. Gamp, he lets loose the desperate claims of sensual appetite and the body in a world of economic scarcity and, beyond that, the voice of ego-boosting fantasy trying to subordinate the whole physical world to the desires of the self and to create self-worth out of the imagination.

Here is Pecksniff, on his way to London for seamy reasons, replying to his daughter, who looks forward to seeing the city:

> "Ardent child! . . . And yet there is a melancholy sweet-ness in these youthful hopes! . . . I remember thinking once myself, in the days of my childhood, that pickled onions grew on trees, and that every elephant was born with an impregnable castle on his back. I have not found the fact to be so; far from it; and yet those visions have comforted me under circumstances of trial. Even when I have had the anguish of discovering that I have nourished in my breast an ostrich, and not a human pupil: even in that hour of agony, they have soothed me."[86]

He can use anything concrete or abstract—youth, hopes, pick-led onions, elephants, delusions, or ungrateful pupils—to boost his moral confidence game and reflect his benevolence. There is nothing that his speech cannot encompass and transform into an extension of his being. His words are his God. They work miracles: the disappointments of others become a positive plea-sure; his fantasies turn out to be practical triumphs; physical laws are repealed; his breast swells to nourish a big bird. His expression is a hymn of praise to the glory in himself toward which all creation moves in worship. It exalts. It also delights, and not just in the usual way of satire, which makes us see folly and evil in a ridiculous light and flatters our superior moral

99

perception. Pecksniff's talk, like Gamp's, at moments actually generates a positive liberating joy because it conjures up for us evidence of the fantastic resources of imagination.

Mrs. Gamp's speech typically explodes like spontaneous combustion, and when she finishes, and the smoke clears, her words have blasted out a new context, with herself at the center. At the denouement, when nobody is noticing her, we suddenly get this:

> "Which, Mr. Chuzzlewit,...is well benown to Mrs. Harris as has one sweet infant (though she *do* not wish it known) in her own family by the mother's side, kep in spirits in a bottle; and that sweet babe she see at Greenwich Fair, a-travelling in company with the pink-eyed lady, Prooshan dwarf, and livin' skelinton, which judge her feelins when the barrel organ played, and she was showed her own dear sister's child, the same not bein' expected from the outside picter, where it was painted quite contrairy in a livin' state, a many sizes larger, and performing beautiful upon the Arp, which never did that dear child know or do: since breathe it never did, to speak on, in this wale! And Mrs. Harris, Mr. Chuzzlewit, has knowed me many year, and can give you information that the lady which is widdered can't do better and may do worse, than let me wait upon her, which I hope to do. Permittin' the sweet faces as I see afore me." [813–14]

She begins desperately with that poor relative "which," a Trojan Horse of grammatical subordination, which in fact relates to nothing but her will to connect everything to herself, to impose this self on others and release the world-whelming power of her unique language. By talking, she can fulfill her wishes, show her knowledge of birth and death—first things and last things—see bottled fetuses and sideshows, make the external world more grotesque than herself, and elaborate on the imaginary Mrs. Harris so that she can use Mrs. Harris's "conversation" to praise herself and help her keep a job to go on making her living. In Mrs. Harris's verbal universe, Sairey Gamp is the most important and virtuous person. Mrs. Gamp's creation of Mrs. Harris is a brilliant example of the human drive to project and objectify one's desired identity and manufacture a flattering self-image. It is also true that Harris does for Gamp exactly what a successful character in a fiction—such as Mrs. Gamp—does metaphorically for an author—such as Dickens: namely, testify to his excellence and importance.

In these two typical monologues by Pecksniff and Mrs. Gamp and in the life's-a-riddle speech by Tigg, as in so many others in the book, expression itself seems to be their main purpose. Material gain, though important, is only secondary. The great monomaniacal speakers of *Martin Chuzzlewit* are, in fact, capitalists of language, engaging in a private enterprise of words. These would-be monopolists of talk invest in their own fictions, hoping not only to make money but to corner the market and drown out all other competing voices.

The cliché "words to live by" applies literally. Characters good and bad, major and minor, assume vocations to verbal styles and word formulas. They live by, out, and on words, pinning their strategies for survival and profit on them and hoping to give order and the sanction of authority to their being. "Jollity" for Mark Tapley, the testimony of Mrs. Harris for Mrs. Gamp, morality for Pecksniff, "freedom," "country," and "dollars" for various Americans, are the respective stakes in life by which these nominalists try to establish their "credit" and build interest.

IV

The American section of the novel offers some extravagant and prophetic examples of language absorbing life. Dickens used the United States to write a powerful satire on nationalism. The American scenes still constitute a profoundly resonant, if extremely one-sided, assessment of American public life. But it would be a big mistake to see their primary significance as local. America, as Edgar Johnson indicates,[16] is Pecksniff writ large—a land of Pecksniffian manifest destiny. It is to Dickens in *Chuzzlewit* what Lilliput was to Swift: a place where he could isolate and satirize major developments and coming distractions of his world.

The Americans live by the earthshaking new nationalistic version of epic fiction, which makes a verbal equation of self and country. A youth, in the throes of Whitmania, years before Whitman, writes to young Martin Chuzzlewit:

101

Sir,

I was raised in those interminable solitudes where our mighty Mississippi (or Father of Waters) rolls his turbid flood.

I am young, and ardent. For there is a poetry in wildness, and every alligator basking in the slime is in himself an Epic self-contained. I aspirate for fame. It is my yearning and my thirst. . . . In literature or art; the bar, the pulpit, or the stage; in one or other, if not all, I feel that I am certain to succeed. . . .

> Yours (forgive me if I add, soaringly),
> PUTNAM SMIF. [364]

For this original American Dreamer, Putnam Smif—his name implies his thematic relationship to Pecksniff—increasing word power is the key to success, and not just because all the careers he considers depend on rhetoric. Language is the medium of transubstantiation in the modern religion of nationalism. The ego can swell to continental size: *my country and everything in it are epic poetry; I live in my country and am a part of it; ergo I am my country and a self-contained epic* (and when you walk on our soil—as Whitman would later say—look for me under your bootsoles). Something like that is the message of Smif and of Elijah Pogram, a frontiersman who, lauding Hannibal Chollop, a murderous hick politician, speaks what I take to be a parody of Natty Bumpo's dying words in Fenimore Cooper's *The Prairie:*

> "Our fellow-countryman . . . is true-born child of this free hemisphere! Verdant as the mountains of our country; bright and flowing as our mineral Licks; unspiled by withering conventionalities as air our broad and boundless Perearers! Rough he may be. So air our Barrs. Wild he may be. So air our Buffalers. But he is a child of Natur', and a child of Freedom; and his boastful answer to the Despot and the Tyrant is, that his bright home is in the Settin Sun." [534]

In the words of Pogram, Smif, and other Americans, the nation is personalized and selfishness is nationalized. They talk like descendants of the braggart-soldier figure of old stage comedy, but in Dickens's time a person can no longer go about boasting how strong and virtuous he is. Men and women who would not openly brag about themselves can, however, feed their pride by saying, for instance, "My country is the richest, most powerful, and best nation on earth."

Patriotism may have been, for Dr. Johnson, the last refuge of scoundrels, but for Dickens the surging new patriotism of America and the nineteenth century is the first cover for confidence men of all types—power-hungry political exploiters, money-grubbers, land speculators, public-opinion merchants, and the like. He insists that American chauvinism is a huge swindle, but he shows that faith in the United States, even for the relatively innocent, becomes, through the transforming power of language, a kind of self-confidence. Words make the nation-state into a new God, which helps people to transcend their limitations in the natural and man-made wilderness and find the hope of power and immortality. Nineteenth-century religiosity includes Pecksniffian worship of the God of nationalism as well as the old God of theology.

The wildest and most unintelligible voices of all in America are those of the two "transcendental literary" ladies whose talk magnificently mocks popular mysticism. "'Mind and matter,' said the lady in the wig, 'glide swift into the vortex of immensity. Howls the sublime, and softly sleeps the calm Ideal in the whispering chambers of Imagination. To hear it, sweet it is. But then, outlaughs the stern philosopher, and saith to the Grotesque, "What ho! arrest for me that Agency. Go, bring it here!" And so the vision fadeth'" (542–43). Nationalism, resting as it does on a projected idealization and transfiguration of the self, makes the mental climate right for transcendental mysticism. Wild, whirling words dissolve matter and minds and issue in advertisements for solipsistic selves. Their abstract diction and chaotic, bombastic grammar and syntax inflate the egotism of person and nation into an egotism of the universe. From the language of transcendental idealism, they can form a fiction that disposes of the world of facts and bothersome others, leaving nothing but self.

In the *Chuzzlewit* world of commercials for ego, America, the land of publicity, is a superpower. One of the most remarkable moments in the novel occurs when young Martin and Mark first land in New York, and the cries of the newsboys greet them:

"Here's this morning's New York Sewer!" cried one. "Here's this morning's New York Stabber! Here's the New York Family Spy! Here's the New York Private Listener! Here's the New York Peeper! Here's the New York Plunderer! Here's the New York Keyhole Reporter! Here's the New York Rowdy Journal! Here's all the New York papers! . . ."

"Here's the Sewer!" cried another. "Here's the New York Sewer! . . . with the Sewer's own particulars of the private lives of all the ladies. . . . Here's the Sewer! . . . Here's the Sewer's exposure of the Wall Street Gang, . . . and the Sewer's exclusive account of a flagrant act of dishonesty committed by the Secretary of State when he was eight years old; now communicated, at a great expense, by his own nurse. Here's the Sewer! Here's the New York Sewer, in its twelfth thousand, with a whole column of New Yorkers to be shown up, and all their names printed! . . . Here's the Sewer, here's the Sewer! Here's the wide-awake Sewer; always on the lookout. . . . Here's the New York Sewer!" [255–56]

The medium here is truly the message: Dickens seems to say, "I have seen the future and it shouts." Steven Marcus writes, "Dickens is here satirizing a society in which individual life tends to be increasingly public and politicized, in which private and personal matters are turned into public acts."[17] Such a society no longer appears peculiarly American but peculiarly modern, and we have in this first verbal assault of the New World something far more important than an incidental satire on American journalism. In the ridiculous frenzy of voices screeching for attention, repeating their top-of-the-lungs importunities to the public, advertising the scandalous, lying fiction of profit-mad opinion-shapers, reducing people to potential consumers of words that foist on them silly news, views, and moral judgments, we have the world of the novel epitomized. A welter of insistent language pours forth, impinging on consciousness, polluting the society, screaming, above all, the fact that words are for sale. The miraculous thing is that Dickens's comic imagination can make this world and these words outrageously entertaining—that calling a sewer a sewer can be such a satisfying and liberating expression.

v

All the dinning voices in America and England, all this verbal exhibitionism in the novel, must be seen, in part at least, as humanity's reaction to the terrifying otherness of the world, to that huge bulk of "naked aggressive existence" that seems in *Chuzzlewit* to threaten the self with disintegration. The well-known view from Todgers's illustrates the dizzying menace of external phenomena in a world that seemingly lacks order:

> [T]here were things to gaze at from the top of Todgers's, well worth your seeing too. . . . [T]here were steeples, towers, belfries, shining vanes, and masts of ships: a very forest. Gables, housetops, garret-windows, wilderness upon wilderness. Smoke and noise enough for all the world at once.
>
> . . . Yet even while the looker-on felt angry with himself for this, and wondered how it was, the tumult swelled into a roar; the hosts of objects seemed to thicken and expand a hundredfold; and after gazing round him, quite scared, he turned into Todgers's again, much more rapidly than he came out; and ten to one he told M. Todgers afterwards that if he hadn't done so, he would certainly have come into the street by the shortest cut; that is to say, head-foremost. [130–31]

In stressing the importance of this vision in Dickens, J. Hillis Miller comments: "This alien world, this collection of objects which has no relation to the observer, and no meaning for him, rushes into the inner emptiness, and swamps and obliterates his separate identity. . . . The ultimate danger is that the looker-on will fall headforemost into the hosts of things, and lose himself altogether." And he adds, "Mere passive observation, it seems, will not do."[18]

Words are the means in *Chuzzlewit* for breaking down the frightening mass of not-self into manageable parts, for dividing, categorizing, and reducing it into units that the self can somehow control—or at least vent its feelings upon. Mrs. Gamp looks out the window at a view like the one from Todgers's and

105

fashions a soothing, preposterous fiction in her own verbal style: "I'm glad to see a parapidge, in case of fire, and lots of roofs and chimley-pots to walk upon" (411). Those orgies of nouns in which Dickens indulges himself are signs of a basic strategy for trying to know and master the world:

> Tiers upon tiers of vessels, scores of masts, labyrinths of tackle, idle sails, splashing oars, gliding row-boats, lumbering barges, sunken piles, with ugly lodgings for the water-rat within their mud-discoloured nooks; church steeples, warehouses, house-roofs, arches, bridges, men and women, children, casks, cranes, boxes, horses, coaches, idlers, and hard-labourers: there they were, all jumbled up together, any summer morning, far beyond Tom's power of separation. [622]

Far beyond Tom's power, but not that of Dickens. This torrent of words, this primal act of calling things by names, celebrates the first power of mankind over matter. In *saying,* the self somehow comprehends the things spoken. Paradoxical though it may be, expression in Dickens is a way of internalizing and possessing the world.

MORAL RHETORIC

> Mr. Pecksniff was a moral man. . . . His very throat was moral. [12–13]

> "What's Pecksniff, who's Pecksniff, where's Pecksniff, that he's to be so much considered?" [663]

Dickens's comedy works to free us from moral tyranny. *Chuzzlewit* ridicules all who assume moral superiority and the gullibility of those who take moral authority at face value. We must see the changes in human feeling and understanding that he is imagining. In *Emma,* Knightley speaks in the name of morality; in *Chuzzlewit* the voice of morality is Pecksniff's. He is "the most moral man alive," and America is the land of "moral sensibility." The comedy of the novel desanctifies moral authority. Dickens's uncanny ability to imagine from a child's point of view made it possible for him to keep and render our early sense that morality is, as I have said, "first of all the will of others set forth in language."

I

"Moralise as we will," says Tigg, "the world goes on." *Martin Chuzzlewit* continually elaborates on these words: people *will* always moralize, and morality *will* always be the product of their *wills*. They will ineluctably seek to give moral authority to what they feel to be in their own personal or collective interest by adapting or inventing fictions that somehow identify the way they want things to be with what is absolutely good and right. The idea of imposing morality stands exposed in Pecksniff's speeches as a ludicrous hoax for manipulating and coercing others:

> "Even the worldly goods of which we have just disposed," said Mr. Pecksniff, glancing round the table when he had finished, "even cream, sugar, tea, toast, ham,—"
> "And eggs," suggested Charity in a low voice.
> "And eggs," said Mr. Pecksniff, "even they have their moral. See how they come and go! . . . If we indulge in harmless fluids, we get the dropsy; if in exciting liquids, we get drunk. What a soothing reflection is that!"
> "Don't say *we* get drunk, Pa" . . .
> "When I say we, my dear, . . . I mean mankind in general; the human race, considered as a body, and not as individuals. There is nothing personal in morality, my love." [14]

Pecksniff's dialogue points out both the emptiness of the abstract moral system in which he operates (it is a manner of speech and reflection that has nothing to do with his ethics) and the ironical fact that morality is, in fact, very personal, in the sense that it is often used for self-enhancement. "There is disinterestedness in the world, I hope?" he says. "We are not all arrayed in two opposite ranks: the *of*fensive and the *de*fensive. Some few there are who walk between; who help the needy as they go; and take no part with either side. Umph!" (15–16). Like most public moralizing, this puts the moralizer on the offensive, others on the defensive, and creates a moral hierarchy. Moral rhetoric is a weapon in *Chuzzlewit,* used to increase personal power or lessen that of others. Any act of selfishness can and will be justified morally if the people who benefit from it are clever with language. Says Pecksniff, having bilked John Westlock of his funds, "Money, John, is the root of all evil" (19). The language that Pecksniff speaks is the language of evangelical Christian moral rhetoric, and the present time of the book is called "the Pecksniff era." Dickens gives him the pastoral sermonizing voice and makes him represent the institution of morality in the world. Pecksniff is always quoting or referring to Scripture and calling upon Providence; wearing "an apostolic look," he is called "good Christian stranger" and "a perfect missionary of peace and love," who delivers "such moral reflections and spiritual consolation as might have converted a Heathen." We cannot help but see that the satire on Pecksniff touches the whole religious structure of the age.

Since characters are continually committing all kinds of wickedness in the name of morality, Dickens's comedy tends to ridicule any moral institution or concept of abstract morality. Anyone in the novel who uses the word "moral," or has it applied to him, turns out to be a fraud. Presumption of morality eventually leads to persecution of the weak by those in power, such as Pecksniff and various American bullies. Those who are deemed immoral can be victimized in good conscience.

II

There is, however, another side to the comedy of moral rhetoric, and that is the combination of exhilaration and cynical, knowing pleasure that Dickens can make us feel at the ingenuity and mesmerizing bravado of the moralist's performance. Slandering Tom Pinch, Pecksniff cries, "I wouldn't have believed it, Mr. Chuzzlewit, if a Fiery Serpent had proclaimed it from the top of Salisbury Cathedral. I would have said . . . that the Serpent lied. Such was my faith in Thomas Pinch, that I would have cast the falsehood back into the Serpent's teeth, and would have taken Thomas to my heart" (496). The comedy is feeding off the tradition of popular Christian oratory, but its main effect is to make us realize how people use imaginative power and linguistic freedom to assert the superiority and righteousness of their egos.

Dickens, of course, is as much a moralizer as Pecksniff, and his ostensible moral purpose in *Chuzzlewit* is to separate Christian ethics from false moral authority and to rehabilitate true

Christian faith. The comedy, however, disorganizes the overt moral structure of the novel itself. It releases such a flood of mockery against the moral language that bombards us all the time, and it provokes such delight in us at all the canting ingenuity with which people try to disguise and make respectable their selfish will, that it drowns Dickens's own moralizing—especially since so much of his moral rhetoric is couched in Pecksniffian language.

Here are two passages addressed to Tom Pinch, whom Dickens presents as the moral center and true Christian of the novel:

> "Old Tom Pinch!...Ah! It seems but yesterday that Thomas was a boy, fresh from a scholastic course. Yet years have passed, I think, since Thomas Pinch and I first walked the world together!...And Thomas Pinch and I...will walk it yet, in mutual faithfulness and friendship!" [80]

> Ah Tom, dear Tom, old friend! Thy head is prematurely grey, though Time has passed between thee and our old association, Tom. But, in those sounds with which it is thy wont to bear the twilight company, the music of thy heart speaks out: the story of thy life relates itself. [836]

The first speaker is Pecksniff; the second is the narrator at the end. Why should we trust or take seriously a voice that falls so completely into the patronizing Pecksniffian manner? Warned by Pecksniff's example, we recognize the tones of the confidence man.

The final Christ-like, Mary-like ascension into heaven of Tom and his sister reads like a hilarious parody of Pecksniff. Since language is inherently deceiving, Dickens decides that Tom's voice shall speak primarily through the music of his organ, but the narrator can't resist translating it into Pecksniffese:

> ...the music of thy heart speaks out: the story of thy life relates itself....
> And coming from a garden, Tom, bestrewn with flowers by children's hands, thy sister, little Ruth, as light of foot and heart as in old days, sits down beside thee. From the

Present, and the Past, with which she is so tenderly en-
twined in all thy thoughts, thy strain soars onward to the
Future. As it resounds within thee and without, the noble
music, rolling round ye both, shuts out the grosser pros-
pect of an earthly parting, and uplifts ye both to Heaven!
[836–37]

How do we account for the blatant contradiction between
Dickens's comic moral rhetoric and his conscious moral intentions? One way is to see that his imagination was more anarchic and rebellious than he could consciously admit to himself
and others; another is to understand that he might sense that
existing moral structures were reactionary and corrupt and yet
long wistfully for moral order and stability. Certainly he had
made morality pay off. Pecksniff, like Pip, is one of Dickens's
major figures of self-revelation. Great satirists' targets are
always somehow deeply rooted in themselves as well as their
societies, and their satire works on a psychological principle of
the scapegoat: they objectify in their imagination the traits they
find most threatening in their own personalities and in the
world, the traits they would most like to purge.

In Pecksniff, Dickens parodies not only the hypocrisy that he
finds inherent in moral rhetoric but, perhaps unconsciously,
Dickens the cheap moralizer, repeatedly taking self-righteous
moral positions that cost him nothing and usually resulted
in immense personal profit. His ethical ideal was the selfless person who lives for the good of others, and, according
to the plots of his novels, happiness and progress depend on
breaking the chain of selfishness and giving up self-interest. In
the characterizations of Tom Pinch, Mark Tapley, Young Martin, Scrooge, Little Dorrit, Joe Gargery, and many others, he
says this explicitly. Yet he is caught in a Pecksniffian pose; for
while he professes selflessness, his art, as I have said, insists
forcefully that humanity grows—and perceives reality—in the
subjective, alienating medium of language, which invariably, if
unintentionally, shapes self-consciousness and is shaped by
self-will. His most virtuous characters are relatively inarticulate,
rarely pass moral judgments, and never claim to be moral. Unselfish Mark Tapley, for example, makes a point of saying he is
helping others out of purely selfish motives, "for credit." The
moral conversions in his books, e.g., of young Martin, Dick

Swiveller, Arthur Clenham, and Pip, are nearly all miraculous and involve losing consciousness—dying to the world of words, as it were. But try as he would, Dickens could not escape his dilemma: to write about selflessness is to dissolve it. Once selflessness is put into words, given a voice, and a moral is drawn from it, it turns into a verbal fiction that can and will be exploited by self-interest and power, as Tom Pinch is used by Pecksniff and patriotic sacrifice by American land-sellers. The devil loves to use Scripture—even comic scripture. When Dickens moralizes, he turns into Pecksniff, and some subversive, mocking side of him knew it and made sure that we would, too.

III

Pecksniffian language teaches skepticism and ought to make us ask, when we hear about morality, "Who benefits? What is the Pecksniffian motive behind any moral assertion or stance?" To swallow moral rhetoric unquestioningly is to play the game of power-loving dictatorial egos. An underlying motive that comes through in *Chuzzlewit*'s satire on moral authority is an impulse in Dickensian comedy to break the monopoly of Christians and Christianity on morality. It may be hard for people who hunger for ethical direction, in a time when the effective authority of Christianity and its churches over moral life has dwindled, to imagine the stifling and reactionary influence that Christian rhetoric might be perceived to have in the world. That, however, is exactly what Dickens does when he creates Pecksniff and his speeches. And the satire on America, where the moral sense is as pervasive and unwholesome as smog, indicates that in this comic world the professed morality of the nation or any other social institution has no more absolute validity than that of the moral egoist or the voice of religiosity.

As Dickens's comedy reduces (or blows up) to absurdity one moral pose after another, a universe of moral parody emerges. Every moral stance or pattern that he holds up for esteem he also makes fun of or shows being perverted. Dickens even scoffs at notions of tragic destiny in this book. Tragedy is literally self-centered, and talk of tragic fate disguises a moral evaluation in which the small self presumes to find fate—i.e., all experience, everything that exists—not right, lacking, immoral, because it doesn't measure up to that self's standards. Belief in a

111

tragic universe, which Pecksniff shares, can lead to a comfortable self-pity and self-centeredness. It can mean the smugness of *fatalism*. Dickens builds a comic universe in *Chuzzlewit* that mocks a tragic sense of life as one of the ego's more astounding and laughable moral judgments: "'As Hamlet says....'" We seem to be left with a moral agnosticism, but even that position is parodied when Tigg, while cadging money, attacks materialism: "I do feel that there is a screw of such magnitude loose somewhere, that the whole framework of society is shaken, and the very first principles of things can no longer be trusted. In short, gents...I reject the superstitions of ages, and believe nothing. I don't even believe that I *don't* believe, curse me if I do!" (103).

So we are left with the morality of existence, of Tigg's "moralise as we will, the world goes on," and his "Ha! ha!" expressing the joy, confusion, and odd jollity of the world. It would be hard, I think, not to see the liberating effect that Dickens's humor can have. Again and again it seems to say, "Look! Here is your world, where moral imperatives, in one form or another, are constantly being thrust at you and various moral judgments can seem so daunting. Yet, prescribing morality is nothing but a vocation of self-interest followed by people who, in their presumption, are fit only to be the butt of jokes."

No doubt, attacking and mocking the morality of existing authorities and institutions can be dangerous and unpredictable. But the comedy of expression can free individual men and women to think what hasn't been thought, to imagine the world for themselves, and to invent the voices of the future.

FOOD, DRINK, AND APPETITE

"And eggs," said Mr. Pecksniff, "even they have their moral." [14]

If the characters are not speaking, they are likely to be eating or drinking. Mouths, which open to ingest external nature and to emit personal voice, are always busy in the oral universe of *Martin Chuzzlewit*. More food is consumed here than in any other novel I know. In this book Dickens imagines the menace of a radical rift between inner and outer life (Pecksniff, the complete narcissistic self, on the one hand, and the view from Todgers's, on the other, show the danger clearly). Food, however, like language, mediates between individual flesh and the world. It proves that the self and the not-self do connect.

I

Dickens continually uses food imagery and eating and drinking scenes to shape the tone and themes of the comedy and to judge the quality of his characters' lives. They may express the sensual joy of being, as in the feast of Tom, young Martin, and John Westlock in chapter 12, or they may satirize the crudity of a culture and point up the driving, insatiable hungers of people, as in this American boarding-house scene: "All the knives and forks were working away at a rate that was quite alarming; . . . everybody seemed to eat his utmost in self-defence, as if a famine were expected to set in. . . . The poultry . . . disappeared as rapidly as if every bird had had the use of its wings, and had flown in desperation down a human throat. . . . Great heaps of indigestible matter melted away as ice before the sun" (270–71). Food and drink images may reveal the enormity of individual appetite and at the same time convey the fun of the clever, brazen audacity by which a person goes about satisfying it, as in almost any soliloquy by Mrs. Gamp. They may convey domestic virtue and the sweetness of life, as in this picture of Ruth preparing a pudding: "It was a perfect treat to Tom to see her with her brows knit, and her rosy lips pursed up, kneading away at the crust, rolling it out, cutting it up into strips, lining the basin with it" (603). In sum, they show a world of consumption and the diverse nature of a consuming race.

Dickens has been accused of being obsessed with food, and it appears that he had an abnormally strong oral fixation. His orality might help to explain not only his passion for creating so many different speech patterns and making language such an important subject matter but also the displacement of sex by food and the strange pregenital nature of love between male and female that we continually find in his fiction. He did draw an extraordinary number of figures who have what Freudians have called recognizable oral character structures. These psychological types are distinguished either by their extreme innocence and passive, almost infantile, dependence (popular wisdom coincides with psychoanalytic theory by calling such people "suckers"), e.g., Tom Pinch, Smike, Little Nell, Paul and Florence Dombey, Little Dorrit, and Esther Summerson, or by fierce aggressiveness (the biters), e.g., Pecksniff, Mrs. Gamp, Jonas Chuzzlewit, Tigg, Quilp, Squeers, and Carker. Whatever the value of such speculation, the fact is that all humanity has an oral fixation of some sort and is necessarily obsessed with feeding. Dickens, though unique as a novelist in the amount of space he devotes to eating, gives it no more attention than it gets in real life. As Tigg says, "the world goes on," and what sustains it is food.

The Victorian suppression of sex in respectable literature undoubtedly has much to do with the prominence of eating in Dickens. V. S. Pritchett writes: "What replaced the sane eighteenth-century attitude towards sex in the comic writing of Dickens? I think probably the stress was put on another hunger, the hunger for food, drink and security, the jollity and good cheer. Domestic life means meals. Good food makes people good. To our taste this doesn't seem very amusing."[19] Perhaps not, but at least it gave Dickens a way of approving and expressing sensual gratification. If there is something innately funny about sex, food is inherently comic too, and every meal is a potential comedy. Just as our survival as a species depends on sexual intercourse, so our survival as individuals depends on eating. And both are highly pleasurable acts. Comedy may well have begun in ritual rejoicing at the existence of food. If that is true, Dickens's comedy retains much of that origin by expressing pleasure at the means of nourishment and in celebrating the will of people not only to stay alive but to revel in their sensual appetites.

TIME

From the Present, and the Past ... thy strain soars onward to the Future ... and uplifts ye both to Heaven! [837]

there was a wild hurrying on to Judgment [721]

Major comic writers try to imagine victories over passing time. Austen stretches the inner time of a mind, and Peacock dissolves time into an enduring image of humanity—wine. In

Chuzzlewit, as in most of his novels, Dickens tries to shape a moralized, poetically just time, but here his comic expression works to demolish his overall plan. He conceives of time as a turbulent linear progress culminating in a revelation when hidden information is divulged, the meaning of events is cleared up, and a benevolent order is imposed. This kind of time is a paradigm of earthly existence in Christian divine comedy, the traditional fiction of the pilgrim's progress through the world to last judgment and happy eternity: witness the fantastic ending with the assumption of Tom and Ruth into heaven. Comic speech, however, ruins the emphasis on the future by creating an intensely vivid present. Time in *Martin Chuzzlewit* is actually vanquished in the comic moment rather than in the comic myth.

Dickens's conceptualized time, like Austen's, is future-oriented, but it is not her time of personal reflection and projection. His time moves toward an external, absolute imposition of meaning and moral judgment. Austen's characters look forward to specific things, like dances and proposals, but Dickens's characters have vague "great expectations" or, less grandly, the nebulous faith that "something will turn up." Tom Pinch's situation, working for an unknown employer, doing ill-defined duties, waiting for the disposer of his fate to appear, is typical: "Every day brought one recurring, never-failing source of speculation. This employer; would he come to-day, and what would he be like?" (618). We could almost be in the world of Kafka or Beckett, except that finally old Martin does show up to set things right and explain them, remarking, "You have expected me a long time." Dickens unfolds a predetermined and arbitrary destiny and makes his characters relatively impotent to change or affect the course of events.

What his time scheme shows, of course, is how much he longed for an all-inclusive religious vision of a human destiny that finally transcends death and time. But those voices speaking out of his "disorderly genius"—especially Pecksniff's—both highlight and mock the selfish motives of such visions. When, for instance, we look at Pecksniff's "silent tomb" speech to old Martin (quoted above, p. 98), we see Dickens shattering notions of time as prelude to pie-in-the-sky. Like Pecksniff, most people imagine revelation and fate as the inevitable settling of accounts in their favor or, more subtly, as the inevitable coming-to-pass of what they deem should happen (consider, for example, such phrases as: "God will not be mocked," "History will show . . . ," "Time will prove . . ."). Moralized time is usually an assertion of somebody's self-seeking will and desire.

Living for the future can debase the present. It leads to a demoralizing anxiety and an alienation from what is actually happening, as the description of Tom Pinch at his job shows. What Dickens's comic expression can do is take us out of time altogether. In a moment of comic release, when a performer like Pecksniff, Mrs. Gamp, or Young Bailey has aroused the emotions of laughter, the sense of chronology in the novel is annihilated. Present mirth has present laughter, and time becomes the time of the performance.

> "Mine," said Mrs. Gamp, "mine is all gone, my dear young chick. And as to husbands, there's a wooden leg gone likeways home to its account, which in its constancy of walkin' into wine vaults, and never comin' out again 'till fetched by force, was quite as weak as flesh, if not weaker." [625]

While Mrs. Gamp speaks, I hang on her words and do not care what will happen to her later or whether she is a bad nurse and a selfish person. Dickens's comic language forms spots of time, or rather spots of timelessness, in which I can lose myself. Like no other Victorian novelist, and few writers of any era, Dickens is capable of transmitting a comic ecstasy that obliterates self-consciousness. His comic moment, stimulating, concentrating, and discharging an immense amount of thought and emotional energy, intensifies a sense of being in the immediate present—a feeling we normally have only in the social context of wit, joking, and live comic performance. It wards off the main burden of time, which is an awareness of moving toward an end. Expression itself becomes Dickens's revelation, in which, for a time, we forget time.

The range of speech then seems inexhaustible, and the imagination, it appears, can shape the past or the future freely, into any pattern it wants. But language is always spoken and heard in the present. Mark Tapley, the man/verb of Dickens's comedy of expression, claims all life for the present tense.

SPACE

countless miles of angry space [245]

Space in *Martin Chuzzlewit* is the large global space of an expanding, developing world. Stretching across both hemispheres, encompassing the wilderness of metropolis and unpopulated land, filled with an infinity of people, objects, sights—natural and manufactured phenomena of all kinds—it is nothing like the confining, familiar space of Austen or the limited, symposium setting of Peacock. In Dickens, the mobility of his characters and the profusion of the physical world stand out, and both contribute to the rich variety and threatening disorder of his fiction.

Motion and travel—rides, walks, voyages, mad dashes, sudden flights—take up much of his narrative. As the characters in *Chuzzlewit* move—on foot, in coaches, gigs, trains, ships, or riverboats—space and its contents seem to whirl around and past them, and we have those panoramic visions of a moving, sweeping eye that mark Dickens as a progenitor of the movies. These are apt, however, to be menacing scenes of chaos and meaninglessness, like the view from Todgers's or this vision of the Atlantic: "the sea . . . leaps up, in ravings . . . and the whole scene is madness. On, on, on, over the countless miles of angry space roll the long heaving billows . . . ; incessant change of place, and form, and hue; constancy, in nothing but eternal strife" (245).

At first, mobility seems to promise characters the freedom to move on to better circumstances and also, by seeing more, to extend their consciousness; but the more they see, the harder it is to assimilate it all. The sheer immensity of what is can intimidate the relatively small self and make it seem powerless. Ease of travel can separate friends and relations and disrupt pleasant modes of life. Tom Pinch yells to the coach, "I can hardly persuade myself but you're alive, and are some great monster who visits this place at certain intervals, to bear my friends away into the world"(24).

The counterpart to alienating distance in this world is its density of phenomena, especially in the city, with its huge population of private selves that do not touch and its largely impenetrable mass of buildings and streets. Here people dwell

117

surrounded by what they can only partially see and can never fully know or understand.[20] This massive space has a kind of irrational force of gravity that can absorb the individuality and humanity of people, as it does in America and in London, turning them into things and setting them into seemingly random motion, where they repel one another and then diverge, like senseless particles of matter.

Dickens's comic expression humanizes this space and helps to break its gravity. After that chaotic vision of the ocean, Mark Tapley says: "the sea is as nonsensical a thing as any going. It never knows what to do with itself. It hasn't got no employment for its mind, and is always in a state of vacancy. Like them Polar bears in the wild-beast shows as is constantly a-nodding their heads from side to side, it never *can* be quiet. Which is entirely owing to its uncommon stupidity" (247). The agile brain and tongue can use simile and analogy on the very vastness and strangeness of the world in order to play with the mindlessness of matter.

Dickens often follows his most disturbing visions of hostile space and uncontrollable matter with his wildest comedy. After the view from Todgers's, where the menace of space threatens to send the onlooker tumbling to death in the street, he develops the character of Young Bailey: "the youthful porter . . . being of a playful temperament, and contemplating with a delight peculiar to his sex and time of life, any chance of dashing himself into small fragments, lingered behind to walk upon the parapet" (131). Young Bailey literally defies gravity and makes what had just seemed deadly the medium for his fun. Gravity cannot touch his mood: "If any piece of crockery . . . chanced to slip through his hands (which happened once or twice), he let it go with perfect good breeding, and never added to the painful emotions of the company by exhibiting the least regret" (145–46). The anarchy, the motion and swarm, of existence cannot be controlled, but expression can comprehend and articulate them. The comic imagination may play with the randomness of things and make droll the crazy vitality and inclusiveness of space.

IMAGINATION, FANTASY, AND REGENERATION

the gift of the gab [430]

In doing what Conrad says is the novelist's job of making us see, Dickens is unsurpassed. One reason why his prose remains so powerful is that he convinces readers that we can see, through his imagination, what various psychological and social conditions and processes would look like if they could take visible shape. What do our sadistic impulses look like? Like Quilp in *The Old Curiosity Shop.* What does the false humility of ruthless, sycophantic ambition look like? Like Uriah Heep's autonomous, writhing, sweaty hands. What might the amoral process of collective human life look like? Like Mrs. Gamp feeding, moving about from birth scenes to death scenes, and comically asserting herself. Visualizing what is not, we more precisely realize what is. For Dickens, imaginative fantasy is a way of realizing life, and also of enjoying it. He has influenced, and helped to form, directly or indirectly, the comic vision of British culture for nearly a century and a half.

I

An irritated Mrs. Gamp, answering her bell, asks, "What is it? Is the Thames a-fire and cooking its own fish, Mr. Sweedlepipes?" (749–50). This offhand, fantastic vision of a river turned gigantic skillet suddenly puts us into a world of imaginative freedom, and it is typical of Dickens's comedy. Nothing—not the aptness of his satirical targets nor the speech mannerisms of his characters—contributes more to the force of his comic expression than his powers of fantasy, this ability to work verbal miracles and transmit mental images of things that never have been or could be. Fantasy permeates the language and life of *Chuzzlewit,* and Dickens renders language itself as the grand utilitarian fantasy of mankind. Expression is an airy nothing in which people try to preserve and stabilize their material substance, by which they can imagine what is not, and through which they can see and shape new connections between ideas and things and new perspectives that continually change the world.

Fantasy soars into wish-fulfillment, and yet, though it *is*

119

escapist, it clarifies reality also. Take another remark by Mrs. Gamp, " . . . we never knows wot's hidden in each other's hearts; and if we had glass winders there, we'd need keep the shetters up, some on us, I do assure you!" (464). Glass windows don't exist in people's chests, but the fantastic image may convey vividly, as no "realistic" statement could, the necessary secretiveness and isolation of our lives.

Mrs. Gamp has the freedom of the artist to put words into the mouths of fantasy people and corroborate a vision of life through imaginary being. She also has the novelist's addiction to what is not, and her fantasies both honor and satirize illusion.

> " . . . and often have I said to Mrs. Harris, 'Oh, Mrs. Harris, ma'am! your countenance is quite a angel's!' Which, but for Pimples, it would be. 'No, Sairey Gamp,' says she, 'you best of hard-working and industrious creeturs as ever was underpaid at any price, which underpaid you are, quite diff'rent.' " [704]

Dickens's fantasy confronts us with the depth, the amoral perversity, and the glee of our rebelliousness against what is. In Mrs. Gamp's talk of the nonexistent Mrs. Harris, we find something rarely expressed but real enough, and that is our urge to revolt against coherent personality and to seek pleasure by splitting identity—in other words, to yield to the attraction of schizophrenia. (Let those who doubt the pleasures of split personality—which Mrs. Gamp reveals and which children instinctively seek when they pretend in their play to be different people—try the experiment of inventing their own Mrs. Harris. Let them set down and read over words of praise and sympathy for themselves and see if those words don't bring real pleasure.)

II

The comic fantasy of *Chuzzlewit* expresses, in ways that amuse, unconscious or suppressed wishes, dangerous impulses, and deep fears. That is why it can have such strong impact. Dickens is full of so-called "black" and "sick" humor, which, despite moralists, is for many people, almost by definition, the funniest kind. When a subject that normally resists humorous treatment can be made comic, the release of psychological pressure can be very exhilarating. No comedy could be more macabre, savage, and "orgiastic,"[21] or further from the tradition of "amiable humor," than the linguistic flights of Dickens's great comic speakers, such as Gamp, Pecksniff, Sam Weller, and Mr. Micawber. In *Chuzzlewit,* Dickens, for some, makes wildly funny such images as bottled dead babies, gagging and smothered children, husbands laid out dead with pennies on their eyes and wooden legs beside them, pregnant women frightened into labor by dogs and locomotives. He imagines and plays with fantasies of aggression—particularly against children and parental figures—and of madness, omnipotence, liberty, sex, anarchy, and—most important of all—death. In Dickens's comedy, the expression of a character becomes the occasion for this sort of complicity, and the character who bears the onus for our "fantasy-charges" allows us, as Frederick Crews puts it, to "diffuse responsibility and stake out some unconscious territory free from the taxation of conscience."[22]

"To Dickens," writes V. S. Pritchett, "as to all primitive natures, there was something comic in death."[23] There is, however, something "primitive" in most of us that needs to find comedy in death: an infantile impulse endures to wish away into nonbeing those competing and annoying others. Humor can be a civilized way of facing up to, and facing down, that recurrent impulse. Pritchett also says, in a lovely phrase, that the great writer must find "the means of forgiving life," and, if that is so, then he must somehow pardon death.[24] Dickens's comic expression, from Jingle's decapitation jokes in *Pickwick* to Sapsea's hilarious epitaph for his wife in *Edwin Drood,* makes death subject to comic utterance. Joking about death can help in purging murderous instincts and also in pardoning life for giving us the consciousness that we must die. In comic expression that makes fun of death there is a principle of regeneration at work that makes death the property of the living by translating it into their fictions and containing it in their word fantasies.

W. H. Auden calls "true" laughter "simultaneously a protest and an acceptance."[25] *Martin Chuzzlewit*'s comedy gives us a laughter *at* and a laughter *with,* an exaltation of and a satire on, subjectivity. In the language of Pecksniff and others we hear what fun it would be to act like the only self in the world and also how ludicrous people are when they talk and act as if they were the only self in the world. Dickens offers us the laughter that laughs at men's self-delusions and also a laughter that laughs with self-delusion, because fantastic self-delusion, inherent in our linguistic natures, is finally what makes individual life possible and the world bearable.

III

I want to conclude by offering the figure of Young Bailey as the fantastic image of Dickens's comic language:

> Mr. Bailey's genius . . . now eclipsed both time and space, cheated beholders of their senses, and worked on their belief in defiance of all natural laws. He walked along the tangible and real stones of Holborn Hill, an under-sized boy; and yet he winked the winks, and thought the thoughts, and did the deeds, and said the sayings of an ancient man. There was an old principle within him, and a young surface without. He became an inexplicable creature: a breeched and booted Sphinx. [422–23]

He is a sphinx, a riddle, a wordplay, asking and answering, just as his name, spawned from Old Bailey, shows, the question, "Why's a man in jail like a man out of jail?" In his paroxysms of movement, pantomime, and speech, he mimics the world, parodies its clichés, makes visible its silliness, mocks its citizens' pretensions of dignity, exposes their egocentric dreams and the deceiving nature of their words, and yet he embodies and glorifies the eternal impetus toward freedom and pleasure. See and hear him:

> "Why, it ain't you, sure!" cried Poll. "It can't be you!"
> "No. It ain't me," returned the youth. "It's my son, my oldest one. He's a credit to his father, ain't he, Polly?" With this delicate little piece of banter, he halted on the pavement, and went round and round in circles, for the better exhibition of his figure. [420]

Into Bailey, the unpredictable, ageless wise-child; skeptical and satirical of authority, affectations, conventional notions of identity and reality; unpredictable; totally self-indulgent, yet able to imagine the conditions of others and touch them, Dickens has portrayed his comic art and the comic bias of his own personality.

After Bailey's apparently fatal accident, Dickens's comic fantasy assimilates and revives him. Sweedlepipe, Bailey's prophet, announces the gospel of his resurrection:

> "Is there anybody here that knows him?" cried the little man. "Is there anybody here that knows him? Oh, my stars, is there anybody here that knows him?" . . .
>
> As the barber said these words, a something in top-boots, with its head bandaged up, staggered into the room, and began going round and round and round, apparently under the impression that it was walking straight forward.
>
> "Look at him!" cried the excited little barber. "Here he is! That'll soon wear off, and then he'll be all right again. He's no more dead than I am. He's all alive and hearty. Ain't you, Bailey? . . . I ask your pardon, ladies and gentlemen, but I thought there might be some one here that know'd him!" [812–13]

What are we to make of Bailey's comic rising from the dead? It has nothing to do with the plot, but somehow it is climactic, proclaiming a farcical triumph of human liberty and the will not to die. The novel's comic action begins with Pecksniff's tumble, a burlesque of Satan's fall, and culminates in the happy travesty of Bailey's resurrection. His regeneration shows the malleability of received words and fictions. Bailey, giddy and shook, is an outward and visible sign of Mark's jollity and his identification with language, and he is the gloss on Tigg's exclamation "Ha! ha!" The unkillable figure going round in circles, to whom "all the wickedness of the world is print," is a speaking image of comic expression itself, that glorious, ridiculous resource of language, at once personal and communal, by which pleasure, selfishness, fantasy, and individualism are renewed and made immortal.

5

THACKERAY'S *VANITY FAIR* (1847–48)

The Comedy of Shifting Perspectives

In comedy, therefore, there is a general trivialization of the
human battle.
                    Susanne K. Langer[1]

Vanity Fair makes a mockery of life in a capitalizing world.
Thackeray's comic vision works to create perspectives that free
consciousness from the vanities of a commercial and competitive
society. Though this world may betray, hurt, and even kill us, it
is, above all else, ridiculous; since we can see its follies and
make fun of its ways, it need not enthrall our minds. Such, in
brief, is the argument and the release that *Vanity Fair's* comedy
offers.[2]

A novel of shifting, sometimes confusing, perspectives, it
gives its readers just what it demands from them: a flexible
and subtle way of seeing and judging the world. I want to get at
Thackeray's comic vision through two crucial passages from
Vanity Fair. The first is the famous ending of the novel: "Ah!
Vanitas Vanitatum! Which of us is happy in this world? Which
of us has his desire? or, having it, is satisfied?—Come children,
let us shut up the box and the puppets, for our play is played
out."[3] That sums up the situation in "this world," i.e., the particular kind of world that he has just defined for us in hundreds
of thousands of words. The conclusion implies possibilities of
liberation from it, if we see it in proper perspective.

Words like "perspective" and "focus" come naturally in discussing Thackeray. Optics, point of view, reflection, and composition fascinated this illustrator of his own books and
would-be painter, as the second passage shows. Thackeray is

124

describing a room in the Osbornes' house: "The great glass over the mantle-piece, faced by the other great console glass at the opposite end of the room, increased and multiplied between them the brown Holland bag in which the chandelier hung; until you saw these brown Holland bags fading away in endless perspectives, and this apartment of Miss Osborne's seemed the centre of a system of drawing-rooms" (42:414–15).[4] This paragraph serves nicely as a metaphor for the novel and its structure: reflections on reflections amid the mirroring vanities of man. Here we have changing frames of reference, important allusions in visions of trivia, and a whole social system revealed by glittering surfaces. In the reverberation and cross-tension of opposing views, we get the literal belittling of a society, expanded dimensions of meaning through optical analogy, and a converging of audience and scene in the narrative point of view. What comic expression is to Dickens, comic perspective is to Thackeray: the thing that makes life bearable.

REFLECTIONS

The world is a looking-glass [2:19]

Good God dont I see (in that may-be cracked and warped looking glass in which I am always looking) my own weaknesses wick-
ednesses lusts follies short-comings?
Thackeray, *Letters*[5]

Vanity Fair is the Versailles of novels; it features conspicuous looking-glasses, both metaphorical and real. Fittingly, the frontispiece shows a lounging performer in motley peering into a cracked speculum. A *mirror*—one of the meanings of the "vanity" of the title—is a miracle of artifice that allows us to go out of ourselves. Looking at it, one becomes both viewing subject and visualized object, both in and beyond what one sees. In its shiny surface, this tool of reflection multiplies eyes, selves, and perspectives.

For Thackeray, the complex process of reflection defines human life. Mind, world, and art are mirrors reflecting upon one another, and every reflection for him is a reflection both *of* and *on* something. That is why the Osborne glasses make such a

perfect symbol for his art. When he reflected, he saw contradictions in himself and his world, and they take form in the
mirroring polarities that give the novel its dialectical tension
and emotional force: for example, Becky/Amelia, cynicism/
sentimentality, stasis/progress, resignation/rebellion, characters/
audience. He organizes and develops in *Vanity Fair* reflections
of and on his era, his self, and the myths, modes, and concerns of previous literature.

I

Specifically, a massive and conscious reflection on two major religious texts, the Book of Ecclesiastes and *The Pilgrim's Progress,*
forms the basis of the novel. It mediates and secularizes through
comedy the cosmic fatalism of the one and the apocalyptic fervor of the other. Like them, it offers the pleasures of condemning the world, but it also makes the world laughable.
Thackeray insists on making explicit the growing tendency of
comic fiction to reflect and perform the traditional functions of
religious faith. He claimed for himself and other humorists the
office of "week-day preacher": "our profession seems to me to
be as serious as the Parson's own," he said of all "who set up as
Satirical-Moralists."[6] "One is bound to speak the truth as far as
one knows it, whether one mounts a cap and bells or a shovel-
hat; and a great deal of disagreeable matter must come out in
the course of such an undertaking" (8:80). This apostle of
humor as moral strategy, as that frontispiece shows, comes to us
as Ecclesiastes in long-eared livery and John Bunyan trans-
ported through the Victorian looking-glass.

Thackeray's "Ah! *Vanitas Vanitatum*" recalls its source in
Ecclesiastes, shedding light on his content and purpose:

> Vanity of vanities, saith the Preacher, . . . all is vanity. [Ec-
> cles. 1:2]

> I have seen all the works that are done under the sun; and
> behold, all is vanity and vexation of spirit. [Ibid., 1:14]

> Vanity of vanities, saith the preacher; all is vanity. And
> moreover, because the preacher was wise, he still taught
> the people knowledge; yea, he gave good heed, and sought
> out, and set in order many proverbs. The preacher sought

to find out acceptable words: and that which was written was upright, even words of truth. The words of the wise are as goads, and as nails fastened by the masters of assemblies. [Ibid., 12:8–11]

"Yesterday's preacher," writes Thackeray in *The English Humorists,* "becomes the text for today's sermon."[7] The text is Ecclesiastes' skeptical world-view, the sermon is *Vanity Fair,* and the comic "week-day preacher" renders the meaning and form of *vanitas vanitatum* for his time.

The title and concept of the novel, of course, come from the Vanity Fair passage in *The Pilgrim's Progress from This World to That Which Is to Come.* This original fair is first of all a place of buying and selling, and Thackeray magnifies and develops every nuance and implication in Bunyan's description: "at this fair are all such merchandise sold, as houses, lands, trades, places, honours, preferments, titles, countries, kingdoms, lusts, pleasures, and delights of all sorts, as whores, bawds, wives, husbands, children, masters, servants, lives, blood, bodies, souls, silver, gold, pearls, precious stones, and what not."[8] He expands and makes specific for his century this allegorical vision of the world as one vast commercial enterprise. Every item that Bunyan lists as merchandise is bought and sold in the novel.

II

Vanity Fair is epic; it is the history of a culture—what Thackeray calls his "little world of history" (1:14). But it is an epic that mocks and mimics, the true comic epic in prose that Fielding had called for a century before. The opening reflects Victorian civilization as surely as Achilles' shield reflects the heroic age, but it also has an undertone of ridicule:

While the present century was in its teens, and on one sunshiny morning in June, there drove up to the great iron gate of Miss Pinkerton's academy for young ladies, on Chiswick Mall, a large family coach, with two fat horses in blazing harness, driven by a fat coachman in a three-cornered hat and wig, at the rate of four miles an hour. A black servant, who reposed on the box beside the fat coachman, uncurled his bandy legs as soon as the equipage drew up opposite Miss Pinkerton's shining brass plate, and

127

as he pulled the bell, at least a score of young heads were seen peering out of the narrow windows of the stately old brick house. [1:11]

The definitive first clause, linking the story to the entire era, claims historic sweep and connects the whole century to the teenage girls, Becky Sharp and Amelia Sedley, for whom the coach has come; but it also mocks epic pretentiousness by personifying the century irreverently as a teenager. What then follows previews the qualities that Thackeray would relentlessly satirize as characteristic of his age. We have the heavy stress on material substance ("iron . . . brass . . . brick"), on quantification, on the graceless display of opulence by the socially ambitious, and even on the trappings of imperialism ("black servant"). Implied are the moral flabbiness and ugly physical imbalance that the repeated adjective "fat" connotes. Notice also the almost mechanical behavior of people in this scene. In fact, *"Something mechanical encrusted on the living"*[9] (Bergson's famous definition of the comic, from the end of the century, is a *cri de coeur* of modern life if ever there was one) exactly reflects the feeling of this paragraph and of much of the novel's puppet-like world.

Miss Pinkerton's is really a kind of factory for producing and selling gentility. This refinery has turned out "the Amelia doll," which the Sedley coach comes to collect for that "system of drawing-rooms." Many Victorians believed as an article of faith that upper-class women were meant to preserve and embody civilization. Passive, conventionally good Amelia and scheming, active Becky Sharp, "the Becky puppet" who necessarily "accompanies" her friend, do indeed embody and reflect their civilization, and that is why they matter.

By splitting the protagonist's role into two contrasting female characters, Thackeray made sure that a strong sense of the contradictory nature of life would result.[10] The first chapter ends, "The world is before the two young ladies," and, as chief products of that fallen world, they will mirror it and each other. Becky and Amelia reflect a world of radical incoherence and cultural schism; switching the perspective back and forth between them works metaphorically to give a feeling of life in a society that professes, and makes use of, both a Christian and a "success" ethic but cannot logically reconcile them. These twin nineteenth-century antiheroines project and reflect, of course, deep strains of Thackeray's own personality, particularly the cynicism and sentimentality that he knew existed strongly in himself. But he shrewdly sensed that these figures, coming out of his deepest psychological experience, were types for his whole culture and could thus make clear certain general characteristics of nineteenth-century European society.

They are types, too, of women—or, more precisely, they typify certain influential male conceptions of women as incomplete personalities. Together they synthesize masculine condescension to, and fear of, women. But the joke is that feminine insufficiency and feminine destiny reflect upon men, mimicking their own fates and parodying the stories they tell themselves. To parody is to cast reflections. Amelia is a parody of the myth of goodness, the legend of the patient Griselda, selfless virtue-rewarded-and-rewarding. Becky parodies the myth of advancement and success, the Cinderella-Pamela myth of deserved rise from humble to high station. People actually base their lives on these fictional patterns, but Thackeray finds them sentimental and deceiving. The new Cinderella turns out to be a comic avatar of the wicked stepsister; the new Griselda proves a hapless saint of ignorance and misplaced love. Becky can see reality, but she cannot love. Amelia can love, but cannot see the truth. Together they mime the history and obsessions of that infamous divided self of the nineteenth century.

Amelia is a practicing Christian; Becky is a practicing comedian. Amelia's prayers and simplistic pieties are nearly always shown in a context that points up both their ineffectuality and their intellectual shallowness.[11] Religion does not provide the knowledge and insight of a large and subtle comic vision, but neither does the comic perspective for Thackeray as yet lead to a sustaining faith sufficient to replace Christianity. He reveals, however, in a passage of high significance to my study as well as to *Vanity Fair,* his conviction that the sense of humor has a truly sacred office to perform. After Becky satirizes the Crawley ménage and the hypocrisy of household prayers at old Sir Pitt's, the narrator backs away from her sentiments, but he also names one of her major functions in the comedy:

> . . . you might fancy it was I who was sneering at the practice of devotion, which Miss Sharp finds so ridiculous; that it was I who laughed good-humouredly at the reeling old

Silenus of a baronet—whereas the laughter comes from one who has no reverence except for prosperity, and no eye for anything beyond success. Such people there are living and flourishing in the world—Faithless, Hopeless, Charityless: let us have at them, dear friends, with might and main. Some there are, and very successful too, mere quacks and fools: and it was to combat and expose such as those, no doubt, that Laughter was made. [8:81]

By the end of this paragraph, the purpose of the comic is to establish faith, hope, and charity. Notice the contradictions here: what starts out as a slap at irreverent comedy, a rebuke to Becky, and lip service to established religion concludes by implicitly approving Becky's satire, since it is she who exposes quacks and fools and asserts the moral function of harsh "Laughter." Thackeray, not wanting to appear the foe of organized Christianity, tries to bring comedy under its control, but, through Becky, he cannot help ridiculing it.

III

Becky Sharp is justly one of the most famous characters in fiction. Thackeray made her both the primary agent and object of his comedy and concentrated in her the glamorous vanities of the nineteenth-century Western world. She acts out its restless force, and, miming its magnetic dream of the ambitious self pursuing a career, she performs "all manner of charades," in which we can find reflections of capitalism, Cinderella, Pamela, Napoleon, Thackeray himself, the function of comedy and satire, and much more. "Energy," says Blake, "is eternal delight," and that explains a good deal of Becky's appeal.

She makes the intellectual abstractions of nineteenth-century history live. Take, for instance, this piece by the young Marx, discussing emergent capitalism in the decade of *Vanity Fair*'s publication: "Under private property . . . every person speculates on creating a *new* need in another, so as to drive him to a fresh sacrifice, to place him in a new dependence. . . . Each tries to establish over the other an *alien power,* so as thereby to find satisfaction of his own selfish need."[12] Early in *Vanity Fair,* George Osborne is speaking of Dobbin to the ladies in the Sedley house: "'There's not a finer fellow in the service . . . nor a better officer, though he is not an Adonis, certainly.' And he looked towards the glass himself with much *naïveté,* and in doing so, caught Miss Sharp's eye fixed keenly upon him, at which he blushed a little, and Rebecca thought in her heart, '*Ah, mon beau Monsieur! I* think I have *your* gage'" (5:52). It is a moment of literal reflection, typical of Becky and of the novel.[13] The glass catches a detail that epitomizes and animates a century. Becky exposes the vanity of this world of speculation, but she is the chief speculator. George turns a charitable remark to his own credit, and she decides she can capitalize on his egotism.

She is also Thackeray's reflection upon Napoleon Bonaparte. The main action begins with a comic version of the change from "classic" to "romantic," from *ancien régime* to modern Europe. Becky throws "Johnson's Dixonary," the talismanic gift of the pretentious little Pinkerton hierarchy, right out the window. It is a revolutionary act, desecrating decorum and the authority of the past. Almost immediately she launches a tirade against Miss Pinkerton and shouts to Amelia, "*Vive l'Empereur! Vive Bonaparte!"* (2:19). Dr. Johnson is gone; Napoleon rules.

Becky's cry reverberates in the novel and in Thackeray's whole era. In the nineteenth-century imagination Napoleon seemed to personify the apotheosis of individualism, for good or evil. This emperor of personal will fascinated and challenged writers as diverse as Stendhal, Carlyle, Tolstoy, Dostoyevsky, and Hardy. His career seemed almost an experiment in modern egoism: how far could the single self go in breaking free of traditional authority, and what did his fate mean? Thackeray continually associates and compares Becky and Napoleon. For example, he refers to Becky as an "upstart" and Bonaparte as the "Corsican upstart" in the same chapter (34). Note, also in chapter 34, "He [Rawdon] believed in his wife as much as the French soldiers in Napoleon." The most striking comparison of all is in Thackeray's drawing of Becky as Napoleon wearing a three-cornered hat and holding her hand under her coat at the opening of chapter 64, "A Vagabond Chapter."[14] If she is a mock Napoleon, he is an overblown Becky Sharp. Her life comments on the hollow vanity of his. Like him, she subverts privilege, exploits the weakness and idiocy of a hereditary aristocracy, manipulates social institutions, and campaigns daringly for victory and success. But, like him, she remains finally a ridiculous prisoner to "this world," a barren St. Helena of self.

Thackeray, unlike Stendhal and Dostoyevsky, through their respective characters of Julien Sorel and Raskolnikov, makes his meditation on the meaning of Napoleon comic. Becky is a serious judgment on Bonaparte, but she is meant to lampoon all that he stands for. And in Thackeray's comedy we can perhaps see the large implications of comic reflection as a British strategy for dealing with the threatening appeal of amoral personal ambition and worldly power that the French Revolution and Napoleon had symbolized for many.

Becky also acts out the mentality that holds that diamonds are a girl's best friend; however, the person who thinks this way usually becomes like her friends: "Sometimes, when she was away, . . . he [Becky's son, little Rawdon] came into his mother's room. . . . There was the jewel-case, silver-clasped: and the wondrous bronze hand on the dressing table, glistening all over with a hundred rings. . . . O, thou poor lonely little benighted boy! Mother is the name for God in the lips and hearts of little children; and here was one who was worshipping a stone!" (37:369). That is not, as it may at first seem, merely sentimental. Thackeray purposely identifies Becky with diamonds and stones, and she mirrors perfectly her society in succumbing to an epidemic of petrifaction.

There is sublime satire in the phrase "a heart of gold," a condition that is often correctly ascribed to whores of all kinds. The Midas touch gilds, then kills. Thackeray mocks himself and his readers in showing how Becky's whorish values permeate our world. She sits in a shambles after Rawdon has cast out Lord Steyne and left her: "The French maid found her. . . . 'Mon Dieu, *Madame,* what has happened?' she asked. What *had* happened? Was she guilty or not? . . . but who could tell what was truth which came from those lips; or if that corrupt heart was in this case pure? All her lies and her schemes, all her selfishness and her wiles, all her wit and genius had come to this bankruptcy" (53:516–17). We are left wondering: Did Steyne get what he paid for? Did he actually have her? Did he possess her?—left wondering, that is, in a manner that makes the sexual act an object for us as well as Becky. This passage has been criticized as equivocal scene-flinching, but it should be read as a subtle and deft satire on what civilization has done to sex. In the history of the world—i.e., Vanity Fair—a woman's sexuality has been transmuted into a possession, a thing on which to capitalize.

IV

Becky defines the way of Thackeray's world. Nearly every passage about her moves explicitly to reduce her life to money or commodity, deadening her vitality. Look carefully at what happens in one of the novel's most famous passages:

> "It isn't difficult to be a country gentleman's wife," Rebecca thought. "I think I could be a good woman if I had five thousand a year. I could dawdle about in the nursery, and count the apricots on the wall. I could water plants in a green-house, and pick off dead leaves from the geraniums. I could ask old women about their rheumatisms, and order half-crown's worth of soup for the poor. . . . I could go to church and keep awake in the great family pew: or go to sleep behind the curtains, with my veil down, if I only had practice. I could pay everybody, if I had but the money. . . ." And who knows but Rebecca was right in her speculations—and that it was only a question of money and fortune which made the difference between her and an honest woman? If you take temptations into account, who is to say that he is better than his neighbour? A comfortable career of prosperity, if it does not make people honest, at least keeps them so. An alderman coming from a turtle feast will not step out of his carriage to steal a leg of mutton; but put him to starve, and see if he will not purloin a loaf. Becky consoled herself by so balancing the chances and equalising the distribution of good and evil in the world. [41:409–10]

In this first paragraph, the life Becky imagines is not, as Arnold Kettle says, the "worthless" life of Miss Bates;[15] rather, it is the exact life of Emma, and Becky's balanced and witty intelligence here is like Emma's. Only someone who cannot imagine the pleasures of a secure social position or of gardening could find this life simply worthless. Becky, like Emma before her, sees its mixed values—cloying, charming, ridiculous, kindly. She both parodies and expresses her desire for a certain respectable life-style and, in doing so, reveals the tension and ambivalence

133

within a highly intelligent nineteenth-century woman. But as Becky's speculation continues, it takes on a literal and reduced meaning; her knowing irony and sensitivity turn to this: "'Heigho! I wish I could exchange my position in society, and all my relations for a snug sum in the Three Per Cent. Consols'; for so it was that Becky felt the Vanity of human affairs, and it was in those securities that she would have liked to cast anchor" (42:410). Notice the play on words: "consoled" becomes "Consols," means become ends, thought and life become ownership, and Becky's mind, unlike Emma's, tends to close out imagination:

> It may perhaps have struck her that to have been honest and humble, to have done her duty, and to have marched straightforward on her way, would have brought her as near happiness as that path by which she was striving to attain it. But,—just as the children at Queen's Crawley went round the room, where the body of their father lay;—if ever Becky had these thoughts, she was accustomed to walk round them, and not look in. She eluded them, and despised them—or at least she was committed to the other path from which retreat was now impossible. [41:410–11]

Such virtuous reflections—as that surprising simile proves—are not of "this world," though they occur. They take one out of Vanity Fair, the real reductive world in which Becky must live. The movement of this whole passage is from flexible intelligence to the mechanical operation of the mind. Compare Emma and Becky, those two bold and agile-brained women: one typically moves through the process of reflection and experience to greater knowledge; the other slides into stale, puppet-like speculation. Becky's charming spontaneity habitually metamorphoses into some form of inanimateness or conventional calculation.

What is true of the particular passage is true of the whole book. Becky gets stuck, trapped by the values and life that she herself has exposed as sham. "She has her enemies. Who has not? Her life is her answer to them. She busies herself in works of piety. She goes to church, and never without a footman. Her name is in all the Charity Lists. The Destitute Orange-girl, the Neglected Washerwoman, the Distressed Muffin-man, find in her a fast and generous friend. She is always having stalls at Fancy Fairs for the benefit of these hapless beings" (67:666). Becky has been a prime agent in her author's radical criticism of "this world," but she does not wish to change or renounce it. She wants to make the system pay her. Just as Napoleon, despising the crowned heads of Europe and making them wag with fear, nevertheless chose to become one, so Becky, full of spite against the doyennes of propriety, still seeks to assume their roles. Resentment may be the sincerest form of flattery, because it so often leads to imitation.[16]

It is so easy to sentimentalize Becky. (See, for example, Dorothy Van Ghent.)[17] She has—and at special moments even personifies—"good humour," and she carries with her the promise and illusion of freedom. The idea of the career open to talent has fired every liberation movement since the French Revolution, and Becky at times seems to embody that hope. She can prick nerves of feminist sympathy as she rips away stifling conventions. Scorning marriage and motherhood, scheming, gambling, carousing, flaunting sex, joking, meeting setbacks and danger with courage—this behavior can look very much like liberty in a world that smothers or channels the potential of women's lives. But the fact that Becky's career has the scope of a man's makes the failure of her constricting "success" only that much more biting and relevant as satire. Equal opportunity in the age of individualism can lead finally to that gilded cage of hypocrisy, a dull stall in Vanity Fair.

And yet, though she is cast in the role of villainess and mistreats innocent good will, there still *does* seem to be more hope in Becky than in the other characters. Unlike almost all of them, she has the capacity for pleasure, and we see her having the most fun just when she ought to be down and out, disgraced: "Becky had found a little nest;—as dirty a little refuge as ever beauty lay hid in. Becky liked the life. She was at home with everybody in the place, peddlers, punters, tumblers, students and all. She was of a wild, roving nature, inherited from father and mother, who were both Bohemians, by taste and circumstance: if a lord was not by, she would talk to his courier with the greatest pleasure" (65:630–31). This is one of the few times we see somebody happy in *Vanity Fair*. Such a paragraph shows Thackeray groping to imagine a fellowship of outsiders. The feeling and energy here create exactly the same sort of

spirit that we find in Robert Burns's *Jolly Beggars* or—
sometimes—in twentieth-century countercultures.

One of the fine comic moments in the novel comes when Jos
Sedley visits Becky in her disreputable third-rate lodgings. As
Jos comes up the stair, "Max" and "Fritz," two students, are
trying for an assignation with her:

> "It's you," she said, coming out. "How I have been waiting
> for you! Stop! not yet—in one minute you shall come in."
> In that instant she put a rouge-pot, a brandy bottle, and a
> plate of broken meat into the bed, gave one smooth to her
> hair, and finally let in her visitor. . . . And she began forth-
> with to tell her story—a tale so neat, simple, and artless,
> that it was quite evident, from hearing her, that if ever
> there was a white-robed angel escaped from heaven to be
> subject to the infernal machinations and villany of fiends
> here below, that spotless being—that miserable, unsullied
> martyr—was present on the bed before Jos—on the bed,
> sitting on the brandy-bottle. . . .
>
> So Becky bowed Jos out of her little garret . . . ; and
> Hans [sic] and Fritz came out of their hole, pipe in mouth,
> and she amused herself by mimicking Jos to them as she
> munched her cold bread and sausage and took draughts of
> her favourite brandy-and-water. [65:631–33]

We are beyond good and evil here; for the moment, amoral
comic pleasure reigns. Jos somehow deserves what he gets, as
Becky puts him on; and her performance for the students
sketches both a resentment and a transcendence of circumscribed roles for women. Brains, appetite, frank companionship with men, along with the right and ability to make
fun of gross male stupidity, could just possibly be part of a
woman's experience.

In chapter 51, Becky, lisping sweet vacuities, sings a song that
parodies the sentimentalization of women, "The Rose upon My
Balcony":

> The rose upon my balcony the morning air perfuming,
> Was leafless all the winter time and pining for the spring;
> You ask me why her breath is sweet and why her cheek
> is blooming,
> It is because the sun is out and birds begin to sing. . . .

That song is a takeoff on Amelia and also on woman as a performing object. Becky makes her audience see the *joke* of innocence when it is equated with ignorance and sentimentality. The sticky words of the song explain nothing and communicate nothing true except that such idiocy invites and makes possible a world of exploitation (which is why Thackeray is so ruthlessly satirical toward even well-intentioned dupes and fools). Sentimentality too is a kind of vanity; feeling is showered upon what is hollow, and the one who feels congratulates himself on having fine sentiments and equates good intentions with virtue. Becky's show mimics her society's penchant for self-deception. The sunshine in the song, as it does so often in *Vanity Fair*, reflects the sun that "also rises" in Ecclesiastes on the vain world.

V

Thackeray's habitual parody reflects upon itself and the vanity of human wishes. Amelia shows Dobbin a theme by Georgy, whom she has turned over to old Osborne:

> This great effort of genius, which is still in the possession of George's mother, is as follows:
> *On Selfishness.*—Of all the vices which degrade the human character, Selfishness is the most odious and contemptible. An undue love of Self leads to the most monstrous crimes; and occasions the greatest misfortunes both in *States and Families.* As a selfish man will impoverish his family and often bring them to ruin: so a selfish king brings ruin on his people and often plunges them into war.
> Example: . . . The selfishness of the late Napoleon Bonaparte occasioned innumerable wars in Europe, and caused him to perish, himself, in a miserable island—that of Saint Helena in the Atlantic Ocean.
> We see by these examples that we are not to consult our own interest and ambition, but that we are to consider the interests of others as well as our own.
> GEORGE S. OSBORNE.
> *Athenè House, 24 April,* 1827.

"Think of him writing such a hand . . .," the delighted mother said. "O William," she added, holding out her hand to the Major—"what a treasure Heaven has given me in that boy! . . . he is the image of—of him that's gone!" [58:567]

I take it that Barbara Hardy had such passages in mind when she wrote that *Vanity Fair* deprives us of "intellectual flattery, moral superiority and emotional indulgence."[18] What starts as a parody of school compositions and youthful naïveté turns out to be a satire on what Joyce would call "the inanity of extolled virtue"[19] and the futility of condemning vice. All literature of valid ethical insight—including *Vanity Fair*—is, from a certain perspective, as absurdly ineffective as Georgy's words in making humanity better: our behavior does not fit our moral knowledge. Saying what is right, we do what is wrong and yet take pride in our beautiful moral sense. The satire mocks the literary imagination, which feeds ethical expectations that mankind can never meet.

The theme and Amelia's response to it both show people uttering truths without knowing what they mean. Georgy's allusion to Napoleon sets off important reverberations, and he concludes with the sum of human wisdom; yet Thackeray has clearly made him a chip off his father's block of selfish vanity. Credulous Amelia becomes crucial. She has no perspective on reality, no way of discriminating between sentiment and fact. When she says that Georgy is the image of George, she has no idea of what she utters. She can only see in the glass of her own defensive idolatry.

Such a moment lets us see why Amelia is such a subtle triumph of characterization and also why she is so unpleasing. Loving, well-meaning, grateful for the sugared lie, gullible and content to be so, she shows us an abiding part of human nature. Historically, most people—certainly most women—for good or ill have resembled Amelia more than Becky and lived lives of visionless quietism. Many more have passively accepted social conventions, have let things happen to them, have moldered in states of intellectual torpor, allowing themselves to be used by the noisy and aggressive, than have tried to shape their lives and put the stamp of their unique being on the world. Amelia naggingly reminds us of that wide sheepish streak in ourselves that asks to be fleeced and that eschews the taxing effort it takes to quit the herd mentality.

Docility has its own forms of vanity. Amelia may not have the magnetism or vitality of Becky, but she has the resonance. Becky's son is merely an object for Becky to use in trying to augment her own worth; she doesn't love him as Amelia loves her boy. And yet, in the proud-mamma passage, look how Amelia, too, turns Georgy into "a treasure" and uses him as a prop to her own vanity. In fact, Amelia is echoing her own thought, at the time when she agreed to give the boy over to old Osborne, so that he might grow rich: "Her heart and *her treasure*—her joy, hope, love, worship—her God, almost! She must give him up" (50:478; italics mine). Thackeray never impugns Amelia's sincerity or the depth of her love, but he shows her worshiping false idols. She makes a commercial bargain that separates her from her son.

What happens to young George of course reflects a pattern in upper-class British life. Boys were separated early from their families. The culture insisted that, if they were to become successful, they must quickly begin to learn the workings of discipline, competition, and power in a masculine environment. Thackeray's closest relationship in life was with his mother, who loved him with Amelia's passion but sent him thousands of miles away from her, back to England from India, when he was six. (That helps account for the idealization of motherhood, the split image between a "good" and a "bad" woman, the absence of a mother at crucial times from the lives of Georgy and little Rawdon Crawley, and the pathos the narrator feels for Amelia and for young Rawdon, unloved by his mother.) Becky is a bad mother. She neglects her child, placing ambition and money before maternal love. As an agent of sharp intelligence in the novel, however, she symbolically acts out the Establishment's priority. And we must see that Amelia, though against her will and from purer motives, does exactly the same thing.

Almost against his will, Thackeray distances himself from Amelia and judges her. When Dobbin turns on her and frees himself from his own lifelong obsession, it is climactic:

"I know what your heart is capable of: it can cling faithfully to a recollection, and cherish a fancy; but it can't feel such an attachment as mine deserves to mate with, and such as I would have won from a woman more generous than you. No, you are not worthy of the love which I have devoted to you. I knew all along that the prize I had set my life on was not worth the winning; that I was a fool, with fond fancies, too, bartering away all of truth and ardour against your little feeble remnant of love. I will bargain no more: I withdraw." [66:647]

That denunciation is iconoclastic but not antifeminist. Just the opposite: Thackeray shows up as worthless an ideal of womanhood that excludes the full potential of consciousness. He breaks the thrall of the idolatry that equates virtue and ignorance. He criticizes, as Meredith would, what his civilization had done to women and to love.

A few pages later he parodies the happy ending of romantic fiction and the vanities of love in the Western world. Amelia and Dobbin are reunited:

She was mumuring something about—forgive—dear William—dear, dear, dearest friend—kiss, kiss, kiss, and so forth— . . .

. . . The bird has come in at last. There it is with its head on his shoulder, billing and cooing close up to his heart, with soft outstretched fluttering wings. This is what he has asked for every day and hour for eighteen years. This is what he pined after. Here it is—the summit, the end—the last page of the third volume. Good-bye, Colonel—God bless you, honest William!—Farewell, dear Amelia— Grow green again, tender little parasite, round the rugged old oak to which you cling! [67:660–61]

That mocks the idolatrous love dreams of author and audience, especially the powerful illusion that bliss lies in the condition of possessing or being possessed by another. The word "parasite" sets off an explosion of ironical meaning, opening up new perspectives on cultural psychology and history. Amelia is often a painful and ambivalent subject, but, by the end of the novel, Thackeray, letting loose his hostility and satire against her, can fit her into his comic vision.

VI

To recapitulate: Everything in *Vanity Fair* depends on reflecting the great world in the little world of dolls, puppets, artifacts, small histories, and private matters. But this unimposing little world actually radiates with meaning. Superficiality *is* historical reality. Fat Jos Sedley, a fleshbag of conspicuous consumption, mirrors the grotesque side of British imperialism.[20] The mythical minikingdom Pumpernickel, satirized in chapter 64, reflects the farcical history of European nationalism and civilization. Surface is meaning; physical detail reflects the world. The substance, the commodity, the composition of things, characterize life and, by allusion and connotation, also assess it.[21] A high point of Thackeray's mode of reflection comes in the long description in chapter 24—too long to quote in full—of old Osborne's study, its contents, and the relation of the man to his surroundings. The prose makes a whole world come alive:

> Hither Mr. Osborne would retire of a Sunday forenoon when not minded to go to church; and here pass the morning in his crimson leather chair, reading the paper. A couple of glazed book-cases were here, containing standard works in stout gilt bindings. The "Annual Register," the "Gentleman's Magazine," "Blair's Sermons," and "Hume and Smollett." From year's end to year's end he never took one of these volumes from the shelf; but there was no member of the family that would dare for his life to touch one of the books, except upon those rare Sunday evenings when there was no dinner party, and when the great scarlet Bible and Prayer-book were taken out from the corner where they stood beside his copy of the Peerage, and the servants being rung up to the dining parlour, Osborne read the evening service to his family in a loud grating pompous voice.... George as a boy had been horsewhipped in this room many times; his mother sitting sick on the stair listening to the cuts of the whip. The boy was scarcely ever known to cry under the punishment; the poor woman used to fondle and kiss him secretly, and give him money to soothe him when he came out.

Such writing releases huge quantities of meaning from everyday Victorian objects. Here is the crucial passage:

> George's father took the whole of the documents out of the drawer in which he had kept them so long, and locked them into a writing-box, which he tied, and sealed with his seal. Then he opened the book-case, and took down the

great red Bible we have spoken of—a pompous book, seldom looked at, and shining all over with gold. There was a frontispiece to the volume, representing Abraham sacrificing Isaac. Here, according to custom, Osborne had recorded on the fly-leaf, and in his large clerk-like hand, the dates of his marriage and his wife's death, and the births and Christian names of his children. Jane came first, then George Sedley Osborne, then Maria Frances, and the days of the christening of each. Taking a pen, he carefully obliterated George's name from the page; and when the leaf was quite dry, restored the volume to the place from which he had moved it. Then he took a document out of another drawer, where his own private papers were kept; and having read it, crumpled it up and lighted it at one of the candles, and saw it burn entirely away in the grate. It was his will; which being burned, he sat down and wrote off a letter, and rang for his servant, whom he charged to deliver it in the morning. It was morning already: as he went up to bed: the whole house was alight with the sunshine: and the birds were singing among the fresh green leaves in Russell Square. [24:222–24]

Old Osborne lives at the center of a system that makes life a ledger; only accounts are real to him. Human will is reified and institutionalized. Religion too is reified and shut up in a book of gold. That frontispiece in the Bible, Osborne's sacrifice of George to Mannon, and George's later death at Waterloo help define a culture by showing that it will trade its children's lives for gold. Casually but firmly, Thackeray alludes to a terrible fact of social life, namely, the existence of human sacrifice, which endures though its forms change. Sensing and expressing links between evangelical religiosity and capitalism, between the heritage of militant British Protestantism and bourgeois righteousness, he condemns, implicitly, stern Jehovah, that capricious, Calvinistic Nobodaddy, on whose terror so much of religion's authority depends. The efficiency, the decorum, the ruthless, quiet power of a mindset on which capitalism and all ideologically triumphant systems have often depended come through in these words. The son has turned into a bad deal that must be liquidated. Thackeray imagines a world—and it is our world—where obliteration may follow on the stroke of a pen.

But the vision and the meaning of the paragraph change radically with the amazing last sentence, which suddenly flashes a comic perspective. There comic faith flourishes. The sunshine plays off the gold, the green leaves mock that pretentious flyleaf, and the tenor of experience is changed. That sunshine, as I said, reflects the sun of Ecclesiastes, and it rises, sets, and shines on an endless flow of being that overwhelms the cruelties and vanities of people or even of civilizations. There is a whole universe of creation that exists beyond the perverse power of men, or even of son-sacrificing, anthropomorphic gods, to control or ruin it. Inner and outer life seem totally alienated, and that may be lucky, since Osborne's murderous wrath cannot stop the rising sun, the coming of spring, or the instinctive gaiety of being. The writing shows that a human mind can imagine the meaning of the sunshine and project a god's-eye vision—or, more accurately, a perspective from the revolving sun—which comprehends the alienation of Osborne, the follies of society, and the vanity of human wishes. That final sentence mocks solipsism and even cultural chauvinism: the mood of the individual and the values of a ruling class are not universal. The religion of gold pales in the sunshine, and vitality returns. "Moralise as we will, the world goes on." The switch in perspective reflects a comic vision and gives intimations of a kind of immortality: suddenly I see the sun and its spawn of natural existence, and I sense a fertile resource of mind that can perceive the almost infinite variety and wonder of ontology, even at a moment of spiritual death.

THE VANITY OF THE WORLD

a deal of disagreeable matter must come out [8:80]

In *Little Dorrit,* Dickens pinpoints and attacks what is most daring and controversial about Thackeray's vision: according to *Vanity Fair,* when we look at the state of the world, the differences in moral quality and motives among people may hardly matter at all. Describing the amiable, lazy, cynical character Henry Gowan—generally thought to be a satire on Thackeray—Dickens puts these words in his mouth: "I am happy to tell you I find the most worthless of men to be the dearest old fellow too; and am in a condition to make the gratifying report, that there is much less difference than you are inclined to suppose between an honest man and a scoundrel." Dickens then comments: "The effect of this cheering discovery happened to be that while he seemed to be scrupulously finding good in most men, he did in reality lower it where it was, and set it up where it was not."[22] Putting aside the pejorative rhetoric, we can see that this does shrewdly get at the logic of Thackeray's moral vision. *Vanity Fair* confirms that "there is much less difference than you . . . suppose between an honest man and a scoundrel." Moreover, this tough conclusion *is* ultimately a "cheering discovery" for Thackeray. The terror at not having done what we ought to have done, the immense chagrin at the waste of our lives, the envying comparisons with our fellow beings, the fierce competition with others for money, for God's glory, or for earthly proof of God's favor—these horrors fade if we and all the world are vain and moral distinctions among people are illusory. If the race of life is a rat race, not winning is no loss at all.

I

In *Vanity Fair,* as in Ecclesiastes, it hardly signifies whether those who strive under the sun are moral or immoral, wise or foolish, benevolent or selfish—all, in the end is vanity, vanity. Greedy Becky, loving Amelia, kind Dobbin, or the virtue-praising narrator—all of them help shape the world into an emblem of vanity to the superlative degree: *Vanitas Vanitatum.* Moral pride becomes farcical, good intentions delude, and, at the end, all the main characters are either vaguely discontented or dead.

"Has" and "having" are crucial words. In *Vanity Fair,* all desire turns into the desire for possession. To want is to want to have something, and that is true for all the characters, not just the immoral ones. Thackeray calls his characters "puppets," not just because he pulls their strings, but because the system of "this world" mocks free will and mechanizes human behavior. Dobbin, intelligent and genuinely moral, has about as much free choice and knowledge of the consequences of his actions as Pinocchio. In a neat touch, Thackeray makes him responsible for the bad marriage of Amelia and George, which brings

144

calamity to everybody: "Without knowing how, Captain William Dobbin found himself the great prompter, arranger and manager of the match. But for him it would not have taken place" (20:186). The determinism of his action and the commercial idiom here characterize the life of this society.

Dobbin, the best of this world, is a gentleman but not a hero. This good man soldiers in the service of vanity, fighting for leeches like the Osbornes, Jos Sedley, and the "august jobbers" who rule the empires of the globe. The dream of being a gentleman, a concept terribly important to Thackeray and the Victorians, is in part a dream of moral innocence and rectitude. The ideal gentleman lives well, both materially and ethically, without doing harm to others; he follows a code of courteous and decent behavior, which leaves him beyond valid moral reproach. But the dream and the ideal are vain. Dobbin is as implicated in the system of crimes and follies of *Vanity Fair* as the arrantest knave, and such a man cannot be a hero.

Pride in personal virtue may be one of the strongest of vanities. *Vanity Fair* ends with the Dobbin family meeting Becky at a fair and refusing to speak to her:

> Emmy, her children, and the Colonel, coming to London some time back, found themselves suddenly before her. . . . She cast down her eyes demurely and smiled as they started away from her; Emmy skurrying off on the arm of George (now grown a dashing young gentleman), and the Colonel seizing up his little Janey, of whom he is fonder than of anything in the world—fonder even than of his "History of the Punjaub."
>
> "Fonder than he is of me," Emmy thinks, with a sigh. But he never said a word to Amelia, that was not kind and gentle; or thought of a want of hers that he did not try to gratify. [67:666]

Such is the foolish, fond fancy of the gentleman and gentility: not to know, not to be connected with the amoral energy and basic force of the world. Hide your daughter from Becky Sharp, but immerse yourself in the history of continental plunder and epic greed. What vanity!

Even love is quantifiable in this world, and for Amelia as well as Becky. She ends by envying her own daughter because Dobbin loves the girl more. "I want to leave everybody dissatisfied," said Thackeray, "and unhappy at the end of the story—we ought all to be with our own and all other stories."[23] Yet there is a certain justice in the ending, poetic and moral, that makes it "happy" in the sense of "proper" and "fitting." About *Vanity Fair* and its function, Thackeray wrote: "We must lift up our voices . . . and howl to a congregation of fools: so much at least has been my endeavour. You have all of you taken my misanthropy to task—I wish I could myself: but take the world by a certain standard (you know what I mean) and who dares talk of having any virtue at all?"[24] Thackeray transmutes the theology of Calvin, disparaging the presumption of human goodness, into cynical comic fiction.

II

The ending begins with the biblical *Vanitas Vanitatum* and concludes with biblical echoes in the word "children," which connotes both condescension and a slight hope for the future—i.e., children may grow up. Inhabiting *Vanity Fair,* his audience finds itself in the childish state that Paul laments: "When I was a child, I spake as a child, I understood as a child, I thought as a child" (1 Cor. 13:11). Rendering life foolish and undignified—especially for those who claim dignity—and showing that it is full of humor, that it contains resources of perspective and seeds of progress that can sometimes bring pleasure and glimmers of hopes, Thackeray names existence a comedy.

The pleasures of cynicism, skepticism, and nihilism are vastly underrated. "Everybody is striving for what is not worth the having!" exclaims Lord Steyne (48:465), and, if so, everybody must be ridiculous. Prove that the fox is right and that the grapes are indeed sour and you turn the fable into a genuine comedy with a happy ending. Take these two typical remarks by Thackeray:

> Always to be right, always to trample forward, and never to doubt, are not these the great qualities with which dullness takes the lead in the world? [35:345]

> . . . yet he failed somehow, in spite of a mediocrity which ought to have insured any man a success. [9:84]

These maxims justify our feelings of spite toward the world and let us rid ourselves of them in good conscience. Sneering nihilistically, we respond properly to a vain and empty world.

Behind nihilism, of course, lurks a totalitarian spirit of righteousness, and Thackeray's comedy lays claim to both the vision and the judgment of a God for the human imagination, though it ridicules such presumption too: *I find the world worthless, and I am justified in doing so.* That attitude can be liberating. The doctrine of *Vanitas Vanitatum* can mean a titanic upsurping of authority. On the one hand, it keeps the world from intimidating us and it legitimizes hostility. We can think ourselves better than the world because we can see the shame and delusions of authority's structures and imagine a better order of things. But, on the other hand, vanity-of-the-world also means, among other things, liberty, fraternity, and equality in absurdity. We are all in the same boat. From one perspective, we are all bound together in a fellowship of fools, but from another point of view we can become like gods, knowing and judging good and evil, making our own consciousness the ultimate moral authority. We are both children who can grow and develop and puppets whose fate is sealed. Our play is and must be played out, but a new one is about to begin.

III

At the heart of *Vanity Fair* lies sacrilege and iconoclasm, and we distort Thackeray if we do not recognize this. He meant it when he said that he usurps the role of the preacher for himself, the humorist. Of the novel, he wrote that he wished "to make a set of people living without God in the world,"[25] and the reason is that he no longer felt God moving positively in his world. Look through the conduct of religious enterprise in the book, note the religious allusions, and you find that vanity-of-the-world includes just about anything to do with God or religion. An undertone of blasphemy is unmistakable in words such as these: "The hidden and awful Wisdom which apportions the destinies of mankind is pleased so to humiliate and cast down the tender, good, and wise; and to set up the selfish, the foolish, or the wicked" (57:552).

Thackeray reveals much about himself and about *Vanity Fair* in his emotional prose on Swift:

   . . . Swift? . . . He could see forward with fatal clearness. In his old age, looking at the "Tale of a Tub," when he said,

147

"Good God, what a genius I had when I wrote that book!"
I think he was admiring not the genius, but the consequences to which the genius had brought him—a vast
genius, a magnificent genius, a genius wonderfully bright,
and dazzling, and strong,—to seize, to know, to see, to
flash upon falsehood and scorch it into perdition, to pen-
etrate into the hidden motives, and expose the black
thoughts of men,—an awful, an evil spirit.

Ah man! . . . what made you to swear to fatal vows, and
bind yourself to a lifelong hypocrisy before the Heaven
which you adored with such real wonder, humility, and
reverence. . . .

It is my belief that he suffered frightfully from the consciousness of his own scepticism, and that he bent his pride
so far down as to put his apostasy out to hire. . . .

And dreadful it is to think that Swift knew the tendency
of his creed—the fatal rocks towards which his logic had
desperately drifted. That last part of Gulliver is only a
consequence of what has gone before; and the worthlessness of all mankind, the pettiness, cruelty, pride, im-
becility, the general vanity, the foolish pretension, the
mock greatness, the pompous dulness, the mean aims, the
base successes—all these were present to him; it was with
the din of these curses of the world, blasphemies against
heaven, shrieking in his ears, that he began to write his
dreadful allegory— . . .

His laugh jars on one's ears. . . . He was always alone—
alone and gnashing in the darkness, ... An immense
genius: an awful downfall and ruin. So great a man he
seems to me that thinking of him is like thinking of an
empire falling. We have other great names to mention—
none, I think, however, so great or so gloomy.[26]

He projects himself into Swift's life and writing, and what he
says about *A Tale of a Tub* and *Gulliver's Travels* applies perfectly to *Vanity Fair*. The overwrought tone betrays, I think, an
intense personal identification. He chooses to stress the dilemma of the humorist and skeptic who, in his heart and in his
greatest work, doubts God and the faith that he nominally professes. Like Swift, Thackeray sees the horror of vanity and the
self's isolation, but he cannot find God or a celestial plan to

148

redeem the world and join the self to an eternal order. He too is an apostate satirist who subverts the Christian Church, though he mouths its pieties and truly would like to believe its creed. The insight of this comedy also leaves people with nothing but the vanity of the world and their own consciousness. We can imagine "heaven," we can and do imagine a scheme of things, better than reality, by which to measure the folly of our lives; but this standard, this something better, which allows for the implicit comparison inherent in satire, exists only in our minds, and no divine intervention can attain it for us. Nothing exists beyond this world. There is no God, only comic insight, to judge the world and offer salvation. The tempered fury and frustrated alienation in this passage, in Swift, in himself, and in *Vanity Fair,* come from the knowledge that the kingdom of heaven is truly within us, and Thackeray cannot have faith in it. If we are in the world and the world is given over to vanity, then redemption, resurrection, and Christian dogma are part of vanity. Once men and women were not alone because they had God; but that communion turned out to be a vain illusion. No one has intercourse with a personal God except in his own worldly head. That is my sense of this comment on Swift.

v

A loss or a changing of faith is momentous and very painful, but the universal vanity in Thackeray's novel—the bad news—can point the way to a comic gospel—the good news. The stress in Western religious thought—especially Protestantism—on the individual's relationship with God and on God's image as a rewarder and punisher has tended to make people see themselves as competitors for divine attention and favor, like moral equivalents of modern studio-audience members writhing and waving to catch the attention of a television cameraman. But without a personal God, people would need more than ever to find ways of transcending self, and the new dream of salvation lies in the unification of mankind. The beginning of unity is to perceive our commonality. "O brother wearers of motley! Are there not moments when one grows sick of grinning and tumbling, and the jingling of cap and bells? This, dear friends and companions, is my amiable object—to walk with you through the Fair, to examine the shops and the shows there; and that we should all come home after the flare, and the noise, and the gaiety, and be perfectly miserable in private" (19:180–81). If nothing else, we live as a brotherhood of fools.

In his introduction to *The English Humorists of the Eighteenth Century,* Thackeray says:

> Harlequin without his mask is known to present a very sober countenance, and was himself, the story goes, the melancholy patient whom the Doctor advised to go and see Harlequin—a man full of cares and perplexities like the rest of us, whose *Self* must always be serious to him, under whatever mask or disguise or uniform he presents it to the public. And as all of you must needs be *grave* when you think of your own past and present, you will not find, in the histories of those whose lives and feelings I am going to try and describe to you, a story that is otherwise than *serious* and often very sad.[27]

The way of the self is the way of vanity and death. Vanity-of-the-world points toward the necessary breaking-down of vain distinction. The characters of *Vanity Fair*—and for Thackeray they include both author and reader—live in a world where most people pride themselves on the possession of qualities or substances they hope make them somehow special. But the book is meant to teach us our common fate. No power beyond the vanity of this world is going to reward us for distinguishing ourselves. "Alone," we are "gnashing in the darkness"; "in private" we are "perfectly miserable"; the "Self" is tragically "serious"; we are deadly "grave" when we deem and use our lives as possessions on which to capitalize. All of this vanity and worship of individuality is ludicrous, and we all participate in it. We are all a part of one silly congregation, and no one is excepted.

"Come children, let us shut up the box and the puppets, for our play is played out." Each of us is an immature little being in the family of man, and the parade of mechanistic behavior, the money system, the mirror of art, the novel as a fetish of escapism, ought, by the end, to have had their effect. We are tossed back into the vanity of the real world, where we are not alone.

NARRATOR AND AUDIENCE

I appeal to the middle classes [9:87]

"I" is here introduced to personify the world in general.
[36:350]

"The novelist, it has been said before, knows everything," says Thackeray (36:351). If that is in any sense true, then the novelist is like a god, and readers must take revelation and judgment from him, the creator of the fictional world. But an audience is, for the writer, like a god too, determining his fate, passing judgment, taking or rejecting his offerings. It must somehow be appeased. The model of literary enterprise for the Western world and for Thackeray is the Bible, the word of God, which readers should use to find out vital information, interpret meaning, and improve their own lives. *Vanity Fair,* in this sense, is mock scripture as well as a mock epic. Thackeray, the narrator, much more resembles Zeus or some trickster deity than Jehovah, as he takes different shapes to seduce and work his will on us.[28] He wishes to implicate himself as well as his audience in his "comic history," and he claims to be not a creator but a reader of the scene—a comic preacher interpreting comic creation for a comic congregation.

I

The assumptions of authority—even narrative authority—need to be ridiculed and broken down because they have made the social structure into a modern Midas-touch system. All, including both producer and consumers of the book, are part of *Vanity Fair.* The comedy sucks both narrator and audience in and gives them shifting identities. Everywhere, as we have seen, Thackeray breaks down distinctions, even those between writer and reader. He insists that he, like his readers, is a spectator of what he presents, and he often asks us to shape the meanings and draw the analogies between his story and our lives. Truth is not revealed from an authority on high. It must be actively sought, and, like thought and reflection, it tends to be process rather than possession.

The rhetoric of Thackeray's fiction pushes us to identify with the flexible consciousness of the narrator rather than with the characters. Of course, the narrator does not "know everything."

He is by turns cynical, ironical, credulous, witty, startlingly wise, and fatuous. He makes mistakes, speaks unreliably, contradicts himself, gives way to priggish moralizing, folly, and prejudice, forgets, bullies, cajoles, lectures, and shirks responsibility. Sometimes he is the reader's friend, sometimes he is objective. Sometimes he is third person, sometimes first person. He is a clown and a Jeremiah too. In short, he is more like the world and like us than an omnipotent, all-knowing God.

Structurally, the narrator works to create the psychic distance from experience and characters necessary to satiric comedy and also to establish an intimacy between performer and audience. Information comes from a protean point of view external to the imagined lives of the story, and we are not allowed to identify for long with the emotions of any one character or to develop the kind of subjective sympathy that would distract us for long from the corrupt farce of *Vanity Fair* as a whole.

The narrator's shifting perspective and identity also teach us practical lessons in epistemology and in the necessity of skepticism. Our sources of information in real life are various and disorderly: gossip here, observation there, memories, reading, hearsay, eyewitness accounts, the dogmatic assertions of absolutists, experiments, guesses, careful study, wish-fulfillments—how we come to know things, as Thackeray stresses, is an amorphous comedy of uncertainty and multiplicity:

> How does Jenkins balance his income? I say, as every friend of his must say, How is it that he has not been outlawed long since; . . . "I" is here introduced to personify the world in general. . . . [36:350]

> The before-mentioned Tom Eaves, . . . had further information . . . which may or may not be true. . . . (the reader must bear in mind that it is always Tom Eaves who speaks) . . . [47:453]

> It was on this very tour that I, the present writer of a history of which every word is true, had the pleasure to see them first, and to make their acquaintance. [62:602]

> Ah, gracious powers! I wish you would send me an old aunt . . . how my children should work workbags for her, and my Julia and I would make her comfortable! [9:87]

The present historian can give no certain details regarding the event. [64:626]

... the moralist, who is holding forth on the cover (an accurate portrait of your humble servant), professes to wear neither gown nor bands, but only the very same long-eared livery in which his congregation is arrayed. [8:80]

... It is not from mere mercenary motives that the present performer is desirous to show up and trounce his villains; but because he has a sincere hatred of them, which he cannot keep down, and which must find a vent in suitable abuse and bad language. [8:81]

The novelist, it has been said before, knows everything. [36:351]

This self-conscious narrator and his incremental mocking of novelistic conventions stress the complexity of perception. He urges a self-reliance on us; we must examine what we know, question authority, see the subjectivity and relativity of truth, see how foolish monolithic views of life are, and understand the motives of those who would form our minds. Questions are raised: Who is Tom Eaves? Why does the narrator have a wife named Julia when Thackeray's wife was Isabel? Why does he personify himself as Folly? Cumulatively, this shifty narrator steers us to a kind of Heisenberg principle: in assessing reality, it is impossible to separate the fact from the observer and inter-preter of fact. Moreover, since reality is always determined by shifting perspective, change perspective and you may change reality. That is the one hope of this comedy. The conglomerate narrator becomes a model for the reader's consciousness and for his opportunities for perspective.

II

Thackeray also *imagines* his readers and tries to create a congre-gation that might begin to transcend the individualism in which he sees men and women caught. When the narrator cries, "I appeal to the middle classes" (9:87), he describes his readers historically, points out where the power lies in his world, de-lineates the social function of the novelist, and ridicules class chauvinism. When he says, "I warn my 'kyind friends,' then, that I am going to tell a story of harrowing villany and complicated—but, as I trust, intensely interesting—crime" (8:81), that "kyind friends" mocks his readers but also satirizes the novel-writer as combination con-man barker and canting parson. (Say "kyind" out loud and you hear the voice of the hustler.) It says, in effect, I'm a rogue and you're another, and we all live in Vanity Fair. The undertone in such phrases and poses calls upon us to share his cynical knowledge and pain and to confess both our scorn for Vanity Fair and our involvement in it. The rhetorical strategy moves us toward mutual confession.

In the first pages of the novel occurs a remarkable interjection. Introducing Amelia, the narrator interrupts himself with a passage of Nabokovian subtlety:

> All which details, I have no doubt, JONES, who reads this book at his Club, will pronounce to be excessively foolish, trivial, twaddling, and ultra-sentimental. Yes; I can see Jones at this minute (rather flushed with his joint of mutton and half-pint of wine), taking out his pencil and scoring under the words "foolish, twaddling," &c., and adding to them his own remark of *"quite true."* Well, he is a lofty man of genius, and admires the great and heroic in life and novels; and so had better take warning and go elsewhere. [1:15]

Thackeray wants to disarm criticism by setting up a straw man, and he wants to claim importance for his subject. He means to forge an audience rhetorically that will be nimble enough to see why Amelia and the heroless Vanity Fair where she dwells signify. He draws Jones, the potentially hostile reader, into the satire. A foolish devotee of Vanity, Jones serves as an example of the reader who wishes to be told what he already knows. On another level, Thackeray is showing the inevitable partnership of author and reader in the making of fiction: reading is no passive activity; every reader is in some way both a coauthor and a character in the book. Note that Jones actually composes what he reacts to and what he ascribes to the author. Note also that what he says about Amelia and her life does have much truth, though he fails to see that it applies equally to himself and to what he admires. Art here becomes a two-way mirror; perspective oscillates, and, momentarily, the supposed narrator becomes audience for the authorship of the reader. Among other things, this tricky passage turns out to be a metaphor for the psychological labyrinth of literary transaction.

The passage also says "Pay attention!" The unpredictable narrator might lash out anytime at anyone—even you. The skilled satirist builds a relationship to his audience that bizarrely mixes hostility and friendliness. Like a good comic, Thackeray seems to anticipate reactions, to get ready for hecklers and make them part of the show. In fact, Thackeray resembles more closely that startling phenomenon, the modern comedian, than almost any other novelist I can think of. The poses, the direct appeals to the audience, the confessional mode, the "inside" jokes, which create a special sense of fellowship—these traits of Thackeray are now the property of the best comic monologists. He ingratiates himself and, like a performer, acts as if he could almost look and talk back at us from the lines on the page.

Thackeray's comic perspective is one way of letting people become their own audiences. The narrator wants the readers to reflect back and forth between their own experiences and *Vanity Fair*. In that resonant last sentence, "Come children, let us shut up the box and the puppets, for our play is played out," he addresses and diminishes the audience but at the same time identifies with it ("us" and "our") and implies that we have also been the creators of "the play." Progress and fate lie in the interplay of writer and readers and in the identification of each with the other. Furthermore, we must learn to move easily between being authors and audience, between active and contemplative experience, between the truth-telling illusions of literature and the lies of the real world.

SPACE AND RANGE

Bon Dieu, I say, is it not hard that the fateful rush of the great Imperial struggle can't take place without affecting a poor little harmless girl of eighteen, who is occupied in billing and cooing, or working muslin collars in Russell Square? [18:167]

Space is global in *Vanity Fair*, as it is in *Martin Chuzzlewit*, but it is also, explicitly, the arena of imperialism. "When the eagles

155

of Napoleon Bonaparte . . . were flying from Provence, where they had perched after a brief sojourn in Elba, and from steeple to steeple until they reached the towers of Notre Dame, I wonder whether the Imperial birds had any eye for a little corner of the parish of Bloomsbury, London, which you might have thought so quiet, that even the whirring and flapping of those mighty wings would pass unobserved there?" (18:167). Thackeray's perspective combines the Ecclesiastes vision of everything under the sun as eternally vain with a nineteenth-century Anglo-Indian's historical view of the world as empire. The narrator's imperial eye sees Vanity Fair expand and extend across continents and oceans to support that "system of drawing-rooms." Resources of plunder—including human plunder, like the black heiress, Miss Swartz, and Sambo the servant—pour into London. All the major characters travel widely. The men go to the corners of the earth to build and rule the empire; Becky tries to capitalize in all the major cities, from London to St. Petersburg; even Amelia uses Europe for her recreation.

Imperialism means mastering and making capital of the world, and that is what the novel, on an imaginative plane, does. Thackeray shrinks the world and burlesques it. He can annex a whole state, Pumpernickel, and exploit it for comic capital in the way that Great Britain could annex and exploit some choice piece of territory. The range, rapidity of movement, and startling juxtapositions of his prose reflect imperialist perception even while he mocks and derides the system. Actually, Thackeray has little of the traveler's interest in place or surroundings per se. He takes pains with physical description, but he uses it almost always as a metaphorical way of assessing moral value or pointing up the opportunities for the capitalizing will to speculate. He knows well the interrelatedness of the world, and especially the financial consequences of international action: "So imprisoned and tortured was this gentle little heart, when in the month of March, Anno Domini 1815, Napoleon landed at Cannes, and Louis XVIII. fled, and all Europe was in alarm, and the funds fell, and old John Sedley was ruined" (18:169).

One of Thackeray's most famous sentences shows his panoramic sweep and range: "Darkness came down on the field and city: and Amelia was praying for George, who was lying on his face, dead, with a bullet through his heart" (32:315). He meant that to be pathetic and shocking, but the mode of perception is free-ranging and powerful. He expropriates the god's-eye vision that liberates us from a narrow perspective. Distances are nothing to Thackeray, who perceives like one of those "imperial birds." His medium of expression records, transmits, and juxtaposes far-flung images almost instantaneously, as if it were a harbinger of television, bringing "the whole world into our living-rooms." And, of course, it is, since both are based on the globalization of perspective that is imperialism's legacy. Imperialism in whatever form is always in part reductive, centralizing the world, glorifying possession, making all places the same place, and eventually trying to standardize life. It is Osborne's domestic system operating on a world-wide scale.

But Thackeray uses its reductive tendencies to minimize Vanity Fair. If the epitome of imperialism is man stepping onto the moon and planting a paltry flag on its surface, the ultimate anti-imperialistic vision is the reverse image of the earth as seen from outer space. Viewing it, we may be reminded that we are frail, tiny creatures who inhabit, for a short time, a little sun-warmed ball spinning through a mysterious universe. It is this kind of manipulation of space and range, through marvelous resources of perspective, and this rendering of the earth and its population as a diverting bauble of vanity that Thackeray's book suggests to me.

TIME

> While the present century was in its teens. . . . [1:11]

> It was but this present morning, as he rode on the omnibus from Richmond . . . [that] this present chronicler . . . marked three little children playing in a puddle. [23:217–18]

People live in a jail of years, and, for many, religious faith has seemed to offer an escape from time into eternity. Thackeray offers no exit, but his comedy does show how large and various the prison of time can be. It also holds up to ridicule many of the ways we measure duration. He makes time manifold and subjective. *Vanity Fair* includes characters' time, the narrator's time, and the audience's time—none of which is uniform. Time becomes career, history, memory, earthly cycle, generation, and even consciousness.[29]

I

The chronological narrative follows the personal histories of Becky and Amelia and, less fully, Dobbin, Jos Sedley, and Rawdon Crawley from about 1813 to 1831. Their time consists of that search for private fulfillment that the Declaration of Independence precisely calls "the pursuit of happiness." Time is made into a career, a form of personal possession, and Thackeray describes it as a movement from anticipation and expectation to some form of disillusionment or resignation. In fiction, the analogue of the successful pursuit of happiness—goal-oriented time—is the happy ending, which, as we have seen, Thackeray parodies (see p. 140, above). The pleasures of attaining goals may be disillusioning because they are "transitory" (51:485). Or happiness may have nothing to do with what people want or think they want: "Perhaps it was the happiest time of both their lives indeed, if they did but know it—and who does? Which of us can point out and say that was the culmination—that was the summit of human joy?" (62:602). Also, the concept of linear time for the individual inevitably implies the dissolution of happy states and the disintegration of self.

The book radically criticizes the pursuit of happiness (i.e., time as a capital investment) as an organizing principle of life, notably in the vague discontent of Amelia and Dobbin at the end and, perhaps most powerfully, in the ironic happy fate of Becky Sharp. Her banal goal has always been wealth, and finally she gets it. In the end she uses her wiles and criminality to turn Jos Sedley's life and fortune into the insurance policy upon which she capitalizes after his sordid death. Thackeray's penultimate sketch of the self-possessed Becky, looking smugly content and modestly coy before the blank gaze of Amelia, bears the title *"Virtue rewarded; A booth in Vanity Fair."* The happy ending, the secular version of God's moralized time (the good life on earth is rewarded, the bad life punished), becomes a farce.

II

All of the characters both embody and are determined by the public time that in retrospect we call history. History is the

158

offspring of chronology wedded to power, and in imperialistic eras it tends to be emphasized. Making people conscious of living in and being a part of history is a way of organizing and manipulating them, but history is also time speculated and capitalized upon for the single soul. Historical consciousness, particularly in modern times, has been a means by which people can appropriate racial and national experience to themselves and project themselves into a larger life.

Thackeray ridicules history and its uses. Though he recognizes the past as part of himself, he does not revere it; his attitude is much closer to Joyce's Dedalus ("History is a nightmare from which I am trying to awake")[30] or T. S. Eliot ("that immense panorama of futility and anarchy which is modern history"),[31] than to Scott, whose novels celebrate and popularize history. Skeptically, he sees it as another commodity in *Vanity Fair*. The Waterloo chapters, especially, show history to be both deadly and farcical. That kind of history—collective time as a possession to feed national vanity—must be ridiculed so that it will lose its murderous hold. Napoleon and Becky must be shown to reflect each other. Waterloo, in fact, becomes an object for personal profit, as the hawkers and guides who conduct old Osborne and the narrator around the battlefield, and Jos, who capitalizes on his cowardice and lives out his life in India as "Waterloo" Sedley, demonstrate. History—what happens and reports of what happened—is shaped, according to Thackeray, by the structure of Vanity Fair. His century—the history that he knows—is Vanity Fair itself.

III

Thackeray tries to get free of both the determinism of history and the closed end of linear time by giving his narrator a synchronous sense of time. He breaks the narrative's chronology whenever he wants to, ranging back and forth, fitting time to his imagination and making the past serve the needs of present states of mind. His consciousness controls chronology; in one paragraph he can use incidents separated by fifty years to make a point or achieve an effect. Telling of old Sedley's bankruptcy, the narrator typically breaks off to interject: "Edward Dale, the junior of the house, who purchased the spoons for the firm, was, in fact, very sweet upon Amelia, and offered for her in spite of all. He married Miss Louisa Cutts (daughter of Higham

159

and Cutts, the eminent corn-factors), with a handsome fortune in 1820; and is now living in splendour, and with a numerous family, at his elegant villa, Muswell Hill" (17:163–64). The shift from past into the present makes Dale a contemporary and suggests that our histories are, in many ways, as ridiculous as his. The juxtaposition also subtly changes our sense of the narrative, making it more comic: love is not forever, disappointment is not the end of the world, careers exist to be parodied. The narrator's time switches are a way of changing focus, and his method serves as a model for ourselves and our own histories.

Thackeray keeps referring to mid-nineteenth-century historical time, when the novel was written and first read, but he also alludes to any reader's time: "Some people consider Fairs immoral. . . . But persons who think otherwise . . . may perhaps like to step in for half an hour" (1:5). That half-hour is the time of reading, a special kind of time, bracketed off, but still a time of actual experience. Reading for a while, I may follow Becky's adventures, learn about an incident in Thackeray's early life, contemplate George IV's inanity, compare, at the narrator's urging, my own experience with events and characters in the story, ponder the similarity of human concerns in all ages, and, at the author's rhetorical insistence, think simultaneously both how much and how little times change. Such a period is an analogue of the multifariousness of actual time.

All these strands of time meet in that final sentence: "Come children, let us shut up the box and the puppets, for our play is played out." It suggests meanings as diverse as these: "The age of individualism is exhausted, and a new era should begin"; "The time for our trivial concern with comic fiction is over, and we must move back to serious reality"; "An immature society may now progress beyond its vain outmoded illusions"; "I, the author, have played out my creative powers and vision"; "It is possible for the agile mind, after using the resources of a period of time, to move on to some new and promising mixture of subjectivity and spatial duration." The sense of this ending— and the sense of time in general in *Vanity Fair*—confirms George Eliot: "Every limit is a beginning as well as an ending."[32]

STYLE

the style is the man.
Buffon

Thackeray is a great stylist, and by this I mean that his prose continually works to make striking and exactly clear the complexity and moral ramifications of his subject matter. It specifies and illuminates the ambiguities and the organic nature of the life he depicts, and it insists on connecting the novel to the reader's experience. It points toward the commercialism and folly of the world and reflects the ingenuity that one needs for living in such a world. This style is equivocal, allusive, rapid, ironic, subversive, and tough-minded. It allows for many moods and shifts in tone, and, because it defines Vanity Fair, it is often hostile and bitter. The wonderfully exact diction is steeped in the idiom of a ready-money society.

I

Trite talk of Victorian novels as "loose, baggy monsters" is especially misleading in the case of a precise and original stylist like Thackeray. He stresses the composition of his prose, compressing and concentrating realms of experience and meaning in a single paragraph. I want to quote two passages that, like the "system of drawing-rooms" piece and "Ah! *Vanitas Vanitatum*," represent the major qualities of Thackeray's style; but even such suggestive excerpts barely indicate the range of significance and the vast structure of culture that the prose of the whole novel embodies. The first example is from the "charade" chapter; the second is from the description of Osborne's study in the disinheritance scene.

(1)   If every person is to be banished from society who runs into debt and cannot pay—if we are to be peering into everybody's private life, speculating upon their income, and cutting them if we don't approve of their expenditure—why, what a howling wilderness and intolerable dwelling Vanity Fair would be. Every man's hand would be against his neighbour in this case, my dear sir, and the benefits of civilisation

161

would be done away with. We should be quarrelling,
abusing, avoiding one another. Our houses would become caverns: and we should go in rags because we
cared for nobody. Rents would go down. Parties
wouldn't be given any more. All the tradesmen of the
town would be bankrupt. Wine, wax-lights, comesti-
bles, rouge, crinoline-petticoats, diamonds, wigs,
Louis-Quatorze-gimcracks, and old china, park hacks,
and splendid high-stepping carriage horses—all the
delights of life, I say,—would go to the deuce, if
people did but act upon their silly principles, and
avoid those whom they dislike and abuse. Whereas,
by a little charity and mutual forbearance, things are
made to go on pleasantly enough: we may abuse a
man as much as we like, and call him the greatest
rascal unhung—but do we wish to hang him therefore? No. We shake hands when we meet. If his cook
is good we forgive him, and go and dine with him;
and we expect he will do the same by us. Thus trade
flourishes—civilisation advances: peace is kept; new
dresses are wanted for new assemblies every week;
and last year's vintage of Lafitte will remunerate the
honest proprietor who reared it. [51:491]

(2)   There was a picture of the family over the mantel-
piece, removed thither from the front room after
Mrs. Osborne's death—George was on a pony, the
elder sister holding him up a bunch of flowers; the
younger led by her mother's hand; all with red cheeks
and large red mouths, simpering on each other in the
approved family-portrait manner. The mother lay
under ground now, long since forgotten—the sisters
and brother had a hundred different interests of their
own, and, familiar still, were utterly estranged from
each other. Some few score of years afterwards, when
all the parties represented are grown old, what bitter
satire there is in those flaunting childish family-
portraits, with their farce of sentiment and smiling
lies, and innocence so self-conscious and self-
satisfied. [24:222–23]

This style provokes enough trains of thought to expatiate upon for hours—for example, in the first passage, the role of luxury in a market economy, the benefits of hypocrisy, economic uncertainty, wine, envy, and privileged-class power and, in the second passage, the ravages of time, the motives of pictorial representation, and the failure of family life. Think of the allusive power of the word "civilisation" in the first excerpt or, in the second, the stab of recognition that Thackeray's sarcasm on family portraits brings if we remember those family Christmas-card photos. Thackeray alludes to something, then quickly moves on. The prose runs one jump ahead of despair. The rationalizations of the narrator appear to mix sophistry and sense, as Thackeray intends; one has no choice but to deal with the horrors of life as best one can, but the inadequacy of our existence is clear. The style displays the free-associating improvisational abilities of a clever mind—the full range of mood, reference, and intelligence that we need if we are to live in Vanity Fair. But at the same time, all the allusions keep rubbing our noses in the vanity of "this world." Those topics that seem to be so casually introduced, those mental leaps, the specific images and details, together build a whole organic composition of life as a vain commodities market. In Osborne's portrait, Thackeray's use of a carefully composed picture to characterize a society and its moral tone epitomizes perfectly the nature of his art.

II

Diction: Thackeray's habitual use of the collective pronoun binds the life of the novel to the life of its audience, but he also uses recurrently an acid diction that alienates readers from the life of the book. Terms like "simpering," "red mouths," "smiling lies," "silly principles," and "our dear Becky" are meant to make us reject the values and sentimental veneer of this society. Words like "whimpering" and "blubbering" often stand out in Thackeray's descriptions of emotional scenes, and cumulatively they help to create a critical, almost criminally savage perspective on a society whose gestures of pathos seem only to perpetuate the Midas system. The diction of cruelty reflects the underlying cruelty of "this world." Also, what Engels called the "spirit of petty bargaining"[33] everywhere marks

163

Thackeray's word-choice, as we have seen. The language and the economic system are merged; words like "share" and "interests" occur even when the subject seems far from financial transactions.

How expert and suggestive Thackeray's diction is hardly needs mentioning. In our two examples, notice "large red mouths," "flaunting childish family-portraits," "we may abuse a man as much as we like," "simpering"; they seem exactly the right descriptive words and phrases to shape our moral attitudes toward the depicted object or experience, but if we imagine ourselves trying to compose these pieces, his skill in word choice can seem dazzling.

Equivocation: We are taught to despise it, yet the craving for certainty is another example of humanity's unwillingness to face reality, which *is* equivocal. Surety is, in fact, ridiculous. "But who could tell what was truth . . . ?" (53:517), far from being an evasion by Thackeray, is his most responsible assessment of life. In the first example, irony subverts static authority. As we read, the ground shifts and the meaning oscillates: "every" debtor is not "banished from society," but some are; "every man's hand" is and is not "against his neighbour"; Vanity Fair is "a howling wilderness," but "our houses" are not "caverns"; material possessions are, and are not, "the delights of life"; "civilisation advances" and does not advance; "peace is kept," and it is broken; the story of Becky does and does not "console." This style is basic training in the modern requisite of having to live with doubt, and it tauntingly devastates any form of smug absolutism. It equivocates and disconcerts with a reverberating irony that exposes the contradictions inherent in our culture.

Life in *Vanity Fair* is full of conflicts, and to know it we need an overall ironic perspective. Thackeray uses irony to study the contradictions not just between appearance and reality but in reality itself. His irony, like Jane Austen's, gives us multiple perspectives; but he shows these perspectives to be logically in conflict, and his irony questions the ultimate value of life itself, as hers does not. It points to an incoherence that is inevitable in the tyranny of materialism and possession. Much more than Austen, Thackeray directs his irony against his audience and himself. Hers is aimed at making proper discriminations, seeing clearly, and moving pragmatically forward. His expresses a basic disorder in things. It is confessional and universal; it does not imply "some people are moral dolts who do these ridiculous things" but "we all are moral dolts who do these ridiculous things." At bottom this irony endorses defiance of the world: existence itself is absurd; it gives us the moral imagination to dream of the good life, but the nature of being in society makes this good life unobtainable. Austen's irony points out contradictions that are not perceived or understood; Thackeray's points up the innate illogic in being.

Vanity Fair's irony shows how much and how little we have to lose. To live at all well, we must both accept and renounce the world. Appearance must be taken at face value and rejected too. The "truth" is that conditions may be both tolerable and intolerable, statements true and false, our beliefs and assumptions somehow wrong and right at the same time. The style is like a verbal equivalent of those trick badges that, from one angle, show a woman fully clothed but, from another, show her naked. His irony says that, in this world of vanity, reflections, and multiple perspectives, whatever we may think, the opposite may also be true. That is unsettling but, on reflection, comic, since it undercuts intellectual affectations and dogmatism and frees us from the hobgoblin of foolish consistency.

Thackeray's style is his message: life itself demands a style of consciousness that, like this prose, can incorporate and deal with contradictions. We have to know that we need real hope and belief that things will change for the better, together with the hard knowledge that they will not. We need both defiance and fatalism. We have to be able to accept the corrupt world, and we have to mock and condemn it, too. Experience is both a pilgrim's progress and a *Vanitas Vanitatum*. There is, in the prose, in the author, in the novel, a longing for transcendence from "this world" and the recognition that such transcendence is impossible. Thackeray's strong will to faith is stymied, but in *Vanity Fair*'s wide range of psychic perspectives, he creates his comic vision.

6

TROLLOPE'S *BARCHESTER TOWERS* (1857)
Comic Reformation

> Institutions establish the community of men: a "church" means
> that many men have had an idea of goodness, but it is part of that
> goodness to perpetually need to be rediscovered and re-
> established in the flux of history and of changing, "reforming"
> society, in each individual situation.
> Ruth apRoberts[1]

Trollope's *Barchester Towers* is at the heart of the great comic
tradition.[2] It brings together religion and comedy and implicitly
juxtaposes prayer and laughter. The most obvious thing about
the novel is also the most important: the ecclesiastical
establishment is made the subject of comedy, and Trollope's
imagination establishes a comic church. The allegiance of Barchester's religious institution and its members has quietly
passed from God to humanity, but its corporate structure remains, and Trollope respects it.

His humor, however, dissolves the aura of divinity around
the church, and no matter how he might wish to deny it, the
logical drift of this book implies that nothing, theoretically, is
sacred—nothing, that is, is beyond comic scrutiny. Though
there is no direct scoffing at the church and little that a confirmed Anglican could resent, the novel is in the broadest sense
irreverent. It makes theological presumption seem ridiculous.
What religious feeling there is resides not in "orthodox Christian supernaturalism"[3] but in Trollope's comic vision of life. He
values, and projects fictively, community, tolerance, love between men and women, the dialectical workings of social institutions and history, and humor itself.

I

Trollope, like Thackeray, thought of himself as a "weekday preacher" ("the novelist," he said, "if he have a conscience, must preach his sermons with the same purpose as the clergyman, and must have his own system of ethics"),[4] and he found his humor in the "preachers" and the milieu of the church. His way of mastering the submerged spiritual tumult of his age and reconciling the clamoring religious strains in his society with the demands and realities of the changing Victorian world is to subsume and fuse ecclesiastical affairs, organized Christianity, and the energies of secularization into a wide comic perspective. In *Barchester Towers,* he imagines a comic reformation taking place.

For Trollope, change in personal and social life—the inevitable flux of circumstances and disruptions large and small—demands constant processes of reformation, i.e., perpetual readjustments of personality and behavior and continual efforts at reestablishing authority and equilibrium in the fluidity of being. These processes are the stuff of his novels. His comedy of change is especially alive to the increasing will to independence of strong-minded women and to the tensions, problems, and incongruities that new female assertiveness and ambition cause when they clash with conventional notions about feminine decorum and "a woman's place." *Barchester Towers* shows us both private and social reformations in the relationships between the sexes happening against the setting of the church, that bastion of male primacy.

Trollope's fiction is so understated and his narrative voice so unassuming that we need to keep in mind just how important his material is. In *Barchester* and its short predecessor, *The Warden,* he creates a religious, provincial society that has to adapt itself to the world's accelerating rate of change and secularizing thrust and find ways of retaining and developing its moral values, its continuity, its harmonies, and its faith. His tone is lighthearted, but it would be hard to think of a more consequential subject. It has been said that "the drama of the modern era is the decline of religion,"[5] but, more precisely, this drama lies in the reshaping and reformation of religious drives and impulses.

167

II

Reading Trollope's comedy of clergymen makes it easier to see in retrospect how English novelists have played with the repressions of religion and with the gaping disparity between Christian profession and the practice of nominal Christians in the world. Superficially, Fielding's Parson Adams, Goldsmith's Vicar Primrose of Wakefield, and Sterne's Yorick and Dr. Slop may have influenced *Barchester Towers;* their authors, however, do not really make fun of the workings of the church or of the ecclesiastical world, nor do they have Trollope's communal focus. There is something of Peacock's spirit of communion in the parties that highlight *Barchester,* but Trollope has a much stronger feel for the particularity of life and of history. Like Dickens, he detested and wished to expose the Pecksniffian moral tyranny in his society, but he had more interest in conserving a moral tradition and a much greater faith in institutional life.

Of the comic writers, he owes most to Austen and Thackeray. From Austen he learned to develop a comic dialectic between character and community (including the importance of dialogue in representing change) and to render the intensity of personal relationships. Like her, he realized that a community without comic imagination can be stagnant, empty, and dangerous. *Barchester Towers,* like *Emma,* offers the blessings of grace upon humanity, but that grace is a gift of the author's comic understanding, not of God.

From *Vanity Fair* he learned the comic resources of shifting perspective. *Barchester Towers* treats a subject and a variety of characters of broad significance within a limited scope. As Thackeray shrinks Napoleon into Becky and the nineteenth century into his Vanity Fair, reducing and controlling them in his comedy, so Trollope shrinks the religious controversy, church factionalism, and secularization of his age into Barset. Thackeray continually brings to bear on his world the perspectives of Christian idealism in order to satirize it. Trollope's comic dialectic absorbs absolutist Christian visions and materialist points of view into a worldly perspective and makes theological views, including *contemptus mundi* and evangelicalism, part of the historical processes of the world.

From Thackeray, also, he seems to have gotten the idea of

carrying over characters from one novel to another; but what was for Thackeray a minor and casual device for reminding people of his earlier books becomes in *Barchester Towers* a major innovation in British fiction[6] and one crucial to Trollope's vision of life as a shifting but continuous communal process. By taking the characters and the setting of *The Warden* and expanding the Barchester world, Trollope turned out to be a chief English progenitor for the countless writers since who have preserved and developed their characters and fictional communities from novel to novel, e.g., Galsworthy, Ford Madox Ford, Mann, Proust, Faulkner, Powell, Lawrence, Waugh, even Joyce and Beckett—to say nothing of the lesser legion that has spawned hundreds of sagas, series, and soap operas.

Barchester Towers, with its continuing life, reflects an urge to break through the constructions of enclosed literary forms, with their traditional endings. It shows the appeal of a fantasy life that goes on and on. Trollope creates a human comedy of developing characters who interact with their evolving community and its institutions. That comedy is social but not impersonal, and it expresses both a desire and a way of seeking for permanence in the world. Extending the fictional structure beyond the covers of a single book or the limits of a single artwork is now so commonplace that we hardly give it a thought, but it says a lot about our longings for imaginative transcendence. I think it likely that the evolution of the modern fictional series has to do with secularization and a need to supplement or replace the "other world" of religion and the figures of religious myth with another kind of enduring, institutionalized fantasy life that one can somehow identify with and find some sort of psychological solace in. If there is any truth in that idea, it would seem apt that a novel and a series that chronicle the secularizing of the church should figure prominently in extending the formal domain of fiction. "We wish," says novelist John Fowles in words that fit Trollope neatly, "to create worlds as real as, but other than the world that is."[7] That expresses a religious impulse, but the wish would not exist in anyone who had perfect faith in God's creation of this world and the world to come.

III

The opening chapter of *Barchester* is both an overture and a précis for the comic vision and mood of the whole book. "A novel," says Trollope, "should give a picture of common life enlivened by humour."[8] What matters most, then, is the total image of the community in action, but what gives life to the whole are the personal traits and whims of its members, set off against each other. *The Warden* centers on one man, and its first words are "The Rev. Septimus Harding..."; but *Barchester Towers* is to be the story of a community: "In the latter days of July in the year 185–, a most important question was for ten days asked in the cathedral city of Barchester, and answered every hour in various ways—Who was to be the new Bishop?" The novel is set in moving time and poses a public question in the undifferentiated but various voices of the whole town. Before we read a proper name, we have the concern with social function and the sense of communal urgency.

> The death of old Dr. Grantly...took place exactly as the ministry of Lord —— was going to give place to that of Lord ——....
>
> It was pretty well understood that the out-going premier had made his selection, and that if the question rested with him, the mitre would descend on the head of Archdeacon Grantly, the old bishop's son.

It is a wonderfully conceived situation; public and private life are inseparable. Trollope's artistry here is so delicate that it can easily be missed. Taking us into the mind of his ambitious archdeacon, he carefully balances the initial public question with a private question:

> The ministry were to be out within five days: his father was to be dead within—No, he rejected that view of the subject....
>
> He tried to keep his mind away from the subject, but he could not....He knew it must be now or never....Thus he thought long and sadly, in deep silence, and then gazed at that still living face, and then at last dared to *ask himself* whether he really longed for his father's death.
>
> The effort was a salutary one, and *the question* was an-

swered in a moment. The proud, wishful, worldly man, sank on his knees by the bedside, and taking the bishop's hand within his own, prayed eagerly that his sins might be forgiven him. [Italics mine.][9]

The exact nature of Grantly's answer may be ambiguous, but what then results shows how richly complex even a blunt personality can be. Trollope internalizes the principle of equivocation that animates Thackeray's world-view. Grantly shows himself capable of wishing for his father's death and wishing for him not to die also. The hand that he grasps is tellingly called "the bishop's" even in the moment of the son's repentance and atonement with the father. The archdeacon longs for preferment in the church and in the same instant longs to live up to Christian principles of humility too.

Harding comes in to see his officious son-in-law praying, and he is touched. Each is moved to "fellowship," and together they witness the passing of the old bishop. The "fellowship" is real, but it doesn't last. Trollope denigrates neither the dying of the gentle bishop and the passing of his pastoral way of life nor Grantly's moment of guilt and his spiritual crisis, but he revives the comic motions of worldliness and makes them follow fast upon prayer and death:

"You cannot but rejoice that it is over," said Mr. Harding. . . .

But how was he to act while his father-in-law stood there holding his hand? how, without appearing unfeeling, was he to forget his father in the bishop—to overlook what he had lost, and think only of what he might possibly gain?

"No; I suppose not," said he, at last, in answer to Mr. Harding. "We have all expected it so long." [1:5]

That "it," which unwittingly encompasses both the father's death and a bishopric, shows Trollope's genius for revelation in dialogue. But just as important is the internal dialogue here. The nub of experience in this book is the comedy of people having to relate to other people unlike themselves. They must define and express their desires in the context of their professional and personal relationships with others—often incongruous others—as Grantly does here in tandem with Harding.

In the presence of death, life and the hunger pangs of ambition assert themselves, and Trollope makes it funny. The comic rhythm increases, and we move back into the public world. Grantly cajoles Harding into sending the useless telegram to the newly fallen Conservative government. Trollope shifts to the world of publicity, as various newspapers speculate on who the new bishop will be. The announcement then comes that the new Liberal government is sending Bishop Proudie down from London. Death has become an aspect of the endless corporate processes of society and a cause of the comic reformation of the Barchester community.

The narrator, at the close of the chapter, returns to the private hopes of the archdeacon, now dashed, and he tentatively sympathizes with him and his worldly ambition:

> Many will think that he was wicked to grieve for the loss of episcopal power, wicked to have coveted it, nay, wicked even to have thought about it, in the way and at the moments he had done so.
>
> With such censures I cannot profess that I completely agree. . . . A lawyer does not sin in seeking to be a judge, or in compassing his wishes by all honest means. A young diplomat entertains a fair ambition when he looks forward to be the lord of a first-rate embassy; and a poor novelist when he attempts to rival Dickens . . . commits no fault, though he may be foolish. Sidney Smith truly said that in these recreant days we cannot expect to find the majesty of St. Paul beneath the cassock of a curate. If we look to our clergymen to be more than men, we shall probably teach ourselves to think that they are less. . . .
>
> Our archdeacon was worldly—who among us is not so?
> [1:8]

That is the prose of a man whose heart belongs to the world and who puts faith in a career. The telling comparison of the priesthood to other professions cannot help but make the religious calling seem like any other calling. Vocation in Trollope's vision is the call of the world, and the church offers, beyond spiritual guidance, professional opportunity where one may find satisfaction, a living, and possibly distinction for oneself. Not holiness and inspiration but professional competence and humanity are the ideal qualities that emerge here for a churchman.

Notice the linkage in the passage: Grantly's emotions and wishes, which, after all, Trollope imagines, take on public significance within the world of the novel but also within the world of author and reader. The archdeacon's ambition is a subject, and so is the putative reader's response to it. Everything relates character to community, including the supposed community of readers. Grantly implicates us in Barchester, and, in a larger sense, Trollope implicates us, too, in a life made not by God but by men and women.

CORPORATE CHARACTERS AND COMMUNITY

People must be bound together. They must depend on each other.

Trollope, *Doctor Thorne*[10]

All the main characters of *Barchester Towers* are relative creatures who together create its vision of community and comic reformation. Trollope insists on the interrelatedness of life. Hope for the future and for personal happiness lie in the flourishing of social life. Imagining how people interact, how they perceive others, how they touch and change each other, how their obsessions and individuality affect their society, how their roles and activities come to be shaped and defined, how they all work together as a collectivity—that is what fascinates him in Barchester. He would later create characters of greater depth and bring readers closer to individual men and women than he does here, but he would never imagine a more resonant community.

I

When I call his people "corporate characters," I mean that he sees them as parts of a functioning whole society and also that he represents individual and communal life as formed by, and inseparable from, corporate organization. Not coincidentally, this comedy was written at just that time in history when the modern corporation was being developed. The church in Trollope sometimes looks as if it were the corporation of a higher agency, since its ends, though moral, are worldly. In his Palliser series and in the chronicles of Barset, Trollope understands and

173

makes art out of two major facts of modern life: (1) Lots of people find—or try to find—success, identity, meaning, and even a kind of transcendence in the corporate structure with which they associate themselves. (2) The dominant corporate structure in a community, though itself a constantly changing entity, sets the tone and the dramatic framework for the people of that place and tends to determine their groupings and their particular destinies. (For example, the conflict in the church in the Barset novels brings Eleanor Harding both her husbands.) Whether Trollope is relating his characters to the church, Parliament, government, or the bureaucracy, he is busy creating the epic of organization men and women.

Barchester is dominated by the institution of organized religion. A Church of England company town, Trollope means it to be typical of an important part of the nation. Like any other institution, the church is made up of worldly and comic people of all kinds. Trollope shows how everybody, from the free-thinking Stanhopes and the old-fashioned Thornes of Ullathorne to the Barchester tradesmen and leader-writers of the London *Jupiter* (i.e., the *Times*), have a stake in Barset clerical life and the currents of ecclesiastical opinion.

He grounds the novel solidly in the religious history of its time and reflects comically the era's theological parties and strife. Slope and Mrs. Proudie represent the church's Evangelical wing; Bishop Proudie, appointed by the reforming Liberals, is a "political" bishop, willing to take orders from the government—a type very familiar in the mid-Victorian age. Grantly stands for the "high and dry" church;[11] Dr. Arabin comes out of the Oxford Movement and champions its Anglican ideals. Even some of the particular incidents of the book had their real-life analogues; e.g., the coincidence of a falling government and a dying bishop; debates about whether cathedral services should be chanted; newspapers meddling in diocesan affairs.[12] All of this goes to show, however, that religious affairs are part of the human comedy. For Trollope, the most important moral and religious truth—the existence of faith, hope, and charity—lies in communal life, not in theological policy or opinion.

Trollope's church is not so much a model of Anglo-Catholic faith as it is a model for displaying a secular catholic version of humanity. It loosely holds together a motley collection of mutual-interest groups and serves as the institutional body within which the maneuvering for power, influence, and security can take place. Egos shape institutions, but institutions can control and soften egoism and keep open the options and possibilities for connection between individuals. The Barchester towers express a common human idealism and give continuity to the changing scene. They are signs and physical evidence that people aspire, despite their worldly folly, to sustain and develop the moral value of their lives and of the civilization to which they belong.

II

Much of the moral equilibrium and integrity of Barchester depends on Harding, whose courtesy and innocent faith put the querulousness of the Proudies, Grantly, Slope, and the rest into perspective. He is the moral link between orthodox religion and the secularizing world—between past and future. A deferential man, Harding lacks the conventional strong qualities of a hero. The narrator, however, calls Harding "a good man," exactly what James Joyce would call Leopold Bloom, the great and ridiculous hero of his modern epic, and we can see Harding as a figure who connects the "foolish" Christian faith of Erasmus's *Praise of Folly* to Joyce's secular comic faith in *Ulysses*. Trollope uses Harding to relate his readers to *his* faith, which is based on kindness and sympathetic fellow-feeling. There is a touch of the holy fool about Harding and his innocence. He functions as a kind of conscience to Grantly, the Oxford clerics, and the public men of London, his very being reminding people that disinterested virtue *can* exist. His special qualities— mildness, patience, tact, sensitivity to others, and a positive will *not* to dictate to them—his very *harmlessness*—are the qualities that make life tolerable in any age. He brings heart to the novel and, in fact, *is* its moral heart.

But Harding is not a symbol. He works in a practical way to preserve good relations. Breaks between people, sudden ruptures of tradition, sectarian enmity, distort the corporate nature of being. He smooths the way generously for the Proudie appointment, Quiverful, to take over as the new warden, and, feeling himself too old and passive to be dean of Barchester, he convinces others that Arabin, the only other character in the novel who shows true piety, should have the office.

175

He moderates the contentiousness of the community and helps to join its generations.

I cannot make the significance of Mr. Harding any clearer or show how necessary he is to Trollope's communal faith than by quoting William James, in *The Varieties of Religious Experience,* when he discusses modern secularizing society's view of saintly humility:

> Here saintliness has to face the charge of preserving the unfit. . . . "Resist not evil," "Love your enemies," these are saintly maxims of which men of this world find it hard to speak without impatience. . . .
>
> And yet you are sure, as I am sure, that were the world confined to . . . hard-headed, hard-hearted, and hard-fisted methods exclusively, . . . the world would be an infinitely worse place than it is now to live in. The tender grace, not of a day that is dead, but *of a day yet to be born somehow,* with the golden rule grown natural would be cut out from the perspective of our imaginations. [Italics mine][13]

Without the faintly ridiculous Harding there could be no moral imagination and no hope of virtue in the emerging society of the present and the future.

III

What is so impressive about the Barchester community is the way it can include so many kinds of people and points of view. Archdeacon Grantly, Dr. Slope, and Bishop Proudie are all in their own ways members of a new institutional breed, completely different from Harding. Political beings, they would be just as recognizable in pin-stripes, gray flannel, or Soviet serge as in clerical garb. Grantly is an administrator jealous for the undiminished power of his profession and, like Slope, "anxious that the world should be priest-governed"; he "really understood the *business* of bishoping" (italics mine). Eager Dr. Proudie, following the main chance, "early in life adapted himself to the views held by whigs on most theological and religious subjects." A good committeeman and amenable to "those who were really in authority," he serves the reforming governmental interests that work to bring the church under the control of the modern state. In the unscrupulous and pushy Slope, Trollope gives us a fine portrait of a climbing organizational infighter, as ruthless as any beast in the modern corporate jungle. These earthy men make a mock epic of church affairs. They also show how the collective ambitions of people in the same organization can be balanced off. Trollope uses their desires to animate the community. Ironically, what results from their corporate battle is, on the whole, good. In Barchester, corporate life keeps the individual will to power in check.

The real apostle of Evangelical thought and action is Mrs. Proudie, one of the most genuinely religious people in the novel. With her sense of moral duty, her reforming obsession, her earnest inner certitude, and her utter lack of humor, she represents that oppressive, puritanical side of religion, which just asks to be ridiculed. In her unctuous language, Trollope parodies the offensive tone of certainty that marks the smug proselyte of a "higher morality." She also stars in *Barchester Tower*'s comic version of the Samson theme. The traditional sexual roles often get reversed in the novel, and not only the bishop's wife but also the Stanhope girls, Mrs. Quiverful, Miss Thorne, Susan Grantly, and Eleanor seem to shear away strength from men. It is fitting that, in this novel of clerical life, women, for so long discriminated against and relegated to secondary status by the church, should romp like so many modern Delilahs through this ecclesiastical community.

Trollope often ridicules feminism, but it would never occur to the son of Frances Trollope that a woman is less important than a man. It is true that he does not imagine women leading successful independent lives or having identities that do not relate closely to men's. What we must also see, however, is that in Barchester he cannot imagine men leading lives of value that are not closely related to, and dependent upon, women's. Arabin can find fulfillment in his professional and private life only by marrying Eleanor and thereby relating himself to the community. Trollope puts a premium on the corporate relationship of the sexes, and that may be why he is without peer among English novelists in portraying marriage and in exploring the psychological connections between men and women, as the Palliser novels, for example, show.

IV

One thing missing from Barchester before the radical and provocative Stanhope family returns is a candid sense of the ridiculous, playing, from within the community, on its establishment figures; another is the alluring sport of sexuality. The reformation of Barset calls for both sex and comedy; by creating Signora Madeline Stanhope Vesey-Neroni, Trollope sets in motion both the mocking critical spirit and the farce of sexual attraction that the place needs. William James, expressing the conventional wisdom of the nineteenth century, says that "religious experience" must be "solemn": "For common men 'religion,' whatever more special meanings it may have, signifies always a *serious* state of mind."[14] For Trollope, religion without joking will no longer do: it cannot properly put down pride, i.e., *Proudieness*.

Madeline, in her aggressive, witty talk and her sardonic laughter, exactly fulfills the definition and function of what George Meredith would later describe as "the Comic Spirit": "whenever they [people] wax out of proportion, overblown, affected, pretentious, bombastical, hypocritical, pedantic...; whenever it sees them self-deceived...drifting into vanities, congregating in absurdities..., plotting dementedly; whenever they are at variance with their professions; are false in humility or mined with conceit, individually, or in bulk; the Spirit...will look humanely malign, and cast an oblique light on them, followed by volleys of silvery laughter."[15] This "spirit" is epitomized by a scene at Mrs. Proudie's reception, where the seductive but lame signora insists, as always, on languishing, courtesan-like, on a sofa. Mrs. Proudie, livid with raging moral prudery because her protégé, Slope, has succumbed to the siren, orders him to leave the couch.

> "Is she always like this?" said the signora. "Yes—always—madam," said Mrs. Proudie, returning; "...always equally adverse to impropriety of conduct of every description."...The signora couldn't follow her.... But she laughed loud, and sent the sound of it ringing through the lobby and down the stairs after Mrs. Proudie's feet. Had she been as active as Grimaldi, she could probably have taken no better revenge. [11:97]

Madeline, like Becky Sharp, excels at badinage and at playing charades with the sentimental idiocies of her time. She uses role-playing and jesting to make fun of contradictions, hidden immoralities, and unconscious motives in the world. By expos-

178

ing Slope, for example, and making us realize that he is the same grubby, greedy poseur in church affairs that he is in love affairs, she lets us infer the common connection between a drive for power over moral institutions and a thwarted infatuation with sexual sin. The "proper" men of Barset flock around her couch, and there she behaves with a flamboyance that kids and even makes a mockery of sex, in much the same way, and with much the same effect, as the comedienne Mae West would later do in the movies: she stimulates and then laughs at the male libido, which prudery can never quite hide.

Trollope hints that Madeline's early life included a pregnancy and the Victorian equivalent of a shotgun wedding. An internal moral censor evidently told him that the flaunting of sex, though necessary to his story, must be punished, and he made her a cripple. Though not fully realized, Madeline is one of the most interesting figures in the book. Trollope lavishes care on her speech and gives her, along with her brother Bertie, by far the best dialogue. She has a continually probing, iconoclastic wit. Like her nonconforming siblings, Bertie and the managerial Charlotte, she takes her living from the corporate church, which supports her, freethinker though she is. She is a daughter of the church, "one of the chapter," she says, and she strikes me as emblematic of the marriage that *Barchester Towers* accomplishes between the Anglican tradition and comedy. Like comedy, Madeline isn't quite respectable; but just because she is beyond the pale, "beyond the reach of Christian charity," as Mrs. Proudie puts it—*not serious*—she can send out the peals of laughter that Barset needs for renewing itself.

In the antiheroine, Madeline, whose repartee needles stuffed shirts and slaughters sacred cows, and the plot's heroine, Eleanor, we see that ingrained Victorian tendency to regard moral virtue as incompatible with critical, satirical intelligence in a woman. Again and again, Trollope, as he does here in *Barchester,* pays lip service to conventional notions of what a woman ought to be: obedient, pliable, the demure angel-in-the-house; a sweet, nurturing, familial creature who depends for her opinions and outlook on a man—someone who will "love, honor, and obey." In England, the ultimate sanction for this view of women's role lies in Christian doctrine and practice—in the church. Trollope wants to believe in the conventional Victorian ideal of womanhood; in fact, in novel after novel he says he does. He then goes right on, in the same books, to depict over and over the dilemmas and talk of those stifled, rebelliously witty women who fired his creative imagination.[16] (Later in his fiction Trollope would bring virtue, humor, ambition, biting wit, intelligence, and vulnerability together in Glencora Palliser, Madame Max Goesler, Violet Effingham, Mabel Grex, and a host of other intelligent and whole figures in what is very likely the finest gallery of female characters ever created by a male novelist in English.)

What makes Trollope's conflict interesting, of course, is that it was—and is—cultural. What could and should women do in the world? The development and the integrity of the social community needed the full potential and participation of women of various talents. The changing status of women was and is one of the greatest social and personal problems of modern life, and Madeline's voice, her satire of conventional hypocrisy, and her immobile, crippled being bring it home to Barchester.

v

Madeline and her Bohemian brother Bertie don't take life seriously; they keep looking for amusement, and they work in dialectical fashion to give the Barchester world what it lacks: skepticism, flash, drama, a love of pleasure, and a touch of frivolity. Trollope stresses their good nature, but he calls them "heartless," which means, as he uses the word, that they cannot love or feel deeply. That lack distances them from us and makes them subjects as well as instruments of satire. Bertie, for example, flits idly about Europe and the Near East, dabbling in art and religion but sticking to nothing and doing no one any good. The Stanhopes look like literary ancestors of Evelyn Waugh's Bright Young People and P. G. Wodehouse's charming parasites. (That hugely famous but critically underrated antihero of twentieth-century comic fiction, Bertie Wooster, could almost be Trollope's Bertie transposed into Jeeves's company.)

Bertie shows, even as a lazy dilettante, that bohemianism can mean comic gaiety, unexpected insight, and tolerance as well as irresponsible arrogance and cultivation of the ego. Eleanor likes him because, full of candor and fun, he never professes to be moral, nor does he preach sermons at her. He acts as an agent for Trollope's subtle, but important, comic devaluing of doctrinal dispute in religion (a devaluing that implicitly means a downplaying of Christian doctrine). Clowning about comparative religion to the bishop and the Barchester clergy, he blurts such things as "I was a Jew once, myself," sapping theology of its intimidating seriousness. Creed, for him, as it has for so many others, becomes fad and entertainment. Through Bertie, Trollope expresses something that endures in the British comic tradition and, I may say, in any lively society, and that is a hedonistic longing for pleasure and jokes, for idylls of irresponsibility. Even the brains of the industrious, when they dream, enjoy fantasies of effortlessness and ambassadors from lands of milk and honey.

Trollope carefully balances the Stanhopes and their disrespectful, campy humor with another brother-and-sister pair, the anachronistic Thornes of Ullathorne. (Ullathorne, a wordplay on extreme religious conservatism, was the title of a noted reactionary Roman Catholic bishop of the day.) The Thornes—typically, Miss Thorne is much more formidable than her bachelor brother—are unashamedly reactionary and try to shut out the present by living in the past. Trollope treats them affectionately. A community, for him, is not only a gathering of people but a gathering-together of customs and mores from different times. It has temporal variety as well as human variety and stretches across years as well as land. Since it is made from the past, it must be tolerant of the past in order not to rend itself. In a rich and good culture, there must be men and women who dedicate themselves to preserving the ideals and values of other times, as do the Thornes. Trollope conceives of the Thornes, like his other characters, as typical and having communal meaning: "Such a year or two since were the Thornes," he writes, ending his slightly patronizing chapter on them. "Such, we believe, are the inhabitants of many an English country home. May it be long before their number diminishes" (22:204). He knew he was being nostalgic. Neither of the Thornes marries; they have no descendants. They do, however, aid in making the match between Arabin and Eleanor. They too are part of the comic reformation of Barset and the catholicity of Trollope's outlook.

VI

Trollope's Barchester world goes to church and goes to parties, but going to parties predominates, and he gives over nearly a third of his text to them. Miss Thorne's party, welcoming Mr. Arabin, and Mrs. Proudie's party, when her husband becomes bishop, are central to the novel. Barchester social life revolves about institutional appointments and relations, and that is how Trollope perceives all society, as he shows later in the Palliser novels. He is the novelist laureate of parties, and social gatherings are his forte. His parties, however, are not the gluttonous feasts of Dickens or the festive comic communions of Peacock but the occasions when much important social business gets done: personal fate turns, relationships are rearranged, and characters and community, in signs, words, and gestures, reveal their real being. At parties men and women get a chance to talk to each other, courting takes place, sexual tension makes the blood jump, and the human comedy surges.

Trollope's comedy reads as if he were intending it to bring about a reunion of the diverging meanings of words by which modern society organizes itself. I mean such words as "party," "company," "corporation," "union," and "class," which have been losing their connotations of mutuality and human solidarity and now often suggest partisanship, private advantage, exclusion, and even social enmity. His parties in Barchester conserve the communal relationship and the social wholeness that potentially inhere in those words. He has a tribal sense of life, and he cares about preserving some sort of corporate integrity. Failure for him means not being able to connect with others. That is why he loves to bring people together, even very disparate people, and conjoin them in what he calls the social "sports."

Barchester's whole is greater than the sum of its parts. The life in the book has an attractiveness and a worthiness that few of the characters have if we look at them separately. Most of them—like the Proudies, Slope, the Stanhopes, Grantly, and Tom Towers—are not very nice or admirable people at all, and even Arabin, Eleanor, and Harding have their glaring shortcomings. The whole cast is not much better ethically than the figures in *Vanity Fair*. And yet the life in *Barchester Towers* seems infinitely sweeter and finer than in Thackeray's novel.

182

The reason is that Trollope finds a value, a joyousness, and an intensity in social relationship that Thackeray does not. I am not saying that Trollope's vision is better or truer or even more conducive to great comedy; but in this novel he is much more optimistic about how people complement and compensate for each other. Henry James calls Trollope's great virtue as a writer his "complete appreciation of the usual."[17] The meaning of that praise becomes clearer if we say that Trollope had a transfiguring faith in the usual and a talent for illuminating the wonder of it. Life, for him, is energized and made diverting by the spark of human interaction, by continuing encounter with the material world, and by the knowledge that human destiny is to be part of a community.

On almost every page he manages to convey a deep and almost obsessive interest in the minutiae of the social structure and the animation of communal relationships. His careful descriptions, for instance, of the mood and talk of different people at gatherings, of movement and positioning at parties, of the surroundings at Ullathorne and St. Ewold's parsonage, of the nagging worries that people have about what others are thinking, of the subtle nuances of behavior in social and professional hierarchies—all contribute to the *bricolage* that builds up an elaborate, thick, personal world.

VII

The title of one of the finest chapters, "The Bishop Sits Down to Breakfast and the Dean Dies," conveys the insistent linkage that operates in the Barchester world. It begins, "The bishop of Barchester said grace over the well-spread board in the Ullathorne dining-room; and while he did so the last breath was flying from the dean of Barchester as he lay in his sick room" (38:364). Trollope's corporate imagination finds apparently separate pieces of information to be part of a communal system that involves the characters featured in the chapter: "When the bishop of Barchester raised his first glass of champagne to his lips, the deanship of Barchester was a good thing in the gift of the prime minister." Everything connects and ramifies, but it doesn't lose its personal meaning for the characters. The syntax here shows an intermeshing social life that seems to function smoothly, like the Newtonian universe, except that there is

183

nothing mechanical about it. The breakfast, as it happens, will be instrumental in determining who will be the new dean, but we do not see this until much later. Trollope, as usual, however, wants to implant the idea of connection.

The body of this chapter concerns itself with what might appear to be a trivial conversation between the signora and Arabin. Actually it is a penetrating account of corporate characters in action and the fateful nature of particular social intercourse, with its strange harmonies:

> "Why, what ails you, Mr. Arabin? . . . Your friend Mr. Slope was with me a few minutes since, full of life and spirits; why don't you rival him?"
>
> . . . Mr. Arabin winced visibly before her attack, and she knew at once that he was jealous of Mr. Slope.
>
> "But I look on you and Mr. Slope as the very antipodes of men. . . . He will gain his rewards, which will be an in-sipid useful wife, a comfortable income, and a reputation for sanctimony. . . . You will see all this, and then—"
>
> "Well, and what then?"
>
> "Then you will begin to wish that you had done the same. . . . Is not such the doom of all speculative men of talent?" said she. "Do they not all sit rapt as you are now . . . ?" . . .
>
> Who was this woman that thus read the secrets of his heart . . . ? The signora went on—"The greatest mistake any man ever made is to suppose that the good things of the world are not worth the winning. . . . You try to de-spise these good things, but you only try; you don't suc-ceed."
>
> "Don't I?" said Mr. Arabin, still musing. . . .
>
> "I ask you the question; do you succeed?"
>
> . . . It seemed to him as though he were being inter-rogated by some inner spirit of his own. . . .
>
> "Do you not as a rule think women below your notice as companions? Let us see. There is the widow Bold looking round at you from her chair this minute. What would you say to her as a companion for life?" . . .
>
> "You cross-question me rather unfairly," he replied, "and I do not know why I answer you at all. Mrs. Bold is a

very beautiful woman, and as intelligent as beautiful. . . . One that would well grace any man's house."

"And you really have the effrontery to tell me this," said
she; "to me, who, as you very well know, set up to be a
beauty myself, . . . you really have the effrontery to tell me
that Mrs. Bold is the most beautiful woman you know."

"I did not say so," said Mr. Arabin; "you are more
beautiful— . . . perhaps more clever."

"Not a word further. . . ."

"But Madame Neroni, Mrs. Bold—"

"I will not hear a word about Mrs. Bold. Dread thoughts
of strychnine did pass across my brain, but she is welcome
to the second place."

"Her place—"

"I won't hear anything about her or her place. I am
satisfied, and that is enough. But, Mr. Arabin, I am dying
with hunger; beautiful and clever as I am, you know I
cannot go to my food, and yet you do not bring it to
me." . . .

It was quite clear that Mr. Arabin was heartily in love
with Mrs. Bold, and the signora, with very unwonted good
nature, began to turn it over in her mind whether she
could not do him a good turn. [38:368–75]

By the end of this tête-à-tête, the comic reformation of Arabin
and of Barchester clerical society is all but assured: Madeline,
this latter-day Eve—with whose teachings, ironically, Trollope
agrees[18]—has preached the value of the world and cleverly
taught him to heed his own longings for pleasure, the flesh, and
relationship. Miss Thorne's breakfast turns out to be an act of
comic communion that promises the renewal of Arabin's faith
in worldly life and the resurrection of the apostolic dean of
Barchester in the person of Arabin.

A comic and worldly church sponsors this scene and party,
with its happy consequences. It countenances and uses the
humor of a vain woman to further its own regenerative ends and
processes. All the characters, likable or not, function in concert
to create hope and faith for the future of the community. Even
though Slope and the Stanhopes leave Barchester in the end,
they have played their parts in its ongoing life, and they still

take their living from the same corporate body that sustains the cathedral town. It might seem, therefore, that this church is no less wondrous, and at least as charitable, as the church of the supernatural God.

CAREER AND VOCATION

My heart's at my office, my heart is always there—
My heart's at my office, docketing with care;
Docketing my papers, and copying all day,
My heart's at my office, though I be far away.
Trollope, *The Three Clerks*

For Trollope, one of the most important goals in life is a successful career, and a modern career, as he imagines it, is very likely to mean a career within an institutional or professional framework. The chance to fulfill oneself through one's vocation is as good an opportunity to find happiness and purpose as life offers. The idea of career is, for him, the secular concept in which the claims of individualism and the claims of society can best be met and reconciled; culturally, I need hardly say, it is still an immensely powerful one. Thinking in terms of career may give a wholeness to life—a wholeness that can seem precious as belief in one's self as an immortal soul fades. It can also give a sense of permanence in this way: one may hope to contribute to, and achieve prominence in, a profession that benefits society and goes on existing though its members die. One then would be a part of something immortal though not supernatural; old Bishop Grantly, for example, dies, but his life has merged with a corporate body that keeps on living.

Ideally, a professional career could satisfy the two Victorian imperatives to do good for others and to grow rich and successful. In both the Barchester and the Palliser series, Trollope describes the interplay of vocation and career (when he comes to write his autobiography, he sets his own life down primarily as a successful writer's career, complete with payments received for his books and a professional code for novelists). Men like Harding, Grantly, Arabin, Dr. Thorne, Phineas Finn, Plantagenet Palliser, and Lord Chiltern, in their own manner, find moral dignity, usefulness, self-sufficiency, and communal responsibility in their careers.

186

I

Barchester Towers, as Slope, Dr. Proudie, and Grantly prove, shows the weakening, for the clergy, of the sense of vocation as a holy calling. But, it also implicitly enhances the status of other professions by showing priests as professionals and by recognizing and honoring the modern sense of vocation. Trollope's comedy dramatizes the historical change from "profession," meaning the professing of religious faith and doctrine, to "profession" connoting a significant occupational career, demanding high competence, for which one is paid.

The big trouble, however, with making career the focal point for faith and hope is that it may tend to glorify professional success at the expense of other kinds of desirable experience and lead to narrow ambition. Stress on career can also, obviously, create huge problems in the relationship between the sexes. If vocational career is what we have instead of God, so to speak, where does that leave women? For many, as Trollope so well depicts, it leaves them filled with conflicts and wanting their own careers. The successful career, in his view, must be something more than a game of king-of-the-vocational-mountain. It requires love, or some sort of emotional and affectionate binding of self to others that resembles love, and it must be a cooperative venture.

Ideally, he says, a man's career ought to include his wife and family, and a woman's career should be to attach herself to her husband and his familial interests and, by supporting him and fulfilling the traditional feminine generative and nurturing roles, find her own successful vocation. That is his normative answer to the problem of women's place. It ran counter, however, to his own deepest experience and to his sense of the tensions in the lives of talented women. He doesn't blink away the emotional turmoil that the blocked access to careers for women can cause. His own experience and his mother's made him understand the powerful appeal of a professional career—its glamor and opportunities—and the inevitable frustrations that women felt in reconciling their conventional place in society with their potential abilities and their rising ambitions.

II

In *Barchester,* the two major figures in his comic vision of career are Arabin and Mrs. Proudie. Arabin's history is a success story

187

about achieving a balance between worldliness and idealism in vocation and life. He is the one character in the novel who combines religious dedication, professional zeal, energy, and open-minded curiosity. If Barchester is to be anything more than an amusing but trivial place, his career must bloom there. When he comes to Barset, he is an advocate for a religion that doesn't satisfy him and, it is important to see, of a kind that Trollope finds sterile. A veteran of the Oxford Movement and a skillful polemicist on matters of abstract theological dispute, he is divorced from the world and celibate. He lacks personal connection to others. We need to see exactly what happens to him. When Grantly brings him to the community to combat Slope and Proudie, he is dispirited; "He was tired of his Oxford rooms and his college life. He regarded the wife and children of his friend with something like envy. . . . The daydream of his youth was over, and at the age of forty he felt that he was not fit to work in the spirit of an apostle. He had mistaken himself, and learned his mistake when it was past remedy" (20:177). Trollope shows him becoming not only a happier man but a better churchman by listening to Madeline and by loving and winning Eleanor. When Harding finds his daughter is to marry Arabin, he arranges for him to become dean of Barchester, thus increasing Arabin's moral influence. Personal and professional life are necessarily connected, and a proper career is an open process of development.

One passage on his attitude toward women before coming to Barset illuminates the antifeminism of the clerical tradition out of which Arabin comes and gives us an example of what is still, fundamentally, the most influential and pervasive form of intellectual sexism: "He looked on women . . . in the same light that one sees them regarded by many Romish priests. . . . He talked to them without putting out all his powers, and listened to them without any idea that what he should hear from them could either actuate his conduct or influence his opinion" (20:175). He and that clerical tradition must be reformed if his career and his faith are to flourish, and, by the end, Madeline and Eleanor both act to change his conduct and opinion.

Late in the novel, Arabin complains to Eleanor, "It is the bane of my life that on important subjects I acquire no fixed opinion. I think, and think, and go on thinking; and yet my thoughts are running ever in different directions." Surety is easy, uncertainty hard; but Arabin actually expresses one of the distinguishing characteristics—I would say glories—of a pragmatic, system-wary British intellectual tradition that has grown out of the Anglican clerical heritage. "England," says Barbara Tuchman admiringly, "dislikes the definitive."[20] Arabin is not a fully developed character like Palliser or Josiah Crawley of *The Last Chronicle of Barset,* but in him Trollope sketches out his vision of the open-minded intellectual career. Life controls and modifies doctrine and ideology. Proper thinking, like a proper career, avoids fixity and leaves open possible ways of approaching the future profitably.

All the trends and factions in the community work for the good of Arabin's career. Such diverse influences as the signora's cynicism and sexuality, Harding's quietism, Miss Thorne's feudal instincts, and Eleanor's eligibility and inheritance all combine to favor him. At the end, only half-facetiously, Oxford refers to him as an "ornament of the age," and Trollope calls him "a studious, thoughtful, hard-working man" who lives "in mutual confidence" with his wife. In Arabin, Trollope shows that vocation and faith must be joined to community; to have a successful career, we must have, quite precisely, *faith in the world.*

III

If Arabin shows the blessings of a career, Mrs. Proudie shows its possible drawbacks. Behind the stock comic figure of the virago, we see Trollope's comedy working to ridicule and restrain a woman's drive for professional career and power. Mrs. Proudie, "a would-be priestess," wants to be bishop of Barchester. At the end she is: "in the beginning...three or four were contending together as to who, in fact, should be bishop....Each...now admitted...that Mrs. Proudie was victorious" (51:489). She comes across as a figure of modern comic myth inspired by social change and male anxiety; she is a caricature of militant feminism. Trollope also has another rationale in making fun of her, which runs something like this: men are tending more and more to make their goal the wielding of power in a corporate structure and turning institutional life into a competitive jungle; God forbid, for the sake of civilization, that women should do likewise.

In his burlesque of the would-be career woman, Trollope

parodies male careerism and projects a comic switch on one of the common sins of male professional ambition. *She* tyrannizes over *her* mate and in her drive for power tramples on his dignity and self-esteem. She treats him, in other words, like a long-suffering hapless wife. The satire on her expresses the incipient fear of women set loose to compete, but it also contains Trollope's basic criticism of all careerists: Mrs. Proudie can't relate to others. Through her he mocks those who identify power—especially power within an institution—with success in life.

The surprising thing about Mrs. Proudie is not that she is such a ridiculous termagant but that she is so successful. Except for the brief farce of her torn dress and the lovely mockery of her by Bertie and the signora, she does *not* come out second-best. Trollope's harsh criticism of her ambition, combined with her success at getting her way, suggests that his divided feelings about his mother might have led him to purge resentment by creating the comic Mrs. Proudie. Something he says in his autobiography reveals an almost filial feeling toward her: "I have never dissevered myself from Mrs. Proudie, and still live much in company with her ghost."[21]

In *Barchester Towers* Trollope's last words on this woman are full of odd ironies: "As for Mrs. Proudie, our prayers for her are that she may live for ever." There is a sly mockery of the efficaciousness of prayer here, and Trollope's faith in both prayer and personal immortality seem highly suspect. In *The Last Chronicle of Barset* he does kill off Mrs. Proudie, and he tells about it with relish in the autobiography. These "prayers" look like a kind of facetious joking. It is true, however, that in *Barchester Towers* there is no killing off what she represents: the growing wave of feminine assertiveness, the impulse to make a vocation of moral bullying, and the use of the insolence of office to equate personal pride with righteousness and one's authority with God's command. She lives as an inevitable part of the enduring human comedy, but Trollope controls her by imagining a comic church, broad enough to include her career and, for the social good, to support, extend, and balance the careers of Arabin, Harding, Grantly, Slope, Dr. Proudie, and all the other Barchestrians as well. The prayers are the prayers of a comic faith that can turn to laughter what is at first sight obnoxious. Prayer, then, in the career of Mrs. Proudie—and of Trollope—in essence merges with laughter.

190

DIALOGUE AND UNDERSTATEMENT

The dialogue is generally the most agreeable part of a novel: but it is only so long as it tends in some way to the telling of the main story.[22]

Trollope, *An Autobiography*

Dialogue, the verbal interchange of various points of view, *is* "in some way" the "main story" of Trollope's fiction. It is there we mainly find the graceful spontaneity and comic creativity of the Trollopean world. He sees the evolving human condition as one of dialogue, a continuing synthesis of voices—often incongruous voices—within the community. Character reveals, defines, and redefines itself in the interplay of conversation. The most important times in life, as he depicts it, come when people talk; in many of his best passages, the author seems to fade out as the characters go on speaking, interacting, and influencing the nature of their society. The characters' talk shapes and clarifies their ideas, expresses their ruling passions and full selves; and it also reveals the processes and themes of the book.

I

Here, from Mrs. Proudie's party, is a conversation between Bertie and the bishop:

"Do you like Barchester on the whole?" asked Bertie.

The bishop, looking dignified, said that he did like Barchester.

"You've not been here very long, I believe," said Bertie.

"No—not long," said the bishop. . . .

"You weren't a bishop before, were you?"

Dr. Proudie explained that this was the first diocese he had held.

"Ah—I thought so," said Bertie; "but you are changed about sometimes, a'nt you?"

"Translations are occasionally made," said Dr. Proudie. . . .

"They've cut them all down to pretty nearly the same figure, haven't they?" said Bertie.

To this the bishop could not bring himself to make any answer. . . .

"Is there much to do here, at Barchester?" . . .

"The work of a bishop of the Church of England," said Dr. Proudie, with considerable dignity, "is not easy. The responsibility which he has to bear is very great indeed."

"Is it?" said Bertie, opening wide his wonderful blue eyes. "Well, I never was afraid of responsibility. I once had thoughts of being a bishop, myself."

"Had thoughts of being a bishop!" said Dr. Proudie, much amazed.

"That is, a parson—parson first, you know, and a bishop afterwards. If I had once begun, I'd have stuck to it. But, on the whole, I like the church of Rome the best."

The bishop could not discuss the point, so he remained silent. . . .

"By the bye, do you know much about the Jews?"

At last the bishop saw a way out. "I beg your pardon," said he; "but I'm forced to go round the room." [11:85–86]

That comic dialogue shows a whole comic reformation taking place in the community. Bertie's glib talk defines his dilettante charm and his brash, baiting humor. Trollope makes Proudie's talk an inconsistent mixture of indirect and direct discourse, stock response, surprised exclamation, self-serving platitudes, passive phrasing, and transparent attempts to impersonate the voice of ecclesiastical authority. This intricately devised dialogue of the bishop reflects perfectly his discomfort and his effort to distance himself from what he takes to be Bertie's impertinence and disgraceful sincerity. Such dialogue-to-avoid-dialogue is, of course, a staple of British life and comedy, but, beyond that, the whole incongruous conversation lets us see Trollope's willingness and power to mock the dignity of the religious establishment. A church that has so pompous but weak a spokesman as Proudie, and that must suffer its poor prelate to be mocked by the likes of Bertie, suggests a religion that is losing its traditional power to daunt.

II

Trollope almost always leaves it to readers to infer the full significance of what his characters say, and the prominence he gives to dialogue is what sometimes gives his fiction the illusion of being an unmediated vision: nothing appears to stand between us and the characters. Neither the characters nor the author will *seem* to have the grasp that readers can have on the meaning and consequence of what has been said. Dialogue, then, is what makes Trollope's novels so subtle, so full of nuances, so much more intelligent than anyone would gather from the narrative commentary. It often conveys important information and profound psychological and social insight in a seemingly offhand way. In dialogue we find his characteristic and telling mode of understatement.

Understatement, a famous trait of British humor, is a comic device for slipping things past a moral censor, internal or external. It is also a *modus vivendi,* a way of making light of life's outrageousness, of not seeming to be distressingly serious and, hence, a bore; of not, in Trollope's revealing words, "seeming to have a design upon the reader." It is a mode of irony but an *indirect* mode, one that assumes a bond of communication and a superior understanding and sympathy between like-minded people attuned to recognizing and putting down crude hyperbole and self-dramatization. Understatement relies on, and encourages, a community of shared perspective.

To be good readers of Trollope's novels, we have to learn to make independent judgments about the dialogue. Look again at the talk between Eleanor and Arabin at the pivotal time of their courtship:

> " . . . old-fashioned things are so much the honestest."
>
> "I don't know about that," said Mr. Arabin, gently laughing. . . . "Some think that we are quickly progressing towards perfection, while others imagine that virtue is disappearing from the earth."
>
> "And you, Mr. Arabin, what do you think?" said Eleanor. . . .
>
> "What do I think, Mrs. Bold? . . . It is the bane of my life that on important subjects I acquire no fixed opinion. I think, and think, and go on thinking; and yet my thoughts are running ever in different directions. I hardly know whether or no we do lean more confidently than our fathers did on those high hopes to which we profess to aspire."
>
> "I think the world grows more worldly every day," said Eleanor.
>
> "That is because you see more of it than when you were

younger. But we should hardly judge by what we see,—we
see so very very little." [48:469–70]

This conversation passes without Trollope's comment, but it
is remarkable. It shows that Arabin has a wise and interesting
mind: what he says about thinking and about point of view is
surprisingly candid and profound; he understands that truth
may be indeterminate and relative but that one needs to seek it
anyway. His talk lets us know that he is honest enough to
express doubt, that he senses the stagnating effect of absolutist
thought, and that he has enough confidence in Eleanor to confess to her what many would regard as weakness and to tell her
what truly bothers him in his intellectual life. It shows that he
has changed since coming to Barchester and can now speak
"with his full powers" to a woman. Her talk reveals a very
conventional mind; there is great irony in her trite but idealistic
sentiment, "I think the world grows more worldly." The growing worldliness of the world has brought her a large income and
now, with Arabin growing more worldly, a fine new prospective
husband. The statement, however, implies an innocence that
charms Arabin. If we compare this dialogue with that between
Arabin and Madeline, who has helped to teach him to love and
enjoy the world, including rich, pretty widows, we see that, for
the most part, he listens to the signora but dominates the talk
with Eleanor. She allows him to express himself more comfort-
ably and fully, and the implication is that he will have little
trouble making her of one mind with him. It is easy to love
those who are solicitous of our ideas and whose opinions we can
help to mold.

III

Arabin's point about the diversity of his thinking identifies a
key aspect of Trollope's fiction: for him, dialogue is an internal
as well as external process. The indirect interior monologue,
which becomes so important in his later novels, often takes the
form of indirect inward conversation—self-dialogue. His typical
characters are made up of many different, changing, sometimes
conflicting social voices and parts, and he uses the method of
internal debate and dialogue to help him with his characterization.

Here is a passage on Arabin's interior life that contains typical
internal dialogue and understatement:

194

He had, as was his wont, asked himself a great many questions, and given himself a great many answers. . . . Then he asked himself whether in truth he did love this woman; and he answered himself, not without a long struggle, but at last honestly, that he certainly did love her. He then asked himself whether he did not also love her money; and he again answered himself that he did so. But here he did not answer honestly. It was and ever had been his weakness to look for impure motives for his own conduct. [34:323]

Notice that what the narrator says about Arabin's answer—that he does, indeed, love Eleanor's money—is *not* the truth that emerges. We have before us the unequivocal answer of Arabin's mind: he *does* love the idea of her money, and nothing that he says or does in the rest of the book, nothing that happens, supports the authorial comment that "he did not answer honestly." The narrator may not understand that the love for a woman and the love of her wealth can be tied to each other, but Arabin does, Trollope does, and so do we. We also learn from this internal dialogue and from several other conversations that "looking for the impure motive" in one's conduct is not a weakness but a great strength and spur to progress.

IV

The stress on both inner and outer dialogue pulls us into a dialogue with the book. Trollope presents this seemingly casual talk among some Barchester clergymen who are visiting the old, dying dean:

"Poor Dr. Trefoil; the best of men, but—"
"It's the most comfortable dean's residence in England," said a second prebendary. "Fifteen acres in the grounds. It is better than many of the bishops' palaces."
"And full two thousand a year," said the meagre doctor.
"It is cut down to £1200," said the chancellor.
"No," said the second prebendary. "It is to be fifteen. A special case was made."
"No such thing," said the chancellor.
"You'll find I'm right," said the prebendary.
"I'm sure I read it in the report," said the minor canon. . . .

"What do you say, Grantly?" said the meagre little doctor.

"Say about what?" said the archdeacon, who had been looking as though he were thinking about his friend the dean, but who had in reality been thinking about Mr. Slope.

"What is the next dean to have, twelve or fifteen?"

"Twelve," said the archdeacon authoritatively, thereby putting an end at once to all doubt and dispute among his subordinates as far as that subject was concerned. [31:296–97]

It is a typical moment in a Trollope novel.

Reading this without direct authorial guidance, I have the illusion of being not only a witness but as credible an interpreter as the narrator of what this conversation signifies. I infer that in the midst of death we are in life, that institutional identity provides continuity of life, that professional people are fascinated by the status and pay of their fellows, that the modern church is a very worldly organization, that an organization's pecking order functions even in extraordinary times, and that Grantly knows everything about the temporalities of his calling. This chatter makes fun of the religious institution, but it shows the animation of profession and the life-force even at death's door. In the fictive understatement of the dialogue I find Trollope's essential humor and comic vision.

NARRATOR

Our doctrine is, that the author and the reader should move along together in full confidence with each other. [15:130]

...readers must make the judgment that the slippery narrator refuses to provide.

U. C. Knoepflmacher[23]

The messenger of momentous tidings of change does well to tread softly and speak ingratiatingly. The best comedians often assume a self-deprecating style and throw out audience-flattering lines in order to keep their comic license to make daring jokes and do thought-provoking routines. The narrator of *Barchester Towers* is self-effacing, disingenuous, shifty, playful and deferential. Trollope has to be careful of alienating his readers because he is making fun of many of the pieties of his age and is imaginatively chronicling major changes. In the communal process that shapes the world and defines life, as he renders it, there is a dialectical tension between the conventional and the unconventional, between old traditions and the uniqueness of particular new circumstances. Trollope wants to engage his readers in this process; he tries to establish community with them and mediate conflicts between what ought to be and what is. He takes his audience to be relatively conformist, poses as conventional himself, and then shows how conventions either need reforming or are shifting.

I

Like Thackeray's narrator, Trollope's narrator works to make us a congregation; but Trollope needs and assumes a much more diffident persona. He is preaching the possibility of a fruitful fusion of spirituality with worldly corporation and a faith in the changing earthly community, not the vanity of the world and the dismaying sameness of life. He has to be more tactful than Thackeray, who was dealing for the most part with lay sinners, that "set of people living without God in the world." He can't afford to say shocking things, as Thackeray can and does. Trollope, treating clergymen and their milieu—a very risky thing to do—has to handle his subject with kid gloves if he wants a broad audience to accept his comic faith.[24]

Not wanting to make a head-on assault against sentimental conventions, he poses as independent from his characters; he lets people like the Stanhopes express unpopular ideas, while he himself makes inoffensive remarks that contradict the tenor of the text and leaves it to the readers to draw controversial conclusions. A "novelist," he says, must sometimes "submit" to his characters, by which he means that their personalities must sometimes seem strong enough to overwhelm the author's opinions and conceptual desire (e.g., Arabin *does* love Eleanor's money), and the audience must take the responsibility for judging the truth and significance of what is put before it.

197

II

Though he denies or obfuscates it, our narrator is often anti-clerical and even antiecclesiastical. Notice the ambivalence and possible irony in his disclaimer of impiety:

> In endeavouring to depict the characters of the persons of whom I write, I am to a certain extent forced to speak of sacred things. I trust, however, that I shall not be thought to scoff at the pulpit, though some may imagine that I do not feel all the reverence that is due to the cloth. I may question the infallibility of the teachers, but I hope that I shall not therefore be accused of doubt as to the thing to be taught. [6:45]

Throwing out that sop to orthodoxy, Trollope almost immediately launches into a denunciation of preaching:

> There is, perhaps, no greater hardship at present inflicted on mankind in civilised and free countries, than the necessity of listening to sermons. . . . No one but a preaching clergyman can revel in platitudes, truisms, and untruisms, and yet receive, as his undisputed privilege, the same respectful demeanour as though words of impassioned eloquence, or persuasive logic, fell from his lips. . . .
>
> To me, it all means nothing; and hours are too precious to be so wasted—if one could only avoid it. [6:47–48]

The narrator's stance is: *I ridicule human frailties but leave sacred doctrine untouched.* The disparaging of sermons and services, however, strips away sanctity from church and priest and carries at least a hint of scoffing blasphemy.

Shortly after, Trollope uses a mock-epic style to describe a meeting of the Grantly forces. He parodies *Paradise Lost* and tacitly compares Religion and Church in Miltonic England with their role in Barchester: "Then up rose Dr. Grantly; and, having thus collected the scattered wisdom of his associates, spoke forth with words of deep authority. When I say up rose the archdeacon, I speak of the inner man. . . . His hands were in his breeches pockets" (7:52).[25] The narrator's mock-heroic voice works to ridicule those who would claim their experience to be extraordinary and elevated above the social norms that govern the world of the reader. Trollope uses snatches of mock epic carefully to satirize those who presume to have an intimate relationship to "celestial minds": Grantly, Mrs. Proudie, and Slope. An archdeacon puts his hands in his pockets; a bishop's wife tears her dress; a chaplain gets his face slapped; and the narrator, using a mock-heroic style, points out ironically the common humanity of the clerical community's leading personages; their behavior is as silly and banal as other people's.

III

Everything about the narrator goes to prove that he too is a part of a corporate existence. Even when he intrudes in order to joke about the fictional nature of the book, he is implying that there is something so true to life and independent about the characters that certain things cannot be manipulated to satisfy his own whim. He is not always an omnipotent author. "But let the gentle-hearted reader be under no apprehension whatsoever. It is not destined that Eleanor shall marry Mr. Slope or Bertie" (15:129). Trollope scoffs at fiction that stresses outcomes and upshots: "Nay, take the last chapter if you please— learn from its pages all the results of our troubled story, and the story shall have lost none of its interest" (15:130). When he twits novelistic conventions, he makes fun of himself, but he is also laughing at those who prefer the conventional pap of illusion in fiction.

The narrator mocks arbitrary finalities and the disposition of private fates in novels because it is in *concluding,* in closing the book, that the analogy to reality that Trollope tries to create breaks down. The conventional, arbitrary, happy ending distorts his sense of life as a continuum. For him, the vitality of living—its meaning, its goodness and pleasure—lies not in ends but in the social dialogue and the continuing interrelationships. The last chapter of *Barchester Towers* begins, "The end of a novel, like the end of a children's dinner-party, must be made up of sweetmeats and sugar-plums" (53:502). That mocking sentence says that our craving for happy finalities is childish, and it implies also that the fantasies of fiction may bring us real pleasure as long as we don't take them too seriously. Trollope usually downplays his endings, returning again and again to the same characters, writing series, imagining a second generation of fictional families; he does so because he is striving to make his fiction conform to the book of the world, and the book of the world cannot be closed.

TIME AND PLACE

> Throughout these stories there has been no name given to a fictitious site which does not represent to me a spot of which I know all the accessories, as though I had lived and wandered there.
>
> Trollope, *An Autobiography*[26]

Trollope begins with a specified time, "In the latter days of July in the year 185–," and a place, "the cathedral city of Barchester." That fixity of time and setting immediately commits him to historical verisimilitude; it claims, in effect, that imaginative fiction is a real part of human annals and that what happens in this novel is typical of the sort of thing that could and would have happened in the Victorian fifties. In this story about the spiritual profession, it says that life is time-bound, that people share a chronology and certain historical circumstances. The quick merging of history with locality, however, gives intimations of communal solidity and continuity in the flux of time. Trollope would call the Barset novels *chronicles,* a word connoting a series of objective historical events and a record of the times of a lifelike community. Temporal fate is defined by where people are and what kind of place they live in, even as the times shape and modify individual communities and particular places. History, the times, chronology have no meaning for Trollope in the abstract. Time must, in that revealing phrase, *take place.*

I

Time in *Barchester Towers* is partly the flowing currents of church and social history, but it is delimited, starting in "185–" with the narrator's assurance of an ending: "our present business at Barchester will not occupy us above a year or two at the furthest." The plot is structured by the time, jointly, of Eleanor's courtship and of the upheaval in Barchester clerical politics that resolves itself in "the present arrangement of ecclesiastical affairs"—Arabin becoming dean and Mrs. Proudie confirmed as *de facto* bishop. The focus on arbitrarily chosen segments of time, whether they are stipulated by process (e.g., the defeat of Slope and the marriage of Arabin), by incident (e.g., Miss Thorne's party), or by duration (e.g., "a year or two"), is what makes the visions of comic form convincing.

Trollope's time is public, linear, and progressive, a time of consecutive social incident—"Ullathorne Sports," Acts I, II, and III. His time is a process of development presented, loosely, in the form of a social calendar of Barchester's clerical community—a history of its conclaves, parties, and interviews that gently parodies the battles and gatherings of historical chronicles and annals. Trollope gives a mock-epic spirit to the novel but also intends it to be, in its comic fashion, a true Anglo-Saxon chronicle of the mid-Victorian world.

History—communal time—is real and inescapable, but it is subjective. It catches up the characters, but it manifests itself in particular ways for particular people in a particular locale. Characters define themselves by their attitudes toward passing time and by identifying with or rejecting parts of the historical process: Eleanor likes everything "old-fashioned," the Thornes detest modern history, Slope likes new men, and Tom Towers likes to see things changed. The comic incongruities of character, for Trollope, not only depend on the accidents of history, they also depend on personal attitudes toward the passage of the world through time.

All the characters, however, are moving from the past into the present—from their time, and the time of the author, to the reader's time. Once balance and accommodation are reached, Trollope leaves us in the present tense: the fictional world and its people are transmuted into the time of the audience's consciousness: "As for Mrs. Proudie, our prayers for her are that she may live for ever"; "One word of Mr. Harding, and we have done. He is still Precentor of Barchester. . . . The Author now leaves him in the hands of his readers." Later, of course, Trollope reclaims time from the reader and, with his deep-seated sense of mutability and his vision of personal life as career, continues the Barset chronicles. He mirrors perfectly the tension, in the typical conception of comedy, between the longing for happy finality and the hope for unending life—the paradoxical and contradictory human wishes for a liberation from time and for eternal immersion in time, that split desire that fundamentally links comedy to religion.

201

Hawthorne's famous description of Trollope's fiction, "as real as if some giant had hewn a great lump of earth and put it under a glass case,"[27] gets at the important "time-capsule" aspect of Trollope's fiction. The time-capsule mentality, even at its most naïve, indicates a desire to master time and become part of an immortal process. People pack up pieces of their culture as a way of speaking to the future; they express faith in a continuing community of human consciousness; their significance will live again and be part of future minds. Trollope intends to transmit an accurate picture of contemporary life for posterity because he has strong faith that it matters, that all life is finally connected and communal—especially imaginative life.

Wanting it known exactly what he was hoping to do, he, the most modest of great novelists, in his autobiography quotes Hawthorne: "The criticism, whether just or unjust, describes with wonderful accuracy the purport that I have ever had in view in my writing. I have always desired to 'hew out some lump of earth', and to make men and women walk upon it just as they walk here among us,—with not more excellence, nor with exaggerated baseness,—so that my readers might recognise human beings like themselves."[28] "Like," here, is a most telling word. His aim in fiction is to make a community with his reader and to show how the past is part of the present and how the imagined life of comic, antiheroic characters, with mixed moral natures, touches and includes the reader's life. People must perceive their commonality across time and space.

II

Trollope specifies and delimits place as he does time, though he makes it an imaginary and composite "cathedral town." He focuses closely on Barchester. All the action, except for brief excursions to Oxford and London, which he does not describe, takes place in Barset. There is no global movement or reporting, as in Thackeray and Dickens. People do travel abroad and move away, unlike the characters of Austen's Highbury world; but when the Stanhopes, the Proudies, or Slope leave Barchester, the narrator's eye does not follow them into new settings. Barchester is caught up and changed by the disturbing rhythms of the world of London and the acceleration of life they are foisting on the country; but by focusing exclusively on Barchester, Trollope shows it preserving its integrity.

In the mobile twentieth century, the longing for the supposed sureties of physical community has been a source of Barchester's appeal. Nostalgic for place and roots, the modern sensibility has endowed Barset with an idyllic quality; witness the resurgence of interest in Trollope during wartime that Elizabeth Bowen and others have noted.[29] In times of urban anonymity and social turbulence, Barchester feeds a hunger for images of solidity and "home." Place seems able to control the frivolous swirls of time.

Focus on a specific community is also a good method for isolating and making clear the great changes taking place in the larger world. As Slope says, "things are a good deal changed in Barchester.... And not only in Barchester... but in the world at large" (12:102). Barchester, like Scott's Scotland, Hardy's Wessex, Faulkner's Yoknapatawpha, and even Garcia Marquez's Macondo, is a fully imagined rural region that betrays the human need and passion for locality. All these novelists, of course, chronicle the changes that are transforming these places even as they assert the tremendous world drama of preserving distinct personal and communal identity in the face of massive amalgamating social forces. Barchester, quiet and nonviolent, partakes of the pastoral mode, and it, like any idyllic setting, becomes in part analogous to *one's own garden* as well as to the broader world. Region, in modern fiction, turns out to be like a modern self, under continual pressure from a changing world, who strives for some sort of stable integrity while having to reconcile with history and the passage of time. Ending in the present tense and the tension of the present, *Barchester Towers,* for me, becomes finally a metaphor for the human comedy of one's own time and place and for that reformation and re-cultivation of one's communal garden upon which civilization depends.

7

MEREDITH'S *THE EGOIST* (1879)

The Comedy of Egoism

Thus civilization has to be defended against the individual.
Sigmund Freud[1]

We have had comic pulpits, for a sign that the laughter-moving
and the worshipful may be in alliance.
George Meredith[2]

George Meredith is the first major British novelist explicitly to
reject and ridicule the dogmas of Christianity and to set up
comedy as a rival to religion. He revered the idea of comedy,
and *The Egoist* is the testament of his comic faith.[3] It insists
upon the energy and creative power of self-criticism that our
comic sense can generate. Its "Prelude" asserts that comedy can
best express the most important things that men and women
can think and know. That mankind should have a sense of
humor filled Meredith with genuine awe, and he became the
conscious apostle of what he called "the comic spirit."

I

This comic spirit, the "Sword of Common Sense," "the sacred
chain of man to man,"[4] became for him the quintessence of
what is holy and permanently valuable in life, since he saw it
both protecting *and* embodying vital communal culture and
allegiance to the progress of humanity. He moralized comedy.
Our common sense of the ridiculous replaced for him the
Judeo-Christian concept of a monotheistic, supernatural God as
the great civilizing moral force and controller of egoism in life.
The time had come when secular comedy, not anachronistic
religion, could best teach proper morality: namely, respect for,
and identification with, cumulative reason and the processes of
civilization.

In Meredith's comic vision, modern egoism ironically generates the growth of new community and fellowship. Playing on
the rapacious, possessive "one" and "I" of his century, he
imagined that "our united social intelligence, which is the
Comic Spirit,"[5] might possibly evolve pride in collective life, a
rational feeling of unity with nature, and the liberty, fraternity,
and equality of the two sexes.

His ode "To The Comic Spirit" makes clear his almost
metaphysical devotion to comedy and his hostility to organized
religion. Like other establishments of undeserved privilege,
Christian worship has sunk into regressive institutionalized
egoism and become a fit object for derision: the human
"heart . . . of its old religion . . . has doubts"; and the poem continues:

> . . . nor much resents,
> When the prized objects it [the heart] has raised for
>   prayer,
> For fitful prayer;—repentance dreading fire,
> Impelled by aches; the blindness which repents
> Like the poor trampled worm that writhes in mire;—
> Are sounded by thee [the comic spirit], and thou darest
>   probe
> Old institutions and establishments,
> Once fortresses against the floods of sin,
> For what their worth; and questioningly prod
> For why they stand upon a racing globe,
> Impeding blocks, less useful than the clod;
> Their angel out of them, a demon in.[6]

One "demon" in religion was the selfish longing for personal
salvation in eternity; it made morality into a glorified commut-
ers' competition for places on a celestial express: "a quivering
energy to jump / For seats angelical."[7] Another was sexism—
the unfair, antifeminist assumptions that men, through the ages,
had built into their religious structures, e.g., "He for God only,
/ She for God in him."[8] Feminism Meredith saw as the index and
hope for advancement in his time, and he found in comedy the
form that both traditionally and potentially seemed to accommodate, better than any other, the aspirations and humanity of
women.

Egoism, feminism, and a comic sense of life form the conceptual basis of *The Egoist* and its imaginative vision. Relentlessly, but comically, the novel assaults human pride and the male ego. For Meredith, the essence of egoism is to think and act as if people have reality only in respect to one's self. Egoism denies the separate being of others and regards them as instruments or possessions for promoting self-esteem. Sexism, that structure of customs and mores that insists on women as adjuncts to male being, becomes the epitome of historical and cultural egoism in his novel. Sexism is to society what selfishness is to the individual personality. The mentality of egoism results from psychological self-division, just as much of human behavior results from the biological division into sexes. Traditionally, societies have used women as chattels, as objects of trade, and as pets to enhance men's lives. A good way, then, to dramatize egoism in action is to focus on the egoist's attempt to make and keep women extensions of himself and tools of his will. But simply denouncing egoism is not Meredith's aim; he wishes to show how much value and good, such as feminine emancipation, can actually come out of an egoist's fatuousness.

II

Egoism is the idea of the self; it is universal and inherent in language and the conceptual imagination. When the self thinks of its own being, it necessarily splits into subject and object—into that duality that is our fate. Entering his protagonist's mind, Meredith writes, "this [trial] worked in the Egoist to produce division of himself from himself, a concentration of his thoughts upon another object, still himself, but in another breast" (23:275). He is obviously talking about alienation, which, as we have been told, was felt more sharply in the nineteenth century than before but is, Meredith holds, the natural by-product of the human mind's verbal and rational powers: "To begin to think is the beginning of disgust of the world" (3:21). Egoism, though it can be frightful, is inseparable from human psychology and history.

Meredith takes a relative and evolutionary view of egoism. At first it was necessary as a kind of human instinct for self-preservation and as the crude basis for the pride, pleasure, and permanence of culture. But with generation following generation, that schizoid being, the universal egoist, creates and projects himself into such entities as gods, goddesses, totems, tribes, nations, public opinion, honor, law, art, and institutions. As time passes and social institutions develop, he demands not merely sensual gratification but such intangible prizes as respect, credit for virtue and civilization, eternal existence, adoration, metaphysical love, and beauty. And the myriad-minded egoist not only has selfish desires that conflict within himself; he also finds himself inhabiting a world filled with other egoists. The modern egoist wants to have his self-esteem flattered by the good opinion of others, and he discovers more and more good things for which he longs. These needs make possible the comic vision of *The Egoist*. The gist of Meredith's whole elaborate comedy of egoism lies in the remarkable chapter "In the Heart of the Egoist," from which I excerpt the following passage:

> Consider him indulgently; the Egoist is the Son of Himself. He is likewise the Father. And the son loves the father, the father the son; . . . Are you, without much offending, sacrificed by them, it is on the altar of their mutual love, to filial piety or paternal tenderness: . . . Absorbed in their great example of devotion, they do not think of you. They are beautiful. . . .
>
> The Egoist is our fountain-head, primeval man: . . . He is not only his own father, he is ours; and he is also our son. We have produced him, and he us. . . .
>
> But society is about him. . . . [H]e has become the civilized Egoist; primitive still, as sure as man has teeth, but developed in his manner of using them. . . .
>
> . . . Sir Willoughby was a social Egoist, fiercely imaginative in whatsoever concerned him. He had discovered a greater realm than that of the sensual appetites, and he rushed across and around it in his conquering period with an Alexander's pride. . . . [I]n the case . . . of Miss Middleton it is almost certain she caught her glimpse of his interior from sheer fatigue in hearing him discourse of it. . . . He slew imagination. There is no direr disaster in love than the death of imagination. He dragged her through the labyrinths of his penetralia, in his hungry coveting to be loved more and still more, more still, until imagination gave up the ghost, and he talked to her plain hearing like a monster. [39:475–77]

I take this reflection to be crucial. It binds God, Sir Willoughby, and the reader in a trinity of human egoism. With that wittily blasphemous parody of Christian theology in the first paragraph, Meredith lays claim to vital significance for his comic novel and its subject matter. Like Sir Willoughby, the Christian God himself is a pattern of egoism; our notions of the highest good and the ethos of our whole civilization have been, and are, necessarily tainted by monomaniacal self-centeredness, by self-division and its inevitable contradictions, and by an innate sexism (like God, the egoist is Father and Son, not Mother and Daughter). The "comic spirit" gently mocks the loving relationship of God and Christ and the ineffable beauty of the godhead as they have shone forth in Scripture and Christian history. What kind of being is it who, self-divided and self-devoted, craves adoration and is careless of others except as they can contribute to its greater glory? The answer is a Supreme Egoist, created by man in his own image—an abstract of his desires and fears. This being, like his creator, is a split personality, incomplete, alienated, needing insatiably the worship that betrays his weakness and insecurity. And the egoist— Willoughby, and Jehovah as well—is both child and father of our consciousness and our lives.

We have here the plan of Meredith's comic dialectic of egoism: his optimism, his belief in progress, and his challenge to each of us who reads it. We must "consider" the egoist "indulgently," since he is part of us and we of him; we can't escape our kinship except by lying or obtuseness. The selfish fool, "coveting to be loved more and still more, more still," is myself, as well as Willoughby. Paradoxically, that ego-mad animal, the human being, has the ability to detach itself from its own errant behavior through a kind of confessional exorcism. We can abstract and describe certain troublesome qualities, instincts, or actions and thus work to purge them.

III

Dickens's protesting cry in *Martin Chuzzlewit* of "Self, self, self, nothing but self," echoes everywhere in nineteenth-century life and literature. The mysterious force of rampant individualism, which the Industrial Revolution somehow released and intensified, seemed a berserk Frankenstein monster. Meredith reveals it as part of a comic pattern: the philosophy of egoism is self-consciousness and solipsism; its style is uniformity—all otherness being drowned in an ocean of self; its morality is institutionally sanctioned appetite, personal well-being, and tortuous self-justification; its social organization is built on hierarchical caste and sexism; its political ethic is imperialism and economic exploitation of others; its recreation is self-pity and self-expression; its setting—as Thackeray shows—is a house of mirrors on an island of alienation; its occupation is power-seeking and ownership; and its aim—literally—is to get the best of everybody. But its fate is self-exposure: the egoist makes an ass of himself. Though egoism never disappears, the egoist himself dissolves in the flux of changing human relationships and revolutions of the earth. New combinations of reason and impulse in the mutable roles of the sexes, together with the intelligence, passion, and love of other beings in the world, overwhelm him.

PATTERN, ABSTRACTION, AND CONDENSATION

And if there is a man who can follow Sir Willoughby's twists without acknowledging some kinship with himself, one must doubt either his intelligence or his candor.
Joseph Warren Beach[9]

Comedy . . . condenses whole sections of the Book in a sentence, volumes in a character. ["Prelude," p. 3]

Pattern is the key word. It forms the character, plot, method, and moral of *The Egoist.* We need pattern in order to make sense of life; without it, reality remains a chaotic mass of sense impressions, and our lives seem disconnected and purposeless. Yet we must try to escape the tyranny of imposed pattern, which robs our lives of freshness, growth, and change. In his "Prelude" to *The Egoist,* Meredith announces that comedy can give us the pattern of social life, can explore what we have in common. It can also discover ways of subverting patterns of egoism. Egoism is universal, but it manifests itself in a definite context.

The comic "situation" is simple, and the characters are relatively few. Sir Willoughby Patterne is engaged to a beautiful and intelligent girl, Clara Middleton, daughter of a wealthy classical scholar, Dr. Middleton. Clara comes to realize how odious Willoughby would be to her as a husband and struggles to break free of him. He tries desperately to hold her. Finally, hoping to preserve his dignity, the egoist, motivated by jealousy and spite and believing that he is losing his fiancée to his friend and rival, Colonel De Craye, helps to arrange a match for Clara with his cousin, the intellectual Vernon Whitford, who is the very man she loves. At the same time, Patterne begs, bullies, and bribes a poor faded woman, Laetitia Dale, whom he has often spurned, to marry him. By the end, Laetitia, his one-time worshiper, neither loves nor admires him but consents to wed. Unwittingly, Willoughby, in trying unjustly to punish a guileless boy, Crossjay, his relative, exposes his own selfishness and double-dealing folly. Several ladies, of various social stations, serve as comic commentators. The story takes place in a few days' time within the confines of Patterne Hall and its environs.

I

Sir Willoughby Patterne, the egoist, is a way of understanding things. He is a pattern of human nature, of nineteenth-century history, of social privilege, of male chauvinism, of an English gentleman, of an ass, of a joke, and of the specific psychological makeup of the author and ourselves. The author calls him a "microcosm" and makes him the humor of egoism incarnate. That Patterne is a metaphorical abstraction is the donnée of a book entitled *The Egoist*. Everything about him illustrates some aspect of egoism. His name explains his function. It alludes to the story of the Willow Pattern, from which the novel takes its plot,[10] and it clearly is meant to suggest the paternal nature of our whole culture as it has developed.

Like Thackeray, Meredith finds comic reflection the way to truth, but, like Peacock, he rejects the wide panorama and the details of realism. Patterne becomes a vision of self and society in which the pompous conceit of our egos turns into high farce. For Meredith, comedy, like science, should have as its aims knowledge and betterment, and his concept of comedy in the "Prelude" reads like a description of an experiment under laboratory conditions. It takes place under strictly controlled circumstances, but its import may be universal. The overall pattern is the breaking of Willoughby's hold on the other characters, and the goal of Meredith's plot is the same as his goal for the reader and the aim of his whole comic method: to set the egoist at a distance, to abstract and compress him psychologically in order to put him in perspective and be free of him—at least temporarily.

He begins, and sets the tone of the book's action, with a banal piece of social cruelty. Willoughby, having read about the military heroics of a distant relative, Crossjay Patterne, and having bragged about his kinship with him to friends and to his first fiancée, Constantia Durham, invites the marine to Patterne Hall. But when he catches sight of the man, he decides to have him sent away: "Not at home," is his order (1:9). That rudeness defines the pattern of egoism. The egoist is top dog and a rabid, if unconscious, defender of the class system, no matter what historical form it may take: "Nothing can be done with a mature and stumpy Marine of that rank. Considerateness dismisses him on the spot, without parley. It was performed by a gentleman supremely advanced at a very early age in the art of cutting" (1:10).

The "Prelude" tells us that comedy is the medium of allusion, and we ought to find here a comic version of the proud man's contumely. Also, according to Meredith, unless we find our own countenance in the scene, we have not read properly. We need to recognize and question the forms of social cutting and snobbery that some of us indulge in, such as averting eyes, ignoring calls, omitting introductions, dropping friends, and thinking ourselves better than others because we fancy ourselves more intelligent. What causes such behavior, and what are the assumptions of the world and the social systems in which it takes place? Not to see or feel the humanity of another is a political act of the highest consequence. Later, Willoughby will act or threaten to act with the same high-handedness toward the lieutenant's son, young Crossjay, and toward Flitch, the employee who dared to leave Patterne. Arbitrary and hard toward those beneath him and vindictive when he can be, Willoughby is a pattern of foolish ruling-class tyranny. Meredith ridicules the whole class system in him.

211

II

After Constantia has jilted him, Willoughby, the egoist, tours the world and then returns to find Laetitia Dale and a band of schoolgirls gathering wild flowers for May Day:

> "Laetitia Dale! . . . And you are well?" The anxious question permitted him to read deeply in her eyes. He found the man he sought there, squeezed him passionately, and let her go, saying, "I could not have prayed for a lovelier home-scene to welcome me than you and these children flower-gathering. I don't believe in chance. It was decreed that we should meet. Do not you think so?" . . .
>
> He begged her to distribute a gold coin among the little ones; asked for the names of some of them, and repeated, "Mary, Susan, Charlotte—only the Christian names, pray! . . . *I* shall see you soon. *I* have much to talk of, much to tell you. *I* shall hasten to call on your father. *I* have specially to speak with him. *I*—what happiness this is, Laetitia! But *I* must not forget *I* have a mother." [4:29–30; italics mine]

That flash of sardonic genius, "he found the man he sought there, squeezed him passionately, and let her go," proves, devastatingly, Meredith's claim that comedy "condenses whole sections of the Book in a sentence." It tells us all we need to know about Willoughby's relationship to Laetitia, but it may tell us more than the egoist in each of us wants to know about the nature of love, friendship, and sex: We adore flattering mirrors and sometimes love passionately so that we may find a lovable self-image. Love objects serve, at least partially, as metaphors for self. Willoughby longs to find and fondle a marvelous self in the other; but the reality of the other interferes with omnipotence of the self, and so the egoist strives to block that reality. "Only the Christian names, pray"—no surnames; in other words, he values the little girls merely as picturesque objects that will set off his glory. Think of all those murderous dictators whose paths anonymous little girls have strewn with flowers: that is the kind of historical absurdity that Meredith wants to bring out.

By the end of the interview, Willoughby's speech has degenerated into a mantra chant of the first-person pronoun, and in these "shrieks of the lamentable letter 'I'" (11:131) we find the literal pattern of egoism and the subject of the egoist's every utterance. In an earlier chapter Meredith had written of Willoughby "straightening his whole figure to the erectness of the letter I" (3:19) and had then observed ironically, "The pleasure of the world is to bowl down our soldierly letter I" (3:21). This "I" of *The Egoist*—it may be the funniest phallic symbol in literature[11]—is an alphabetical priapus, popping up again and again in Willoughby's conversation to identify egoism with the preening of male vanity. More precisely, it is a comic symbol of men's absurd phallic pride. Much later, Meredith makes this obvious in the climactic scene in which Willoughby implores the sickly maid Laetitia to marry him: "I promise it. If you imagine you want renewing, *I* have the specific. I, my love, I.... I will cure you, my Laetitia. Look to me, I am the tonic.... I, my love, I" (40:486–87). The egoist thrusts his "I" at Laetitia and the world as if he were out to commit verbal rape—which, of course, he is. But since he loves only self, any real intercourse with another is impossible, and what we really have is an exhibition of linguistic masturbation. "I" stands alone, a clown's stick beating time across the page, exposing the sheer monotony of egoism, the pattern of the self foolishly trying to stamp its tiny monogram on the universe.

III

The pattern of the egoist's speech is always comic exposure. Under stress, he indulges in mind-boggling flights of megalomania and delusion that seem even more astounding when we recognize that they describe common feelings and wishes. He is at his most ludicrous when, full of intimations of mortality, he anxiously talks with Clara, his new fiancée, and asks her to swear she will not remarry should he die.

"Is it not possible that I may be the first to die?" said Miss Middleton....
"And I helpless! The thought is maddening. I see a ring of monkeys grinning. There is your beauty, and man's delight in desecrating. You would be worried night and day to quit my name, to...I feel the blow now. You would have no rest from them, nothing to cling to without your oath!"

213

"An oath!" said Miss Middleton.

"It is no delusion, my love, when I tell you that with this thought upon me I see a ring of monkey-faces grinning at me; they haunt me. But you do swear it! . . .

"An oath?" she said. . . . "To what? what oath?"

"That you will be true to me dead as well as living! Whisper it."

"Willoughby, I shall be true to my vows at the altar."

"To me! me!"

"It will be to you."

"To my soul. . . .

"Our views of the world are opposed, Willoughby."

"Consent; gratify me; swear it. Say, 'Beyond death.' Whisper it. I ask for nothing more. Women think the husband's grave breaks the bond, cuts the tie, sets them loose. They wed the flesh—pah! What I call on you for is nobility: the transcendent nobility of faithfulness beyond death. . . ."

"My vows at the altar must suffice. . . . Think; question yourself whether I am really the person you should marry. Your wife should have great qualities of mind and soul. I will consent to hear that I do not possess them, and abide by the verdict."

"You do; you do possess them!" Willoughby cried. "When you know better what the world is, you will understand my anxiety. . . . But try to enter into my mind; think with me, feel with me. When you have once comprehended the intensity of the love of a man like me, you will not require asking. . . . [O]nly, I see farther than most men, and feel more deeply. [6:58–60]

The immediate target here is male totalitarianism, and the most obvious pattern in this conversation is the clear pattern of the book as a whole: Willoughby makes a self-defeating attempt to absorb the soul and individuality of a woman and in doing so teaches her the necessity of her independence for self-preservation. As Clara says elsewhere, "how must a man despise women, who can expose himself as he does to me!" (10:111). The modern rage of intelligent women at men, whether justified or not, historically speaking, comes from the disgraceful evidence that male testimony and confession, oral and written, have provided.

Such words as Clara hears show Willoughby as a character of mythic proportions. Behind his shrill comic ravings, thrilling in their fatuousness, lies the urge for immortality and the hysterical self-delusions that knowledge of death foists upon humanity. How can we, and why should we, take seriously a being—and, of course, the being is part of ourselves—who worries about life's assault on his consciousness *when he will no longer have any consciousness?* Meredith satirizes the egoist in us that wants to tie everybody and everything to us forever and transfix the world permanently at the moment of death. We may not be able to take it with us, but how we long to!

The egoist's speech tells us of patterns within and without. His claim that he is somehow better and more sensitive than the rest of the world, his naked sentimentality about himself, expresses messages of our own egos. The canyon between what he thinks and says and what he does is the same one that each of us fails to cross. But in Willoughby's presumptuous talk of how the world is, in his generalizations, assumptions, and self-serving morality, we can also read and hear that din of external voices desperately bellowing at us to see and do things their way. Comedy can produce certain effects on us akin to those traditionally associated with religion. Comic monologues by foolish types like Willoughby or Pecksniff can for a time purge us of the fools within—*comic confession*—and raise us up above the fools without—*comic election and justification*—by ridiculing the hypocrisies and pretensions of those importuning others of the world.

Particularly in talking to Laetitia, whose respect he takes for granted, Willoughby displays the presumptuousness of people who assert views and moralize with no conception of how their pronouncements relate to reality or apply to themselves. The ring of monkeys grinning at Willoughby is the group of comic imps from the "Prelude" who "love to uncover ridiculousness in imposing figures" (p. 5)—specifically, here, by provoking him to inane bombast:

> "Reverting to that question of deceivers: is it not your opinion that to pardon, to condone, is to corrupt society by passing off as pure what is false? . . .
>
> Deceit and sincerity cannot live together. Truth must kill the lie, or the lie will kill truth. I do not forgive. All I say to the person is, go! . . .

Do not set me down for complaining. I know the lot of man. But Laetitia, deceit! deceit! It is a bad taste in the mouth. It sickens us of humanity. . . .

For when I love, I love. . . . my friends and my servants know that. There can be no medium: not with me. I give all, I claim all. As I am absorbed, so must I absorb. . . . The selfishness of love may be denounced: it is a part of us! My answer would be, it is an element only of the noblest of us! Love, Laetitia! I speak of love. But one who breaks faith to drag us through the mire, who betrays, betrays and hands us over to the world; whose prey we become identically because of virtues we were educated to . . . possess: tell me the name for that! [31:374–82]

The funniest, as well as the most frightening, thing about this passage is that in moments of candor and passion we really are capable of thinking and uttering such self-dramatizing idiocies. The egoist constantly rails at others for doing what he himself does, and sooner or later his audience cannot help but see it. When Willoughby woos Laetitia while still holding Clara to her vow and nevertheless talks of deceit and love, he convicts himself. See and hear, says Meredith, the contradiction between doing and saying and between the conflicting desires of egoism. Loving his own voice, the egoist records the tapes that lead to his own exposure.

IV

The egoist is a sponge and a parasite. We must take him at his word when he prates about absorbing others; our egos tell us we are more important than others and that they ought to please us. "We are all of us born in moral stupidity," says George Eliot, "taking the world as an udder to feed our supreme selves."[12] The patterns of human inequality may develop naturally in individual minds; but inequalities of class, sex, and wealth, institutionalized and perpetuated by leeching selfishness, must be shown up for the terrible practical jokes that they are. Imploring Laetitia to marry him, Willoughby spouts, "You were a precious cameo, still gazing. And I was the object. You loved me. You loved me, you belonged to me, you were mine, my possession, my jewel; I was prouder of your constancy than of anything else that I had on earth" (40:487). To the egoist, the proper function of others is either to pay him homage or to be a precious thing that he owns. His treatment of women as objects and his high-handed behavior to everyone who must depend upon him show this. He represents the institutionalized patterns of money privilege and patriarchical primogeniture, and in him Meredith ridicules as mean little games these methods by which society has been organized.

The pattern of inequality abnegates large numbers of people and breeds a slave mentality. Willoughby's aunts, Isobel and Eleanor, reflect the kind of world the egoist wants. They depend totally on him, talk only of him, and have no personal identity. Though these two are wonderfully comic figures, their satellite being, like that of Rosencrantz and Guildenstern, helps to define a social culture. Actually, as Françoise Basch points out, there were hundreds of thousands of such women in Victorian Britain: "In the middle classes the old maid led a withdrawn, melancholic, embarrassed existence. A contemporary saw her as a sad shadow who, having renounced all personal existence, consoled, listened, helped, and resigned herself to living through others and then effaced herself more and more, as if to excuse her existence."[13] Meredith uses them as a comic chorus:

> They took to chanting in alternation.
> "—We are accustomed to peruse our Willoughby, and we know him by a shadow."
> "—From his infancy to his glorious youth and his established manhood."
> "—He was ever the soul of chivalry."
> "—Duty: duty first. The happiness of his family: the well-being of his dependents." . . .
> "—When he was a child he one day mounted a chair, and there he stood in danger, would not let us touch him because he was taller than we, and we were to gaze. Do you remember him, Eleanor? 'I am the sun of the house!' It was inimitable!" [44:549–50]

This comic paean brilliantly ridicules egotistical desire. Egoism, consciously or not, longs to reduce everyone else to adoring ciphers. And yet the logic of that wish, as these chanting figures show, would make us live in vacuity, masters of nothing but emptiness. What good is such idolatry? How foolish to be a "sun" in a "house of mirth" (Eccles. 7:4)!

The nullity of the egoist's imagination and the pointlessness of his life come through in Willoughby's weird projections into the future. They consist of mean-spirited victories over others. The most elaborate and ridiculous occurs in his reverie about a chastened, repentant Clara:

> "No, Willoughby; the irreparable error was mine, the blame is mine, mine only. I live to repent it.... Oh, that eyes had been mine to know the friend I had!—Willoughby, in the darkness of night, and during days that were as night to my soul, I have seen the inexorable finger pointing my solitary way through the wilderness from a Paradise forfeited by my most wilful, my wanton, sin. We have met. It is more than I have merited. We part. In mercy let it be for ever. Oh, terrible word! ... Willoughby, we part. It is better so."
>
> "Clara! one—one only—one last—one holy kiss!"
>
> "If these poor lips, that once were sweet to you ..."
>
> The kiss ... was intended to swallow every vestige of dwindling attractiveness out of her, and [it] satisfactorily settled her business. [23:270–71]

This is dialogue of the ego, by the ego, and for the ego.[14] Think of all that mental activity, fantasizing what will not happen and would not satisfy if it did. Such a literal rendering of the desire for revenge in love and for social triumph reminds us, like projected images of ourselves in an afterlife, of the infinite silliness of the egoist in us.

And yet, after all the triviality of Willoughby, *The Egoist* may be truly epic. Freud and Lévi-Strauss, among others, trace the beginnings and defining characteristics of human culture in the ways and means by which men dispose the fates of women. A famous *New Yorker* cartoon shows two club-bearing cavemen shaking hands, and the caption reads, "Og's the name, and conking dames is the game." That hoary pattern endures in Willoughby, but Meredith senses a fading of male supremacy and cultural sexism. The powerless—women, the child Crossjay, and the intellectual Vernon—ally with each other to break the hold of the autocratic egoist.

218

The developing independence of Clara and Laetitia means progress; but since inflexibility marks the egoist, this change drives him to paroxysms of desperation and high comedy:

"You loved me devotedly. . . . You loved me. . . . You never loved me, you shallow woman! . . . As if there could be a cessation of love! What are we to reckon on as ours? We prize a woman's love; we guard it jealously, we trust to it, dream of it; *there* is our wealth; . . . women—women? Oh! they are all of a stamp—coin! . . . they cannot love! They are shadows of men. Compared with men, they have as much heart in them as the shadow beside the body! Laetitia! . . . You loved me. . . . Then you confess it was a love that could die! Are you unable to perceive how that redounds to my discredit? You loved me, you have ceased to love me. In other words, you charge me with incapacity to sustain a woman's love. . . . I could recount . . . victories. Quite another matter! But they are flies. . . . I love you. . . . I come to you, I sue you, and suddenly—you have changed! . . . And you say you do not know what love is— avowing in the same breath that you did love me! Am I the empty dream? [40:488–90]

"Am I the empty dream?" Egoism is the empty pornographic dream of the marvelous "I," rigid forever before the perpetual harems of adoration. The egoist's fantastic dream reduces other people to "shadows," "wealth," "coin," "victories," and "flies." Fortunately, the dream turns to farce as the egoist babbles on, making himself ridiculous. The pattern of life is change and evolution. Willoughby moves from this: "Allow me once more to reiterate, that it is repulsive, inconceivable, that I should *ever, under any mortal conditions, bring myself to the point of taking Miss Dale for my wife*" (13:154–55), to this, "I offer you my hand and name, Laetitia!" (40:484). Man is a giddy thing, and life is flow.

v

For Meredith, comedy depends upon and honors our powers of abstraction. Abstraction might seem a cold and forbidding word, but it is just this quality that gives *The Egoist* its extraordinary warmth and generosity; for I am convinced that the major pattern of the book, the control and transcendence of self through comic vision, grew out of its author's ability to abstract and transform a shameful part of himself and his life. The inspiration for Sir Willoughby was surely autobiographical, as the story of Meredith's disastrous first marriage reveals. He wooed Mary Ellen Nicolls, Thomas Love Peacock's widowed daughter, and, refusing to take no for an answer, he finally won her. After a few unhappy years of marriage, she left him and their child for Henry Wallis, an artist, by whom she had a baby. They also parted; Meredith, for a time, refused permission for her to see their son, and she died in lonely and tragic circumstances. Reflecting upon the whole miserable affair, he found a pattern of egoism in his own conduct and, surprisingly, a pattern of comic faith in his ability to criticize and mock himself.

The idea that Meredith could generate comedy from such experience may seem strange, even heartless, but doing so actually showed great courage and self-control on his part.[15] And it illuminates what is most interesting and original about him. Public opinion in the Victorian age would have been much harder on Mary Ellen than on him, and conventional morality would have fed his sense of self-righteousness. She broke all the rules of feminine propriety, and Meredith suffered great anguish and public humiliation as a result of her actions. Nevertheless, the passage of time and his ability to get outside his former self let him see not only the awful selfishness in his own relationship to her but also a microcosm of the egoism infecting the Victorian personality and human culture generally. That he could abstract and deride the egoist in himself and other men who victimize women when he had been so badly hurt by Mary Ellen shows a remarkably liberal and secure spirit. Thinking on the crazy twists of the ego in love and the barbarous imagination of jealousy seems to have stirred sympathy in him for the woman.

What was it about his own self and about the system of self in which he lived that could make a woman so desperate to flee him? In *Modern Love,* he directly explored this sorry affair, but *The Egoist* transmutes it into something less subjective and, as he hoped, more universal. Willoughby is an abstract expression by Meredith of his own foolishness and also a pattern of modern selfishness. The brilliant chapter "An Aged and a Great Wine" (20:224–37) shows clearly Meredith's skill at creating comedy of historical and intellectual significance. About drinking port, this chapter is also about the civilizing power of comedy itself to function as a criticism of life, and it comes straight out of the most painful and grievous episode in Meredith's life. "An Aged and a Great Wine" was born in his guilt over the way he and his father-in-law, Peacock, had treated Mary Ellen Meredith. It becomes a comic meditation on the male ego.

The setting is this: Clara Middleton, seeing her mistake in accepting Willoughby, has begged him to let her go, but he has refused; she has also asked her father to take her away from Patterne Hall for a short time. Dr. Middleton has no idea of her real feelings and still considers the match set, but he has promised to take her away. To Clara, escape is everything, and she waits in the evening for her father to name the hour of leaving the next day.

The chapter begins with a portrait of Middleton: "The Rev. Doctor was a fine old picture; a specimen of art peculiarly English; combining in himself piety and epicurism, learning and gentlemanliness" (20:225). He is strikingly like Peacock's chief epicurean characters, Dr. Folliot and Dr. Opimian, but is even more like Peacock himself.[16] To understand the larger patterns developing in this scene, we need to keep in mind that Peacock was Meredith's mentor in comedy and the author who most deeply influenced him.[17] Peacock mocked the quirks of egoists, valued social intelligence, excelled at condensing masses of meaning, and revered the comic spirit. In his works and in person he baptized Meredith in the communion of comic faith. For Peacock, as we have seen, wine was metonymically civilization, and its very existence demonstrated man's metaphorical powers as well as his capacity for sensual enjoyment. Meredith, however, makes of wine a comedy of egoism, not a communion.

Willoughby uses "an aged and a great wine" to bribe Dr. Middleton not to leave. The facetious tone of the chapter does not hide the fact that Willoughby is sleazily trying to buy hymeneal blood with a ninety-year-old port.[18] The subject of wine is introduced reverently, and Meredith sets up a train of associations with the double and triple meanings that link wine, women, sex, and religion. Unconsciously the doctor compares the wine cellar to a womb, "This cool vaulted cellar, and the central square block, or enceinte, where the thick darkness was not penetrated" (20:228). We then get the essential image of Peacock's comic communion, as I have described it, in

Nightmare Abbey: "Dr. Middleton's musings were coloured by the friendly vision of glasses of the great wine; his mind was festive" (20:228).

But Meredith spots a fatal flaw in comic communion: it excludes women:

> "But here [says the doctor] is misfortune of a thing super-excellent:—not more than one in twenty will do it justice.... Women, for example...."
> "This wine would be a sealed book to them." [20:229]

Like priests celebrating Mass, the ceremonious wine-drinkers have been men only, and privileged men at that. After dinner the egoist, dismissing the others, orders two bottles of the exquisite port to drink with the father. The scene builds its comic resonance, with Middleton in ecstasy at the wine and Willoughby promising him the run of the cellar:

> "Note the superiority of wine over Venus!—I may say, the magnanimity of wine; our jealousy turns on him that will not share! But the corks, Willoughby. The corks excite my amazement!"
> "The corking is examined at regular intervals...."
> "It must be perilous as an operation for tracheotomy; which I should assume it to resemble in surgical skill and firmness of hand, not to mention the imminent gasp of the patient." [20:232]

The quick turn from Venus to corks and bottles reminds us just what sort of transaction is taking place here and, beneath the veneer of propriety, reminds us in the most insistent biological terms. Egoism confuses people with things. It sacrifices others to its appetites, and in the elaborate comparison of women to wine and in the parallel ways men think about and handle them we find the heart of cultural egoism. "A fresh decanter was placed before the doctor. He said: 'I have but a girl to give!' He was melted" (20:232). Though not meant entirely in earnest, that typical joke of carousal flashes with truth: old wine in old bottles; patriarchal history in the vials of egoism. Wine seals a male alliance in a ritual from which women are barred. Once, wine replaced blood as the symbol of human sacrifice, but in this scene it tempts sacrifice:

Sir Willoughby replied: "I take her for the highest prize this world affords."

"I have beaten some small stock of Latin into her head: and a note of Greek. She contains a savour of the classics. . . . but she is a girl. The nymph of the woods is in her. Still she will bring you her flower-cup of Hippocrene . . . [even in delicate classical allusion, there lurks the euphemistic vampire of sexism, identifying rare wine with virgin blood]. She goes to you from me, from me alone, from her father to her husband." [20:232–33]

This whole scene becomes a model of ruling-class arrangements—how business gets done in the patriarchy—but it is not quite as sordid as it may seem. We need to make a distinction between Willoughby and Dr. Middleton, who, though self-indulgent and potentially destructive, is also loving, in his fashion. He is not really selling his daughter here, only patronizing his ego. Compare the previous passage of genteel paternal sexism with Willoughby's reaction: "His offended temper broke away from the image of Clara, revealing her as he had seen her in the morning beside Horace De Craye, distressingly sweet; . . . sweet with the sharpness of young sap. Her eyes, her lips, her fluttering dress that played happy mother across her bosom, giving peeps of the veiled twins; . . . all her terrible sweetness touched his wound to the smarting quick" (20:233). This is prurient, funny, and damning at the same time: the drinking egoist reduces the classically accomplished woman to that staple of male desire, a pair of luscious breasts.

When Willoughby, who falsely makes Middleton believe that Clara and he have made up, has the doctor both tipsy and sentimental, he plies his corrupt strategy:

"What shall I do to-morrow evening!" he exclaimed. "I do not care to fling a bottle at Colonel De Craye and Vernon. I cannot open one for myself. . . . When do you bring me back my bride, sir?"

"My dear Willoughby! . . . The expedition is an absurdity. I am unable to see the aim of it. . . . I have ever maintained that nonsense is not to be encouraged in girls. . . . And I stay." [20:233–34]

Behind the communion of Willoughby and the doctor lies the earlier communion of Peacock and Meredith, whatever its precise nature, and such communion needed to be ridiculed by the "united social intelligence." According to *The Egoist,* the major weaknesses in Peacock's literary comic vision, which has in it so much that is good and wise, are that it does not allow for historical change and progress and that its epicurean pleasures can become the property of a tyrannical egoism.

Meredith's chapter, however, though describing potential evil and growing out of the author's sense of personal sin, is neither bitter nor sardonic; in fact, it shows his balance and optimism. At its end, male pretentiousness and the frivolity of egoism lie exposed. Clara sees that she cannot trust the patriarchy. The comedy of egoism activates her powers of mind and independence, and the result is the fine ensuing chapter of discovery and growth, "Clara's Meditations" (21:237–51). The ridiculous drinking bout leads to the blossoming of Clara's understanding. The pattern of the novel, and of comedy, is renewal and change. The egoist's selfishness becomes so blatant that it forces positive change on others; he is always the butt of an ongoing situation comedy. "An Aged and a Great Wine" marks the cultural pattern of the ego's obsessive desire, the abstraction of the egoistic communion of mankind, and the condensation of Meredith's own grapes of wrath to comic vintage.

SEXISM, FEMINISM, AND LOVE

The love-season is the carnival of egoism, and it brings the touchstone to our natures. [11:130]

The Egoist, who is our original male in giant form, had no bleeding victim beneath his paw, but there was the sex to mangle. [23:277]

Of all literary and intellectual forms before this century, the novel has shown the most responsible and probing concern with the tenor and meaning of women's lives. The movement of the human imagination from Richardson's victimized Clarissa and her tragedy of entrapment to Meredith's Clara and her comedy of liberation carries high hopes. Meredith sees comedy flourishing only when and where women's general status has some dignity, and comedy for him is both means and evidence of feminine progress. One of the great dramas of modern history is played out in *The Egoist:* women's struggle toward freedom against the imperium of male egoism. But it is the finely fluctuating state of war and peace between men and women, not simply the battle of the sexes, that makes Meredith's comedy. Romantic love naturally brings into play the most intimate emotional desires of personality, and he finds in it the epitome of both paternalistic culture and feminist aspiration.

Love may be either the purest form of selfishness or the best way out of solipsism; Meredith does not prescribe what the proper outcome of "the love-season" might be. Love is a subjective thing: the phenomenon may be universal, but the experience is always personal: "For these mysteries, consult the sublime chapter in the GREAT BOOK, the Seventy-First on LOVE, wherein Nothing is written, but the Reader receives a Lanthorn, a Powder-cask, and a Pick-axe, and therewith pursues his yellow-dusking path across the rubble of preceding excavators in the solitary quarry" (29:345). A rational, passionate love helps Clara; an irrational love hurts Laetitia. Willoughby, self-divided, does not love anything beyond himself and sees others only as love tokens to give to himself. If love leads one to cherish the precious individuality of another, it is joyous and good; but when it seeks to swallow and absorb the other, it is foolish.

I

For the egoist, love is always talk, possession, and incorporation: "He desired to shape her character to the feminine of his own . . . for he wanted her simply to be material in his hands for him to mould her" (5:52). Willoughby, a Pecksniff of the heart, feels it a pity that Clara would not, "by love's transmutation literally be the man she was to marry" (6:54). Meredith carefully links sexism and other forms of exploitation. Patronizing Clara and trying to bend her to his will, Willoughby instructs her: "As to our peasantry, we cannot, I apprehend, modify our class demarcations without risk of disintegrating the social structure" (7:71). Like a greedy imperial power, he drains Laetitia, and the author writes an epigram for collective as well as personal egoism: *"Possession without obligation to the object possessed approaches felicity"* (14:156).

225

One of the more subtle but far-reaching forms of sexist oppression was the demand that women be morally superior. Egoism's schizophrenia shows through in that strange combination of prudery and prurience that characterizes the Victorian obsession with female purity. Nowadays we are used to the idea of exploitation of women as sex objects. But nineteenth-century sexism did more: it made them virtue objects as well. That frenzy for the suppression of sexuality and the longing to adore the spiritual essence of femininity helped to remove women's bodies from their own consciousness. If it degrades women to be judged continually by their beauty and sexual desirability, like flesh in the market, imagine how it feels to be expected to live up to, and even personify, impossibly high moral standards. Think of the onus on people when they are made to function as chalices of virtue.

Insisting on innocence, male egoism inculcated ignorance. Do not talk about bodies, repress frankness about sex, make of women "good souls," and you eliminate a good deal of that troublesome otherness of being that egoism detests. Meredith gets the whole subject down in a profound paragraph:

The capaciously strong in soul among women will ultimately detect an infinite grossness in the demand for purity infinite, spotless bloom. Earlier or later they see they have been victims of the singular Egoist, have worn a mask of ignorance to be named innocent, have turned themselves into market produce for his delight, and have really abandoned the commodity in ministering to the lust for it, suffered themselves to be dragged ages back in playing upon the fleshly innocence of happy accident to gratify his jealous greed of possession, when it should have been their task to set the soul above the fairest fortune, and the gift of strength in women beyond ornamental whiteness. Are they not of a nature warriors, like men?—men's mates to bear them heroes instead of puppets? But the devouring male Egoist prefers them as inanimate over-wrought polished pure-metal precious vessels, fresh from the hands of the artificer, for him to walk away with hugging, call all his own, drink of, and fill and drink of, and forget that he stole them. [11:131–32]

226

What we have here is an anatomy of Victorian spiritual pornography. The reverse of sexual pornography, it just as clearly shows the impulse to use another, without limit, for personal gratification. Moreover, it is just as demeaning. Wanting to seem attractively pure, women have had to neglect their potential of mind and spirit. They think they should be innately pleasant, innocent, and moral, but, knowing they are not, they sham. Prostitution of the soul flourishes as well as prostitution of the body. Male egoism, full of contradictions, wishes to turn soul into possession and equate the two. The egoist longs for a robot sex of women and mechanically tries to foist mechanical behavior on them. They are to be machines of pleasure and virtuous ornaments as well. It is ridiculous, but, in Meredith's comedy, the dilemma of these outrageous expectations comes through: the egoist wants to preserve his image of "the constant woman." The grand joke of the book, however, is that women will not stay still: Constantia elopes; Clara breaks free; and Laetitia leaves her illusions behind.

Meredith explicitly ties feminism in *The Egoist* to the achievement by women of comic perspective. The right to be irreverent is one of the major tests of liberty; a quest for freedom often starts with a joke. Laetitia begins as a relatively humorless character, but as she develops her powers of irony and playful mockery, she develops her independence. Clara uses her wit like a magic potion to relieve the pressures of her intolerable state and to steel her courage. And Mrs. Mountstuart Jenkinson, whose deadly wit and epigrams Sir Willoughby fears so much, is not accidentally a woman and a devotee of the comic spirit.

II

The sexist tries to pit woman against woman (for Laetitia, Clara is "the chosen rival," and, for Clara, Laetitia is exhibited as a model of "constancy" and deportment). But Clara has a great talent for making alliances and undermining the egoist's reign. She touches Laetitia and begins to break through her reserve;

> "...Women who are called coquettes make their conquests not of the best of men; but men who are Egoists have *good* women for their victims; women on whose devoted constancy they feed; they drink it like blood...."

227

Clara stopped. "I have not your power to express ideas," she said.

"Miss Middleton, you have a dreadful power," said Laetitia. [16:191]

This is the germ of militant feminism, and its political import is obvious. We know, reading this, that somehow these women will never allow Willoughby to consume their blood like so much wine.

Female sexism, however, is not the answer to male sexism. Meredith warns: "Movements of similarity shown in crowned and undiademed ladies of intrepid independence, suggest their occasional capacity to be like men when it is given to them to hunt" (23:277). Feminism should be something better than reverse sexism, something that opposes the stasis of the egoistic imagination with its fixity of vision. Life should be animate and flowing like Clara, whose being sings a whole litany of what can make humanity admirable:

The sight of Miss Middleton running inflamed young Crossjay with the passion of the game of hare and hounds. He . . . flung up his legs. She was fleet; she ran as though a hundred little feet were bearing her onward smooth as water over the lawn and the sweeps of grass of the park, so swiftly did the hidden pair multiply one another to speed her. So sweet was she in her flowing pace, that the boy, as became his age, translated admiration into a dogged frenzy of pursuit, and continued pounding along, when far outstripped, determined to run her down or die. Suddenly her flight wound to an end in a dozen twittering steps, and she sunk. Young Crossjay attained her, with just breath enough to say, "You are a runner!" . . .

"Now you must confess that girls run faster than boys."

"They may at the start."

"They do everything better."

"They're flash-in-the-pans."

"They learn their lessons."

"You can't make soldiers or sailors of them, though."

"And that is untrue. Have you ever read of Mary Ambree? and Mistress Hannah Snell of Pondicherry? . . . And what do you say to Joan of Arc? What do you say to Boadicea? I suppose you have never heard of the Amazons." . . . She rose and took his arm. "You shall row me on the lake while I talk to you seriously."

It was she, however, who took the sculls at the boat-house, for she had been a playfellow with boys, and knew that one of them engaged in a manly exercise is not likely to listen to a woman. . . .

"I like brave boys, and I like you for wanting to enter the Royal Navy. Only, how can you if you do not learn?" [8:79–81]

That is the work of a master novelist trying to make us sense why we should care about his story. If life does have value, Clara must thrive; her great potential must not be destroyed by the egoist. That crinoline flowing over the green in the first paragraph quickly conveys an image of beauty and grace in action. Then we see her spontaneity, her wit, her ability to think, her coquettish side, and her vulnerability. Meredith gets at her deep dissatisfaction with a parrot-cage existence. A confirmed feminist, she takes the war of the sexes as inevitable, and yet she can laugh at it and live in it as a kind of happy warrior. Most crucially, this scene renders one good human being going out to another—an unrelated boy—and caring for his well-being. Clara personifies the marvelous decency and gay fineness on which Meredith builds his comic faith and vision.

III

The most important bond of the plot ties Clara to Vernon Whitford, who is explicitly made a feminist: "he was quite equal to a philippic upon woman's rights" (29:354). Clara and Vernon both help to loosen the hold of the egoist on each other. They need each other as anyone who would be free and independent requires another's love and concern. She confirms him in his decision to leave the patronage of Patterne, and he confirms her resolve to break the silken noose of sexist pampering. He pushes her to show strength of mind as well as heart, and she is grateful: "My appeal is always to reason," he says; "I have not 'the lady's tongue.'" "I loathe 'the lady's tongue,'" she answers (27:329). He builds her confidence, talks to her of such things as political philosophy, makes her face up to her responsibility like a competent being: "She was to do everything for herself, do and dare everything, decide upon everything" (21:242).

What is most important and interesting about Vernon is his talk with Clara—not his history, and not what others say about him, not the fact that he was supposedly based on Virginia Woolf's father, Leslie Stephen, not that he, the formal hero of the plot, is overshadowed by Willoughby. He and Clara meet and touch in probing comic dialogues that jump with their need for, and delight in, each other (see, e.g., 12:140). They draw each other out and fill each other in. Sometimes they speak the comic tongue of *double-entendre* and latent sexuality, but this talk does away with the nuances of possession that we saw in "An Aged and a Great Wine."

> "I assure you," said Vernon . . . , "it's not the first time I have thought you would be at home in the Alps. You would walk and climb as well as you dance."
> She liked to hear Clara Middleton talked of: and of her having been thought of, and giving him friendly eyes, barely noticing that he was in a glow, she said, "If you speak so encouragingly I shall fancy we are near an ascent."
> "I wish we were," he said.
> "We can realize it by dwelling on it, don't you think?"
> "We can begin climbing."
> "Oh!" she squeezed herself shadowily.
> "Which mountain shall it be?" said Vernon in the right real earnest tone.
> Miss Middleton suggested a lady's mountain first, for a trial. [12:139]

This lovely teasing reads like elegant verbal foreplay. They are physically drawn to each other, and their mutual love of exercise has sexual as well as feminist connotations.

The best antidote to sexism is the sort of comradeship that grows between Clara and Vernon, as they share interests and values and move toward union. In the "Essay on Comedy," Meredith writes that as men and women, "however divergent, both look on one object, namely, life, the gradual similarity of their impressions must bring them to some resemblance. The comic poet dares to show us men and women coming to this mutual likeness; he is for saying that when they draw together in social life their minds grow liker."[19] That perfectly describes the relationship of Clara and Vernon. At the end, they sit together on an Alp, next to the comic muse, having achieved ascent and perspective.

IV

One of the most famous passages in the novel—and justly so—occurs at the end of the chapter "The Double-Blossom Wild Cherry-Tree," where Meredith brilliantly analyzes the experience of falling in love and the meaning of love itself:

> Coming within gaze of the stem she beheld Vernon stretched at length, reading, she supposed; asleep, she discovered: his finger in the leaves of a book; and what book? She had a curiosity to know the title of the book he would read beneath these boughs, and grasping Crossjay's hand fast she craned her neck, as one timorous of a fall in peeping over chasms, for a glimpse of the page; but immediately, and still with a bent head, she turned her face to where the load of virginal blossom, whiter than summer-cloud on the sky, showered and drooped and clustered so thick as to claim colour and seem, like higher Alpine snows in noon-sunlight, a flush of white. From deep to deeper heavens of white, her eyes perched and soared. Wonder lived in her. Happiness in the beauty of the tree pressed to supplant it, and was more mortal and narrower. Reflection came, contracting her vision and weighing her to earth. Her reflection was: "He must be good who loves to lie and sleep beneath the branches of this tree!" She would rather have clung to her first impression: wonder so divine, so unbounded, was like soaring into homes of angel-crowded space, sweeping through folded and on to folded white fountain-bow of wings, in innumerable columns: but the thought of it was no recovery of it; she might as well have striven to be a child. The sensation of happiness promised to be less short-lived in memory, and would have been, had not her present disease of the longing for happiness ravaged every corner of it for the secret of its existence. The reflection took root. "He must be good . . . !" That reflection vowed to endure. Poor by comparison with what it displaced, it presented itself to her as conferring something on him, and she would not have had it absent though it robbed her. [11:134–35]

231

Note carefully the sequence of Clara's consciousness here: curiosity about another person; overpowering wonder at the natural beauty and luminous ecstasy in being; a real, if brief, feeling of transcendence; happiness; reflection; articulation of memory through simile and metaphor; loss of the ecstatic moment; a positive judgment about Vernon based on her assumption of shared values and perceptions; and a moral, passionate, involuntary decision to keep alive somehow the transcendent experience through affectionate faith in another.

These words move far beyond Clara's particular experience. They describe that passing of ecstasy—including, I think, sexual ecstasy—that frustrates the romantic quest for sensation; they recapitulate Wordsworthian psychology and anticipate Freudian humanism in a moment. They get at the tension between the longing for permanent perfection and the knowledge that this desire can never be fulfilled. They also suggest a whole current of Western intellectual history, from Dante to the present. The heavenly imagery captures momentarily the celebrant spirit of the divine comedy, with its hope and promise of everlasting bliss under God's benevolent order—a hope and a promise in which a modern being like Clara or Meredith cannot sustain belief. This thrilling heaven changes, fades, reveals itself to have been the creation of mortal imagination rather than an absolute deity, and it gives way to humanism. Humanism and civilization, culture and knowledge—they are projects and praxes of the deficient individual personality stuck in a world of flux, seeking fulfillment through faith in the other. In other words, they are products of the same formula as love.

So love comes as consolation for mutability and the alienation that mind, living in time, is heir to. This great and complex paragraph reflects the insufficiency of consciousness and our longings to unite the ego with the world. Love, if I follow Meredith correctly, is sublimation for "a lost oneness with the universe." It seems to spring out of an antecedent wholeness; it is a compromise with the facts of life and is evidence of the failure of the self to maintain a rapturous or integrated existence in the world.

But that makes it sound too bleak. Wonder and happiness trigger love, and love serves as a pledge that these emotional states will come to us again. Fittingly, Vernon calls Clara the "Mountain Echo." Love *is* an echo, voicing the inescapable reality of separate matter outside the boundaries of self, the tremendous reverberations of the past, and the need to feel and continually renew relationship to surrounding being.

Thus self-glorification through love is mere pretentiousness. People like Willoughby may take a crazy pride in love—what they really mean by love is an infinite craving to *be* loved and to be thought lovable—but love inevitably humbles, because it lays bare an ineluctable poverty in one's self. Without knowing and revering qualities that we lack, we individuals can find no satisfying love, nor can we make a soothing collective effort to transcend personal limitations.[20]

Feminism in the novel makes love a positive force; sexism makes it negative. When love cannot see the other, it is truly the blind god. Willoughby's Cupid naturally is "his naked eidolon, the tender infant Self" (29:344). For Vernon and Clara, however, Crossjay functions as Cupid; their care for him—for the good of another—draws them together. Love, a sign of the weakness of individualism, can be a way to strength, both personally and socially if it can be seen and experienced as a means to relationship rather than ownership. Reveries of possession, constancy, and eternity are all parts of the same ideal of ordered immortality, the dream of the possibility of perfect and lasting being. Yet the experience of "the second sex" shows that such dreams can turn to nightmares of enslavement and reification. Losing faith in a stable, divinely arranged universe does bring woe and insecurities to humanity, but change carries the hope of progress. A strong will and a hope of progress run through Clara's thoughts and emotions in the cherry-blossom scene, even as she comes down from euphoria. One compensation for earthly mutability is that the lot and potential of a whole sex may improve in time, and the insight and achievement of the double-blossom-cherry passage might belong to developing feminism.

"Her chief idea," says Meredith of Clara, "was, the enrichment of the world by love" (5:45). Feminism means the liberation of love or it means nothing. *The Egoist* depicts the complete interdependence of each sex on the other. The double-blossom cherry signifies two people, two sexes, two loves, growing and mutually flowering together beyond the static and absurd patterns of the possessive, sexist ego.[21]

NATURE

... she threw up her window, breathed, blessed mankind: and
she thought: "If Willoughby would open his heart to nature, he
would be relieved of his wretched opinion of the world."
[19:217]

Nature, like love, is a touchstone of character in the novel and
an important part of Meredith's comic vision. The world of
nature and the world of man are separate for the egoist but
whole and one for those with the imaginative insight to comprehend the indivisibility of life. The cherry blossoms present
nature not only as a fitting subject for religious feeling but as
means, substance, and evidence of *relationship* as well. Waking
under the tree, Vernon sees "a fair head circled in dazzling
blossom" (12:136), a flower set against flowers. Clara, his
"Mountain Echo" (12:136), echoes his own reverence for the
natural world and its beauty. Awed by something lovely, outside themselves, they are drawn to each other. The human mind
frees itself from its solipsistic maze by sensing the glory and
power of nature and understanding that it, too, is a part of what
it beholds.

Love of nature, like love of God in other times, becomes a
test of virtue, a test that Vernon and Clara pass and Willoughby
fails. Clara's reflection, "He must be good who loves to lie and
sleep beneath the branches of this tree," expresses a strong
sentiment in the history of modern consciousness. That we
know what she means and very possibly agree with her shows
the strength and life of the faith out of which her thinking
comes. It may be no more logical than: "He must be good who
loves to look at Wedgewood porcelain and sleep beneath
panelled ceilings," but it seems more persuasive. True piety has
come to mean feeling the connectedness of all being and revering the whole earth. In an industrial age, the natural beauty
of the world can no longer be taken for granted. The modern
blasphemy for many is against nature rather than God: felling
redwoods, befouling the air, polluting water—these sins of
selfishness are widely felt to be impious now in much the same
way that acts of simony or iconoclasm once were. Vernon's
heart is open to nature; Willoughby's is closed. The man who
can quietly admire the wonder of the tree and immerse himself
in its beauty without needing an audience or having to own the

234

tree and make it an object of his will is a man capable of cherishing Clara and a man fit to be cherished. She sees Vernon doing what she would like to do and knows that they share a community of perception and awe. Her love and respect for the world find an answer in him.

"The tree," says Blake, shedding light on a conflict going on in modern history as well as *The Egoist,* "which moves some to tears of joy is in the Eyes of others only a Green thing that stands in the way."[22] The egoist wants to exploit nature, which is good only insofar as it pleases the "I." Willoughby longs to be beyond nature and above the earth, a superman bending all creation to his personality. "Pedestrianism was a sour business to Willoughby" (4:32). At a preposterous moment he says to Clara, "Come and see me mount Black Norman." He is or would be "the man on horseback" looking down on others—or rather, he is the *reductio ad absurdum* of that fantasy of egoism and all it conveys. Superman lives in the egoist's ridiculous daydreams, and supernaturalism reveals the longings of egoism's idealized megalomania.

Against the manic aspirations of individualism, Meredith's comedy shows that real self-fulfillment comes only through the ego's consciousness of itself as part of the world. Vernon says that we must love the world "in the sense of serving it" (8:86). He gets his identity and his bearings from the earth and its manifold life. In contrast to Willoughby, he "knew that nonsense is to be walked off" (12:137).

Crossjay, the comic imp "plucked out of the earth, rank of the soil, like a root" (4:34), becomes a kind of metaphor of nature; like a force of nature, he exposes Patterne's artificial selfishness and, like a vine, he binds Clara to Vernon. Also, like nature, he needs human cultivation. Meredith, with his love and feel for nature, was groping for a comic vision that would transcend the egoistical basis of both divine comedy and human comedy. He was pushing for a change of allegiance from self to species and world organism: no longer To thine own self be true; instead, Be true to the whole earth and humanity.

In a time of massive change, Thomas Hardy imagined nature ignoring or crushing individual will and from that made pathos and tragedy. From a different point of view, Meredith saw nature confounding the egoist's desires and found in it comedy. Because there was such a broad egoistic streak in the Romantic movement, we sometimes forget that the great impetus for aesthetic pantheism and the cult of nature that have flourished since Rousseau and Wordsworth has come from a desire to combat solipsism and to find a rational outlet for religious impulses. It was as if Western civilization, trying to prove that there really is an objective reality out there, were performing the collective equivalent of Dr. Johnson's kicking a big stone to refute Berkeley's idealism. You could bang up against nature, and also you could agree on its beauties and sublimity; therefore, something outside the head must exist, and sensitive consensus has called it good.[23]

Meredith ends the book in the Alps, with Clara, Vernon, and the comic muse sitting together on a mountain overlooking "the Lake of Constance." The freedom and vision of the comic spirit must be grounded in the hard materiality of the vast world. Nature has the comprehensiveness, endurance, and continuity that make a comic response to life valid.

TIME

> You may as well know him out of hand, as a gentleman of our time and country. ["Prelude":5]

Time in *The Egoist* is compact, but it also is meant to symbolize the essential pattern of modern history. Literally, it is the limited history of a particular situation, the development of events for a few characters. Nearly all of the action takes place within a few days. Time is bracketed and focused in a way that subordinates the single ego to a collective process; it is the duration of a plot, culminating in a happy ending—that is, a state of affairs in which a desired good, as judged by "our united social intelligence" ("Prelude":3) results. Metaphorically, Meredith's time is the modern age, which he conceives of as an era of progress and increasing social control over the forces of egoism. The time that matters is the time of social event, a paradigm of broad historical movement, not personal, psychological, or calendar time. It isn't the time of revolving sun, seasons, and generations; neither is it the supernatural time of God, heaven, and eternity or the sweep of specific historical events. It is linear, positive, communal, figurative, and oriented toward specific social goals.

For Meredith, comedy offers a way of organizing experience that gives us a proper sense of time: namely, as arbitrary segments of being in which some success can be achieved and which can then be understood as part of the historical process of, and progress toward, the common good of the race. Time has become the medium in which the frustration and control of egoism can take place.

The egoist, in modern history, is a monument to stasis. He hates change and finds it terrifying because it threatens him with loss and, implicitly, disintegration and death. Since he sees everyone and everything as actual or potential property, time menaces his possessions. Willoughby, "a gentleman of our time" ("Prelude":5), stands for the historical power and force of the dominant egoism of the nineteenth century, and Meredith sees his conflicts and internal contradictions leading to a changed and changing social order: the time is ripe for an overthrow of sterile individualism. The comedy of Willoughby sets the pattern for the socialization of egoism, and it is rooted in Meredith's historical understanding: once egoism was valuable to mankind and nature; now it is obsolete and harmful. From one point of view, his comic plot reads like a parable of the downfall of ruling-class ideology, and his comic imps function like angels of historical necessity. No wonder Jack Lindsay could see Marxism in Meredith.[24]

SPACE

[T]he world had been his possession. Clara's treatment of him was a robbery of land and subjects. [29:344]

[S]he had housed herself in the imagination of her freedom. [13:146]

Space, like time, is limited in the novel, but it is also symbolic. Nearly all the movement and action of the characters takes place in Patterne Hall or on the Patterne grounds. E. M. Forster criticized Meredith for rendering "the home counties posing as the universe";[25] but, since the provincialism of the self is the

237

subject of *The Egoist,* that is just the satirical point Meredith was trying to make. The world *is* concentrated in Patterne. The setting for the comedy is the property of the Egoist.

The egoist controls space by owning it, and ownership, of course, is one of the most glaring signs of egoism's power in human nature. Except for Willoughby, the characters are almost all guests, tenants, or people in some way patronized. Moving in an area to which they have no claim or legal right, they feel themselves constricted and handicapped—satellites of the sun of egoism. The drive for freedom, the passion for the outdoors, the longings for escape that we see in Clara, Vernon, and Crossjay express discontent at living in another's space. Patterne does reflect the universe, or at least the home counties and the Western world, because much of it is private property, the enjoyment of which depends largely on the whim of the owner.

The characters' predicaments and responses are typical: run off, head for the mountains, go to the city, go to sea, seek money, marry for the estate, flee to the past and live in the calm of antiquity, travel the world restlessly. Metaphorically, the space of the novel is like a despot's country filled with insurrections.

Along with physical space, there exists the inner space of reflection and imagination. For Willoughby, this space, sometimes alienated from the outer world, seethes with turbulence; for Clara, and for the author too, the inner setting is a place where vistas of freedom can expand. True spaciousness in the novel exists in the range of reference of the narrator's imagination, which continually discovers connections and analogies between Patterne and other places and times. The outward setting has the calm of the English manor; the inner setting boils with energy. Meredith's imagery for this interior world describes a landscape full of violence, danger, and high passion. He finds spatial and material terms with which to picture emotional states; jealousy, for instance, becomes "a volcanic hillside where a thin crust quaked over lava" (29:246).

Superficially, the inner space of *The Egoist* might seem like that of *Emma:* what we see of Clara's inner life, for example, is almost exactly like Emma's. The difference, however, is fundamental. The mind of the egoist works to turn everything to objects of his desire. He does not like the free motion of others

238

to exist, but, if it does, he wants it to cease. All is to be regulated by, and around, the sun of the house. That mental space of Emma Woodhouse, on the other hand—prone to selfish error as she is—becomes an arena for relationship, dialogue, and interaction with the world. Emma's mistakes, ridiculous though they may be, result from her imagination's operating on reality and misconstruing it. The egoist, however, in his frustration with reality, doesn't just get things wrong; he dwells from time to time in another world, one that is totally alien to the social world; he projects those wholly imaginary scenes—for example, with Clara crippled, crushed, and contrite. The mind becomes a comic disaster area of egoistic fantasy.

The joke is that his inner space becomes the setting for a perpetual suicide. For the egoist not only turns other people into things; he also makes a fetish of the self, which he victimizes as well. The outer self must keep the inner self hidden so that the social self will stand respected in the world. In order to shine in the outer space, Willoughby must try to keep the inner space closed off and let the split self and its avatars perish again and again in the lonely field of mental alienation.

Finally, Patterne becomes a place that everyone wishes to escape from, even Willoughby, though he must pretend that it is perfect. Therefore, the breaking of confinement is possible. The book ends above and beyond the egoist's inner and outer space on that Alp, which appears as a sanctuary from the real estate of egoism and an international park of the comic spirit.

STYLE

> . . . humorists are difficult: it is a piece of their humour to puzzle our wits. ["Prelude":2]

> Now the world is possessed of a certain big book . . . the Book of Egoism. . . . Comedy . . . condenses whole sections of the book in a sentence, volumes in a character. . . .
> One . . . cries out, in a style pardonable to his fervency: The remedy of your frightful affliction is here, through the stillatory of Comedy. ["Prelude":1–3]

"A style pardonable to his fervency." That describes the judgment many readers of *The Egoist* would pass on the prose of the Comic Spirit's chief prophet. Meredith's style, difficult, allusive, puzzling, at times even precious and self-indulgent, has undoubtedly limited his audience and hurt his reputation. Yet it is inseparable from his vision and his intentions, as the "Prelude" to the novel shows, and it does achieve, as we have seen, varied and magnificent effects. At its best it can express the wholeness and interflow of life in the world, and, in its dialogue, it exposes the rhythms, motives, and mental farce of egotistical speech and desire.

I

The narrator's consciously artificial style—full of visual imagery, metaphors, similes, ingenious comparisons, and marked by unconventional diction and syntax—is meant to make you think and think hard and therefore to evoke respect and careful attention to the insights of comedy. The style condenses the world and pushes us to see connections all through the universe. Meredith uses it to slow the plot by focusing on the meaning of his story and to ward off those allies of egoism, stock response and sentimentality. It is aimed at "our united social intelligence" ("Prelude":3), not at our easily aroused emotions. The continual ellipsis, personification, figurative language, appositions, abstractions, queer vocabulary, delayed subjects, and recondite references make easy reading impossible and force us to use our reason actively.

Comedy, for Meredith, must be cerebral: thought teaches us that we are social beings, and that is our hope. Quick passions reveal us as scared and demanding little selves. Sheer intensity of feeling nearly always goes hand in hand with destructive selfishness. That is no doubt one reason why Walpole said that life is a tragedy to those who feel and a comedy to those who think. The style attacks the monotony and sameness of language and our conventional reactions to it, which reinforce the stagnancy of egoism. It insists on the complexity and the intricate, subtle relationships of all humanity. The mode of the egoist, seeking to reduce all to the self, is simplicity: simple greed, simple solutions, simple slogans, simple patterns, simplemindedness. The antidote to all that is the active intelligence playing on life in relatively disinterested fashion, and that becomes possible only if comic vision, with its distancing of passion and its scrutiny of selfish presumptions, comes into play. The style works to abstract egoism, anatomize it, and put it in a very large social context. It becomes a way of reform and transcendence and a metaphor for controlling the anxious ego. One rises above the self, as Clara and Vernon, in the end, rise, together with the Comic Muse, above egoism's Patterne to see an expanded view of the changing world. Style is thus a part of the whole comic process that turns the mind, with its synthetic reasoning powers, toward continuing social relationships and a sense of responsibility for the future.

II

Finding in comedy the essence of faith was a concept so radical that it needed extraordinary tact and subtlety to make it palatable, let alone persuasive. Since the comic impulse had often been ascribed to the trough of the soul, Meredith used his elaborate style rhetorically to make the comic spirit intellectually respectable. He wanted to show a sophistication and range of learning, and especially a moral sense, equal to any worshiper of high seriousness. His dogmatic ideas about the comic and his stress on its moral dignity make sense when we remember that he saw it taking over the functions of religion. His "Essay on Comedy" and the "Prelude" to *The Egoist* treat comedy in the prescriptive manner of the defender of a faith: there is a hierarchy of comedy, and there is a proper comic mode. Meredith on what comedy should be is like a theologian on what religious faith should be. He is a Jesuit of comic faith seeking influential and talented converts, and, in their own fashion, Wilde, Butler, Beerbohm, Shaw, Firbank, and Joyce prove his success, though in their work they did not always follow his dogma for comedy.[26] I think he meant his style to have a snob appeal. In a way, it is the equivalent of the in-joke, which turns its appreciators into a knowing elite.

But it is important to see that much of what now seems precious and aesthetically elitist was aimed as skewering the philistines, who felt, like Willoughby, that poetic expression was so much bunk, and who used stock verbal formulas and platitudes to reinforce the reign of ideological selfishness. The style points to the possibility of a refined and civilized society in which wit and the fear of appearing an antisocial fool—not superstition, violence, and psychological torture—might coerce proper behavior. A disciplined urbanity and an active life of the mind could be the ethical norms.

The main criticism against the style is that its indirectness and artificiality remove *The Egoist* too far from life and make it irrelevant. Meredith's comedy leaves out the direct shock and pain of life (as he says in the "Prelude," "no dust ... no mire," "human nature in the drawing-room"), but the reason, according to his logic, is that the frightened egoist in us tends to overemphasize these things. Howls about private tragedies of selves distort the more important truth about the continual development of mankind. Look at human history and you see culture, wealth, population, beauty, the arts, and knowledge spreading through the interplay of countless egoists within an evolving social structure. Meredith's elegant and difficult complexity, which seeks to absorb the thrust of aggressive egotism, says that coarse selfishness is literally out of style and that civilization is in.

Ironically, everyone can see the obvious egoism in Meredith's style. It demands that we learn his idiom. That, however, only strengthens the point of the comedy by showing the pervasiveness of an egoism that inevitably exposes itself before the "united social intelligence."

III

The prose in such passages as the cherry-tree piece and the meditation on the Egoist as Father, Son, and ourselves is very far from normal speech, but it achieves both an enormous range and an intense concentration of meaning. Motion and fluidity mark Meredith's style, as we can see in the following description of Willoughby watching Clara:

> He ... doated on her cheek, her ear, and the softly dusky nape of her neck, where this way and that the little lighter-coloured irreclaimable curls running truant from the comb and the knot—curls, half-curls, root-curls, vine-ringlets, wedding-rings, fledgeling feathers, tufts of down, blown wisps—waved or fell, waved over or up or involutedly, or strayed, loose and downward, in the form of small silken paws, hardly any of them much thicker than a crayon shading, cunninger than long round locks of gold to trick the heart. [9:101]

The point of view, as so often in *The Egoist,* is both within and without Willoughby. The vision here becomes dynamic, for his close and admiring look at Clara conveys the effects of her beauty on his thoughts. That hair becomes twining coils of sexuality, which tie him up. The form and motion of the curls loose the flow of lust. And this particular passage, which records minutely the nuances and stream of his consciousness, quickly explodes, with that surprising leap from "root-curls" to "vine-ringlets, wedding-rings," and "feathers," into a larger vision of the universal power of sexuality. A typical emotional jump of the mind suddenly opens up the world of sex, the whole process of regenerative animal nature, and the rituals that socialize the mating urge. The incessant motion and energy of sexual desire in a world that tries to repress it come through in this stylized language. The curls suggest the hair that can be had only in return for a wedding ring; therefore, a "root-curl" somehow becomes the full circle of the wedding ring. Through the whole passage *double-entendre* flashes, and this device of wordplay in itself becomes meaning. The strange comparative, "cunninger," may even be a daring and covertly obscene pun, one that coincides with the style of the egoist and the style of the society. Both try to cover and obscure reality but instead expose it continually to those with a common sense of the ridiculous. As we follow the twists and turns of Willoughby's mind, we gain perspective—through metaphor, precise juxtaposition, and insistent visualization—on what it all means and begin to see why humanity and the comic spirit are inseparable.

The principle of metamorphosis animates Meredith's style and imagination. The figurative language shows things turning into other things. Transformation and continual evolution is the message I keep reading. Curls turn into wedding rings; blossoms become angel wings and then love; the Egoist turns into oneself. Epigrams and aphorisms point to a universal human nature that curbs individual pride. Everything calls attention to our social nature.

One of the major comic achievements of the novel lies in the speech patterns and rhythms Meredith devises for his characters: Dr. Middleton's charming and maddening pedantry, the chanted self-abnegation of the aunts, Colonel De Craye's gay banter, the jibing, rhythmic dialogue of Vernon and Clara. Above all, Willoughby's voice is a comic triumph of the highest order. His talks with Clara and Laetitia reveal a semantics of supreme selfishness and cry out that rhetoric is the inevitable

243

instrument of the ridiculous ego. His speech is a mockery of the personal voice à la Pecksniff, but universalized. Typically, it moves from elaborate disguise to self-revelation; the verbal wrappings of his egoism unwind until the naked shrieking "I" is laid bare upon the page.

Meredith's imagination comes close to making the kinds of identification of being and language that Dickens, Carroll, and Joyce make, except that he premeditates and preconceives the essence of his characters and their situation even before they speak. His prose does filter out the "mire" and give us the verbal equivalent of "human nature in the drawing-room." The style is the book: it is a vision of linkage in the world and a voice mocking the rampant ego, including one's own; it delights in the being and potential of nature and society.

8

CARROLL'S *THROUGH THE LOOKING-GLASS* (1871)

The Comedy of Regression

Life's nonsense pierces us with strange relation.
Wallace Stevens[1]

Lewis Carroll's words and images are to the formulation of a comic faith what Jesus's parables are to Christian doctrine: they create a fiction so radical that it can bring its audience to look with fresh wonder at the structure and meaning of experience. Ultimately, they point to the necessity of faith in humanity's potential. But, unlike Scripture, they also proclaim and make us laugh at the inescapable absurdity of the world.

Carroll's way is the way of regression. By befriending small girls, identifying with them, projecting himself back into childhood, and writing tales explicitly for children, he managed to create two texts that have been, and are, as widely read and quoted, and as influential, as any imaginative literature of the past century. The Alice books do not address our serious, responsible, moral selves; Carroll turns his back on the adult world. Nevertheless, this man who retreats into juvenility and dream states, reverts to play and nonsense, toys with language, avoids any overtly didactic or practical purpose, and escapes from society, history, and "reality" into the fantasy of his own mind appears before us as a comic prophet and a father of modernism in art and literature. From out of the rabbit-hole and looking-glass world come not only such major figures as Joyce, Waugh, Nabokov, Beckett, and Borges but also much of the character and mood of twentieth-century humor and life.

245

I

Writers who last seem in retrospect to have been seers, telling people not just what is passing but also what is to come. The Alice books offer a metaphorical compendium of the obsessions and urgencies of our modern intellectual world; they give us the frightful self-consciousness, the fantastic shapes of the inward journey, the quest for innocence and withdrawal from a grimy and highly organized society; they convey loneliness, the frustration of intimacy, the feelings of living on the verge of hysteria and being in a dream or game whose form is constantly changing. They express our typical ambivalence toward authority, our rage for chaos along with our search to find and keep order and meaning without losing a sense of humor. Carroll imagines the relativity of being, the problems of identity and of split, diced personality. He renders for us the fictional nature of reality as it is registered in the inevitably distorting mirrors of our perception. He shows us our necessarily equivocal fate as logocentric creatures who experience language both subjectively and objectively. And he does all this—and more—in two of the funniest books in English.

These facts are so surprising that they still are not widely acknowledged and can even strike some as outrageous. Is he really a major writer and *Through the Looking-Glass* a masterpiece? To answer is to touch upon many of the most crucial attitudes we hold about the nature of life and literature. If we say no, then, consciously or not, we probably believe in the hierarchy of priorities in human affairs and the conventional assumptions that the book ridicules. Our need for order and surety, our drive to feel that life does or should make sense, can make Carroll seem trivial or uncomfortably subversive. His play and his *reductio ad absurdum* might seem to denigrate the importance and distinctness of individual lives. He can strike some as a messiah of infantilism, irrelevant to our mature interests and therefore easy to dismiss. More ominously, he may seem a piper of chaos. But if we say yes, the reason, if we analyze it, is that his comedy of regression somehow renders for us the absurd truth and strangeness of life and gives us a way of accepting and even reveling in both its senseless conditions and its creative possibilities.

Carroll epitomizes, in himself and his best work, the challenge that the comic tradition in fiction offers to orthodoxy. He personally lived out the change that Trollope had imagined taking place within the culture: "Lewis Carroll" chose comedy, not institutional Christianity, as his light and his true vocation; but to do so, he had to split his identity from his conventional self, the Reverend Charles Dodgson, ordained cleric. I think what allowed him this schism was his rationalization that his comic fantasy could work to preserve the possibility of Christian faith, since it undercuts those very forces that were undermining Christianity: rationalism, science, positivism, utilitarianism, materialism, and the worship of progress. *Through the Looking-Glass* shows exactly why there is real logic behind Tertullian's "I believe because it is absurd." But the main effect of his comic vision is surely to render an absurdist world that makes ridiculous all authority, all dogma, including the traditional Christian brand. "This man," writes Elizabeth Sewell, "who was in Holy Orders in the Anglican Church and who is presented to us by his contemporaries as deeply religious has only to open his mouth to convince us of the insecurity of his beliefs."[2] He found a brilliant art and strategy for preserving faith, but it is comic faith, not Christian.

In *Finnegans Wake,* Joyce parodies the Holy Trinity by inventing the wonderfully expressive Carrollian trinity: "Dodgfather, Dodgson & Coo."[3] This phrase gets at the essential blasphemy that Carroll wrote (compare it to Meredith's mocking of the Trinity), and it illuminates and identifies the means and ends of his comic faith in *Through the Looking-Glass.* Even the order of the syllables sums up the process of Carroll's creative regression: it suggests the drive to escape from the burdens of the father and God, from the fixed single self, from filial responsibility and manliness, and the movement to incorporate the voice of the child in himself with the holy spirit, which ends by discovering God, self, and freedom in comic wordplay. That happy "Coo" signifies the *coup* by which the Holy Ghost, its symbol the gentle dove, and Carroll himself merge into Alice; the company that makes up his metamorphosing plural selves; and the sound that, mocking sentimentality and pretentiousness, connotes healthy skepticism. The sound, however, also bespeaks, in the sometimes awkward and absurd way of language, the tenderness, love, and humor that are part of human aspiration.

II

In all comedy there is something regressive that takes us back to the world of play that we first knew as children. And if all comic literature somehow involves regression, many will naturally find it frivolous. But I see the comic regression in *Through the Looking-Glass* as profound. Regression means a going or coming back; it can be defined as a reverting to earlier behavior patterns so as to change or escape from unpleasant situations. It is both radical and conservative: radical in rejecting the present and in juxtaposing material from both our conscious and unconscious minds; conservative in holding on to time past. In Freudian dream psychology, regression means the translation of thoughts and emotions into visual images and speech when the progress of idea-content on its normal way to consciousness is blocked. It is a way of expressing and elaborating suppressed memories and daring psychic formations from infancy and childhood and letting them play on present realities. Regression can thus be a means of seeing the world anew. The child's fantasy can be father to the adult's changing civilization.

The way to go forward in looking-glass land is to go backward—back to origins, first principles, early years, early pleasures, and premoral states—in order to see with fresh clarity what, through habit and social repression, we have come to accept as absolutely the truth and to find in a place of make-believe that *make-believe* is the essence of our fate and being. The way to freedom and curious wonder is to recognize and comprehend the arbitrary, predetermined, and artificial structures that order our lives. The way to knowledge of culture and society is to explore one's inner fantasy life. The way to honor intelligence is to know and laugh at its limitations. The way to celebrate creation is to play with its silly mysteries. The intention that comes through in *Through the Looking-Glass* is, in effect, the meaning of mankind's comic capacity, and it is this: I will play with and make ridiculous fear, loneliness, smallness, ignorance, authority, chaos, nihilism, and death; I will transform, for a time, woe to joy.

III

Metamorphoses, then—sudden miraculous transformations, conversions, and translations of thought and being, undoings, recombinations, and reinventions of psychic matter—constitute the workings of regression. They also form the basis of jokes, humor, literary transaction, and religious experience. These are all forms of regression, but often positive, socially approved forms. Culture needs an institutionalized fantasy life—be it religion, art, myth, or sports—as a mind needs to dream. We sometimes have to have ways of changing contexts, of changing the past, of reliving it, of mixing the past and present, of moving beyond what we can actually know, or allow ourselves to feel, to what we can imagine. We find in literary art, as children find in fairytales, not only escape but also sanction for our individuality. Psychological criticism has told us that books and authors fulfill parental roles and can serve as fetishes of knowledge and authority. But we also seek in texts foster children to whom we can give our own countenances and in whom we find emissaries of our selves to others—permanent inheritors of our features and our playful imagination. Like the transmitters of myths, legends, sacred writings, parables, and fairytales, Carroll and such modern writers as Kafka and Beckett give people open-ended metaphors—word images that have the suggestive quality of our own dreams and eschew directly stated meanings. Carroll is particularly susceptible to the regressive tendencies of readers who find, in his genius, meanings and emotions that clarify and articulate their own obsessions and visions. He defines us as our dreams do.

Read what has been written about Carroll and you find a zoo of interpretation. It has been seriously argued, for example, that Alice equals a phallus, that her pool of tears represents the amniotic fluid, that *Alice in Wonderland* may contain a secret history of the Oxford Movement, that the "pig and pepper" chapter is a description of toilet training, that the White Queen stands for John Henry Newman, that these tales are dangerous for children, that they are literally nonsense and do not refer to the real world, that Alice is an existential heroine, that Carroll was a latent homosexual, an atheist, and a faithful Christian. Some of this criticism is lunatic, some of it is brilliant, much of it is fascinating, nearly all of it is entertaining, and most of it is offered with the dogmatic surety of Humpty Dumpty.[4] My point is not to condemn other commentators but to show that something in the nature of the writing itself sparks a wide variety of reactions.

The Alice fiction not only deals with the crisis of authority in modern life, it presents one, and readers are drawn into solving it. Like the Bible, the two books call forth hermeneutics and ingenuity but resist definitive interpretations. In the prefatory poem to *Through the Looking-Glass,* Carroll predicts "The magic words shall hold thee fast."[5] These "magic words" are not sacred, but comic, writing. In the crisis of authority, many turn to the comic text for support, finding transfiguring meaning in a sense of humor. "The magic words" somehow mirror one's own wonderland. If I look through the looking-glass, I see reflected in that mirror-vanity the desperate and hilarious comedy of myself coping.

IV

I want to discuss the comedy of *Through the Looking-Glass.*[6] Both Alice books deserve to be seen as fictions of integrity, each standing on its own, but *Looking-Glass* has had little separate attention. On the whole, Carroll's humor, language, vision, and characters seem even more resonant in it than they do in *Alice's Adventures in Wonderland* and even more central to the great modern comic tradition. *Through the Looking-Glass* reads as if Carroll had imagined one of those "children" at the end of *Vanity Fair* climbing through the Osborne mirror. And, even more significantly, the Carrollian elements in Joyce's *Finnegans Wake,* such as the dream philosophy, portmanteau language, the fratricidal Tweedle brothers, Humpty Dumpty, and the play on insect/incest, all come from *Through the Looking-Glass.* It is less sentimental than *Wonderland,* less escapist, more critical of both solipsism and social authority. And since the tensions and conflicts it treats are even sharper than those in the first Alice book, and the threats it poses larger and more insistent, the pleasure and achievement of its comedy—the release it offers—seem to me greater.

CHILD

Be as a child.
Lewis Carroll, "Stolen Waters"[7]

In "The Emperor's New Clothes," a child exposes the ruler's nakedness by cutting through lies and illusions to give people

250

the perspective they need for seeing their own gullibility and the ruses of power. That's how Carroll works. He makes a child his protagonist, pretends that children are his audience, and focuses on childhood so that he can rid himself and others of repression. Through the child, he strips away both personal and social prejudices and pretensions, holds them up to ridicule, and opens up possibilities for the imagination. In the reversed looking-glass of his art, Carroll uses Alice to show up the silly childishness—in its pejorative sense—of the so-called adult world. *Through the Looking-Glass* proves that even in the most outwardly conventional and time-serving of adults there may be a wild and brave child struggling to get out and mock the soul-killing pomposity and rigidities that govern life. Such is the hope of the comedy of regression.

I

One of the comic triumphs in *Through the Looking-Glass* is that Carroll's search for lost time succeeds. Like the White Queen, he lives backwards, and in childhood he finds vitality and creativity. Trying somehow to get back to childhood is one way of reacting to the menace of obliterating time. Carroll's famous twin passions for children and photography are especially revealing because they both reflect and preview popular ways of hanging on to life. What is photography to most of us but a technological process for trying to preserve memories, to reify images from time's flow? And surely the relatively recent fascination with the events and patterns of childhood is an effort to revisit and prolong the time of life that is farthest from death. Making a fetish of personal memory and the history of our childhood, we make consciousness elastic and time expandable.

Carroll imagines his own sort of permanence in the form of a comic picture—almost a photograph—in the memory of a child whom he has invented. This becomes clear in a passage describing the White Knight—a virtual self-portrait:

> Of all the strange things that Alice saw in her journey
> Through The Looking-Glass, this was the one that she
> always remembered most clearly. Years afterwards she
> could bring the whole scene back again, as if it had been
> only yesterday—the mild blue eyes and kindly smile of the
> Knight—the setting sun gleaming through his hair, and

shining on his armour in a blaze of light that quite dazzled her—the horse quietly moving about, with the reins hanging loose on his neck, cropping the grass at her feet—and the black shadows of the forest behind—all this she *took in like a picture*. [307; italics mine]

It is the child Alice who validates and preserves Dodgson-Carroll's being. Notice how he projects himself into her: she takes the picture that is his hope for immortality.[8] He not only loved little girls, he wanted to *be* a little girl, as the choice of his pen name goes to show.[9]

The cult of the child flourished in Victorian times, and other authors, particularly Dickens, exploited to the last emotional pang the sympathy and identification that people had come to feel for children in print, especially orphans and lonely children. Of the major writers in the language, however, only Carroll and Mark Twain used the child *primarily* for comic purposes. This, at first, seems surprising, since the figure of the child would seem ideal for comedy. Natural symbols of hope, children, in modern times normally much closer to birth than to death, live relatively free of the fear of time and give themselves to play, games, and the pursuit of pleasure. Their naïve honesty can make the sophisticated hypocrisy of the world look silly, and they also make good "straight men." And if you write for them, you can give way to fantasy, say things that in another context might be construed as wild or blasphemous, and claim you're doing nothing but amusing children. But before you can fully realize the comic potential of the child, you have to rebel against the powerful idea that adult life is somehow superior to child life. You must choose the child over the parent—even the parent in yourself and the parent that you are in your own imagination. Carroll did. This laureate of growing-up-absurd knew that a part of us resents having to grow up, and he insisted—it is the heart of his vision—that maturity, whatever else it may be, is somehow a sham and a joke.

Such a writer and such a vision can succeed only when there is a deep but repressed questioning of the authoritarianism of the past, both individually and collectively. (Cf. Günter Grass's Little Oscar in *The Tin Drum* in post-Nazi Germany.) The intensive subversion of authority that *Through the Looking-Glass* enacts could take place only when children of God, consciously

252

or unconsciously resentful of His order, were ready to doubt and mock the divinity and omnipotence of the Father.

II

The first chapter establishes a play-frame. It begins with a mawkish description of the child and childhood, as Alice, coyly mimicking adult ways, addresses long, bossy speeches to her kitten. In her cozy setting she represents the Victorian and modern wish to see the time of childhood as a bastion against the dangers and troubles of the grownup world—a paradise at the beginning instead of the end of life. The Victorian girl-child could be seen as a living icon of innocence and as visible proof that in a hard and changing world it was possible to maintain and nurture sweetness and purity. She made an ideal *raison d'être* for life's struggle and also symbolized an escape from it. What is more, with the triumphant development of corporate organization, rationalism, science, and economics, childhood became a kind of wild-life refuge for the fancy and wonder that might seem impractical in adult life. (We ought to note, of course, that our whole conception of childhood and children derives, in some degree, from the imaginative power of such writers as Rousseau, Blake, Wordsworth, Dickens, Freud, and, not least, Carroll.)

Alice's opening monologue reads like a regressive incantation on Carroll's part. It is as if he were trying to become the voice of the most morally unobjectionable being he knew in order to smother his psychic censor in a well of treacle: "I wonder if the snow *loves* the trees and fields, that it kisses them so gently? And then it covers them up snug, you know, with a white quilt; and perhaps it says 'go to sleep, darlings'" (179). A few pages later he devastatingly satirizes such a "pathetic fallacy" in "The Garden of Live Flowers," but here he had to impersonate the sentimental child of Victorian myth.

Watch a child alone at play with its toys, and after a while you may begin to hear and see these figures taking on roles that dramatize aspects of the child's life. Different tones and voices arise, words come out that reveal thoughts and visions neither you nor the child knew it possessed. Carroll's fiction is like that. He can render his deepest insight into the large world only by transferring it to the small. The child in Carroll is the parent in this antiworld, and the creatures are his children.

253

After insulating Alice and making her babble drowsily to Kitty, he reaches the point where she, her playthings, and her surroundings can become mirrors for his imagination. To the child, objects like chess pieces and looking-glasses are not inert. They seem to have autonomous personalities and to give off messages. The signal that we are beyond the double wall of superego and sentimentality in Carroll comes when he gives Alice humor and first shows his own: "once she had really frightened her old nurse by shouting suddenly in her ear, 'Nurse! Do let's pretend that I'm a hungry hyaena, and you're a bone!'" (180). That explodes the sentimentalized little-girl image. From now on, fantasy, wit, play, animation, and manic energy fill the book. Everything flows with uncontrollable life.

Once Alice passes through the looking-glass, we move into a world of reversal and comic revolution: Carroll immediately turns those two great symbols of power, royalty and parenthood, into game objects and comic characters; the red and white kings and queens first appear as befuddled parents and incompetent self-managers. And, almost at once, we get an uncannily apt image of his whole method, one that allows him to say daring things but disclaim responsibility for them:

> Alice looked on with great interest as the King took an enormous memorandum-book out of his pocket, and began writing. A sudden thought struck her, and she took hold of the end of the pencil, which came some way over his shoulder, and began writing for him.
>
> The poor King . . . at last . . . panted out "My dear! I really *must* get a thinner pencil. I can't manage this one a bit: it writes all manner of things that I don't intend—" [190]

The child takes hold and writes what it wants. That is a perfect trope for Carroll's comedy, and it points up the unconscious source of his writing as well as the role of the unconscious in all art; in fact, it could stand for the Freudian definition of art as "regression in the service of the ego."[10]

The White King's words also stress the involuntary nature of life. The book throughout evokes a child's feeling of being manipulated, of neither choosing nor understanding the conditions in which it must act and react. Part of the great appeal of *Through the Looking-Glass* is that Carroll captures and expresses this sense of being a pawn in an incomprehensible game. To the adult, the involuntary can be terrifying, but a child learns to take it in stride. Alice sees her unwilled passage through the mirror as a chance to explore something new. She even finds a kind of liberty in being where, for the moment, "they"—the usual rulers in her life—"can't get at" her. When she holds her book up to the mirror, "Jabberwocky" bursts into her ken, but she reads calmly. "'Somehow it seems to fill my head with ideas—only I don't exactly know what they are! . . . But oh!' thought Alice, suddenly jumping up, 'if I don't make haste, I shall have to go back through the Looking-glass, before I've seen what the rest . . . is like'" (197). We are not to take things too seriously, meanings and certainty are hard to come by, we haven't much free choice about where we are; but there is a lot of exploring to do.

III

With Alice on the mirror's far side, Carroll now develops fully his world of oedipal comedy: in chapter 2, "The Garden of Live Flowers," he lets loose those parodies of authority and happily slays parental figures and their mad pretensions to surety.

Carroll revered and, in his own style, practiced avidly both science and poetry, each in its kind a discipline for interpreting nature and seeking truth. But in his Oxford world he saw how disciplines and vocations have a way of turning into monolithic faiths competing for exclusive power over people's minds. Victorian intellectual life was filled with the self-important voices of sages who professed to speak in the name of science, poetry, and nature. Assuming roles, they identified their egos with cosmic intentions.

Carroll begins by murderously parodying Thomas Huxley, the public champion of science, and Tennyson, the seer of poetry. His weapon is *reductio ad absurdum:* seizing on an authority figure's grandiose words, he takes them literally, like a child, and imagines their full implications to show how ridiculous they are.

The chess-game pattern that structures the book parodies the trite proposition that life is like a chess game and, in particular, the following passage in Huxley's "A Liberal Education and Where to Find It," published in 1868, the year in which Carroll began to write *Through the Looking-Glass:*

Suppose it were perfectly certain that the life and fortune of every one of us would, one day or other, depend
upon his winning or losing a game of chess. Don't you
think that we should all consider it to be a primary duty to
learn at least the names and the moves of the pieces; to
have a notion of a gambit, and a keen eye for all the means
of giving and getting out of check? . . .

Yet it is a very plain and elementary truth that the life,
the fortune, and the happiness of every one of us, and,
more or less, of those who are connected with us, do depend upon our knowing something of the rules of a
game infinitely more difficult and complicated than
chess. . . . The chessboard is the world, the pieces are the
phenomena of the universe, the rules of the game are what
we call the laws of Nature. The player on the other side is
hidden from us. We know that his play is always fair, just,
and patient. But also we know, to our cost, that he never
overlooks a mistake, or makes the smallest allowance for
ignorance. To the man who plays well, the highest stakes
are paid, with that sort of overflowing generosity with
which the strong shows delight in strength. And one who
plays ill is checkmated—without haste, but without remorse.[11]

In the name of science, Huxley professes to know that the
process of being is a game the individual can win, and, instead of
Jehovah or Jesus, he imagines God as a sort of Universal Grand
Master. Walking with the Red Queen, Alice looks about her:
"'It's a great huge game of chess that's being played—all over
the world—if this *is* the world at all, you know. Oh, what fun it
is!'" (207–8). The chess game that the Queen previews for Alice,
and which they join, is absurdist; but it represents life much
more accurately—and it seems to be much more fun—than the
simplistic game analogy that Huxley solemnly draws. Alice
understands, as many of the tribe of Darwinians did not, the
uncertainty of knowledge and the fact that our subjectivity may
deceive us about the nature of reality. If life is a game, we are
counters in the game, not objective players external to it. Even
the most potent piece will eventually be eliminated. Our vision
must always be limited. Science itself is done by beings, not so
different from Alice, the White Knight, and Peacock's Asterias,

who live tumbling in the world, not by precise, stationary titans, who can look down on the earth as if it were a chessboard. The rest of the story gives form and meaning to the chess-game metaphor by taking the part, and the point of view, of a pawn.

In Tennyson's *Maud*, such is the power of human ecstasy that even the flowers can speak rapturously when the protagonist's beloved comes to him in the garden. Nature, reflecting human will, becomes a dummy for the poet's ventriloquism:

> There has fallen a splendid tear
>   From the passion-flower at the gate.
> She is coming, my dove, my dear;
>   She is coming, my life, my fate.
> The red rose cries, "She is near, she is near";
>   And the white rose weeps, "She is late";
> The larkspur listens, "I hear, I hear";
>   And the lily whispers, "I wait."

These verses generated "The Garden of Live Flowers." If nature becomes an extension of humanity and flowers can talk, why shouldn't they be like real people—naughty children, for example—rude, stupid, and full of nonsense? And so they are:

> And here they all began shouting together, till the air seemed quite full of little shrill voices. "Silence, every one of you!" cried the Tiger-lily, waving itself passionately from side to side, and trembling with excitement. "They know I can't get at them!" it panted, bending its quivering head towards Alice, "or they wouldn't dare to do it!" ...
> "Hold *your* tongue!" cried the Tiger-lily. ...
> "She's coming!" cried the Larkspur. "I hear her footstep, thump, thump, along the gravel-walk." [202–5]

It is power, not love, they await—the Red Queen, not Maud.

So much for the pathetic fallacy. Poetry that personifies nature can be an eloquent bullying, a rhetorical and emotional self-indulgence, that seeks to make all being conform to the bard's sensibility. That is the point of Carroll's spoof of Tennyson and also of his later parody, in the White Knight chapter, mocking Wordsworth's obliviousness, in "Resolution and Independence," of everything but the speaker's sublime thought.

Through the Looking-Glass shows the mature poems of honored poets to be deceiving and ridiculous. The verses that tell

257

the truth and prophesy what will happen turn out to be anonymous nursery rhymes (e.g., "Tweedledee" and "Humpty Dumpty"). Carroll embraces the child's poetry and rejects the adult's. That is typical of his subversion, i.e., his turning-around of things from underneath.

IV

The child often experiences authority as a kind of abrupt rudeness. Carroll subverts it by making it look petty; he knew that the exercise of power can simply be the childishness of big beings. The Red Queen is his principal explicit authority figure in the book, and he uses her for satire. He called her "pedantic to the tenth degree, the concentrated essence of all governesses,"[12] which means she must be the essence of government and authority as a Victorian upper-class child first knew it. In the way of most perceived authority, she has a personality but no depth of self; all her being goes into telling others what to do. She has no self-doubt, no disinterested wonder, no hesitancy that might humanize her. Contradictory and rude, like so many of the cocksure characters Alice meets, she asks questions but then gives orders before they can be answered. "Where do you come from? . . . And where are you going? Look up, speak nicely, and don't twiddle your fingers all the time" (206). That may simply caricature the authoritarian type; but her next command, "Curtsey while you're thinking what to say. It saves time" (206), provides a whole comic disquisition on the role of manners as well as a blueprint for success. Her pronouncements come out as a mad strategy for facing the mystery of things. When Alice sets out through the unknown countryside, the Red Queen says, "Speak in French when you can't think of the English for a thing—turn out your toes as you walk—and remember who you are!" (212). As words to live by, nothing could make clearer the capricious and ridiculously inadequate nature of authority and the tragicomic fragility of people who must face their fate without proper knowledge. Yet the Queen's advice makes as much sense as most rules of conduct. Humanity must rely on simplistic formulas, internalized slogans, and funny little gestures as it moves about in its unfathomable game.

Carroll is the don of comic reduction: shrink the essence of authority to a child's scale, diminish the threatening urgencies of society, make jokes of them, show up their triviality—those are his imperatives. Fleeting impressions and images stand for and mock great patterns and manifestations of power. In chapter 3, he manages to fit the mighty clamor of capitalism and industrialism into a single square, through which Alice is rushed—by railway, naturally. A chorus dins at her:

> "Don't keep him waiting, child! Why, his time is worth a thousand pounds a minute!" . . . "The land there is worth a thousand pounds an inch!" . . .
> "Why, the smoke alone is worth a thousand pounds a puff!" . . .
> "Better say nothing at all. Language is worth a thousand pounds a word!"
> "I shall dream about a thousand pounds tonight, I know I shall!" thought Alice. [217–18]

We have the assault of the capitalistic system, the canting hustle of steam and price, as it might be felt by a child with whom we sympathize, but Carroll reduces this financial mania "to child's play, the very thing to jest about." [13]

v

Chapter 4, the great Tweedledee and Tweedledum chapter, treats in the same fashion such matters as fratricide, contradictions in human nature, power struggles, war, and political controversy. Here we have Cain and Abel reduced to puerility: "Tweedledum and Tweedledee / Agreed to have a battle; / For Tweedledum said Tweedledee / Had spoiled his nice new rattle":

> "Of course you agree to have a battle?" Tweedledum said. . . .
> So the two brothers went off hand-in-hand into the wood, and returned in a minute with their arms full of things—such as bolsters, blankets, hearth-rugs, table-cloths, dish-covers, and coal-scuttles. . . .
> Alice said afterwards she had never seen such a fuss made about anything in all her life . . . she arranged a bolster round the neck of Tweedledee, "to keep his head from being cut off," as he said.

259

"You know," he added very gravely, "it's one of the most serious things that can possibly happen to one in a battle—to get one's head cut off."

Alice laughed loud: . . .

"We *must* have a bit of a fight. . . . What's the time now?"

Tweedledee looked at his watch, and said "Half-past four."

"Let's fight until six, and then have dinner," said Tweedledum.

"Very well," the other said. . . .

Tweedledum looked round him with a satisfied smile. "I don't suppose," he said, "there'll be a tree left standing, for ever so far round, by the time we've finished!"

"And all about a rattle!" said Alice, still hoping to make them a *little* ashamed of fighting for such a trifle. [241–43]

Such an excerpt shows the error of those who dismiss the profound seriousness of Carroll's humor. In a way almost unparalleled in literature, he treats comically and succinctly the most momentous subjects and the most terrible problems of humanity. Here his topic and target are, in fact, war and its perpetrators. The comedy controls for the moment the potential horror of battle by putting it in a context of play and asserting that from a certain dispassionate point of view, which we have the power to assume, war means the ridiculous behavior of Tweedledee and Tweedledum. Ridiculing the twins, Carroll withdraws dignity from those who make the highest claim to it but do not deserve it—namely, fighters and force-worshipers of any sort. All our sympathy and our respect in this scene go to Alice.

In "Tweedledum and Tweedledee," Carroll, as usual, reverses roles: Alice, the child, has the maturity and wise judgment that a parent was supposed to have. She does not, however, have the parent's authority or influence. She knows what's right, but she is powerless to stop the inevitable charade of inanity. She cannot control her world, but she can know it, and she survives. At the end of nearly every chapter, including this one, she moves on, away from violence, futility, death, disaster, emerging as an image of the child as refugee and survivor, a figure with a future.

VI

Carroll not only belittles the masters of combat in the Tweedles, he also parodies the arrogance of scientists, poets, and
philosophers. Like a compulsive Coleridgean bard, Tweedledee
speaks the most famous of all nonsense poems, "The Walrus
and the Carpenter," which sounds like an anthem for the new
evolutionary scientists.

> "It seems a shame," the Walrus said,
>   "To play them such a trick.
> After we've brought them out so far,
>   And made them trot so quick!"
> The Carpenter said nothing but
>   "The butter's spread too thick!"
>
> . . . .
>
> "O Oysters," said the Carpenter,
>   "You've had a pleasant run!
> Shall we be trotting home again?"
>   But answer came there none—
> And this was scarcely odd, because
>   They'd eaten every one.
>
>   [236]

Here is a comic microcosm of "nature red in tooth and claw"—a
farcical vision of life as a tricking and trapping of others, as if
Herbert Spencer had been spliced with Machiavelli and then
articulated and rhymed by Edward Lear. In the poem Carroll
mocks the authority of a discipline that finds the basis of existence in conflict and extermination, but he also savagely mocks
the oysters in the poem for being dupes of the authority that
devours them.

The twins try, in fact, in the discussion about the Red King,
to devour Alice through metaphysics, as if she were an intellectual oyster:

> He had a tall red night-cap on, with a tassel, and he was
> lying crumpled up into a sort of untidy heap, and snoring
> loud—"fit to snore his head off!" as Tweedledum re-
> marked. . . .
>   "He's dreaming now," said Tweedledee: "and what do
> you think he's dreaming about?"

261

Alice said "Nobody can guess that."

"Why, about *you!*" Tweedledee exclaimed, clapping his hands triumphantly. "And if he left off dreaming about you, where do you suppose you'd be?"

"Where I am now, of course," said Alice.

"Not you!" Tweedledee retorted contemptuously. "You'd be nowhere. Why, you're only a sort of thing in his dream!"

"If that there King was to wake," added Tweedledum, "you'd go out—bang!—just like a candle!" . . .

"Well, it's no use *your* talking about waking him," said Tweedledum, "when you're only one of the things in his dream. You know very well you're not real."

"I *am* real!" said Alice, and began to cry.

"You won't make yourself a bit realler by crying," Tweedledee remarked: "there's nothing to cry about."

"If I wasn't real," Alice said—half-laughing through her tears, it all seemed so ridiculous—"I shouldn't be able to cry."

"I hope you don't suppose those are *real* tears?" Tweedledum interrupted in a tone of great contempt.

"I know they're talking nonsense," Alice thought to herself: "and it's foolish to cry about it." So she brushed away her tears, and went on, as cheerfully as she could. [238–40]

Nothing could show more strikingly the importance of *not* being earnest. Two axioms emerge from this scene: (1) Recognizing the existence of nonsense can make one laugh instead of cry; (2) the child, having an open mind and a sense of the ridiculous upon which successful living depends, is the most promising and potentially the most rational creature in this world. About the passage, Bertrand Russell remarked, "if it were not put humorously, we should find it too painful";[14] but the point is that there is no other way to put "it" without pretentious lying. Carroll insists upon reducing speculation about reality, identity, and a Supreme Being to the province of Tweedledee and Tweedledum, squabbling sibling rivals. Philosophy appears here as the rather nasty pastime of contentious little know-it-alls who browbeat a nice person into self-doubt. In the humor, we find a novelist's traditional criticism of philosophical theory: Alice is finally right; the Tweedles do talk nonsense because they spout their mock-Berkeleyan idealism in a specific context. She may not be able to refute their argument, but it comes from the mouths of foolish beings who *are* discredited. Ideas exist in a structure, in the world we inhabit, and our view of them cannot be independent from those who hold them and what they do. Alice knows this instinctively, and she sees also that whether her pain is objectively "real" or not, she does feel it and therefore must act as if she really exists and matters. Her doubt may recur—in fact, doubt for Carroll is a necessary prior condition for the acts of faith on which he bases his comic vision—but she lives by an ultimate faith in herself. The quick change from tears to laughter and the resolute cheerfulness typify the child's resilience and mark the comic pattern of the book.

Behind Alice's doubt and unease lie Carroll's skepticism and distrust of any claims to absolute authority; but there is something even more basic showing through the scene: the child's quest to be its own master, which is the germ of all human freedom. The Red King is the closest thing to a father figure in *Through the Looking-Glass,* but he is debased, and the comedy makes it preposterous that this seedy snorer could in any way be sovereign over Alice and her imagination. "No novelist," says Harry Levin of Carroll, "has identified more intimately with the point of view of his heroine."[15] Her fear of existing only in another's dream betrays at bottom, I think, her author's suppressed rebellion at the idea of an omnipotent anthropomorphic God. The device of the Red King's dream satirizes the notions that the cosmos exists only in the mind of a supernatural entity or that we take our being from a whimsical personal God. God is diminished in this episode to an impotent snoozer, not yet dead but surely in a coma.

VII

Alice does have the saving sense of humor that is missing in nearly all of the other characters, and it protects her when her trip threatens to become too painful. In "Wool and Water" she meets the White Queen and again begins to cry:

> "Only it is so *very* lonely here!" Alice said. . . .
> "Oh, don't go on like that!" cried the poor Queen, wringing her hands in despair. "Consider what a great girl

263

you are. Consider what a long way you've come to-day. Consider what o'clock it is. Consider anything, only don't cry!"

Alice could not help laughing at this even in the midst of her tears. "Can *you* keep from crying by considering things?" she asked.

"That's the way it's done." [250–51]

In this comic dither, we find Carroll's strategy for repelling despair: concentrate hard on anything that even temporarily keeps the demons of despondency out of consciousness, identify with the curious child in the self, and see the funny side of life.

In all the encounters that follow, the form of Alice's meeting with the Tweedles is repeated: she can talk to the zany characters with interest, deal courteously with them, even banter and have fun; but, when things threaten, or when her involuntary journey must continue, she can detach herself without useless pain or anxiety. The kind of practicality blended with imagination that Austen found in Emma's charity to the poor Carroll now locates in the wise child.

As she goes from square to square, Carroll turns menace after menace to child's play, e.g., insubstantiality of purpose and being in "Wool and Water," national and epic pride in "The Lion and the Unicorn," and solipsism, idealism, and madness in "It's My Own Invention." Alice's progress through nonsense across the magic chessboard reads at times like a child savior of comedy harrowing the little hells of our fearful hearts.

The destination of the plot seems, until the end, to be the queening of Alice in the chess game, but, when she gets her crown, we have a typical Carrollian reversal. The wish to be a queen in fairytales, says Bruno Bettelheim, means, symbolically, the gaining of self-control;[16] but self-control is just what the queens in *Through the Looking-Glass* lack. If this is growing up, maturity is silly. Everything in the square of the queens, in fact, goes out of control, and Alice finds it the most disturbing place of all. Distinctions of form and being at Alice's coronation banquet disappear, and the chaos finally drives her out of her dream.

The impossible black-comedy world of chapter 9 and Alice's awakening have to be seen, in part, as a flat rejection of growing up and the authority of adult life. Upon waking, Alice is shaking a kitten, instead of the dwindled queen, and posing as an adult before her cats. That puts us right back where we started—with the child at play and mimicking officious grownups. The book ends in regression. What was figurative at the end of *Vanity Fair* turns into Carroll's literal fantasy: protagonist, audience, and author are all children and part of the same story.

> "Now, Kitty, let's consider who it was that dreamed it all. This is a serious question, my dear, . . . it *must* have been either me or the Red King. He was a part of my dream, of course—but then I was part of his dream, too! . . ." But the provoking kitten . . . pretended it hadn't heard the question.
>
> Which do *you* think it was? [343–44]

We end in childish uncertainty, among schoolchildren, as it were, but that is the human condition for Carroll, and not a bad one; he restores us, for the moment, to that time when ignorance is bliss because it carries wide-open possibilities for the future. All is absurd, all is inscrutable, and, therefore, a desperate faith is no more foolish than anything else.

VIII

"The child" for Carroll is what "marriage" is in Austen, what "nature" is to Meredith, what "community" is in Trollope: it sets off thoughts and feelings that bind us to the future. Carroll's creed is that the child is good and that in identifying with the child we grow younger, freer, more hopeful. Says Judith Bloomingdale, "Throughout her journey she has exhibited (to enumerate the qualities Carroll attributes to her) curiosity, courage, kindness, intelligence, courtesy, dignity, a sense of humor, humility, sympathy, propriety, respect, imagination, wonder, initiative, gratitude, patience, affection, thoughtfulness, integrity, and a sense of justice in the face of an outrageous universe."[17] (Note how well this list also describes Clara Middleton.)

Certain psychoanalytic critics note that there is very little mature love in Carroll and that Alice herself expresses little love. That misses the point. He is not out to sentimentalize Alice or himself. What counts is that the comic associations and impressions, which the figure of this girl-child in the text calls up, seem to justify Carroll's faith. In the matrix of her character, she is worthy of our love, and in the intricate web of circumstance and humor that calls her into being and puts her before us there is something worthy of hope and charity. I want to quote two distinguished writers to show not only how Carroll has used Alice to express a sense of faith but also how pervasive and symbolically relevant—I would almost say holy—this child image can be in modern secular civilization:

"Is Alice . . . ," asks W. H. Auden, "an adequate symbol for what every human being should try to be like? I am inclined to answer yes. A girl of eleven (or a boy of twelve) who comes from a good home—a home, that is, where she has known both love and discipline . . . can be a most remarkable creature. . . . [O]ne cannot meet a girl or a boy of this kind without feeling that what she or he is—by luck and momentarily—is what after many years and countless follies and errors one would like in the end to become."[18]

More than a century before Auden, Dickens, in the introduction to *The Old Curiosity Shop,* talking of Little Nell, describes a condition that countless readers and writers since have fantasized as their own: "I had it always in my fancy to surround the lonely figure of the child with grotesque and wild . . . companions, and to gather about her innocent face and pure intentions, associates . . . strange and uncongenial." Of this mass impulse to regression, Carroll made his comedy.

DREAM AND FANTASY

The remarkable fact about Dodgson is that by using the very means of his weakness, by succumbing to his dream and fantasy, he should become so intelligently awake.
Peter Coveney[19]

The Alice books are dream visions and belong to an important tradition. Like the authors of "The Dream of the Rood," *The Pearl, Piers Plowman,* and *The Pilgrim's Progress,* among others, Carroll uses the device of the dream to express what deeply concerns him and to organize and condense broad, significant experience. The dreams of Alice, however, uniquely celebrate whimsy and a comic fantasy life. Carroll brings together the literary convention of the dream vision, the mood and feeling of a real dream, and the full play of his fantasy—and he exploits their potential for comedy. Nobody before had done anything quite like that.

I

Typically, dream fictions presume to show a moral and spiritual reality that supposedly exists but gets lost in daily life. The existence of dreams, like traditional religion, points to an actuality of being beyond the ken of our normal waking consciousness and thus may suggest the miraculous and the supernatural. When we dream, we do truly experience that which is not. Not surprisingly, much dream literature affirms a divine Providence; from the Bible to Jung, we find dream visions being used for religious purposes. Such dream works as *The Pilgrim's Progress* are not, strictly speaking, fantasies at all— unless we call them fantasies of collective wish-fulfillment —since the writers and much of their audience would see them portraying things that are real—at least symbolically —and exist independently of their authors' imaginations. Bunyan, for instance, may be a visionary, but he intends to present objective truth "under the similitude of a dream." He does not doubt that what he sees is there. Implicitly, the dream vision projects its author's challenge: this "dream" is essential reality; mundane living makes you doze to the truth, but everything has its meaning and place here, in the universal order that my vision reveals. The form has a built-in allegorical bias. Every detail, every sense impression, bears a general as well as a particular significance—often a religious significance. Carroll, by stressing the absurd fantasy and anarchy of the dreaming state, in effect parodies the authority of previous dream visions, but his framework, as surely as Bunyan's, also carries universalizing tendencies: Looking-Glass land *is* somehow the world, and Alice's strange journey through it *is* like life. "Life, what is it but a dream?" asks Carroll (345).

Actual dreams, however, are not coherent literary visions, religious or otherwise; they are more like anarchic prayers of the unconscious. Remarkably realistic, Alice's dreams have the fluidity, the tricks of distortion and displacement, the rapid shifts in context, and the relatively passive visualizing center that we recognize in our own dreams. In *Through the Looking-Glass,* the dream flow dissolves and recomposes objects of waking perception in startling ways. Its ambience is unstable, exhilarating, and speedy. Alice does not so much resolve problems and puzzling relationships in her dreams as leave them behind—just

267

as we do in so many of our dreams. Suppressed wishes, division and projections of personality, and many more characteristics of dreaming fill the text.

Through the Looking-Glass also conveys the happy human comedy that lies in the very fact that we dream. Better than any other psychological phenomenon, a dream expresses the tension and strange fusion in life between solipsism and determinism, between our willful subjectivity and the involuntary tenor of our being. It expresses the variety of our intelligence, which uses both logic and intuition, and it plays on conflicts between our past and our future. Not all dream experts agree on their subject, but most seem to believe that (1) dreaming keeps us from going awry by preserving a balance in the awful multiplicity of our being; and (2) dreaming involves some kind of regression, whether to yesterday's events, childhood memories, animated visual fantasies, racial experience, early modes of brain functioning, lost patterns of spontaneity and holistic perception, or what have you. We do not choose what we dream, but somehow it seems that we do. Absolutely private and personal as our dreams are, we still have no conscious say over what they shall be. In them we sense our aloneness and our inescapable individuality, and yet we seem to be pawns in the hand of an alien agency. Everything becomes a part of our internal world, and still we feel separate from what is demonstrably going on within our own heads and nowhere else.

Dreaming—even in nightmares—implies the happy ending of waking, and thus a dream per se signifies the promise of a future and a regeneration. It also proves that we are all seething with creativity. It presents an alternative universe with each dreamer in the role of a god—not omnipotent, but immanent—and it tells us that the resources of imagination are fluid and nearly infinite. Time and space become subjective and relative: inner space and dream time. Dreams, for Carroll, thus sanction fantasy.

II

Human nature itself obviously needs alternative worlds and a fantasy life, and the fantasist, playing at being God, compensates in dreams for the deficiencies of "real" life. It is the precedent and model by which he can defy both physical limitations and the conventional boundaries of thought and moral decorum. Carroll may leave us at the end with the question of "who it was that dreamed it all," but the whole dream is undoubtedly his fantastic wish-fulfillment.

Creating fantasy is, like dreaming, a way of internalizing miracles; but, of course, it is consciously done and historical. Like dream work, fantasies, according to Freud and his followers, grow out of childhood experiences and imaginings. They, too, are animated images of repressed hopes and stifled wishes set free. Fantasy indicates, however, the secularization of wonder, and Carroll is its prophet.

In large degree, fantasy flourishes and fantasy life looms so large in the modern era because the past two centuries have been a time of religious confusion and doubt. People need to believe that the limits and terrors of reality can be changed, that the future can be different and better, that wonderful things can happen; if religious institutions cannot do these things, something else must. "Imagination reshapes the world, and the self, to the desires of the mind. . . . It breaks bounds, emancipates itself from space and time, raises itself above the limiting human conditions, assumes higher powers, subjects things to its own will, makes all perfect." So Stuart Tave, deriving his sense of "imagination" from Coleridge's definition of "fancy," describes exactly how fantasy assumes the role of Providence and its function.[20]

In Carroll's hands fantasy becomes a comic mode to ponder and enjoy; it purges contradictions and hard realities from the mind. His comic fantasy depicts a world so outlandish that it never could be and that therefore provides some escape from social pressures and moral responsibility. But we also find that his preposterous imagination very often gives us exactly the sort of silliness that goes on all the time in the real world. "I've believed as many as six impossible things before breakfast," says the White Queen to Alice (251), and "The rule is, jam tomorrow and jam yesterday—but never jam *to-day*" (247): fantastic and funny lines, but somehow true to life. Words like the unicorn's to Alice, "if you'll believe in me, I'll believe in you" (287), remind us that we are creatures of social fantasies who need huge amounts of absurd faith just to sustain ordinary life.

The use of fantasy for humor seems so natural now that it comes as a surprise to realize how original the Carroll of the Alice books was. He had few distinguished predecessors in

269

his mode. Cervantes, Swift, Shakespeare (*A Midsummer Night's Dream*), and Dickens, who sets his comic fantasy against a normative background, would seem to be his chief precursors, but they all write in other modes. He is not very close to any of them, except perhaps Dickens, with whom he shares a passion for finding the humor and pleasure in mankind's obsessions with language and a propensity to make fun out of schizophrenic states of mind. Fantasy as a literary subgenre was developed in the Victorian era most notably by Carroll, Thomas Hood, George MacDonald, Charles Kingsley, and William Morris. It grew out of the Romantic movement—specifically from such late eighteenth-century historical phenomena as intensified interest in childhood, the collecting and setting-down of fairytales and nursery rhymes, the revival of interest in beast fables, and the burgeoning of children's literature. It seemed important to some that children's powers of fancy be developed—especially since the Romantics prized imagination—and that people should find ways to stay in touch with the playfulness of childhood. The cult of the exotic, the cultivation of the self's visionary powers, the fascination with irrational states of mind (including dream states), the felt need for new myths and symbols to meet the breakdown of religious orthodoxy and the crisis of faith, all helped to produce the literature of fantasy and to make it respectable. Victorian fantasy proclaims the continuing need for a renaissance of wonder (Carroll at the end of *Wonderland* calls the waking world "dull reality," an astounding assertion if you think about it); in practice, particularly in Kingsley and in Carroll's friend MacDonald, it often deals with religious doubt and theological preoccupations, e.g., the theodicy of death and problems of personal immortality.[21]

Moral controversy swirled about the development of children's literature and fantasy modes. The tales of fantasy seem historically to have been connected with the mythology of superstitions and magical cults—in other words, with outlawed religions. At first, fairytales were condemned for lacking ethical purpose and religious seriousness, but then the guardians of orthodoxy found they could be expropriated and used to inculcate correct behavior in much the same way as traditional Christian dream visions had been used. By the time Carroll wrote the Alice books, most children's stories spread religious and moral propaganda.[22] Fantasy was serving social orthodoxy. (Later, in *Sylvie and Bruno,* Carroll—I should perhaps say "Dodgson"—would use it for the same ends.) *Through the Looking-Glass,* which he calls a "fairy-tale," mocks this sort of thing and claims fantasy, miracle, dream techniques, and religious wonder for comedy.

III

Like his fellow fantastists MacDonald and Kingsley, Carroll faces the subject of death; in *his* fantasy, however, it isn't God, but the power of humor, that takes away death's sting:

> "... you may observe a Bread-and-butter-fly ..."
> "And what does *it* live on?"
> "Weak tea with cream in it."
> A new difficulty came into Alice's head. "Supposing it couldn't find any?" she suggested.
> "Then it would die, of course."
> "But that must happen very often," Alice remarked thoughtfully.
> "It always happens," said the Gnat. [223]

Death jokes are actually resurrection jokes. They announce that there is nothing which the life-force of the mind can't transform into vital pleasure. They do, of course, release the hostility that builds up against others by playfully letting us feel how nice the demise of beings not ourselves can seem. Macabre humor, though, does much more, and few mental processes are more complex: it integrates death into life, shockingly reminding us, like the religious *memento mori* of another age, of death's ubiquity and of life's sweetness, prodigality, and doom. And, most important of all, it revels in the ability of consciousness to transubstantiate dead bodies into living waves of joy—laughter. Black comedy, with its fantasies of death, flourishes in modern times, and the reason must be that it somehow works to reconcile people to dying and to offer them intimations of immortality. We cannot understand the prevalence of black humor—any more than we can understand the belief in hell—without seeing that it performs a kind of theological function. Joking about death is one of the most sophisticated ways that we have of combating its menace—of accepting it and defying it at the same time.

271

Carroll's cartoon-like fantasies of the last words and actions of Humpty, the Tweedles, and the Gnat, along with all the death and decapitation gags in both Alice books, are extremely important in showing why so much comic death fantasy has come to permeate high- and low-brow literature and art, ranging from comic books and cartoons to Samuel Beckett. "One short sleep past, we wake to eternity," wrote Donne; but for Carroll the "short sleep" is an almost infinitely malleable comic dream—or series of comic dreams—showing the resources of consciousness for creating fantastic worlds where death's power is circumscribed.

Death humor may seem callous, but its fantasies are really no more cruel—in fact, they are much less so—than the doctrines of heaven and hell, which stimulate images that, for a believer, are psychologically similar in effect to morbid "black comedy," though to my mind they are much more sadistic and vengeful. Humanity needs to fantasize victories over the grave and find ways of imagining that either death does not end life, or, if it does, then it's a happy ending. If religious dogma fails to do the job successfully or becomes unconvincing, the sense of humor can use death to create a feeling of regeneration and well-being. Even though this feeling may not last for long, its existence and recurrence serve as proof and analogue of the indomitable spirit of life and the wild animation of reality.

IV

Animation, the breath of life, motivates most black comedy and also gives us a key to Carroll's comic dream and fantasy world: he animates fantastic images. Nursery rhymes, words, thoughts, poems, animals, chess pieces, and flowers all come alive, take visual shape, move and talk. As everything in a dream is part of the dreamer, so everything in the looking-glass world is part of the fantasist's personality. His imagination animates new forms of life in every square. Harry Levin notes the "evanescent . . . cinematographic movement of dreams" in Carroll;[23] it is the movement of animation. The illustrations to *Through the Looking-Glass*—Carroll's fussiness about them nearly drove Tenniel out of his mind—are more important to the text than those in any other book I can think of, and the reason should be clear: repressed thought turns to visual images, and these images move and live in Carroll's fantasy. Try to think of Humpty

Dumpty without benefit of the Carroll-Tenniel image and you can see the force of Carroll's animation. If you could combine his fantastic literary animation with his photographic interest, you would get motion pictures, and certainly he has a right to be called a direct ancestor of the sensibility that created the aptly named "movies"; specifically, he is spiritual father, as surely as any technological innovator, to that revealing progeny of the twentieth century, animated cartoons.

The movie-cartoon world, full of animism and violence, comes right out of *Looking-Glass* life. In these visions, horrendous falls, accidents, explosions, murderous intentions, and carnivorous frenzy seem not only harmless but funny. Animation by definition excludes death, and these visual fantasies—classic examples of comic regression—give us a world in which mortality and pain have no sway. Viewers can work off violent impulses without worrying about guilt or moral responsibility. Humpty Dumpty, the Walrus and the Carpenter, the Tweedles, the White Knight, and the Queens are the forerunners of Donald Duck, Road-runner, the Pink Panther, and all those other creatures from the happy realm of innocuous cruelty and miraculous regeneration that is popular comic animation.

It may be that one of the greatest sources of pleasure in animation is that it seems to take us back to a time in childhood when we felt ourselves to be the center of life and made no distinction between the self and the other—when everything we knew was alive and personal, and we had no need to care for the alien. The animation of all, the personalizing of anything, may express a craving to be all, to ingest all, and to obliterate all boundaries—between people and things, between stories and life, between kinds of animal life, between child and mother. Carroll indulges in a chaotic urge for formlessness, but he mocks that urge also. In the climactic chapter of the dream, "Queen Alice," the crescendo of anarchic life peaks. Nothing remains inanimate; everything storms with personality; distinctions fade; anything becomes anybody; and the fantasist imagines all life in motion:

> At this moment she heard a hoarse laugh at her side, and turned to see what was the matter with the White Queen; but, instead of the Queen, there was the leg of mutton sitting in the chair. "Here I am!" cried a voice from the

soup-tureen, and Alice turned again, just in time to see the Queen's broad good-natured face grinning at her for a moment over the edge of the tureen, before she disappeared into the soup.

There was not a moment to be lost. Already several of the guests were lying down in the dishes, and the soup-ladle was walking up the table towards Alice's chair, and beckoning to her impatiently to get out of its way. [335–36]

Explicit comic regression in this chapter has gone very far: the scene of Alice's last supper seems to me to recapture and give voice to such experiences as infantile table behavior, animism, and early identity crisis. The comic fantasy manages to articulate the joy, the potential menace, and the powerful emotional charge that a human being in his early stage of life must feel—no mean feat of writing. The absence of order satisfies some deep urge in us to be free of all restriction, but it also threatens to destroy the child's hard-won self-consciousness and growing independence:

"'I can't stand this any longer!' [Alice] cried, as she jumped up and seized the tablecloth with both hands: one good pull, and plates, dishes, guests, and candles came crashing down together in a heap on the floor" [336]. Absolute regression and the formless animation of everything to the point of complete instability mean loss of character and madness. The dream is never more entertaining than in this chapter, and the breakdown of conventional structure, the defiance of authority, and the wild nonsense conversations open up new worlds and create a heady atmosphere of inspired play and anarchic freedom; but the child must finally act to be kept from being overwhelmed by the frantic energy and animism of the fantasy.

v

Everything in this whole chapter rushes with the jumbled urgency and affect of a vivid dream. It epitomizes the Looking-Glass world. Much of what has come before tumbles together in the manner of dream logic and dream-within-a-dream distortion. It has, like a dreaming mind, a kaleidoscopic coherence, rearranging the book's contents; Carroll carefully refers to motifs, characters, imagery, subjects, and words from

274

all the previous chapters and gives the book a greater unity than it is usually credited with. For example, Alice attains the ultimate goal of a pawn—Queenhood—but her victory becomes a nightmare; the autocratic Red Queen and the sappy White Queen turn into a comedy team that continues the satire on authority; the obsession with fishes becomes explicit; the snore of the Red King reappears as the snore of the two queens; the pudding course, invented by the White Knight, now banters with Alice; the White Queen talks of Humpty; Tweedledee's "shrill voice" welcomes Alice to her banquet; the Gnat's pun on "horse" turns up in the Frog's throat; the Bread-and-butter-fly and the "Brown bread and butter" of "The Lion and the Unicorn" become a part of Alice's "examination" dream; and, of course, the "dream-rushes" turn, by wordplay, into the rushing of this dream.

The comic fantasy of "Queen Alice" has the brilliant improvisation and invention, irreverent hilarity, and manic Dionysian upswing of the best modern comic ensembles, such as the Marx Brothers and *Monty Python's Flying Circus,* who are so obviously in the tradition of Carroll (see, in particular, the dialogue of pp. 327–30). This whirling world of mad whimsy, wisecracks, nonsense talk, and puns overthrows the drabness of predictability and keeps us off balance. It holds the fascination that our dreams have for us or that any great live comic performance has. One reason for the surge of liberation that comedy can stir in us is that so much gets covered so fast, and we must race our brains to keep up: we feel that we are mentally flying. To follow, to stay on top of what's happening, to "get it," to "get the joke," we have to rivet our attention on the winging moment and focus on the particularity of what we are sensing, living fully and intensely in a speedy present. In our usual mental set, we are partially abstract beings who keep fitting the data of the moment into the conventional framework of past experience. What can happen in flights of inspired comic nonsense is that the normal connections we make between present, past, and future break. Carroll's wild dialogue can still the consciousness that goes beyond the unique reality of "now" by shattering our expectations of what is to follow and our assumptions about the meaning of the past. Such talk seems to stimulate a sense of alert well-being, and, temporarily liberated

275

into a vitality of the moment, we feel the joy of free play and the power of imaginative originality.

Edmund Wilson says that "the creatures that [Alice] meets, the whole dream, *are* Alice's personality and her waking life,"[24] but, of course, they are Carroll's personality and life too. Carroll ends his fantasy by stressing the dream: the last chapter, "Which Dreamed It?" concludes with a question seeking the identity of the dreamer of the imaginary world: "Which do *you* think it was?" It draws us in and, making us a part of his fiction, leaves us wondering. The rhetoric claims that it is our dream as well as his, for, if we enter it, we must be involved in it.

VI

Out of Carroll's dream world, out of the weird projections of his own odd character on the screen of his fantasy life, have come comic figures who take on the proportions of mythic figures for our era and point up the potential for self-transcendence that his art finally shows. I want to end this section by looking at three more of his great autobiographical characters: Humpty Dumpty, the White Knight, and the Gnat.

A rude, arrogant, intellectual and the original egghead, Humpty is doomed to crash in a farcical version of the Fortunate Fall (in *Finnegans Wake,* Joyce makes him central to his vision of the world). He embodies perfectly the brittle vulnerability of hubris. He's a pattern of egoism—like Meredith's Sir Willoughby living inside an eggshell. Carroll forms a punning dream equation that makes Humpty a tottering hieroglyph of pride: Egg + 0-shape = EGO (in dream logic such associations happen all the time, and Carroll uses such tricks of a dreaming mind to intensify the aura of a dream—e.g., in "Wool and Water," "sheep" changes to "shop" and then to water, i.e., to "ship," and, in "Looking-Glass Insects," "goat" becomes "gnat," metamorphoses based on the similar letter structures of words). *Through the Looking-Glass* infuses the Mother Goose character with the force of vital myth—*comic* myth. In an age of growing democracy, flaunted egoism must be shattered and ridiculed: the fall of the proud becomes comic, not tragic. People need to feel that even the pompous wizards of selfishness get their comeuppance and that fate is, at least sometimes, fair in punishing conceit and special privilege. The image of Humpty objectifies

276

and makes funny the downfall of intellectual presumptuousness and the tyranny of ego.

In part, Carroll revenges himself on his Oxford enemies and on donnish fatuousness, but, in the main, Humpty Dumpty is a fantasy projection of Carroll himself. Like his author, Humpty studies logic and semantics; he, too, is obsessed with mathematical problems. He has at times a brilliant Carrollian skepticism that cuts through stupid convention to a profound truth:

> "I don't know what you mean by 'glory,'!" Alice said.
> Humpty Dumpty smiled contemptuously. "Of course you don't—till I tell you. I meant 'there's a nice knock-down argument for you!'" [268–69]

Like Dodgson, he enjoys confusing a child with conundrums, and he also has the imagination to animate language:

> "They've a temper, some of them,—particularly verbs: they're the proudest—adjectives you can do anything with, but not verbs—however, *I* can manage the whole lot of them! Impenetrability! That's what *I* say!"
> "Would you tell me, please," said Alice, "what that means?"
> " . . . I meant by 'impenetrability' that we've had enough of that subject." [269]

He, too, is a great fantasist who rebels against reality:

> "That's just what I complain of," said Humpty Dumpty. "Your face is the same as everybody has—the two eyes, so— . . . nose in the middle, mouth under. It's always the same. Now if you had the two eyes on the same side of the nose, for instance—or the mouth at the top—that would be *some* help." [276]

Comic fantasy playing on the conventions of the dream vision allowed Carroll to abstract the mental overreacher in himself, put it in a big doomed egg, and so transcend Humpty Dumpty through self-knowledge, a humorous sense of his own fallibility, and an ultimate allegiance to the child and what she stands for. The myth of Humpty Dumpty still possesses us, but not merely because we love to witness the richly deserved splat of fatuous, self-absorbed authorities; it lives also in the slapstick farce of one's own alienated intellect, bragging of its resourceful brilliance just when it is falling blindly against hard realities.

VII

The White Knight, of course, is Carroll's fantastic, wish-fulfilling self-portrait, but he is also Humpty Dumpty revisited and sentimentalized. This kindly Quixote of whimsy serves the girl child faithfully; that distinguishes him from Humpty and shows how much Carroll valued in himself his imaginative ability to cherish and amuse the child and all she represents. But the knight, like Humpty, spouts nonsense to Alice with bland assurance, uses words any way he wants ("the wind is . . . as strong as soup"), and dabbles in semantic logic, poetry, and impractical ideas. He, too, has a habit of falling, and he shows how ridiculous the Victorian mind-body split could be: "He . . . instantly rolled out of the saddle, and fell headlong into a deep ditch. . . . 'What does it matter where my body happens to be?' he said. 'My mind goes on working all the same'" (303–4).

Unlike Humpty, he is the intellectual seen through the light of amiable humor. His friendly behavior toward Alice means that even mad genius can be domesticated and socialized; it need not always be broken. (Nowadays, his descendants show up in popular comic figures, such as the absent-minded professor, the bumbling idealist, the cheerful visitor from another planet, and the blue-sky dreamer who befriends children.) Actually, the Knight doesn't get hurt falling, because he has no real physical being, no material self. Carroll's thwarted or stunted sexuality may have had something to do with inspiring such a fantasy, but the self-effacing conception of the character exactly fits his function: as the White Knight of Humor, he exists only to amuse others, a personification of comedy. His true quest, like his creator's, is to *be* humorous.

He seems to me the most insular of the book's major comic figures. The influential and revealing American Oz fantasies of Frank Baum feature characters like him, but his spirit flourishes mainly in the English public-school tradition of whimsical nonsense, in the cultivated zaniness of upper-class English families, in writers like Wilde, Beerbohm, Wodehouse, and Waugh, in public figures like the elderly Bertrand Russell and Aldous Huxley, and, generally, in the English tolerance for cranks. The

White Knight, in fact, champions the informal institution of British eccentricity, and the main point of comic eccentricity lies in its effect on others. It makes people realize how daffy life can be, and it reminds them how relatively well adjusted and tolerant they themselves are. But it also lets them glimpse the potential of being free from the tyranny of public opinion and breaking loose into a comic idyll. It can even give them the very dangerous message that they might have a right to be different, even goofy.

VIII

In maudlin moments, Carroll must have seen himself as a comic martyr, or he couldn't have invented the Gnat—a character whose cultural significance seems out of all proportion to his brief appearance. He does not, however, sentimentalize the Gnat, that gloomy little advocate of comic vision. A joke-maker, a punster, and "a dear friend" of Alice, the Gnat has much in common with Carroll; but when the insect sighs himself out of life, Alice moves blithely on, without the slightest regret. One reason is that Carroll's fantasy can leap beyond self-images like the Knight and the Gnat to identify with the child. Another is that he identifies with the sacrificial nature of his comic role and takes pleasure in finding a way to confess what his place is in the world.

The Gnat first speaks little words to Alice in "an extremely small voice." "You might make a joke on that—something about 'horse' and 'hoarse' you know" (219). Next: "You might make a joke on *that* . . . something about 'you *would* if you could' you know" (220). Their encounter ends quickly with the Gnat's humor, lack of confidence, sorrow, and demise:

> "Well, if she said 'Miss,' and didn't say anything more,"
> the Gnat remarked, "of course you'd miss your lessons.
> That's a joke. I wish *you* had made it."
> "Why do you wish *I* had made it?" Alice asked. "It's a
> very bad one."
> But the Gnat only sighed deeply, while two large tears
> came rolling down its cheeks.
> "You shouldn't make jokes," Alice said, "if it makes you
> so unhappy."
> Then came another of those melancholy little sighs, and

this time the poor Gnat really seemed to have sighed itself away, for, when Alice looked up, there was nothing whatever to be seen on the twig, and, as she was getting quite chilly with sitting still so long, she got up and walked on. [224–25]

The comic performance cannot be sustained, and the comic performer cannot save himself; in Carroll's revision of the Cassandra myth, he will never even be honored, but he does contribute something necessary to life, nevertheless. And if we accept the proposition that we cannot do without a comic perspective, then the Gnat is a wacky new kind of hero. If he is an insect who plays on words, makes jokes, and then must perish, so, in a sense is every human being. Kafka's Gregor Samsa and Joyce's H. C. Earwicker show how ready the modern imagination is to identify with insect life, and the reason might be that, in the wake of ebbing faith in personal immortality, the communal, transitory, and metamorphic nature of human existence becomes more and more inescapable.

Carroll's fantasy no doubt expresses such taboo thoughts as "I am an insect who deserves to be crushed," "I am nothing; this girl child is everything," "I'm a mere gnat compared to this favored and whole being," and maybe even "I am an inverted creature whose passion and inner drives can be symbolized by the word 'insect' serving as a cover for the word 'incest.'" (Insect–incest; that transposition is certainly the way Joyce understood Carroll, and he makes this switch central in his dream of humanity, *Finnegans Wake*.) More importantly, the fantasy says, "I am the sacrificial being whose creation of comic modes and whose ability to make up jokes on the brink of death, and to care about their quality, protects the living."

The Gnat is an embryo comic version of the misfit antihero who suffers to create and of those ill-fated modern gadfly clowns who take away—momentarily—the sins of the world. I see his progeny in comics like Chaplin and the self-deprecating Woody Allen, in writers like Wilde, Joyce, and Beckett, in characters like Bloom, Dedalus, Thomas Mann's Tonio Kröger, and Joyce Cary's Gulley Jimson, and even in cartoon figures like Disney's Jimminy Cricket and Charles Schulz's Charlie Brown.

Just in passing, the Gnat asks Alice, "What sort of insects do you rejoice in, where *you* come from?" (221). The question is fantastic, and it somehow epitomizes the art of comedy. To have imagined people rejoicing in the existence of insects seems almost impossible. Fantasy brought the comic reality of these words into being, and they show that fabulous, ridiculous leaps of faith can be made out of our own subjectivity. Their logic says, in effect, I am an insect and rejoice in the life of my kind, and therefore such rejoicing could be universal; since it is possible to rejoice in the existence of even the lower forms of life, it is thus possible to imagine a world where beings rejoice in other kinds of being. This question out of Carroll's dream baldly assumes that man's fate naturally includes rejoicing. When the Gnat poses the question, he is fanning Alice with his "wings." Something in Carroll's mind, I think, was echoing and reshaping Psalm 63:7, "Because Thou hast been my help, therefore in the shadow of Thy wings will I rejoice." If I am right, he is not merely parodying Scripture and God; in his fantasy of reversal he is proclaiming the sacred function of comedy and the despised comic artist in celebrating the mystery of life.

LANGUAGE

So it seems apparent that language is the theme underlying virtually all the episodes of *Through the Looking-Glass.*
Patricia Meyer Spacks[25]

We live in an absurd comic mystery of language, according to Carroll. In the "wood . . . where things have no names" (225), Alice and a Fawn, unable to remember what they're called, come together:

So they walked on together through the wood, Alice with her arms clasped lovingly round the soft neck of the Fawn, till they came out into another open field, and here the Fawn gave a sudden bound into the air, and shook itself free from Alice's arm. "I'm a Fawn!" it cried out in a voice of delight. "And, dear me! you're a human child!" A sudden look of alarm came into its beautiful brown eyes, and in another moment it had darted away at full speed.

Alice stood looking after it, almost ready to cry with

vexation at having lost her dear little fellow-traveler so suddenly. "However, I know my name now, . . . that's *some* comfort. Alice—Alice— . . ." [227]

This little scene may be sentimental, but as a metaphor for the effect of language it works very well. Linguistic power creates that joyous surge of identity and also that knowledge of alienation. Throughout the *Looking-Glass* we find Carroll rediscovering and stressing both the delight and the farce of misunderstanding that are inherent in words. The text renders what we felt as children struggling to master language; it is slippery, confusing, hard, and frustrating but also creative and pleasurable. Carroll's sense of language is very close to Dickens's: we are members of a species separated from all others by a common linguistic nature. Language proves our social being and determines our fate, but it is also our only means for defining and expressing our individuality and subjective freedom. We live by linguistic fictions. In *Looking-Glass* many of the characters act out verbal structures, e.g., Humpty Dumpty, the Tweedles, and even Alice, whose movement conforms exactly to the predictive words of the Red Queen at the beginning. The essence of word patterns, here usually represented by nursery rhymes, controls destiny and determines what happens in each space and square: Humpty must fall, the crow must loom down on the Tweedles, Alice must be crowned, because all must conform to the social conventions and inherent conditions of language.

I

In trying to replace a divine comedy with a credible human comedy, many modern writers and thinkers have fixed on language. Quest for meaning and permanence has focused on speech and writing as signifying agents and evidence of a kind of immortality: language endures, and, by studying it, one can find meaning and make some sense of life. Literature, linguistics, philosophy, logic, semiotics, and other semantic disciplines become the new theology. Carroll helped to lead in making language a great comic subject for thought and literature, but for him it is nothing to be idealized. It can never be a precise communications system because it is inseparable from its users. Alice's comment on "The Jabberwocky," "Somehow it seems to fill my head with ideas—only I don't exactly know what they are!" (197), describes his sense of language perfectly, provided that we stress that "exactly" and still keep in mind the bizarre richness of those "ideas." The whole book supports Freud's dictum that "Usage of language is unreliable and is itself in need of examination for its authority."[26]

Carroll makes language a more explicit theme in *Looking-Glass* than in *Wonderland,* and, since he links the fate of his characters to preexisting linguistic structures, its world is a more deterministic one than *Wonderland*'s. One reason why the sense of the involuntary seems so much stronger in the second book has to do with the inevitable repeating of patterns in the story—patterns that the "arbitrary universe" of language controls. "Repeat" is one of the key words in *Looking-Glass*. Carroll almost invariably uses it whenever Alice recites poetry or has it recited to her: e.g., "What shall I repeat to her?" says Tweedledee (233); "Who's been repeating all that hard stuff to you?" (272). Carroll stresses that language is repetition. Even poetry, the traditional institution for sublime personal expression, becomes a process of repetition, and this emphasis on the repetitive nature of language and life also shows why there is such a strong desire to break free of linguistic convention and assert personal will over language—even if that will or mastery is almost entirely illusory.

From the first, Carroll tells us that Alice moves in a dream world composed of words that exist independently of personal will. When the White King exclaims of his pencil, "it writes all manner of things that I don't intend" (190), he is talking about the unmanageable nature of language and previewing its role. And, almost immediately, "Jabberwocky" appears to Alice, proclaiming, in effect, that we are in a fictional world of absurdity and wordplay:

> 'Twas brillig, and the slithy toves
> Did gyre and gimble in the wabe:
> All mimsy were the borogoves,
> And the mome raths outgrabe.
> [191]

The poem foreshadows *Through the Looking-Glass*. The extreme tensions in the verse—between the unconventional use of language (invented vocabulary) and the conventional (normal syntax, grammar, rhythm, and rhyme), between referential significance and self-contained nonsense, between order and disorder—define and energize the whole book. "Jabberwocky" mocks such things as the pretensions of poetry, pompous bards, and the sentimentalization of primitivism and violence, but its comic impact comes mainly from the liberties it takes with words. It makes us focus on the *fact* of language itself, whose very existence is just as marvelous as any meanings it conveys.

The comic success and pleasure of "Jabberwocky" would seem to come from its rebellious daring in defying early taboos against free expression, balanced with the sense of mastery of language that the form of its poetry shows.[27] Humpty Dumpty, whom Alice later asks to explain the poem, makes clear the sources of the comic effects and, hence, of Carroll's linguistic comedy as a whole. Humpty arrogantly ascribes his own precise and absolute meaning to what has no objective, impersonal, unambiguous meaning. Words are suggestive: they play on the subjective imagination, and they also feed the deep human need for order and meaning that shows in the mind's propensity to construct from words fictions that make sense. The teasing of nuance and meaning from a nonsense word is only an extreme example of the sort of thing going on all the time: "Well, *'slithy'* means 'lithe and slimy.' 'Lithe' is the same as 'active.' You see it's like a portmanteau—there are two meanings packed up into one word" (271).

II

Humpty's phenomenon, the semantic portmanteau, has profound implications. Not only is it the brick from which Joyce would try to build his Tower of Babel, *Finnegans Wake;* it also indicates the whole modern tendency to apotheosize language as the structure in which all human significance and value exist. The power of God, for Humpty and his spiritual progeny, becomes the potential of the word. When he so eagerly analyzes the concentrations of multiple meaning in a single word, we have a comic preview of the secularization of exegesis and the canonization of literary texts that we find in twentieth-century schools of criticism and semantic study. The use and popularity of terms like "new criticism," "verbal icons," "seven kinds of ambiguity," "the Geneva School," "hermeneutics," and "structuralism," for example, suggest both a reverential interest in linguistic meaning and a shift of religious awe and wonder away from traditional theological subjects toward language. Humpty in his bumptious way shows how literal the search for meaning in life can become, and we can see the portmanteau word itself as a comic verbal icon of our intense concern with signification. "Portmanteau" may stand for comic language and nonsense, but it also may signify the obsessive human drive to gather vast quantities of meaning together and then compress them and store them economically in such things as fetishes, totems, myths, deities, jokes, books, puns, computer systems, and professional comedians.

The configuration of "Humpty Dumpty" symbolizes perfectly Carroll's understanding of life and language: the basic "deep" structure of linguistic ability that defines our species—i.e., the nursery-rhyme "Humpty Dumpty"—predetermines and limits the possible range of human experience; but within this structure there is room for the play of the individual linguistic imagination with words—i.e., Carroll's rendering of Humpty—in order to create a unique and richly significant version of a general fate. The *Looking-Glass* Humpty is himself a portmanteau figure who combines his Mother Goose identity with a farcical reincarnation of a Tower of Babel builder and his fate.

> "When *I* use a word," Humpty Dumpty said, in a rather scornful tone, "it means just what I choose it to mean—neither more nor less."
> "The question is," said Alice, "whether you *can* make words mean so many different things."
> "The question is," said Humpty Dumpty, "which is to be master—that's all." [269]

Alice senses rightly the fallacy in Humpty's logic: no one has the power to make other people accept all his arbitrary meanings for words; no single person *can* so "master" language: suppose this self-proclaimed "master" of language were to "choose" that the word "fall"—as in "Humpty Dumpty had a great fall"—should mean "soar": he still could not keep from cracking up. To make language and meaning uniform and to control them would be to have the absolute authority of a supernatural tyrant and to destroy human individuality. Each person has a separate verbal imagination, and no one can be a God of language. Language, however, confers a kind of immortality—Humpty Dumpty lives in the thoughts, mouths, and books of others—though its workings defeat immutability. Linguistic usage, innately loose, has a lot of "play" in it.

Almost all the characters Alice meets are glib semantic dogmatists, muddled victims of linguistic misunderstandings, or both. The Red Queen, refusing to let Alice correct herself, says, "when you've once said a thing, that fixes it, and you must take the consequences" (323). But language can never be exactly fixed or objectified. Its "consequences" flow subjectively for everybody, everywhere, and it drives the authoritarian mind into spasms of imperative and interrogative nonsense: the Red Queen shouts, "Always speak the truth—think before you speak—and write it down afterwards." (319); and "Do you know Languages? What's the French for fiddle-de-dee?" (323). Until all word-users are made precisely the same, language can never be made perfectly logical and standard, nor can it ever be exclusively private property. Linguistic uniformity and quantifiability are fantasies.

The Gnat speaks out for a hedonistic attitude toward language. Unlike Humpty and the Red Queen, who regard it as something to be mastered and worked, he treats it as something merely to play with, as his ancestor, Aesop's Grasshopper, treats life. It's all puns, jokes, and wit for him. He even perishes of a pun, losing "sighs," i.e., "size," until he disappears. When Alice tells him that she knows the names of some insects but that they don't answer to their names, he says:

> "What's the use of their having names . . .?"
> "No use to *them,*" said Alice; "but it's useful to the people that name them, I suppose. If not, why do things have names at all?"
> "I can't say," the Gnat replied. [222]

Alice, eminently sensible as usual, points out that language, imprecise as it is, does have its pragmatic triumphs.

It overwhelms the White King and Queen, who take it literally and can hardly ever comprehend words and phrases whose meanings, being multiple, depend upon the particular context in which they are used:

286

"I beg your pardon?" said Alice.
"It isn't respectable to beg," said the King. [280]

"Am I addressing the White Queen?"
"Well, yes, if you call that a-dressing," the Queen said.
...."It would have been all the better...if she had got some one else to dress her." [245–46]

Beings who have no sense of the flexibility of words are liable to lose touch with reality and wind up in the soup: "the Queen's...face...disappeared into the soup" (335).

Arbitrary and absurd though it may be, the involuntary nature of language can have very serious consequences. When Alice is introduced to Haigha, we get this: "'I love my love with an H,' Alice couldn't help beginning, 'because he is Happy. I hate him with an H because he is Hideous. I fed him with—with—with Ham-sandwiches and Hay. His name is Haigha, and he lives—'" (279). This wordplay parodies the parlor game "I love my love with an A"; but by calling attention to the confusion of pronunciation between A and H, a linguistic sign that identifies social class and life-style in Britain, it really does point out the huge importance of something as silly as a little matter of pronunciation.

For Humpty Dumpty, words are "hands": "I can manage the whole lot of them"; for the Gnat they are clowns. However, both are wrong: language is neither all work and no play, nor all play and no work.

III

Carroll's comedy of language flashes brightest in dialogue, at which he, like Austen and Trollope, is an expert. In their whirling talk, the characters hardly communicate at all with each other, but they make clear to readers the kinds of nonsense and absurdities that characterize our speech. Conversation best represents for Carroll the verbal energy of the race because he finds language to be the amorphous sum of many voices and of listeners interpreting and misinterpreting these voices. The breathless quality of the dialogue reflects the animation of his whole world, where everything from bugs to mirrors can give and receive word messages. Coming out of her dream, Alice remarks to her kitty, who once spoke as the articulate Red

Queen but now only purrs monotonously, "how *can* you talk with a person if they *always* say the same thing?" (341). The major point here is that predictable utterance is finally boring and, in fact, not human, for people never *do* say or mean exactly the same thing.

A good way to appreciate Carroll's sense of language, which he imagines both fixes us and sends us speeding in innumerable directions, is to look at his use of the word *fast*. Humpty Dumpty describes the urgency that his words convey when he says, "this conversation is going on a little too fast: let's go back to the last remark but one" (265). Carroll says, in the prefatory poem, that against "the raving blast" (of horror, old age, and death) "the magic words shall hold thee fast"—and "fast" turns out to mean not only *rapt* and *motionless* but, because words *are* magic and can do opposite things at the same time, also to connote "suddenly" and even "in a state of acceleration," thus describing the effect of *Through the Looking-Glass* on our minds. The White Knight tells Alice about getting stuck in a helmet:

> "I was as fast as—as lightning, you know."
> "But that's a different kind of fastness," Alice objected.
> The Knight shook his head. "It was all kinds of fastness with me, I can assure you!" [303]

Absurd and wonderful words play with us and hold us, like the Knight, in all kinds of fastness.

PLAY, NONSENSE, AND GAMES: COMIC DIVERSION

Carroll stands by the pervasiveness and humanity of play.
Kathleen Blake[28]

The spirit of play predominates in Carroll's comedy. He is *Homo ludens* asserting his right to divert himself and seek pleasure for its own sake. *Through the Looking-Glass* presents a strategy for mastering experience through play, nonsense, and games. They are modes for temporarily changing and controlling reality, but they also become ways of reflecting and criticizing the arbitrariness and absurdities of life. Something in Carroll and in much of modern comedy says that life is so absurd that only play can illuminate it or make it mean anything worthwhile. Needing to disarm to get a hearing, he offers comic play as a harmless interlude; but, as it does in so many modern writers, it defies the inhibiting social and natural order and flouts the oppressive work of others. Comic play asserts the personal freedom to change mood and perspective. It incorporates time and space into elaborate and shifting games.

I

Diversion, with its sense of pleasing distraction, seems the perfect word for Carroll's play. He begins by offering to divert us from the summons of death—"Come, harken then, ere voice of dread / With bitter tidings laden, / Shall summon" (173)—and then goes on to subordinate death, pride, madness, power, language, chaos, himself, his characters, his readers, "reality," and even his God to his play. He manipulates, for his own amusement, whatever seems threatening. Continually improvising, he makes a comic game of anything, and by doing so he exposes the games of others that set limits on human liberty.

His verbal play and nonsense are full of rebelliousness. "Jabberwocky," as we have seen, expresses a longing to break through conventional language and get to a state of free utterance. One impulse behind it is the implied protest: "I do not have to make sense; I can say anything I like, any way I like." Another is, "I can construct my own language and style for others to decipher." The test for artistic success in nonsense language is whether it suggests pleasing connotations that an audience will be motivated to discover and itself manipulate. That means that it must maintain a poise between mere gibberish and common usage.[29] Carroll's nonsense generally manages to let us experience language as something full of opportunities for play and exhilarating freedom. "O frabjous day! Callooh! Callay!" (197). "Then fill up the glasses as quick as you can, / And sprinkle the table with buttons and bran: / Put cats in the coffee, and mice in the tea— / And welcome Queen Alice with thirty-times-three!" (329). That sort of thing diverts us by breaking down our conventional expectations and drawing our attention, for many reasons, to the joy that we can find in words. We, like the author, play with his language.

But there is an equally strong hostile impulse in

289

nonsense—the desire to satirize the senselessness of the world. The Red Queen sums it up: "You may call it 'nonsense' if you like . . . but *I've* heard nonsense, compared with which that would be as sensible as a dictionary!" (207). As usual in Carroll, what at first seems self-enclosed is, in another light, mimetic and referential. The nonsense poem "A-sitting on a Gate" says in effect that there are things in Wordsworth's "Resolution and Independence" just as absurd as anything the White Knight can devise. Look at these lines:

> His accents mild took up the tale:
> He said "I go my ways,
> And when I find a mountain-rill,
> I set it in a blaze;
> And thence they make a stuff they call
> Rowland's Macassar-Oil—
> Yet twopence-halfpenny is all
> They give me for my toil."
>
> But I was thinking of a way
> To feed oneself on batter,
> And so go on from day to day
> Getting a little fatter.
> I shook him well from side to side,
> Until his face was blue:
> "Come, tell me how you live," I cried,
> "And what it is you do!"
>
> [311]

The verse works in two ways: Its vision is so crazy that we don't have to take it seriously, and it frees us of the pressures and responsibilities of our usual mental life. Nothing can keep the poem's speaker (the White Knight) from trying to invent schemes that no one would have any reason to conceive, and just this motiveless originality taps some source of anarchic sympathy in us. That is the nontendentious side of nonsense. On the other hand, the "aged man" plans and acts in ways just as zany as the Knight's, even if he does so to get paid. Macassar oil really did exist—for greasing hair; and a world that used it must have been as nonsensical as any that could be devised by an author. And the parody of Wordsworth's leech-gatherer seems even more powerful now than in the nineteenth century: what could be more foolish than paying money for leeches to suck sick people's blood? Carroll plays here with literature and language: with himself, in the guise of the nonsense-loving solipsistic White Knight, with the farce of mutually misunderstanding minds, with vocation, and with the queer arbitrariness that calls Rowland's Macassar Oil and leeches sensible and "The Jabberwocky" nonsense. Therefore, the lines also imply: "I write nonsense because nonsense is reality."

II

The way of the *Looking-Glass* world is constant diversion. It turns all sorts of subjects into games that can be played, often simultaneously, and mastered through comedy—e.g., philosophy, semantics, and religion. One of the most important is the mirror game, whose main rule is reversal, i.e., literally considering things from the very opposite of the conventional point of view. All of Carroll's games, however, tend to be fluid, as befits a dream game, rather than fixed and rigid.

He structures the book on the model of a chess sequence, which he controls, and the implications of the game matter a great deal. In his parody of Huxley's universal game, he is the sole player. He accepts the analogy of life to chess but makes it clear that his game, though it usually conforms to chess rules, is a loose, sliding contest ("The *alternation* of Red and White is perhaps not so strictly observed as it might be," says Carroll [Preface:171]; and some of the characters move like chessmen, but some do not). This fussy man of exactitude and logic always notices and insists on the innate sloppiness and imprecision of being. A game, however, does serve nicely to point up the inscrutable, arbitrary nature of things. Carroll's play and game contribute to the insights of modern game theory, which, as Kathleen Blake says, "helps to reveal the literally artificial nature of our mental universes."[30] Games, like language, depend on agreed-upon conventions; but conventions do shift, and people may not be playing the same game by the same rules: in Huxley's chess match, the game of life is played between each person and a supreme being who enforces the fixed laws of nature. In *Through the Looking-Glass,* with the authoritarian, Huxley-like Red (the Red Queen) versus mild-mannered Carrollian White (Alice as White pawn; the White Knight), Carroll rigs it so that White wins. He moves his characters about as if he

291

were omnipotent and makes the game subservient to himself, the player. It provides the framework for the action, but he ignores its status when he wishes; for example, when the Red Queen puts the White King in check, nothing happens.

The chess game is diversion—one more element of Carroll's play, but not usually the primary focus of attention. Its climax, however, *is* crucial and makes for Carroll's version of a happy ending. According to the chess plan, Alice actually wins the match for her side: her sudden move, upsetting the Queen's banquet, eliminates the Red Queen and puts the Red King in checkmate. *The child takes the power.* All these pieces are counters in their author's game. If the Red King in some sense stands for God, as the Tweedles' discussion with Alice indicates, and if Carroll identifies with Alice, then the structure of the game and the plot, as well as the thought and humor of the book, show the child winning out over God, Carroll winning out over the Reverend Mr. Dodgson, and comic regression and reversal winning out over orthodox religion.

The business about the Red King in the Tweedle chapter makes us see the kind of game Carroll was capable of playing with us and, oddly enough, with himself. When Tweedledum and Dee talk of the Red King's dream, they parody Bishop Berkeley's view that all material objects are only "'sorts of things' in the mind of God."[31] In fact, I think Carroll means to associate the Tweedles particularly with Berkeley, who, after all, wrote *Siris,* a tract that began as a disquisition on "tar-water." The monstrous crow of the nursery rhyme, "as black as a tar-barrel," along with the Tweedle travesty of idealism, makes the identification likely. I think, also, that the Tweedles may represent bishops in the chess game; bishops are the only pieces that Carroll fails to mention directly or put on the board, and their absence would be glaring to a gamesman like himself.

It is all very strange but revealing: the author fears to put the word "bishop" in his story, rails elsewhere at looking "at solemn things in a spirit of mockery," yet somehow manages to make God a shabby plaything, whose defeat ends the game happily. To understand the Carroll of *Looking-Glass,* we must see that he not only could and would play with what a part of him held to be most serious and sacred, he would also play with the side of his own consciousness that made a subject taboo for comedy. He will sacrifice anything to his own play here—even the Reverend Charles Dodgson and God—because only the ability to play, in this text, can subject the chaos of reality and the disappointments of life to personal will.

Play, as such games-playing modern authors as Joyce, Nabokov, Borges, and Garcia Marquez attest, is a way of establishing order for the self in the midst of an absurd universe and of asserting one's own unconquered free spirit. Elizabeth Sewell, looking at Carroll from the point of view of an orthodox believer in God, writes: "If Carroll is to play with the whole of . . . life, always to be in control of it as a player must be, and as none other can, then he must be his own God."[32] He usurps the right of deity to play with all creation, and his desperate faith is that he can game and jest with anything, even his doubts.

For upon doubt Carroll builds his *Looking-Glass* house. One important difference between *Wonderland* and this book is that *Through the Looking-Glass* ends with questions rather than assertions: "Which do *you* think it was?" and "Life, what is it but a dream?" In this world, nothing is sure. Such doubt requires diversion and sets the wild comic imagination loose to play with senselessness and folly, which seem to be everywhere. "You might make a joke on *that*" (220) and "Consider anything, only don't cry" (250) are the humble twin commandments of Carroll's comic faith.

9

JOYCE'S *FINNEGANS WAKE* (1924–39)

The Comic Gospel of "Shem"[1]

He saw himself as the *Vates,* the poet and prophet, and his work
as the sacred book of a new religion of which he was the prophet
and priest.

James Atherton[2]

Don't you think . . . there is a certain resemblance between the
mystery of the Mass and what I am trying to do?

James Joyce[3]

James Joyce is a comic writer who fully intends his comedy to
function as religion. In *Ulysses* and in *Finnegans Wake* he tries to
adapt the religious impulses of humanity and the urge for sacred
vocation that he felt within himself to the secular, profane,
matter-of-fact world that history—especially nineteenth-
century history—had bequeathed to the twentieth century. Vivian Mercier has shown how Joyce's anticlerical comedy reflects
oral and cultural traditions of Irish humor, wit, and parody.[4] If,
however, we are to put into proper perspective both his writing
and the achievement of a whole century's best comic novelists,
we must also see and stress his relationship to such major
British comic writers as Dickens, Thackeray, Meredith, and
Carroll. His work features and makes unmistakably clear the
tendencies in nineteenth-century British comic fiction to
criticize and undermine the dogma and institutions of religion
and to put faith in the very existence of comic perspective itself.

Comedy, for Joyce, becomes a new gospel. He expressly rejected the priesthood of the Roman Catholic Church to become
"a priest of eternal imagination,"[5] but that imagination is emphatically comic. To him, the sacred is ridiculous, the ridiculous
is sacred, and both are inseparable. "Comedy," says Richard
Ellmann, "was his true mode";[6] it could embody his creed and
faith. Joyce wants his comic art to be a new catholicism, one
that gets rid of the supernatural, hierarchical, and solemn clap-

294

trap of the Church. He tries, in *Finnegans Wake,* to create a comic Bible. That book offers, in its joking, punning way, knowledge and understanding of all things first to last, promise of aggregate immortality, reconciliation to personal fate, and the experience of holy mystery. It seeks to represent the blending of the particular and the universal, that is, the connections and union between any individual and the rest of humanity, history, and nature. It presents a miraculous sense of humor that can transform, mock, and consecrate almost anything. To Joyce, shit is as sacred as Scripture: according to the *Wake,* each is ineluctably linked to the other, each is ridiculous, and each is deserving of reverence. Scatological eschatology and "pornosophical philotheology"[7] describe the content of the *Wake* and its author's sense of reality.

I

I choose to focus on the "Shem" section of *Finnegans Wake* (Book I, section 7, pp. 169–95) for several reasons. It is, in itself, a comic masterpiece and ought to be better known.[8] It contains the essence of Joyce's comic feeling for the world, and it epitomizes his art as he developed it in the early twentieth century. A short, relatively accessible part of this painfully difficult, neglected, and magnificent book, it illuminates the *Wake*'s vision and meanings. It is also as revealing as anything Joyce ever wrote about his own life, and, moreover, in it he deals directly with all of the themes and motives in the fiction I have discussed. The antiauthoritarian, playful tenor of his later writing, its tremendous scope, its impetus to break free of repression, its satire, its experiments with parody, language, and style, its stress on human communion and on union with nature, and its surprising tolerance, all have precedent in the great comic tradition of the preceding century.

"Shem" is both a farcical portrait of an artist as a ridiculous man and the clownish odyssey of mental and physical wandering from Dublin to Paris to Trieste, from Eden to Dublin, from birth to death and resurrection, from condemnation to redemption, from genesis to revelation, from era to era, from civilization to civilization, from dream stage to dream stage. Like the whole *Wake,* it is the story and vision of a Humpty-Dante,[9] a universal, human—not divine—comedy, telling of a momentous but fortunate and very funny fall. In Joyce, the inferno, purgatory, and paradise are simultaneous, omnipresent, and inseparable.

The chapter consists mainly of a hostile account of the disgraceful career of Shem by his enemy, elsewhere identified as his brother Shaun. The prose weaves together invective and insult directed at this composite character, who is simultaneously James Joyce, Satan, minor devils, persecuted martyrs, various fratricides, outcast shaman figures from different cultures, and low-life nonconformists generally. Much of the abuse is made up of pastiches and parodies based on derogatory reviews of Joyce's books and the remarks and deeds of those who acted toward him with enmity. Shem is an exile, a heretic, a bohemian, a plagiarist, a fornicator, and a fetishist who smells, shirks, refuses to get married, and has delusions of grandeur. According to Shaun, he commits all seven deadly sins and breaks each of the Ten Commandments. He makes ink from his own excreta, writes over his own body, goes whoring, falls into trouble with the law, and finally gets arrested. At this point in the text the accusing narrator turns into "JUSTIUS" (187.24), a composite Inquisitor, confessor, prosecutor, judge, and jury. He abandons his third-person exposition to address Shem directly, continuing the case against him until he finally condemns him as "mad"; Justius then "points the deathbone and the quick are still" (194.28, 29). "MERCIUS," the Shem figure, at last speaks one of the more resonant sentences in literature, and in it the identities of himself and his brother somehow merge, and the voice of his mother, as well, speaks through his consciousness. This voice transforms itself into the expression of the running headwaters of the Liffey River. Mercius then "lifts the lifewand and the dumb speak," and the chapter closes with the babbling-brook word "Quoiquoiquoiquoiquoiquoiquoiq!" (195.5, 6).

II

My summary drastically oversimplifies the text, but it may help to show how "Shem" typifies Joycean comedy. The chapter gives us good news. It moves from banality, solipsistic isolation, and comic abasement through a torrent of abuse to regeneration, flow, and eloquence. It has the sort of comic pattern that we find repeatedly in parts of *Ulysses* and the *Wake* as well as in each book as a whole. The spiteful, combative tone shifts to a mood of ambiguous acceptance, equanimity, and even play, and the future is assured (though we are taught not to hope too much from it).

The young Joyce, calling comedy "the perfect manner in art,"[10] theorized that proper comedy leaves us with a feeling of joy, a joy that arises from the possession of some good. An aesthetic feeling of joy does predominate at the end of "Shem"—and of all of *Finnegans Wake* too—because Joyce stresses that we do sometimes possess language, love, and laughter. This sacred trinity preserves human life and can make it at times valuable and beautiful as well as diverting.

In the perspective of Joyce's major work, however, beauty and goodness can emerge in people only when their lives have been subjected to mockery. They must undergo a comic Calvary of ridicule; otherwise the sham of sentimentality and pride will distort the truth, and without truth art is worthless. A view of life that does not see foolishness in everyone—including the viewer—is unrealistic and fragmentary. Gravity, not levity, pulls everything down. Stephen Dedalus writes nothing of value, but Shem, who is mocked and satirized as thoroughly as any character in fiction, has the power to lift a pen and give a voice to the world. The Joyce of "Shem" and the *Wake,* understanding the farce and folly of his own life, can articulate mercy and sympathy for the ridiculous world and feel his communion with it.

Mockery also shows the power of discrimination and perspective, which allows the individual mind to imagine and judge something as ridiculous. Though we are the products of collective creation, we must perceive life through the self, and the self will always find experience imperfect. Part of each of us has a quarrel with the world and deeply resents our relative powerlessness in it. Refusing to recognize that side of our nature and deal with it can lead to repression and its terrible consequences, as all history, both social and personal, shows. Any conception of life that does not allow a role or outlet for aggressive, bitter humor, wrongheaded though it may be, perverts human nature and invites exploitation by self-seeking authority. Comic ridicule may be disreputable, and reflect discontent, but it can work against totalitarian thought control and energize and democratize life; it shows a defiant drive by the thwarted ego for pleasure and freedom.

Joyce has a genuine reverence for life, but real piety, for him, includes giving the horselaugh to what anyone considers sacrosanct, including himself. Proper reverence includes a sense of the ridiculous. The mocker—e.g., Shaun, Buck Mulligan, the nameless narrator of "Cyclops" in *Ulysses,* Shem at times—plays a necessary if unsympathetic role in *Ulysses* and the *Wake;* Joyce had to learn to incorporate him into his art before it could have the wholeness, harmony, and radiance that he aspired to.

III

Whatever is most beautiful and estimable Joyce grounds in absurdity and "lowness" (170.25). Shem creates immortality and radiance out of his own excrement. Therefore, not only is immortality a kind of joke, but excrement and anuses are part of an immortal comedy. Joyce's supposed cloacal obsession works to integrate digestive and sexual processes into our total picture of life and to make it clear that we all share the destiny of bodily existence and need not be ashamed of our low nature. The power that gives speech and writing to the world develops out of a "perfect lowness" (174.36). "Shem was a sham," says Shaun, "and a low sham and his lowness creeped out first via foodstuffs" (170.25). Moreover, on puns, the proverbial "lowest form of humor," Joyce builds his faith.

This embracing of "lowness" has, in fact, many of the revolutionary implications of Christianity. His comedy, like the New Testament, disdains worldly success and honor. Creating heroes like Bloom and Shem comes from the same kind of thinking that holds that the first shall be last, the last shall be first, the meek shall inherit the earth, and the truth shall make you free. The broadening of human sympathy that *Ulysses* and *Finnegans Wake* enact relates directly to the Christian belief that deems every soul important. Figures like Bloom, Molly, HCE, ALP, and Shem are genuinely heroic because they face up to truth about themselves with remarkable courage and honesty; but even this honesty seems to grow out of a deepening and development of the traditional Catholic practice of confession. Joyce rejects theology, God, the Church, and condemnation of the flesh, but he accepts a humanization of Christian ethics and values and undertakes the religious responsibility to try to mediate and reconcile personal fate and the universal order of things. Artistic and religious goals converge when Shem-

Mercius, at the end of the chapter, causes the dumb to speak. That orphic miracle of resurrection is the heart of Joyce's comic faith.

IV

All the themes of the *Wake* and, indeed, of all of Joyce's other works appear and reappear in the arabesque prose of "Shem," but what makes it most typical of Joyce and his comedy is its dialectical and metamorphic quality. Readers of *Ulysses* know how Joyce's comic dialectic works: juxtaposed polarities (e.g., Bloom vs. Stephen, Bloom vs. Dubliners, Cyclopean giganti- cism vs. Cyclopean myopia, Gerty Macdowell's popular-press prose vs. Bloom's uncensored stream of consciousness) create marvelous absurdities, incongruous images, resonating ener- gies, and multiple perspectives. Shem and Shaun are the quin- tessential comic opposites, reverberating as significantly as Yin and Yang or cerebral bipolarity. They create each other, play off of each other, speak recognizably for and to different sides in ourselves, in the contemporary world, in all history; and out of the implied tension between these mythic figures and their world views comes Joyce's comic vision.

More important even than the Joycean dialectic, but joined to it, is his protean sense of life. Something is always in the process of becoming something else: words turn into other words, meanings become other meanings, people, places, and times become other people, places, and times. Voices, ele- ments, and language are constantly changing and flowing. One of Joyce's names in the *Wake* for the whole circulating, recycl- ing, evolving, dreamlike nature of being is "collideorscape" (143.28). The term connotes the ever-changing patterns of a totality that must, however, be held and perceived by an indi- vidual; it also suggests shifting upheavals of landscape, unity of opposites, noisy crashes, the hazards of life, the continual fu- sions and disintegrations of images, and the infinite malleability of language. It captures perfectly the crux of the protean com- edy of *Finnegans Wake.*

299

PROTEAN IMAGINATION AND FORM

After all, he said to Frank Budgen, "The Holy Roman Catholic
Apostolic Church was built on a pun. It ought to be good enough
for me."

Richard Ellmann[11]

"Never was a man like you, Willoughby, for shaking new patterns
in a kaleidoscope."

George Meredith[12]

Proteus, King of Flux, fascinated Joyce. The myth of the shifty
old man of the sea told him how hard it is to find and hold onto
any meaning and permanence when mind and matter alter
shape so fast. In the "Proteus" episode of *Ulysses,* Joyce gives us
Stephen Dedalus's consciousness, racing hot with energy as he
visits the sea but as yet unable to give form to the whirl of his
brilliant imagination. The contrast between the richness of his
flying thoughts and his artistic production in the chapter—a
callow, pompous, four-line poem, which Joyce compares to a
piece of snot—makes clear that Stephen cannot yet hold Proteus and discover his secret. But bound by the proper art and
form, Proteus might convey the magic of transubstantiation,
which he embodies, and tell us, as he told Menelaus, that we are
"not ordained to die."[13]

In the *Wake* and "Shem," Joyce both animates and controls
the protean imagination by fitting it into his comprehensive
comic "collideorscape," a dream vision embracing the whole
world, and by expressing it in a language of puns and all-
engulfing sentences. He develops the "kaleidoscope" of
Meredith's comic spirit and Carroll's verbal portmanteau to impose a form that seeks both to represent and to contain the
power of Proteus. The pun, one word holding diverse meanings, is a model and a metaphor, showing how things may be
simultaneously discrete and unified, changing and yet the same.
And the kaleidoscope, a revolving instrument of continually
evolving patterns, shows how mutability may be held in a fixed
structure of finitely combining matter.[14]

I

"Shem" begins with names, a verbal comparison making connections with sound, and the comic potential of language:
"Shem is as short for Shemus as Jem is joky for Jacob" (169.1).

In our linguistic realm of being, the word is protean: one name, one idea, one sound suggests others. *Shem* can remind us of James Joyce ("Jem"), of Jacob the Patriarch, of one who *shames* us, of Jacobites and Jacobins, rebellious followers of dangerous and losing causes. Joyce, like Dickens, finds in a name cultural and personal history and first evidence of the inevitably metaphorical nature of life. Names, like jokes, condense and release huge configurations of meaning. The opening of "Shem" resembles strikingly the first chapter of *Martin Chuzzlewit,* which Joyce seems to have known well. He uses not only ideas and themes of Dickens's preface but also specific names, such as "Humphrey" (30. 2) and William the Conqueror ("William the Conk" [31.14]). Both Dickens and Joyce insist on linking biological and etymological heritages. Each relates his particular characters to the farcical story of the whole human race, which they both see as philological comedy, featuring the inherent jokiness and protean shape of language. In the *Wake* as in *Chuzzlewit,* wordplay makes history, funny names make up the family of man, and the expression of language forms the pattern of life.

The second sentence of "Shem" mocks class and lineal pride and makes the bestial Cain-like heritage of Joycean man apparent: "A few toughnecks are still getatable who pretend that aboriginally he was of respectable stemming (he was an outlex between the lines of Ragonar Blaubarb and Horrild Hairwire and an inlaw to Capt. the Hon. and Rev. Mr. Bbyrdwood de Trop Blogg was among his distant connections) but every honest to goodness man in the land of the space of today knows that his back life will not stand being written about in black and white" (169.1–10).[15] The past, which comes to us primarily through language, is part of the present, and we are generated not only out of bloodlines but also out of those impulses, messages, and vital utterances that are implied "between the lines" of everything that has been written and read. Shem-Jem Joyce is created from the line of Adam and Cain and from that of his father, John Joyce ("de Trop Blogg" refers to him), but he also comes out of the comic line of Dickens and of Lewis Carroll. It is no accident that echoes of these masters of comic expression and comic regression appear often in the first two pages of "Shem."[16] Like Jacob and Cain, they helped to form the protean Joyce and his *Wake*. "Getatable" and "Horrild Hairwire" joke about Cain and Harold Hairfoot, king of the Saxons, but they also punningly include Dodgson-Carroll and his strange, outlawed, semiincestuous yearnings and his daring comedy of regression, which so deeply affected Joyce. Look at this teasing passage from the famous child actress Isa Bowman's coy reminiscences of Carroll:

> And if the broken pieces had been get-at-able, he would have made me count them as a means of impressing on my mind the folly of needless exaggeration.
>
> I remember how annoyed he was once when, after a morning's sea bathing...I exclaimed, "Oh this salt water, it always makes my hair as stiff as a poker."
>
> He impressed it on me quite irritably that no little girl's hair could ever possibly get as stiff as a poker. "If you had said, 'as stiff as wires,' it would have been more like it. . . ."
>
> And then, seeing that I was a little frightened, he drew for me a picture of "The little girl called Isa whose hair turned into pokers because she was always exaggerating things."[17]

"Between" these "lines" Joyce seems to have found a progenitor, *double-entendre,* sexual guilt, and the insistent snigger that all pride sooner or later draws.

A man, Joyce writes, is a "hybrid," a protean being; Shem gets formed by "putting truth and untruth together" (169.8, 9). His language tries to accommodate and express that hybrid human condition of fact and fiction, flesh and collective consciousness. The next paragraph features Shem's wordpower and the development of metaphor out of his own body. We are "at the very dawn of protohistory" (169.21), meaning that his history, like all personal histories, is prototypical and that all history is protean. Vico writes that "in all languages the greater part of the expressions relating to inanimate things are [sic] formed by metaphor from the human body and its parts and from the human senses and passions."[18] Metaphor, the life-blood and motion of the mind, begins with the body; Joyce accepts this but, as usual, sees the humor in it:

> Shem's bodily getup, it seems, included an adze of a skull, . . . the whoel of a nose, . . . the wrong shoulder higher than the right, all ears, an artificial tongue with a natural curl, not a foot to stand on, a handful of thumbs, a

blind stomach, a deaf heart, a loose liver, two fifths of two buttocks . . . a manroot of all evil, . . . a bladder tristended. [169.11–20]

This combines Joyce's self-pity for his failing body, his epithet on his own art ("an artificial tongue with a natural curl"), a theory of the sexual nature of original sin ("manroot of all evil"), with the central puns expressing how our physical being shapes language and how our connecting powers of metaphor extend our will and bodily functions into the inanimate matter from which we make our tools. Imagination transforms one thing into another and then into abstractions.

II

Finnegans Wake is a book of changes fixed by ink, but the original ink of Shem's comes, like everything else, from the body. "Shem was a sham and a low sham and his lowness creeped out first via foodstuffs" (170.25, 26). Linguistic process is like digestive process. Consciousness is protean: it includes physical, mental, and creative processes, writing and reading processes. People, language, and matter are constantly metamorphosing into one another. In one of the most exuberant passages in the *Wake,* Shaun takes inventory of "the house O'Shea or O'Shame . . . known as the Haunted Inkbottle" (182.32, 33), where Shem dwells:

My wud! The warped flooring of the lair and soundconducting walls thereof, to say nothing of the uprights and imposts, were persianly literatured with burst loveletters, telltale stories, . . . alphybettyformed verbage, vivlical viasses, ompiter dictas, visus umbique, ahems and ahahs, imeffible tries at speech unasyllabled, you owe mes, eyoldhyms, fluefoul smut, fallen lucifers, vestas which had served, showered ornaments, borrowed brogues, reversibles jackets, blackeye lenses, family jars, falsehair shirts, Godforsaken scapulars, neverworn breeches, cutthroat ties, counterfeit franks, best intentions, curried notes, upset latten tintacks, . . . twisted quills, painful digests, magnifying wineglasses, solid objects cast at goblins, once current puns, quashed quotatoes, messes of mottage, . . . crocodile tears, spilt ink, blasphematory spits, stale shestnuts, schoolgirls', young ladies', milkmaids',

washerwomen's, ... super whores' ... garters, tress clip-
pings from right, lift and cintrum, worms of snot, tooth-
some pickings, cans of Swiss condensed bilk, highbrow
lotions, kisses from the antipodes, presents from pick-
pockets, borrowed plumes, ... princess promises, lees of
whine, ... broken wafers, unloosed shoe latchets, crooked
strait waistcoats, fresh horrors from Hades, ... glass eyes
for an eye, gloss teeth for a tooth, war moans, special sighs,
longsufferings of longstanding, ahs ohs ouis sis jas jos gias
neys thaws sos, yeses and yeses and yeses, to which, if one
has the stomach to add the breakages, upheavals dis-
tortions, inversions of all this chambermade music one
stands, given a grain of goodwill, a fair chance of actually
seeing the whirling dervish, Tumult, son of Thunder, self
exiled in upon his ego, a nightlong a shaking betwixtween
white or reddr hawrors, noondayterrorised to skin and
bone by an ineluctable phantom (may the Shaper have
mercery on him!) writing the mystery of himsel in furniture. [183.8–184.10]

Shaun brands all this as "pure mousefarm filth" (183.4). Like
the earth, the mind of a writer—and language itself, for
Joyce—is dirty, but life grows out of dirt, and "filth" is a part of
fertility: "Dirty cleans," thinks Bloom in *Ulysses* (68).

Actually, Joyce is taking verbal stock of his world, his book,
and his living and working conditions and trying, in fact, to
include everything in words. We have seen this kind of Adamic
naming passion at work before, in Dickens's wild lists of objects
from *Martin Chuzzlewit;* but here Joyce wants to find a way not
just to name the things that surround him but to allude to
everything that could possibly exist and be thought, said, or
written *and to make it funny.* This is a catalogue of both inner
and outer life, a table of contents for his universe. Between
each pair of relentless commas, Joyce casts one more mudpie
brick for his new Tower of Babel, and each one radiates with
meaning and energy. He wants to turn all into comic scripture
and make us participate in a miracle, both sublime and farcical,
in which all that exists in his room, in his mind, in his art, and
and what exists in all languages, legends, and customs from all
time and space, flow continuously together and yet retain their
individuality. That is a worthy and logical goal for a man who had

studied and taken the concept of the Trinity very seriously but saw it also as a great joke.

III

"My wud!" is Shem, Joyce's incarnated logos, and Shem's meaning made manifest. It includes *word, wood, wad,* and *would,* and all that follows in the passage describes it. The *word* is language, Joyce's writing, and *Finnegans Wake* in particular. The *wood* is the wood pulp that contains this word and all writing, the material that houses man, the "wall" that "the handwriting is on," and what Shaun, addressing Shem, calls "the cross of your own cruelfiction" (192.18, 19). The *wad* is the heap of phenomena, "literatured" (183.10) about, in which we live. *Would* is the fact and force of will to give it all shape.

Such a "sentence" makes that glib, stale phrase "a writer's material" live. Food, clothing, garbage, myths, even his fetishes (e.g., women's underwear) turn into prose. As bread becomes the Host and the body of the Word, in the Eucharist, so foodstuffs become language in Joyce's comic consecration: "once current puns, quashed quotatoes, messes of mottage" are ingested by the imagination to nourish the verbal soul of civilization and make a new Bible. But the process is not one-way; the words transmute objects also, as wordpower and linguistic heritage enable new combinations of matter to be formed. Also, the arbitrary distinction we make between actual writing and the signs and messages that objects give off fades here, and Joyce, like Vico or Derrida, imagines that all perceived phenomena have a hieroglyphic effect and function. The "furniture" of life constitutes a script, which can be and ought to be read, "decoded," though it is imbued with the mystery of human creation. In *Ulysses,* Stephen Dedalus notes, "These heavy sands are language tide and wind have silted here" (44). In "Shem," the only difference is that the language of phenomena makes puns and tells jokes.

Look how, in this inventory, language, material objects and circumstance, the human body, literature, the particular artist's work and imagination, and the historical consequences of all of this are all in the process of turning into one another. Everything fuses in the act of creation so that dead objects, clichés, waste products, old words, suddenly convey new life and burn with new meaning and animating mockery.

305

A full gloss on every item in the list, were it possible, would, I am sure, yield a fuller psychological biography of Joyce than any extant. In a sense, the list *is* Joyce's omnivorous imagination, which contains everything from broken condoms ("burst loveletters" = French letters, i.e., contraceptives) to his poetry ("chambermade music"), from the Bible and Vico ("messes of mottage," "vivlical viasses") to Bloom and Carroll ("kisses from the antipodes"), from the Eucharist ("broken wafers") and Christ ("unloosed shoe latchets")[19] to damnation ("fresh horrors from Hades"), from wit mocking Jung and himself (cans of "Swiss condensed bilk") to wit setting forth a somatic theory of human conflict ("war moans" = hormones). This portrait of the artist is highly personal and candid. Nothing could better express Joyce's aims, or the *Wake,* than "imeffible tries at speech unasyllabled."

As revealing and moving as anything here is the fun he makes of the hard-won affirmation at the end of *Ulysses,* "yeses and yeses and yeses." (The flow of the passage repeats that of *Ulysses,* from squalor, banality, and humiliation to those desperate affirmatives.) It's as if he views himself from a distance, amid all his "alphybettyformed verbage," and sees that he is not a Dedalian or Nietzschean Superman—only an alphabet-souperman. Even the self-mockery of the passage, however, does not disguise—in fact, it somehow makes clearer—Joyce's passion for enlightening us with the flash of his generating, creative joke-words.

The last lines of this passage render with all their allusive speed the spinning Joycean collideorscape of life, and they portray Shem the artist as the human kaleidoscope, "the whirling dervish" who writes down the patterns of experience. "Tumult" in one sense is language itself, the offspring, according to Vico and Joyce, of lightning and thunder. Nothing can bind the force of imagination but writing itself, the protean form that holds and reveals the mysterious tumult of the world. Writing for Joyce becomes the shaper of an inscribed punning, which must be read aloud. In the inventory of the haunted inkbottle we may read the comic mass of diversity that composes and writes the tumultuous farce of our own being.

V

Shem, self-exiled "in upon his own ego, a nightlong a shaking," sleeps and dreams, and *dream,* that conflux of the imagination, forms the framework of the *Wake* and makes possible its comic gospel. Like Dante, John Bunyan, and Carroll, Joyce renders his universe "under the similitude of a dream." Not until Shaun-Justius points the deathbone, stilling the quick, and Joyce intones sleepily, *"Insomnia, somnia somniorum, Awmawm"* (193.29, 30), does Shem-Mercius speak directly. This implies that sleep and dreaming give mercy form in the world, that rest is somehow necessary for the generation of new vitality, and that the *Wake* celebrates our capacity to dream and sleep. One meaning of the Fortunate Fall in "Shem" is simply falling asleep.

Dreams, like puns, both represent and give form to the protean nature of things and demonstrate the witty power of the mind. The *Wake*'s punning language, fusing many images and meanings simultaneously, is in one sense a metaphor for the psychological phenomenon of the dream. But dreams diffuse single-minded focus, conventional identity, and personal will; condensing and melding the world into bizarre shapes, they absorb and incorporate life into the space of an individual brain. So it is also true to say that a dream is a metaphor for *Finnegans Wake* and its language. In a way, dreams are pure metaphor, natural psychic tropes that bear a kinship to the reality of the senses very similar to the one books have. Notoriously protean, however, dreams, after superimposing multiple perspectives, fly away, and it seems inevitable that Proteus-haunted Joyce would seek to tie down the reality of dream and night, that part of life so little explored before the twentieth century.

In their little universes of sleep, dreamers are like spectator gods watching their own creations behave, sometimes appallingly, with the gift of free will. Truth in the fuzzy collage of dreams is neither clear nor simple, and often it seems disgraceful. An upright citizen may watch himself star as a sex fiend in a pornographic comedy. That the dreaming mind can work this way struck Joyce as both deeply significant and very funny, and he had to find a way to get the outrageousness of the dreaming psyche into literature.

He knew what Freud had shown: that dreams and joke-wit are intimately connected, that both are forms of psychic release.

Like puns, dreams may be looked down upon, but they flush and cleanse the psyche. Joyce sees and renders dream as a wonderful joke played on proud, narrow rationalism and moral smugness. In the chaos, the homage to the unspeakable, the bawdy sexuality, the uncontrollable absurdity, and the multiple significance of dreams, he finds our common and manifold humanity.

VI

Mercius, at the climax of "Shem," speaks out of sleep and dream the long flowing sentence that ends the chapter. This remarkable piece of prose, to which I will continually refer, breaks down categories, unites contrarieties, jumbles common distinctions between the trivial and important, between high and low, and dissolves the little worldly self and its anxieties as a prelude to resurrection and the recycling of the universal flood of consciousness.

> MERCIUS (of hisself): *Domine vopiscus!* My fault, his fault, a kingship through a fault! Pariah, cannibal Cain, I who oathily foreswore the womb that bore you and the paps I sometimes sucked, you who ever since have been one black mass of jigs and jimjams, haunted by a convulsionary sense of not having been or being all that I might have been or you meant to becoming, bewailing like a man that innocence which I could not defend like a woman, lo, you there, Cathmon-Carbery, and thank Movies from the innermost depths of my still attrite heart, Wherein the days of youyouth are evermixed mimine, now ere the compline hour of being alone athands itself and a puff or so before we yield our spiritus to the wind, for (though . . . all that has been done has yet to be done and done again, when's day's woe, and lo, you're doomed, joyday dawns and, la, you dominate) it is to you, firstborn and firstfruit of woe, to me, branded sheep, pick of the wasterpaperbaskel, by the tremours of Thundery and Ulerin's dogstar, you alone, windblasted tree of the knowledge of beautiful andevil, ay, clothed upon with the metuor and shimmering like the horescens, astroglodynamonologos, the child of Nilfit's father, blzb, to me unseen blusher in an obscene coalhole, the cubilibum of your secret sigh, dweller in the downand-

outermost where voice only of the dead may come, because ye left from me, because ye laughed on me, because,
O me lonly son, ye are forgetting me!, that our turfbrown
mummy is acoming, alpilla, beltilla, ciltilla, deltilla, running with her tidings, old the news of the great big world,
sonnies had a scrap, woewoewoe! bab's baby walks at seven
months, waywayway! bride leaves her raid at Punchestime,
stud stoned before a racecourseful, two belles that make
the one appeal, dry yanks will visit old sod, and fourtiered
skirts are up, mesdames, while Parimiknie wears popular
short legs, and twelve hows to mix a tipsy wake, did ye
hear, colt Cooney? did ye ever, filly Fortescue? with a
beck, with a spring, all her rillringlets shaking, rocks drops
in her tachie, tramtokens in her hair, all waived to a point
and then all inuendation, little oldfashioned mummy, little
wonderful mummy, ducking under bridges, bellhopping
the weirs, dodging by a bit of bog, rapidshooting round the
bends, by Tallaght's green hills and the pools of the
phooka and a place they call it Blessington and slipping by
Sallynoggin, as happy as the day is wet, babbling, bubbling,
chattering to herself, deloothering the fields on their elbows leaning with the sloothering slide of her, giddygaddy,
grannyma, gossipaceous Anna Livia.

He lifts the lifewand and the dumb speak.

—Quoiquoiquoiquoiquoiquoiquoiq! (193.31–
195.6)

"Mummy" is the most important word in the passage; it carries the essence of life, of death, of humanity. It means mother,
dead body, and also memory (cf. "mumorise" [180.29],
"because ... ye are forgetting me" [194.21]). One single term
connotes the fact that out of the mother comes new life,
and out of death comes memory.[20] At the end of the *Wake,*
this mother-river, Anna Livia Plurabelle, now passing on, cries
"mememormee" (628.14). The book is the gift of memory to
the mother and to death. To say the word "mummy"—to let it
resound, to mull and dream over it, to gloss it—is to illuminate
the human comedy and Joyce's way of understanding and rendering it.

He tries to incorporate everything into the language of Mercius and its climax; the huge sentence typically swallows the

whole world and all its processes. Clause piles on clause, relationships and voices multiply, and syntax must wind and
stretch to encompass every possible experience. Mercius's
sentence, like Molly Bloom's sentence, is an emblem of language containing life, and such verbal form is meant to circulate
like water. Joyce wants the last words of *The Wake* "a long the"
(628.15, 16) to flow back into the first word "riverrun" (3.1),
and he wants the end of "Shem"—"...quoiq!"—to flow into
the start of the following Anna Livia chapter, "O" (196.1).

Dreams and dream language show and contain Proteus in
consciousness, but the substance in which he lives, water, does
so materially. His secret is the message we hear in the sound of
running water, quoiquoiquoiquoiquoiquoiquoiq: that fecund
life exists and will continue to exist as long as there is water.
The secret of Proteus, for Joyce, is ultimately knowing how to
make matter and spirit interchangeable. Water turns into consciousness and consciousness turns into water. Thought and
metaphor originate in the body, but the body can be known
only by thought and metaphor. The protean imagination must
be fixed and transmitted by the protean form of material writing, and it is in literature that form and imagination come together.

VII

"Shem" celebrates the power of literature and the transcendence that its very existence suggests. According to Joyce, literature gives us some ground for faith in humanity and its potential because it proves that transubstantiation of meaning and
spirit, as well as matter, is possible. In his comic gospel, the
model for full transubstantiation of life is the mutual metamorphosis between writer and reader and between writing and
reading. Among the dialectical oppositions that Joyce imagines
is Shem as living word, subjective language, devotee and
generator of sound and flowing time vs. Shaun as the arrester of
the word, stiller of creative language, transmuter of subject into
object, and master of sight and space. Shem's lifewand and
Shaun's deathbone, among their other identities, are both pens.
E. L. Epstein speculates on these polarities:

> If the *Wake* is a letter from ALP, nevertheless the voice
> throughout is the voice of Shem, who, as the Penman,

310

creates the words for the voices of nature. In the physical object which is the individual copy of the book *Finnegans Wake*, "Shaun" is the material of the page and binding and the ink on the page, and "Shem" is the "subvocalic" representation of the marks on the page which is the "reading" of the text by the reader. Shaun is an object in space, a book, and Shem is a process in time, a reading.[21]

Each is also a function of speech and writing: Shem is the generative, metaphorical part of language, which brings new knowledge and fresh perceptions; Shaun is the conservative part, which stabilizes meaning, establishes system, rules, and order, and preserves the past. Both, of course, must fuse for any tongue to exist, and literature—though it finally belongs to Shem because, by definition, it is creatively metaphorical—is both matter and spirit.

In the end, after Shem has uttered the word and Shaun has fixed it, Mercius speaks, lifts the lifewand, and we have the speech of the dumb. Shem and Shaun have come together to make literature, but literature—the sleeping beauty of experience—can be awakened only by the alert and venturesome reader. The interplay between text and the reading self animates the reader's mind and continues the streaming dialectic of consciousness in the world ("Quoiquoi..." puns on "stream of consciousness"). Experience flows into the language of the writer and the text and then back into the brains of the living, where it tells tidings of the past, the remote, the dead, the inanimate, the previously unimagined—all the information that we take for granted but that would never reach us without the voice of the creative word. And without that flow, the reader would never, in turn, become the writer of the mystery of himself in his surroundings—never, that is, give the form to his life that he does.

Shem lifts the lifewand of the pen to compose that which will let the world speak, and he also lifts the pen from the page to stop composing, become a reader once again, and hear the sound and see the signs that will stir and renew his creative imagination. Thus one metamorphosis that takes place is between James Joyce and ourselves, and his writing impregnates and shapes our imagination.

Joyce means his protean style to broaden our conception of

311

language until we see that everything is inseparable from language, that we ourselves are flesh-words of multiple meanings, and that there is no such thing as dead language. Mercy, for him, means the union of word and matter and the regeneration of meaning and material being in many forms and sounds. Mercius exclaims, "thank Movies from the innermost depths of my still attrite heart": the idea of cinema, that new form of language sired by technology, combining sound and sight, words and imagery, motion and plot, and including both spatial and temporal dimensions, suggests to Joyce a metaphor for the unfolding of the incarnated word in the world. Movies are motion, yet contain motion, and that is Joyce's sense of literature.

He wants his language to be a form supple enough to include Heraclitus's flux and to express the continuity of life's flow. When, near the end of Mercius's lines, Joyce describes the start of Anna Livia's flow ("with a beck, with a spring, all her rill-ringlets shaking"), he is doing more than trying to imitate the sound of running water (though he is doing that): he strives through sound, rhythm, and imagery to transmute into words and render exactly a common human experience of perceiving running water and to convey the kinds of feeling that such perception generates. He wants the sound of the words to touch and move us as he tries to revive an oral power and influence that have faded in an age of print. He attempts to show that the sound and flow of water and the sound and flow of language can produce precisely the same effect on us and may therefore be interchangeable. Matter speaks through spirit; spirit speaks through matter. Words may express water, water may express words, and both together may express humanity and nature, as this Babel-building brook tells us.

The speech that ends the chapter conveys the all-encompassing joke of imagination and form as well as anything can. Shem, his "joky" quality, Mercius, the lifewand, and the miraculous speech of the dumb culminate in the sound of laughter, what Joyce calls "prolonged laughter words" (600.20): "Quoiquoiquoiquoiquoiquoiquoiq!" Justius had earlier taunted Shem to "move me . . . to laughter" (187.33), and that is just what finally happens. Mirthful laughter expresses vitality and suddenly dissolves the seriousness of the world and its elements into a joyous exclamation of breathy sound. It is the sign of released tension, of motion, change, and play within the mind, of loss of self-consciousness, of a time out of time when being flows outward and no introspection is possible. "He laughed," writes Joyce of Stephen Dedalus in *Ulysses,* "to free his mind from his mind's bondage" (212). Laughter, then, an agent of freedom, a breaker of boundaries, a rescuer from the inhibitions of individualism and univalent meaning, is a mode of transitions. Those prolonged laughter-words of "Shem" sound out, in their convergence and explosions of ridiculous and gay significance, the whole protean potential in the expanding economy of humor. Nothing could be further from the scornful laughter at the end of Chaucer's *Troilus and Cressida,* when Troilus from heaven, looking down on the sham of the world and the flesh, mockingly distances his soul from the corrupt earth. Joyce's laughter proclaims the union of spirit and matter and a transcendence, not of the world, but of single identity. It grows out of the rich process of material life and the fantastic collage of silly and serious earthly possibilities.

Existence is a huge far-fetched pun, and the laughing sound is only one part of the chapter's last word. In "Quoiquoiquoi . . ." we may hear and see also the letters representing the flow of the water, the spurt of semen from the phallic lifewand, the scratch of the pen, the cackle of what Joyce calls elsewhere the "original hen" whose hen-scratch begins literature, the cock's crow hailing the new day, the snore of the dreamer, the flush of the toilet, the French question-word *quoi,* signifying the eternal curiosity and mystery that life holds, the rumble of Viconian thunder, the squawk of a gramophone record beginning, the flapping "murmur" of sound starting the movie of history, and the collective babble of multitongued humanity. However crazy all of this may be, it does go to show that Joyce, in a verbal epiphany, has here tried to pin down language and life, together, in "laughter words."

COMIC HERO AND COMIC CATHARSIS

In what sense, then, is Mr. Joyce's work purgatorial? In the absolute absence of the Absolute. Hell is the static lifelessness of unrelieved viciousness. Paradise the static lifelessness of unrelieved immaculation. Purgatory a flood of movement and vitality released by the conjunction of these two elements.

Samuel Beckett[22]

Shem, like Leopold Bloom, is both comic and heroic. If we are to understand Joyce and the consequences of the whole movement of nineteenth-century comic fiction, we have to see that he embraces a new kind of heroism. He scoffs at the old idea that comedy represents men as worse than they are. Bloom gives aid and comfort to Stephen at the end of "Circe," not in spite of his comic humiliation and the silly shapes that his dreams of fatherhood assume, but *because* of them. Shem lifts the lifewand, not in spite of the fact that he is an alienated, ridiculous scribbler whom normal folks jeer at, but *because* he is. Shaun keeps accusing Shem of being "low" and harps incessantly on this "lowness." A revolution has taken place. Ironically, Joyce is claiming primacy for the "low" form of comedy and his comic hero. Against hierarchy of genre, he sides with the democratic thrust of comedy. Shem, the writer as nonconformist, comic bum, is "the shining keyman of the wilds of change" (186.15, 16) who unlocks the sources of creativity so that they may flow. Characters like Bloom and Shem stand for diversity and the importance of the single soul in civilization, and they show, in the unprecedented candor of revelation about them, a new courage in searching for and facing the truth. Their spirit cannot be stifled, and in the forms of their "confessions" we find a comic catharsis.

I

It seems clear that in the best comic writings the authors always somehow mock themselves. They find ways of rendering in their characters what is ridiculous about themselves. This impulse to creative, regenerative confession points to a fundamental union of certain motives of comedy and religion. Look back at the great comic characters of the nineteenth-century novelists—at Emma, Pecksniff, Becky Sharp, Willoughby Patterne, and Humpty Dumpty, for example—and you see how

314

autobiographical these figures are; often their creators drew and projected them as an inspired means of distancing and exorcising certain objectionable and foolish sides of their own personalities. Shem belongs in this tradition, but Joyce identifies much more closely with him; and without denying Shem's outrageousness he makes him the agent of comic salvation and the promise of the future.

The folly of Shem is explicitly the folly of James Joyce. Joyce does not try to transcend Shem, as he did Stephen Dedalus and Bloom; instead, he incarnates himself in Shem, the comic word ("my wud"). He does not omit the most ridiculous and shameful things about himself, nor does he pretend that he has reformed into respectability, has triumphed and left behind the old flawed self, as the authors of "confessions" so often do (cf. Augustine and Rousseau). He admits his own comic lowness and plays with it without exculpating himself; from his own experience, he shows that we understand the comedy of the world only when we fully imagine the extent and shape of our individual foolishness as it manifests itself in the particular circumstances of our lives. Joyce takes upon himself the jokes of the world in order to release us from the fear of ridicule.

The comic confession through Shem and Shaun becomes a paradigm for generating the sympathy and expressive abilities we need and depend on. Shem, "the tragic jester" (171.15), is a much greater sinner than Bloom, much more harmful, flawed, and desperate (Bloom rarely seems to have murderous thoughts), much less sentimental, but just as ridiculous and even more heroic. He too resists the idiocy and violence of public life, but he has a vocation to literature and truth that nothing, not even his own crazy folly, can quench. Shaun's attack is the comedy of paranoia and schizophrenia, and Joyce, like a masochistic Mrs. Gamp with De Sade for an alter ego, writes the satire on himself with such gusto that it turns confession and self-criticism into a festival of invective, as he meant it to.

But the energy and wild humor of his diatribe ought not to obscure Joyce's remarkable candor about his own follies. He drags up and alludes, directly or indirectly, to everything his disparagers or his conscience ever charged against him: e.g., his alcoholism (176.30–31), his conceit (178.5–7), his laziness (180.17–31), his selfishness (192.5–12), his callous behavior to

315

those who loved him (187.13; 191.9–33), even his incestuous
feelings for his daughter (186.27–28). Much of the comedy and
the confession of "Shem" comes out in Joyce's sexual exhibitionism (see, for example, 181.27–33, 192.23–30). We need to
remember what a pioneer he was in making sex an acceptable
subject for the novel and, particularly and uniquely, for comic
fiction. Not only is Shem a lecherous outlaw who finds sex
pleasurable and various, he also commits the even more terrible
sin, according to an enraged Shaun, who speaks on behalf of the
institutional, social control of sex, of not taking sex and his own
sexual life seriously (see 188.28–189.27).

What may be even more surprising for this artist with the pride
of Lucifer is the ridicule of his own literary ambition and accomplishment. And Joyce is not simply using the "old tactic of
defensive self-mockery"[23] and discrediting his critics by having
the egregious Shaun speak their views. Shaun voices the conventional sentiments about Joyce and *Finnegans Wake,* but many
of the difficulties and problems he points out are real, including
the general estimate and reputation of the book as a failure. It is
part of the drama of "Shem," the *Wake,* and Joyce's comic gospel
that the criticism is in some ways true and must be faced and
accepted. Certainly no critic has written more devastatingly
about the *Wake* than Shaun.

The worst thing that could happen to an experimental writer
like Joyce, who had given his life over to a work that looks insane
to most people, would be to doubt his own sanity and to see
himself, in the world's reflection, as a deluded madman. Shaun-
Justius's final whispered words to Shem end with a terrible last
judgment: "Sh! Shem, you are. Sh! You are mad!" (193.27, 28).
Joyce makes that implicit judgment on the author of "Work in
Progress" the climax of Shaun's attack on Shem because, I think,
he feared it might be true. Shem intends to call his masterpiece
"his Ballade Imaginaire" (177.27, 28) (i.e., the Ballad of Persse
O'Reilly, *Finnegans Wake*), or *How a Guy Finks and Fawkes When
He Is Going Batty* (177.29). The nightmare of the artist-hero
defying the world is to find out that the world is right and he is
insanely wrong, but the best triumph is to find a way of turning
that nightmare into a joke. If the madman is traditionally
alienated from the community, still, he is the one who pro-
verbially hears voices, and to him in the end come the voices of
the dead and of nature and also the power to articulate these

316

strange voices. The whole denigration of Shem and Joyce's self-mockery through him rest on the psychological principle of mastering fear through play.

Joyce describes the writing of *Finnegans Wake* as a solipsistic and scatological farce that is somehow both ludicrous and truly heroic:

> ...when the call comes, he shall produce...from his un-heavenly body a no uncertain quantity of obscene matter, not protected by copriright...bedung to him...through the bowels of his misery,...this Esuan Menschavik ...wrote over every square inch of the only foolscap available, his own body, till by its corrosive sublimation one continuous present tense integument slowly un-folded all marryvoising moodmoulded cyclewheeling history (thereby, he said, reflecting from his own individual person life unlivable, transaccidentated through the slow fires of consciousness into a dividual chaos, perilous, potent, common to allflesh, human only, mortal). [185.28–186.6]

The last part of this quotation articulates with eloquence Joyce's superhuman ambition in the *Wake* (it also exactly portrays the phenomenon of "dream"), but he then follows with an equally extraordinary confession of failure:

> ...but with each word that would not pass away the squidself which he had squirtscreened from the crystalline world waned chagreenold and doriangrayer in its dudhud. This exists that isits after having been said we know. And dabal take dabnal! And the dal dabal dab aldanabal! [186.6–10][24]

His self, his life-blood, passes into his book which has a kind of physical permanence; it is, however, in truth only a written exclamation of babble, a literary screech of gibberish. Joyce, at the very moment when he speaks directly about the great things he hopes to accomplish in the *Wake*—to marry all the voices of history and the earth to his own life and prose—and of the tremendous self-sacrifice that is required, describes it, literally, as a shitty piece of writing and an indecipherable riddle of cacophony. He laughs at his own effort and burlesques his Wakean voice squalling away incomprehensibly to the world. It would be a shame if the usual prejudices against the comic mode and Joyce's reputation as an overly demanding writer were to obscure the passionate drama, the disciplined perspective, and the awesome humility of this passage of art.

III

I want to look closely at the passage in which Shem-Joyce pores over his own literary masterpiece to see how magnanimous Joyce's comedy of confession can be:

> It would have diverted, if ever seen, the shuddersome spectacle of this semidemented zany . . . making believe to read his usylessly unreadable Blue Book of Eccles . . . turning over three sheets at a wind, telling himself delightedly, no espellor mor so, that every splurge on the vellum he blundered over was an aisling vision more gorgeous than the one before t.i.t.s., a roseschelle cottage by the sea for nothing for ever, a ladies tryon hosiery raffle at liberty, a sewerful of guineagold wine with bran-comongepadenopie and sickcylinder oysters worth a billion a bite, an entire operahouse (there was to be stamping room only in the prompter's box and everthemore his queque kept swelling) of enthusiastic noblewomen flinging every coronetcrimsoned stitch they had off at his prob-scenium, one after the others, inamagoaded into ajustil-loosing themselves, in their gaiety pantheomime, when, egad, sir, acordant to all acountstrick, he squealed the topsquall . . . for fully five minutes, infinitely better than Baraton McGluckin. . . . [179.24–180.8]

This view of the century's most formidable author, admiring his famous book in drunken pride, just like any vain hack, has the effect, I think, of humanizing both the writer and literature. It relates us to him by showing that we have in common with him the kinds of motives and fantasies that prod us and feed our ambitions. We get much closer here to the artist and to the humor that prompts artistic creation than we do in *A Portrait of the Artist* or even in *Ulysses*. With the description of the day-dreams that his book sets off, Joyce, in an act of comic charity, makes himself a laughingstock. His fantasies confess that this man of genius is a brother in the community of fools.

The letters "t.i.t.s." stand for *that is to say,* but they mean "tits" too, and they tell us that Joyce's writing gave him the libidinous pleasure of breasts, that it was some sort of happy sublimation for him. They say also that the libido may stimulate the creative activity of genius, that by writing *Ulysses* Joyce found a way back to the mother he had lost, and that, most significantly, he did not much mind people knowing these things. I know that Shaun is the speaker here, but can any serious reader of Joyce doubt the authenticity of the implied confession in this passage? The fantastic reveries here belong to Shem the Penman and to James Joyce, not to some character, like Stephen Dedalus or Willoughby Patterne, whom writer or reader might be able to look down upon with superior detachment. Playing on *Ulysses,* Joyce parodies the "Nausicaa" and "Sirens" episodes and the kinds of Bloomian hallucination we get in "Circe." Shem dreams of an idyllic venereal existence by the sea, of an infinite goldenshower flow of wine, of the sensuous thrill of ladies and ladies' underwear, and of becoming sexually irresistible and omnipotent through the power of his beautiful tenor voice. These joyful visions are complex metaphors for the personal motives that inspired Joyce to create the corresponding episodes in *Ulysses* and also for the pleasurable ends to which his artistic creation was the means. But the fantasies serve also as metaphors for the ways and means that enable art—even "high" art, like *Ulysses*—to fulfill the quirky wishes of our individual psyches. The pleasures of reading and writing merge here in a bizarre comedy of artistic transaction.

Set that study of Shem against the famous lines from *A Portrait of the Artist:* "The artist, like the God of the creation, remains within or behind or beyond or above his handiwork, invisible, refined out of existence, indifferent, paring his fingernails."[25] The comic theories of the genesis of artistic creation and appreciation that Shem's visions of delight imply not only make a mockery of Stephen's pompous words; they also give us a much richer idea of the dialectical relationships between an artist and his work and—what is often ignored—between the different works of the artist. The passage brings out the conflicts and subtle motivations in both the writer and his books, and it also brings out the joyfulness, morally suspect though it might be, that animates so much of *Ulysses* and *Finnegans Wake.*

319

IV

If Shem purges us of embarrassment and guilt, Shaun purges us of resentment and censoriousness. Out of the specter of all criticism, conscience, reproachful superego, and alien authority, Joyce creates Shaun-Justius, the censor within and without and a great comic character in his own right. Through him, Joyce mocks not only the tyranny of others' judgment over ourselves but also our own boiling dissatisfaction with people and our judgmental enmity toward them. Shaun is Justius, the might that makes right, organized religion and the establishment; but he is also the configuration of personal and social forces that create righteousness and institutions of morality and justice. Listen to his voice and tone:

> JUSTIUS (to himother): Brawn is my name and broad is my nature and I've breit on my brow and all's right with every feature and I'll brune this bird or Brown Bess's bung's gone bandy. I'm the boy to bruise and braise. Baus! [187.24–27]

That is the roar of top dog, of machismo, of surety bellowing out alliterative breath. The language and the sound give emotional life to the abstract idea of justice, but they also make it comic. Joyce renders the pose, bluster, and brag lurking in institutional power and moral authority and brings out, in the total effect of the prose, the incongruity between the impersonal façade that authority tries to present and the actual selfishness and sadistic aggression that always—to some degree—motivate those who exercise it.

In the rhetorical irony of Shaun's voice, Joyce justifies our rebelliousness toward the highness that despises lowness: "take your medicine. . . . Let me finish! Just a little judas tonic, my ghem of all jokes, to make you go green in the gazer" (193.5–10), says Justius, trying to execute Shem. The allusion may remind us that it is the Shauns of the world who give the orders to poison Socrates, crucify Christ, stone Stephen, burn Bruno, gas the Jews, and conduct the Inquisition and Party purges. All in all, Shauns have wielded and continue to wield the deathbone with efficiency and good conscience.

Joyce's antiauthoritarianism, which Irish history—personal as well as national—taught him, was confirmed by the regimented slaughter of the Great War. That bloodbath had a much greater effect on his work than has generally been realized. One reason why the comic heroism of Bloom and Shem emerged in the postwar period is surely that the traditional concept of heroism had led to unspeakable disaster.

Orthodoxy threatens physical and spiritual death to those who oppose it; even worse, for Joyce, it bores: Shaun has no mode of metamorphosis: he cannot change, he can only defend and fear for the status quo. He lacks the power of metaphor and poetic fancy that allows Shem to see in the deathbone a lifewand and thus, through imagination, to turn death into life. Shaun's totalitarian righteousness puts the world to sleep. *"Insomnia, somnia somniorum. Awmawm."* Only Shem can make it dream.

The comic irony of Shaun's attack on the creative artist Shem and the reason why Joyce identifies with the Shem principle come out in an instant when Justius is railing at Shem: "nomad, mooner by lamplight, . . . an Irish emigrant the wrong way out . . . an unfrillfrocked quackfriar, you (will you for the laugh of Scheekspair just help mine with the epithet?) semi-semitic serendipitist, you (thanks, I think that describes you) Europasianised Afferyank!" (190.32–191.4). To insult Shem successfully, Shaun must depend on his brother's articulate power.

In one sense, the voice of Shaun is the criticism of James Joyce by Gogarty, Pound, H.G. Wells, Alfred Noyes, Wyndham Lewis, Stanislaus Joyce, and everyone else who ever reproached his art. Shaun alludes to almost every knock that Joyce ever got. But Shaun also expresses the doubt that assails the creative artist; he speaks for the self-doubt, bad conscience, and status quo that the artist must overcome. Two of the strongest enemies that the writer faces are that he has nothing new or important to say and that what he says could not possibly matter. Joyce hated Shaun, but it would be a mistake to identify him solely with Joyce's critics or with the forces he opposed. He could never have made him such a resourceful and entertaining talker and fool if he did not live with Shaun inside himself also.

The accusatory Shaun lurks inside us, too, ready to pounce and scoff. The fault of the mocker, however, does not lie in his belittling humor but in his blindness to his own kinship with the

321

life he mocks. Much of public and private life is spent in passing judgment on others. We think a great deal about how they do not live and act as we would have them; we criticize them and the consequences of their misbehavior. The act of judgment is partially a casting-out. In justice there is always something of that eternal note of strident dissatisfaction that wants to eliminate what is alien to our will. The Justice of the world appears in stone tablets, in heavy tomes, in scales balancing weights, and in signs and instruments of coercion: it has a bias toward the inanimate. Like the judgmentalness in ourselves, it tends to "static lifelessness."[26]

In Justius's denunciation, Joyce explores the nature of justice, the letter of the law, and also the judging side of the brain. Justius denounces his twin, the other, the not-self: "JUSTIUS (to himother)" (187.24). In this pun, "himother," there lies a hostility to *the mother,* to the very system of generation, the natural source of alienation that has expelled the self and made being diverse instead of uniform. Justice cries out with this long-standing resentment and the need for protection against encroachment by another. Justius condemns Shem the Penman, because Joyce knows that the fresh and creative personal use of language—the very nature of language—has always brought doubt, multiplicity, change, and even madness. Justius is inevitable in self as well as society. The voice of justice defines and assesses sin and its consequences in others and institutionalizes punishment and its threat.

V

But Justius, justice, and authority become incorporated, for Joyce, in something larger. Mercius subsumes them. Mercy, for Joyce, is the definition, assessment, and acceptance of sin and its consequences in oneself. Knowing the reality and potentiality of one's own sin and foolishness, one can better empathize with others. Mercy comes out of the recognition that the self includes a mass of shifting identities that swamp moral prescription. Shaun, like the traditional egoist, loves conformity and hates otherness. Unable to change himself, he would change everything into himself or kill it. Shem, the artist, as a man is just as egotistical, but his true vocation as a creator allows him to change himself into everything else, to feel and speak as

322

others, making himself literally the spokesman for all life and being. In his final speech, the comic artist-hero brings the merciful gift of linguistic imagination.

The origins of the whole Justius-Mercius antithesis, and particularly Mercius's speech, seem to lie in Portia's famous speech from *The Merchant of Venice*. Joyce can make us hear, through Shem the comic artist, the quality of mercy; he puns shamelessly: "it falleth as the gentle rain from heaven," becomes "quoiquoiquoiquoiquoiquoiquoiq!" Like Shakespeare, he locates mercy in flow, water, a woman and her voice, and comedy.

In the verbal flow of Mercius, who is mainly Shem, Shaun is momentarily fused with his brother in a Bruno-like coincidence of contraries. Joyce quotes Coleridge on Giordano Bruno: "Every power in nature or in spirit must evolve an opposite as the sole condition and means of its manifestation; and every opposition is, therefore, a tendency to reunion."[27] The comic hero finally includes Shem and Shaun, or rather, to be more accurate if less schematic and symmetrical, Shem must include Shaun. In Joyce's protean art, Shem and Shaun naturally represent many things and different things at different times. Shem and all humanity are "of twosome twiminds" (188.14), according to Joyce, and modern science seems to be confirming his insight by telling us about that left-brain-right-hand, right-brain-left-hand split in cerebral functioning. Our heads appear to be Shem-Shaun bipolar affairs with many of the very same contradictions and tensions that these characters personify in the *Wake*. ("Lefty takes the cherubcake while Rights cloves his hoof" [175.29, 30].)

I find in the Shem-Shaun conflict a symbol of the tension between organized religion and comedy that has been my theme and, in the emergence of the Joycean comic hero at the end of the chapter, a fusion of the comic and the religious impulses. Shaun as Justius, playing the role of confessor and meter-out of punishment, speaks in the name of Holy Church. Whispering to Shem about the terrible judgment that rumor has passed upon him, Justius the priest ends his condemnation: "'That a cross may crush me if I refuse to believe in it. That I may rock anchor through the ages if I hope it's not true. That the host may choke me if I beneighbour you without my charity! Sh! Shem, you are. Sh! You are mad!' He points the deathbone and the quick are still" (193.24–29). The faith, hope, and charity of Christianity have now been perverted in the words of the Church's spokesman: His faith is that his brother is mad and that he is his brother's keeper only in the sense of being the keeper of a madman; his hope is that Shem is a lunatic; and his charity means, for him, payment given to organized religion for spiritual benefits. Shaun could be Pecksniff. In effect, Joyce presents the gist of comic satire, especially the satire of nineteenth-century comic fiction, on the institution of morality in religion. Shem-Mercius, the comic hero, absorbs Justius and expresses the faith, hope, and charity that now belong to Joyce's comic sense of life. Mercy and human salvation lie with the "ghem of all jokes" (193.9).

Earlier, Shaun-Justius, irritated by what he sees as the faith-destroying, Church-wrecking nihilism of this modern agnostic comic artist, cries: "you have become of twosome twiminds forenenst gods, hidden and discovered, nay, condemned fool, anarch, egoarch, hiresiarch, you have reared your disunited kingdom on the vacuum of your own most intensely doubtful soul. Do you hold yourself then for some god in the manger . . . that you will neither serve nor let serve, pray nor let pray?" (188.14–19). The case against Joyce and skeptical secularism (or comic faith, for that matter) could hardly be put more clearly or forcefully. But Shaun's question boomerangs. The very phrase "god in a manger," playing with and using Aesop and Christ and making each reverberate, says that holiness can and does appear in the lowest of the low. The joker-artist-hero comes to disrupt order, blurt the *verboten,* and liberate people from the piety and reverence that congeal metaphorical thought and creative imagination into dogma and authority. When Justius points the deathbone, Shem gets his just deserts, and we must understand the voice of Mercius and the lifting of the lifewand, which follow, for what they are: a drama of merciful regeneration. The comic hero overcomes death and assumes a miraculous protean identity.

In the original draft of the Shem chapter, the Shaun-Justius voice continued to the end, denouncing Shem and telling him that because of his sins his "mummy," whose death-dealing qualities he stressed, is coming to him with the implied booby prize of mortality.[28] Joyce changed his conception completely and made the ending one of his most carefully wrought and radiant climaxes. Shaun the priest, with his priestly function, fades into Shem the joker-artist, and Shem becomes Mercius, the new comic hero. For the time being, Joyce, Shem, and we, the audience, having undergone comic catharsis, are purged of hostility and superiority. Guilt, shame, and aggressions have been raised and flushed, pride dispelled. Shem-Mercius-Joyce can now marry the voices that articulate the eternal circulation of life and the endless patterns of death and resurrection.

VI

Not only does Shem recognize Shaun to be a part of himself, he also experiences his mother's being in his own consciousness. It is important to see that the comic hero briefly metamorphoses into a woman and that Joyce ascribes to a woman the generation of language as well as life. In his most eloquent and emotional moments—in the final pages of *Ulysses,* the washerwoman's dialogue at the end of Book I of *Finnegans Wake,* the Anna Livia Plurabelle monologue in the final pages of the *Wake,* and in this speech—Joyce speaks in the guise of woman. The highest form of heroism for him is the act of creation, and he finds and represents the basis of creativity, not in the male God of Christianity, but in a woman. Thus a true male hero must try to transcend his sex even if this makes him seem ludicrous—like Bloom, Shem, and even Joyce.

Look, in this passage, at the reason that the mother gives for her reappearance and her presence, as her being and words flow into Mercius's language and their identities become, for an instant, one: "because ye left from me, because ye laughed on me, because, O me lonly son, ye are forgetting me!, that our turfbrown mummy is acoming...running with her tidings" (194.20–23) (the changing pronouns show the shifts of identity).[29] "Because ye left from me" signifies parturition at birth, the traumatic pattern for all subsequent partings, and the very nature of our separate existence; it expresses the inevitable leave-taking of the child from the parent. "Because ye laughed on me" means *because you mocked the life of your mother,* as male children of our culture almost inevitably have; but it also means *because laughter, life, and love happened around and on the body and at the breasts of the mother* (in the Joycean tongue, the word "laughed" also says "lived" and "loved"). Inherent also in post-childhood laughter is the idea of comic distance between the laugher and what he laughs at—distance that creates a need to communicate. "Because, O me lonly son, ye are forgetting me" means that the isolated, lonely human being forgets the reality of mother love; the unaided human memory fails. *"Amor matris,"* speculates Stephen Dedalus, "subjective and objective genitive, may be the only true thing in life" (*Ulysses* 207). Because of all this, then, *language,* the matrix of humanity, appears, and it is the gift of the mother. The tidings of life flow from this mass-circulation medium into Mercius: "old the news of the great big world." Since Joyce found the logical basis for human continuity, connection, and hope in mother love, he had to be able to imagine and express, in order to be successful in his calling, the voice of the mother and her metaphorical reality for him. The Holy Roman Catholic Church, he thought, was founded on the mystery of fatherhood, on apostolic succession, on the void. But comic faith rests on motherhood, on generation, on actual nurturing of children, on physical flow, and on the fertility of the word in writing. The tidings borne and uttered by Anna Livia the mother are both tidings of James Joyce and of the news of domestic life traditionally associated with women. The content of all this news adds up to a comic version of Ecclesiastes from the coinciding points of view of James Joyce, an Irish woman like his mother, Vico, and some super-mortal mother-of-the-world whom we might call Mothering Nature, the universal muse.

But the voice of the comic hero does more than transcend personal identity and sex. Joyce tries to go beyond anthropomorphism and give sympathy, identity, and vocal powers to nature in the shape of the running water and the earth's fields. The merciful comic fool is madly trying to create an ecological tongue that will convey messages from external nature to us and complete a communion between animate life and inanimate being: "babbling, bubbling, chattering to herself, deloothering the fields on their elbows leaning with the sloothering slide of her, giddygaddy, grannyma, gossipaceous Anna Livia" (195.1–4). He wants to express an identification with water and earth and, through linguistic power, mediate between the elements and the articulate spirit of humanity. The fields, resting "on their elbows," become humanized, but voice and thought have become hydraulic.

VII

We are left, then, with a version of the pathetic fallacy, but we are meant to see, as Shem lifts the lifewand and makes the dumb speak, that this so-called fallacy is our reality: we impersonate nature, we find that we speak through it and it speaks through us in ways that ultimately depend on linguistic capacity. And Joyce claims for the comic imagination the power of promoting and realizing this mutual interflow and interchange of person and nonperson, of high consciousness and low matter. The function of his babble of sound and writing is both ridiculous and religious. "Quoiquoiquoiquoiquoiquoiquoiq!" equals comic catharsis: a hopeful flow that is laughable. Shem-Mercius is both the true joke and the real comedian that Trevor Griffiths describes in his play *Comedians:*

> A real comedian—that's a daring man. He *dares* to see what his listeners shy away from, fear to express. And what he sees is a sort of truth, about people, about their situation, about what hurts or terrifies them, about what's hard, above all, about what they *want*. A joke releases the tension, says the unsayable, any joke pretty well. But a true joke, a comedian's joke, has to do more than release tension, it has to *liberate* the will and the desire, it has to *change the situation*. [30]

Shem changes the situation from his own scorned lowness and from the just sentence of death—Shaun's killing of the quick—by pointing the way to the future.

327

AUDIENCE: OBSCURITY, INTERPRETATION, AND COMIC EPIPHANY

[T]he art itself must create its audience—must create those who can respond to it and be saved. Not the majority, of course, who have no desire to rise any higher than they must, but the elect, who by their aspiration cut themselves off from the majority.

J. Mitchell Morse[31]

This is the most colossal leg-pull in literature.

Oliver St. John Gogarty[32]

The obscurity and difficulty of punning diction and convoluted syntax require a clerisy to interpret *Finnegans Wake*. Wakean language is to Joyce's comic faith what Latin is—or was—to the Roman Catholic Church: in theory it is an international medium, free of locality, through which truth and sacred mysteries can be universally expressed and communicated; in practice it delivers the keeping of the faith over to a relatively small group of devoted followers. We have seen Meredith's tendency in *The Egoist* to make a religion of comedy and to couch it in a complex style that becomes inseparable from his comic vision and that makes heavy demands on his readers. In Joyce that tendency becomes definitive. As in *The Egoist* and Carroll's "Jabber-wocky," we have to grapple with the language. We can't take it for granted; we have to slow down and struggle with its multi-plicities, its connections, its patterns. Joyce's insiders' language, so hard to follow, implies a militant emotional defiance, "us against the Philistines," a spirit that underlies much comedy as well as religion.

But *Finnegans Wake* not only requires a vocation, it asks for a kind of conversion too. We must become like Shem: lonely, knowing what it is to be called mad and to feel the justice of the charge, identifying with failure—ridiculous. Reading the *Wake* seriously is a perpetually frustrating struggle for meaning and light and a continuing act of faith.

I

Why did a man who came to detest hierarchy, who honored comedy, "lowness," and the uncommon but average little man in the street, who loved the vernacular and was accused of "literary Bolshevism,"[33] write the most inaccessible and esoteric prose of his age? One reason is that he wanted the *Wake* to serve as a metaphor for the full, intricate mystery of the dynamic universe. A doctrine of Joyce's gospel, confirmed by our groping efforts at understanding, is that we can never build the Babel of language to stand firm and still, though we are fated to try. Reality, language, the mind, and the whole self are all astoundingly complicated, and if literature does not convey that complexity, it will not have much lasting value.

If the fate and task of human consciousness is to make form and meaning out of the flux, then Joyce's language turns us into interrogators of Proteus. An author's writing must somehow be able to communicate the truth and significance of his world and thought, but it must also potentially convey, clarify, and *imagine* the reader's life too; and to do that the writer must find the patterns and form that will include the reader and possibly convince him of his involvement in the book. What has sometimes glibly been talked of as a writer's universality is really the dream of Babel; Joyce sought that universality by making his language so rich and polysemantic that he hoped it would have particular relevance for everyone who would read him seriously. To be universal, he believed he had to create a more allusive and multivarious language, fusing many tongues into English, and to use, more fully than anyone had ever done before, the combined resources of sound and print to suggest meaning.

Joyce, catholic (small "c") by temperament and experience, detested provincialism and wanted to find a catholic, internationalist mode of expression that would utter the catholic nature of man. He tried to "render ... the texture of a real polylingual world with a real polylingual history behind it."[34] He wanted to restore and realize the wholeness, the marvel, and the sacred feeling of language. Blasphemy, for him, is taking language obliviously and ignoring its holy and comic nature. "I'd like," said Joyce, "a language which is above all languages, a language to which all will do service."[35] That might seem strange coming from an artist who cried *"Non serviam"* (*Ulysses* 582), but it shows Joyce's messianic side. He wanted a congregation of the faithful, and, what is more, something monomaniacally wild in him sought divinity by making himself into language and language into God.

Although he joked about it, Joyce appears to have hoped that interpretation would be a kind of religious vocation for his readers that might transform them. It would necessarily break down the automatic habits of thinking, the stock responses and verbal channeling, that narrow and deaden our lives. An active search for meaning might lead readers to understand and forge connections between themselves, particular beings, and the flow of words and matter that constitute all humanity and the universe. They would realize not only the wonder of the world but their own remarkable analytical and synthesizing powers—their linguistic fluency—and sense the Joycean word living in themselves. Interpretation would be a subjective act performed upon an objective artifact, the book. Each reader would bring a different life to the text, which is written in a style and language so rich in potential meaning that every interpreter might discover something fresh. The *Wake* would continually yield new meanings and new combinations of meaning that would help to explain life, but the task of interpretation would never—could never—be completed by one person. It would necessarily be both a collective and a particular enterprise, and, as the kaleidoscope of the world and the book keep turning, it would mean continual mental action and vitality. It would clarify, harmonize, integrate, and radiate; and the audience, in reading actively rather than passivly, might find a comic faith.

Remember, Joyce extolled comedy because it leaves us with a joy arising from our possession of something. We can never possess the language of the *Wake* (language is social, not private property), but he hopes that we can possess and take away from his language, as we strive to figure it out, exactly that emotional experience of aesthetic beauty that depends on the existence of wholeness, harmony, and radiance in life.

II

Interpretation can satisfy a craving for order and a need to believe that, if we could know enough, things would make sense. Reading *Finnegans Wake* is a metaphor for the quest for meaning and the accumulation of knowledge. Joyce builds into it puzzles that have answers and holds out to us a joyful dream of salvation through problem-solving: in Wakese, *solvation.*

"Shem" offers innumerable examples of the Joycean "epiphany," a concept and psychological event that splices religion, art, and—in the *Wake*—the sense of humor. The idea of "epiphany," the sudden showing-forth of divinity, moved Joyce, and he adapted the term for his own purposes to mean "a sudden spiritual manifestation, whether in the vulgarity of speech or of gesture or in a memorable phase of the mind itself."[36] The young Joyce, describing this phenomenon, sounds very much as if he were theorizing about audience participation in art, about how meaning is apprehended, and specifically, about reading and literary transaction:

> This is the moment which I call epiphany. First we recognise that the object is *one* integral thing, then we recognise that it is an organised structure, a *thing* in fact: finally, when the relation of the parts is exquisite, when the parts are adjusted to the special point, we recognise that it is *that* thing which it is. Its soul, its whatness, leaps to us from the vestment of its appearance [e.g., from the printed page].[37]

From early on, then, there is a blending of artist and audience in his aesthetic thought, and the distinction between the two blurs. Notice also that he has given us a theory of revelation. We can see what led him to sanctify the pun. In everyday living, the kind of thing he is talking about happens when the light dawns and, seeing the point, we get the joke. And it is remarkable how similar that moment is to accounts of quick, blissful, religious illumination. Though convention has kept them in different categories and they differ in degree, the flash of wit is of a kind with the sudden experience of conversion: *once I was blind, but now I see!*

Every darkly obscure new word in the *Wake* carries with it a potential comic epiphany. Take, for instance, the striking, sprawling pun of Mercius's, "astroglodynamonologos" (194.16–17). The Jesuit scholar Robert Boyle explicates it this way: "Mercius's word for his own artistic vocation, or rather for himself as artist, is drawn . . . from the opening of St. John's gospel with its description of the ideal priest. . . . it combines the words for star, *aster;* cave-dweller (literally, hole-seeker), *troglodyte;* source of power, *dynamo;* lonely speaker, *monologos;* and the word, *logos.*"[38]

To Boyle's components, I would add: "glow," conveying the radiating light of the word; "dynamite," expressing its explosive power; "monologist," which has commonly come to denote a speaker of comic monologues; and the dynamiting of the monologist, i.e., the explosion of the single voice into many. Boyle rightly goes on to stress the religious significance and function of Joyce's word and art, though I do not agree that they can be subsumed into Christian dogma. For Joyce, Mercius's word, fusing spirit and matter, high and low, Christ and Lucifer, heaven and earth and hell, serious and comic, supersedes Saint John's Logos. It contains and reenacts Vico's theory of the origin of language; the flash of lightning and thunder inaugurates (and symbolizes) linguistic capacity and, thus, humanity and history. And it combines the reverence and mockery that characterize Joyce's sense of life.

To the mind striving to comprehend such a word, this pun can come as an epiphany of the energy of words and the range and power of the human brain. What one might get from thinking about and trying to fathom this word and its relations to the context, the book and the world in which it has been spoken, is a sudden feeling for the largeness and inclusiveness of life and language, for their plural, separable, combining, and fluid parts and also for their inexhaustible capacity to generate meaning and wonder. When I grasp such a pun as "astroglodynamonologos," I may realize for an instant the rich totality of meanings that my mind can hold, and in that epiphanic moment Joyce's resonant word is incarnated in me. I experience Joycean *revelation*, a perfect Wakean word, whose sense includes "reveal," "revel," "elation," "relation," and "elevation."

III

All of this may seem pretentious and grimly labored, however, if we forget that interpretation of the *Wake* is a clownish process for a faithful foolish few. Oliver Gogarty, so often wrong about Joyce, was right in calling the book "a great leg-pull." Its readers inevitably become the butt of a joke that gives them the most ludicrous aspects of Shem and Shaun. Like Shem we appear to most of the sensible world to be misguided fanatics devoted to arcane, silly writing. Nearly all who study and write on the *Wake* sometimes feel ridiculous: for whom do we explain things and why? Like Shaun, we become critics analyzing another's "root language" (424:17), knowing that we will never fully understand it, and, like him, we are tempted to become zealots of orthodoxy, pretending to be priests of eternal imagination, whose mysteries we never really can know. No author has had more ingenious or industrious readers within the century of his life than Joyce, but Joycean scholarship and criticism sometimes do seem like Shaun's revenge on his creator. Bad-tempered, sanctimonious attitudes stir in much of the commentary on the *Wake,* and the tone of Joyceans reviewing each other's work often resembles the type of reception that infidels tampering with sacred scripture might expect. (Joyce, getting down both the religious impetus of the *Wake* and the humor inherent in presumptions of sanctity, refers to his book as "secret stripture" [293, n. 2].) Comic material can harden into dogma, and the dogmatic, proprietary pose becomes, in the wake of Shaun, implicit satire. Explication can seem at times to analyze beauty right out of existence, and even the harmless, drudging Shaun-critic of comedy no doubt seems to be murdering humor to dissect it. One of the lessons of the comic gospel is that it can and will often be captured by jealous members of a cult devoted to graven images and idolatry.

But Joyce's ideal reader may also take on the best traits of his twins. The Shauns who explicate texts and compile the concordances, the lexicons, the lists of Lithuanian words, and the readers' guides make it possible to read with the synthesizing power of a Shem. Moreover, the more we know analytically, the greater our pleasure when we put the parts together. For the whole of a pun, the whole of "Shem," the whole of the *Wake* are all more than the sum of their parts: explicating a joke-word is not the same as experiencing the surprising jolt of humor any more than discussing religion is like seeing God. But the language of the *Wake* is one medium in which the pleasure is not permanently spoiled by analysis; analysis helps us in fact to find the synthesis from which the comic epiphany radiates. The more we know of the parts, the more frequent and powerful are the flashes of wit, the illuminating correspondences, and the stimulating creative bursts of energy of the *Wake*—even if we cannot directly communicate them to others.

Joyce, in the last monologue of the chapter, boldly identifies Shem, the bearer of the word, with the audience ("to you . . . to me . . . our turfbrown mummy is acoming"). We too are bearers of the word, then; but, at the very end, as Shem lifts the lifewand and makes us, the dumb, speak, we become, along with Shem and Joyce, the uttered word itself, i.e., the "prolonged" laughter-word, "Quoiquoiquoiq . . ." that conveys

333

bemusement, obscurity, the cacophony of critics, and the babble out of which flow the dialectic of our being and our malleable verbal ability.

SACRAMENTAL HUMOR

He that believeth on me, as the scripture hath said, out of his belly shall flow rivers of living water.
John 7:38

His writing is not *about* something; *it is that something itself.*
Samuel Beckett[39]

The history, explication, and meaning of one single word would sum up all that Mercius's speech represents: the circulation of body fluids, the metamorphosing properties of moisture, the flowing quality of life, the deliverance that mercy brings from cold, immutable facts, the punning facetiousness, the quirkiness of personality, the jocose imagination playing over human nature, the coincidence of elementary matter, eternal waters, language and consciousness, and the spirit of humanity, which transcends the individual being. The word, of course, is "humor." This speech defines, embodies, and celebrates the existence of humor, as a Mass, for a devout Roman Catholic, might define, embody, and celebrate the presence of the living God. By the end of the chapter, comic fiction has become comic faith, Shem has taken over the pastoral functions of Shaun and Christ, and Joyce's humor has become sacramental.

I

As I read "Shem," the comedy of the text becomes the manifestation of an immortal grace of being that is both sacred and profane. Joyce uses and makes fun of the Christian sacraments. We move from a baptism ("Shem is as short for Shemus as Jem is joky for Jacob") to a comic "extreme unction," the final gush of Anna Livia, anointing the sick and the dead ("all inuendation, little oldfashioned mummy . . . rapid-shooting . . . by Tallaght's green hills . . . and a place they call it Blessington" refers to plague victims buried at Tallaght and to the place of deadly wounds, Blessington [Fr. *blesses*]); the flowing-forth of

Quoiquoiquoi . . . , in the midst of death, promises resurrection and new life. In between, he often alludes to and mocks all the other sacraments as well. For example, Penance: "Let us pry. We thought, would and did. *Cur, quicquid, ubi, quando, quomodo, quoties, quibus auxiliis?*" (188.8, 9); Holy Orders: "your birthwrong was, to fall in with Plan . . . and do a certain office . . . in a certain holy office . . . during certain agonising office hours" (190.12–15); Marriage: "the wheeze sort of was you should . . . repopulate the land of your birth and count up your progeny by the hungered head and the angered thousand but you thwarted the wious pish of your cogodparents . . . I'd have been the best man for you, myself . . . accompanied by a plain gold band" (188.33–189.25).

Shaun-Justius both articulates and is a parody of the Church as the Sacrament of Christ's love and word. But Joyce goes beyond parody to bestow his own kind of sacramental blessing and sense of grace. His comic gospel moves to baptize and confirm us into a faith of the living word. It seeks to transform the text eucharistically into the immortal flesh and spirit of existence. It carries the penance of ridicule to hurtful pride, and it works to ordain Shem, Joyce's alter ego, as a comic priest of the eternal imagination. Marrying the word to the world, it rejoices in fecundity. Finally, it intends to prepare one for the round of eternity and immersion in the corporate body of nature. The nature of being for him is both sacred and comic, and it would be neither if it were not also the other. What is holy is the living word, but language is a mutable human joke: wordplay: "astroglodynamonologos."

II

For Joyce, the greatest bearers of the word have been Christ and Shakespeare, and, in the voice of Mercius, he joins himself to them to make a trinity. The sacrament of his humor transubstantiates them into the text of the *Wake*. Mercius's opening, "My fault, his fault, a kingship through a fault" (193:31–32), plays on Shakespeare's pariah king, Richard III, on the liturgical refrain *"mea culpa,"* and on the image of the living waters pouring from Christ's wounds, which signify the hope for eternal life in the kingdom of heaven. Joyce, in Mercius, combines Christ the incarnate Word as merciful savior, Shakespeare's quality-of-mercy speech, and Hamlet's wish—and the consummation of us all—that his "flesh" should "melt, thaw, and resolve itself into a dew."

The Word that Joyce carries is made of nature's moisture and flux, of *humor*. Language articulates moisture and flux. "Shem" and Mericus's voice end with "laughter-words," humor. Humor plus literary form is comedy. Life, for Joyce, is the rhythm of laughter, the burst, complexity, and release of the joke.

"He lifts the lifewand and the dumb speak" (195:5). How is it, after all, that the dumb *do* speak, that the dead and the inanimate do communicate and have life in us? The answer lies in good part in the flow of ink and, nowadays, in the cycles and movement of solidified liquid, products of wax, plastics, and petroleum, combined with the flow of communicating energy currents. That linguistic blend of consciousness, moisture, and matter is mankind's humor, and it is constantly being recycled. I am a speaking, thinking creature of humor whose stream of consciousness may be suggested by the sound and rush of "Quoiquoiquoiquoiquoiquoiquoiq!" That punning voice emerging out of the babble of nature, released by the lifewand of Shem, speaks the message of water: it promises life. It expresses and dramatizes in sound the first word of *Finnegans Wake*, "riverrun," which itself signifies the flow, reverence, punning humor, and transcendent quest that combine in Joyce's faith.

III

I began this inquiry with Joyce Cary's equation of prayer and laughter, and I will end it with a prayer by James Joyce. We may infer the religious nature and meaning of Shem's comedy and the whole intimate connection of comic fiction to the subjects and impulses of religion from the prayer that ends Book II, section 1 of the *Wake*. It recapitulates the drift of Mercius's soliloquy and itself flows out of those "prolonged laughter-words," "quoiquoiquoiq . . .":

> "O Loud. . . . Loud, heap miseries upon us yet entwine
> our arts with laughters low!
> Ha he hi ho hu.
> Mummum. [259.3–10]

"Lord" has metamorphosed into the ambiguous "Loud," a parody of Vico's speech-orginating thunder god and an indefinite part of speech that could be an adverb as well as a noun. God becomes the importuning word and also the agent of modification. The art of laughter unites with a conventional subject of theology—God, arts, and hearts become interchangeable, and the basis of speech and language, the vowels, merge into the sounds of laughter: ha he hi ho hu. *Amen,* the *so be it* of existence, fuses with *mummy* and mother love. And when I say this prayer aloud, I hear at the end "hu-mummmum," a final pun containing "human," "humor," and even "humus"— earth. It is the Joycean union of human flesh, linguistic comedy, and matter in the elementary fluidity of speech.

This fusion of prayer and laughter, this intentional reunion of comic and religious instincts in literature—for Joyce, literature consecrates language—takes us back to the sacred origins of comedy and the comic origins of the sacred, which Christianity had tended to suppress. Let the prayer stand as a metaphor for the comic faith and the comic vision that a great tradition in British fiction has given us.

NOTES

1. INTRODUCTION

1. Aristotle, *Poetics,* in Paul Lauter, ed., *Theories of Comedy* (Garden City, N.Y., 1964), p. 14.

2. F. R. Leavis, *The Great Tradition* (London, 1948), p. 2.

3. Northrop Frye, "The Argument of Comedy," in Lauter, p. 455.

4. George Eliot, *Middlemarch,* Gordon S. Haight, ed. (Boston, 1956), p. 3.

5. Yvor Winters, *The Function of Criticism* (Denver, 1957), p. 57.

6. See my bibliography for a full listing of sources and references for my study of comic theory and history. The following books have been indispensable in helping me to judge where and what the most important information about comedy is, in formulating my own ideas on the subject, and in writing this introduction.

Anthologies of Comic Theory

Robert Corrigan, ed. *Comedy: Meaning and Form.* San Francisco, 1965.

John J. Enck et al., eds. *The Comic in Theory and Practice.* New York, 1960.

Paul Lauter, ed. *Theories of Comedy.* Garden City, N.Y., 1964.

Harry Levin, ed. *Veins of Humor.* Cambridge, Mass., 1972.

Wylie Sypher, ed. *Comedy: "Laughter" by Henri Bergson and "An Essay on Comedy" by George Meredith.* Garden City, N.Y., 1956.

W. K. Wimsatt, ed. *The Idea of Comedy: Essays in Prose and Verse.* Englewood Cliffs, N.J., 1969.

Works by Single Authors Treating the Comic

Mikhail Bakhtin. *Rabelais and His World*. Translated by Helene Iswolsky. Cambridge, Mass., 1968.

Louis Cazamian. *The Development of English Humor*. New York, 1965.

Francis M. Cornford. *The Origins of Attic Comedy*. Cambridge, Eng., 1914.

Sigmund Freud. *Jokes and Their Relation to the Unconscious*. New York, 1960.

Northrop Frye. *Anatomy of Criticism*. Princeton, 1957.

Donald Gray. "The Uses of Victorian Laughter." *Victorian Studies* 10 (1966): 147–76.

Morton Gurewitch. *Comedy: The Irrational Vision*. Ithaca, 1975.

William Hazlitt. *Lectures on the English Comic Writers*. London, 1819.

U. C. Knoepflmacher. *Laughter and Despair*. Berkeley and Los Angeles, 1971.

Ernst Kris. *Psychoanalytic Explorations in Art*. New York, 1964.

Robert M. Martin. *The Triumph of Wit*. London, 1974.

Vivian Mercier. *The Irish Comic Tradition*. Oxford, 1962.

D. H. Munro. *The Argument of Laughter*. Melbourne, 1951.

Richard Simon. "Comedy, Suffering, and Human Existence." Ph.D. dissertation, Stanford University, 1977.

Stuart M. Tave. *The Amiable Humorist: A Study in Comic Theory and Criticism of the Eighteenth and Early Nineteenth Centuries*. Chicago, 1960.

William Makepeace Thackeray. *The English Humorists of the Eighteenth Century*. Vol. 13 of *The Complete Works of William Makepeace Thackeray*, pp. 111–330. Boston, 1889.

7. Wimsatt, *The Idea of Comedy*, p. 7. These words are Wimsatt's summary of Plato's ideas on comedy contained in books III and X of the *Republic* and books VII and XI of the *Laws*.

8. See Wimsatt, p. 2, for a short, clear, and properly tentative statement about the origins of comedy and tragedy in the ritual of the Year God.

9. Mikhail Bakhtin writes that "laughter in the Middle Ages remained outside all official spheres of ideology and outside all official strict forms of social relations. Laughter was eliminated from religious cult, from feudal and state ceremonials, etiquette, and from all the genres of high speculation. An intolerant, one-sided tone of seriousness is characteristic of official medieval culture" (*Rabelais and His World*, p. 73).

10. The exercise of humor and laughter are, as far as we know, unsuppressible. There is no doubt that the comedy of everyday life

flourished in the Middle Ages as in other times. My statement refers to formal comic activity and expression.

Bakhtin says: "Early Christianity had already condemned laughter. . . . Only permanent seriousness, remorse, and sorrow for his sins befit the Christian. . . . But this intolerant seriousness of the official church ideology made it necessary to legalize gaiety, laughter, and jests which had been eliminated from the canonized ritual and etiquette" (pp. 73–74). "Summing up, we can say that laughter, which had been eliminated in the Middle Ages from official cult and ideology, made its unofficial but almost legal nest under the shelter of almost every feast" (p. 82). "And so medieval culture of folk humor was fundamentally limited to these small islands of feasts and recreations" (p. 96).

11. Frye, "The Argument of Comedy," in Lauter, *Theories of Comedy,* p. 456.

12. See Bakhtin: "By the end of the Middle Ages a gradual disappearance of the dividing line between humor and great literature can be observed" (p. 97).

13. Ian Watt, Introduction to *The Life and Opinions of Tristram Shandy, Gentleman, by Laurence Sterne,* ed. Ian Watt (Boston, 1965), p. xxxiii.

14. See Stuart M. Tave, *The Amiable Humorist,* pp. 148–51.

15. Ibid., pp. 140–42.

16. Henry Fielding, "Author's Preface" to *Joseph Andrews* (New York, 1950), p. xxxii.

17. Lawrence Stone, "Death and Its History," *New York Review of Books* 25 (October 12, 1978): 22.

18. Sterne, *Tristram Shandy,* p. 255.

19. Samuel Johnson, *The Rambler,* no. 125, in Lauter, *Theories of Comedy,* p. 254.

20. Northrop Frye, *Anatomy of Criticism,* p. 167.

21. Louis Cazamian, *The Development of English Humor,* p. 3.

22. "Hannah Arendt: From an Interview," *New York Review of Books* 25 (October 26, 1978): 18.

2. AUSTEN'S *EMMA*

1. G. W. F. Hegel, "The Philosophy of Fine Art," translated by F. P. B. Osmaston, in Lauter, *Theories of Comedy,* p. 351.

2. Jane Austen, *Emma,* R. W. Chapman, ed. (Oxford, 1933), p. 343. All subsequent citations to Austen's novels are to this edition.

3. There is a wealth of informative, varied, and provocative critical discussion of *Emma.* Much of the most interesting and important of

this criticism, to which I am greatly indebted, is collected in the following books: John Halperin, ed., *Jane Austen: Bicentenary Essays* (Cambridge and New York, 1975); David Lodge, ed., *Jane Austen: "Emma": A Casebook* (London, 1968); Stephen M. Parrish, ed., *Jane Austen: "Emma": An Authoritative Text, Backgrounds, Reviews, and Criticism* (New York, 1972); B. C. Southam, ed., *Critical Essays on Jane Austen* (London, 1968); B. C. Southham, ed., *Jane Austen: The Critical Heritage* (London and New York, 1968); Ian Watt, ed., *Jane Austen: A Collection of Critical Essays* (Englewood Cliffs, N.J., 1963).

In addition to the writers and critics anthologized in those collections, I also recommend—and am very grateful to—the following authors for their specific criticism on *Emma:* Susan Morgan, *In the Meantime: Character and Perception in Jane Austen's Fiction* (Chicago, 1980); Stuart M. Tave, *Some Words of Jane Austen* (Chicago, 1973); Howard Babb, *Jane Austen's Novels: The Fabric of Design* (Columbus, Ohio, 1962); Lionel Trilling, *Beyond Culture* (London, 1966), pp. 31–55; Malcolm Bradbury, "Jane Austen's *Emma,*" *Critical Quarterly* 4 (Winter, 1962): 335–46; J. F. Burrows, *Jane Austen's "Emma"* (Sydney, 1968); Alistair M. Duckworth, *The Improvement of the Estate* (Baltimore, 1972); Joseph M. Duffy, Jr., "*Emma:* The Awakening from Innocence," *ELH: A Journal of English Literary History* 21 (March, 1954): 39–53; U. C. Knoepflmacher, "The Importance of Being Frank: Character and Letter-Writing in *Emma,*" *Studies in English Literature* 7 (Autumn, 1967): 639–58; J. S. Lawry, "'Decided and Open': Structure in *Emma,*" *Nineteenth-Century Fiction* 24 (June, 1969): 1–15; Robert Liddell, *The Novels of Jane Austen* (London, 1963); David Lee Minter, "Aesthetic Vision and the World of *Emma,*" *Nineteenth-Century Fiction* 21 (June, 1966): 49–59; Marvin Mudrick, *Jane Austen: Irony as Defense and Discovery* (Princeton, 1952); Edgar F. Shannon, Jr., "*Emma:* Character and Construction," *PMLA* 71 (September, 1956): 637–50; Andrew Wright, *Jane Austen's Novels: A Study in Structure* (London, 1953).

4. Jane Austen, *Letters to Her Sister Cassandra and Others,* R. W. Chapman, ed. (London, 1952), p. 443.

5. Ibid., pp. 430, 443, 451, 452–53. My sense of Jane Austen disagrees sharply with that of Marilyn Butler, who tends to see her as an unambiguously conservative novelist in her *Jane Austen and the War of Ideas* (Oxford, 1975).

6. John Henry Newman, *Letters and Correspondence of Newman,* Anne Mozley, ed. (1891), vol. 2, p. 223, cited by Rachel Trickett in B. C. Southam, ed., *Critical Essays on Jane Austen,* p. 176.

7. Anthony Ashley Cooper, third earl of Shaftesbury, *Sensus Communis: An Essay on the Freedom of Wit and Humour* (1709). Cited by Wimsatt in *The Idea of Comedy,* p. 284.

8. Margaret Oliphant, in B. C. Southam, ed., *Austen: The Critical*

Heritage, pp. 216–17.

9. Thomas Hobbes, *Human Nature.* Cited by Wimsatt, p. 284.

10. Emmanuel Kant, "Critique of Judgment." Cited by Wimsatt, p. 285.

11. Mark Schorer, "The Humiliation of Emma Woodhouse," in Lodge, ed., *Jane Austen,* p. 172.

12. Northrop Frye, *Anatomy of Criticism,* pp. 163–66.

13. Wylie Sypher, "The Meanings of Comedy" in *Comedy,* p. 212.

14. Cited by James Edward Austen-Leigh, *Memoir of Jane Austen* (London, 1871; Oxford, 1926), p. 157.

15. My interpretation of this scene runs counter to that of Julia Prewitt Brown, who regards Austen's words about the efficacy of Emma's ministering to the poor as wholly ironic. See her *Jane Austen's Novels: Social Change and Literary Form* (Cambridge, Mass., 1979), pp. 101–27.

16. Cited by Frederick Engels, "Socialism: Utopian and Scientific," in Karl Marx and Frederick Engels, *Selected Works* (New York, 1968), p. 406.

17. See, for example, Schorer, "The Humiliation of Emma Woodhouse," and Edmund Wilson, "A Long Talk about Jane Austen," *Classics and Commercials* (New York, 1950), pp. 196–203.

18. Notice that a rising man, in Emma's world, is sure to want to own a carriage for easier traveling, just as modern affluent people want to travel and have better cars, boats, or even planes as substance and symbol of greater liberty.

19. I am using Marvin Mudrick's excellent discussion of irony. See his book, *Jane Austen: Irony as Defense and Discovery.*

3. PEACOCK'S *NIGHTMARE ABBEY*

1. Sypher, *Comedy,* p. 224.

2. Freud, *Jokes and Their Relation to the Unconscious,* p. 127.

3. Comparatively little specific criticism of *Nightmare Abbey* exists. The book that I have found most useful and informative in writing this chapter is Jean-Jacques Mayoux's massive *Un Epicurien anglais: Thomas Love Peacock* (Paris, 1932), which deals with the full range of Peacock's life, opinions, and writings. Good discussions of *Nightmare Abbey* appear in Carl Dawson's *His Fine Wit: A Study of Thomas Love Peacock* (Berkeley and Los Angeles, 1970) and Howard Mills's *Peacock: His Circle and His Age* (London, 1969). Lorna Sage's edition of *Peacock: The Satirical Novels: A Casebook* (London, 1976) gathers together many significant nineteenth-century appraisals and twentieth-century interpretations of Peacock. The best study in English is Marilyn Butler's *Peacock Displayed: A Satirist in His Context* (London, 1979), which appeared after this chapter was completed. See esp. pp. 133–39 and 264–71.

4. Northrop Frye, *Anatomy of Criticism,* p. 309.

5. Carl Van Doren, *The Life of Thomas Love Peacock* (London, 1911), p. 276.

6. Mills, *Peacock,* p. 1.

7. A. E. Dyson, *The Crazy Fabric* (London, 1965), p. 64.

8. Frank Kermode, *The Romantic Image* (New York, 1964), p. 2.

9. Frank Kermode, *The Sense of an Ending* (New York, 1967), p. 3.

10. Thomas Love Peacock, *Nightmare Abbey,* from *The Novels of Thomas Love Peacock,* David Garnett, ed. (London, 1948), p. 419. All subsequent citations to Peacock's novels are to this edition.

11. Ben Jonson, *Every Man in His Humour,* act 3, scene 1.

12. Humphry House, "The Novels of Thomas Love Peacock," *The Listener,* (December 8, 1949), p. 998.

13. Dyson, *The Crazy Fabric,* p. 64.

14. Mills, *Peacock,* p. 145.

15. Jean-Paul Sartre, *Search for a Method,* Hazel E. Barnes, trans. (New York, 1968), p. 65, n. 4.

16. Mayoux, *Un Epicurien anglais,* p. 278.

17. The fact that part of this speech is a paraphrase of Denys Montfort does not lessen its serious impact.

18. Dyson, *The Crazy Fabric,* p. 65.

19. In *Crotchet Castle* and *Gryll Grange,* Peacock would combine the roles of Hilary and Larynx, the comparatively silent hedonist vicar, in the figures of the reverend doctors Folliot and Opimian—the priests, in effect, of modern epicureanism.

20. Mayoux's phrase is "un sentiment religieux du monde réel et matériel" (p. 614).

21. Mayoux, p. 618.

22. Johan Huizinga, *Homo Ludens: A Study of the Play Element in Culture* (Boston, 1955), p. 158.

23. P. J. Salz, "Peacock's Use of Music in His Novels," *Journal of English and Germanic Philology,* vol. 54 (1955), and Edmund Wilson, "The Musical Glasses of Peacock," *Classics and Commercials* (New York, 1950).

24. Wilson, "Musical Glasses," p. 406.

25. Sigmund Freud, *Wit and Its Relation to the Unconscious,* in A. A. Brill, ed. *The Basic Writings of Sigmund Freud* (New York, 1938), p. 654. I use this edition here because it alone gives the Hamlet speech.

26. Claude Lévi-Strauss, *The Savage Mind* (Chicago, 1966), pp. 23–24.

4. DICKENS'S *MARTIN CHUZZLEWIT*

1. Susanne K. Langer, *Feeling and Form* (New York, 1953), p. 330.

2. Charles Dickens, *The Life and Adventures of Martin Chuzzlewit*

(London, 1951), the New Oxford Illustrated Dickens, p. 733. All subsequent citations are to this edition.

3. See R. G. Collingwood, *Faith and Reason,* Lionel Rubinoff, ed. (Chicago, 1968), pp. 130–34.

4. R. C. Churchill, "Charles Dickens," in Boris Ford, ed., *From Dickens to Hardy* (Baltimore, 1958), p. 120. Steven Marcus, one of the most perceptive critics of *Martin Chuzzlewit,* says of the novel, "It may also be called, as . . . R.C. Churchill . . . called it, the greatest work of comic genius in English literature, which I think it probably is" (*Dickens: From Pickwick to Dombey* [New York, 1965], p. 213). A. E. Dyson calls it "the funniest book in the language" (*The Inimitable Dickens* [London, 1970], p. 71).

5. For illuminating discussions of *Martin Chuzzlewit* see: Marcus, pp. 213–68; Dyson, pp. 71–95; J. Hillis Miller, *Charles Dickens: The World of His Novels* (Cambridge, Mass., 1959), pp. 98–143; Dorothy Van Ghent, "The Dickens World: A View From Todgers's," in George H. Ford and Lauriat Lane, Jr., eds., *The Dickens Critics* (Ithaca, N.Y., 1961), pp. 213–32; Albert J. Guerard, *The Triumph of the Novel* (New York, 1976), pp. 235–61; Branwen Pratt, "Dickens and Freedom: Young Bailey in *Martin Chuzzlewit,*" *Nineteenth-Century Fiction* 30 (September, 1975): 185–199; and James R. Kinkaid, *Dickens and the Rhetoric of Laughter* (Oxford, 1971), pp. 132–62, whose excellent study I read after my own was completed (Mr. Kinkaid has pointed out the centrality to the comedy of Tiggs's "moralise as we will" speech).

6. Barbara Hardy, *The Moral Art of Charles Dickens* (New York, 1970), pp. 119, 121.

7. V. S. Pritchett, "The Comic World of Dickens," in Ford and Lane, eds., *The Dickens Critics,* p. 310.

8. See John Forster, *The Life of Charles Dickens* (London, 1966), vol. 2, p. 271.

9. Ibid., vol. 1, p. 273.

10. Freud, *Jokes and Their Relation to the Unconscious,* pp. 125–28.

11. Taylor Stoehr, *Dickens: The Dreamer's Stance* (Ithaca, N.Y., 1965), p. 54.

12. Ibid., pp. 77–78.

13. See Barry Westburg, *The Confessional Fictions of Charles Dickens* (De Kalb, Ill., 1977), pp. 121–24, for an illuminating discourse on the importance of names and pronunciations to Pip in *Great Expectations.*

14. Marcus, *Dickens: From Pickwick to Dombey,* p. 217.

15. Henri Bergson, "Laughter," in Sypher, ed., *Comedy,* p. 84.

16. See Edgar Johnson, *Charles Dickens: His Tragedy and Triumph* (New York, 1952), vol. 1, pp. 473–77.

17. Marcus, pp. 244–45.

18. Miller, *Charles Dickens: The World of His Novels,* pp. 117–18.

19. Pritchett, "The Comic World of Dickens," p. 313.

20. J. Hillis Miller, in his excellent discussion of *Martin Chuzzlewit,* to which I am indebted, says that Dickens's world "has no center, but is an unimaginable number of plural and interchangeable objects" (p. 113).

21. Pritchett, p. 309.

22. Frederick C. Crews also writes: "Since our common plight is to be forever seeking acquittal from the fantasy-charges we have internalized as the price of ceasing to be infants, we share an eagerness for interpsychic transactions that seem to promise such an acquittal, or at least an abatement of guilt by means of establishing a confessional bond. Rather than being merely an unconscious release within the author or a similar release within the reader, literary process establishes a transitory complicity between the two" ("Anaesthetic Criticism: II" *New York Review of Books* 14 [March 12, 1970]: 52).

23. Pritchett, p. 318.

24. Ibid., p. 310.

25. W. H. Auden, "Concerning the Unpredictable," *New Yorker,* February 21, 1970, p. 124.

5. THACKERAY'S *VANITY FAIR*

1. Susanne K. Langer, *Feeling and Form* (New York, 1953), p. 349.

2. The shelves groan with critical discussion of Thackeray's *Vanity Fair,* but a surprising amount of it seems to me confused and wrongheaded. Even outstanding critics, such as Dorothy Van Ghent and Arnold Kettle, fail to do it justice. The reason for this critical ambivalence and muddle is due mainly I think to the difficulties readers have in dealing with Thackeray's comic fatalism, his equivocal style, and the class and political antipathies that he seems to exacerbate. There has, however, been acute and illuminating criticism written on this novel—criticism that has made my study of Thackeray's comedy of shifting perspectives possible. I am deeply indebted to G. Armour Craig's "On the Style of *Vanity Fair*" in M. G. Sundell, ed., *Twentieth Century Interpretations of Vanity Fair* (Englewood Cliffs, N.J., 1969); A. E. Dyson's "*Vanity Fair:* An Irony against Heroes," in *The Crazy Fabric* (cited in chap. 3, n. 7); Barbara Hardy's *The Exposure of Luxury: Radical Themes in Thackeray* (London, 1972); U. C. Knoepflmacher's "*Vanity Fair:* The Bitterness of Retrospection," in *Laughter and Despair* (cited in chap. 1, n. 6); John A. Lester Jr.'s "Thackeray's Narrative Technique," in Robert O. Preyer, ed., *Victorian Literature: Selected Essays* (New York, 1966), pp. 159–81; John Loofbourow's *Thackeray and the Form of Fiction* (Princeton, 1964); Juliet McMaster's *Thackeray:*

The Major Novels (Toronto, 1971) and her "Thackeray's Things: Time's Local Habitation," in Richard Levine, ed., *The Victorian Experience: The Novelists* (Athens, Ohio, 1976); Jack P. Rawlins's *Thackeray's Novels: A Fiction That Is True* (Berkeley and Los Angeles, 1974); Winslow Roger's "Thackeray's Self-Consciousness," in Jerome Buckley, ed., *The World of Victorian Fiction* (Cambridge, Mass., 1975); Geoffrey Tillotson's *Thackeray the Novelist* (Cambridge, Eng., 1954); and James H. Wheatley's *Patterns in Thackeray's Fiction* (Cambridge, Mass., 1969). Each of these works has brilliant and original insights into the power and greatness of Thackeray's best book.

I have found three collections of critical comment to be of great help and convenience: M. G. Sundell, ed., *Twentieth Century Interpretations of Vanity Fair;* Geoffrey Tillotson and Donald Hawes, eds., *Thackeray: The Critical Heritage* (London and New York, 1968); and Alexander Welsh, ed., *Thackeray: A Collection of Critical Essays* (Englewood Cliffs, N.J., 1968).

3. William Makepeace Thackeray, *Vanity Fair: A Novel without a Hero,* Geoffrey and Kathleen Tillotson, eds. (Boston, 1963), chap. 62, p. 666. All subsequent citations (by chapter and page numbers) are to this edition.

4. See G. Armour Craig, who also discusses the importance of this passage ("On the Style of *Vanity Fair,*" in Sundell, ed., *Twentieth Century Interpretations,* pp. 56–57).

5. *Letters and Private Papers of William Makepeace Thackeray,* Gordon N. Ray, ed. (Cambridge, Mass., 1946), vol. 2, pp. 423–24.

6. Ibid., p. 282.

7. Thackeray, *English Humorists of the Eighteenth Century,* p. 114 (see chap. 1, note 6).

8. John Bunyan, *The Pilgrim's Progress from This World to That Which Is to Come* (New York, 1963), p. 91. See William Marshall, *The World of the Victorian Novel* (London, 1967) p. 245, who quotes this passage in his interesting study of *Vanity Fair* (pp. 245–60).

9. Henri Bergson, "Laughter," in Sypher, ed., *Comedy,* p. 84.

10. Thackeray's most important precursors here were, I think, De Sade in *Juliet* and *Justine* and Jane Austen in *Mansfield Park.*

11. See, for example, chap. 26, p. 251; chap. 31, p. 298; chap.38, p. 380.

12. Karl Marx, *Economic and Philosophical Manuscripts of 1844,* Dirk J. Struik, ed. (New York, 1964), p. 147.

13. See Dorothy Van Ghent, *The English Novel: Form and Function* (New York, 1961), p. 145, who points out the importance of the incident.

14. See *Vanity Fair* in *The Complete Works of William Makepeace Thackeray* (Boston, 1889), vol. 2, p. 271.

15. See Arnold Kettle, "Thackeray: *Vanity Fair*," in *An Introduction to the English Novel* (New York, 1960), vol. 1, pp. 164–65.

16. If I am right in identifying Becky with a large strain in Thackeray himself, then that final description of her contains a remarkable metaphorical insight into what his own career was to become. Like her, he would take an honored place in Vanity Fair and mute his cynical, rebellious genius, his Becky wit encrusted by barnacles of respectability.

17. Van Ghent, *The English Novel*, pp. 141–45.

18. Hardy, *The Exposure of Luxury*, p. 33.

19. James Joyce, *Ulysses* (New York, 1961), p. 734.

20. See Van Ghent, *The English Novel*, p. 146, for a discussion of Jos.

21. For a fascinating discussion of materiality in Thackeray, see McMaster, "Thackeray's Things," in Levine, ed., *The Victorian Experience*, pp. 49–86.

22. Charles Dickens, *Little Dorrit* (London, 1953), book 1, chap. 17, p. 205.

23. Thackeray, *Letters*, vol. 2, p. 423.

24. Ibid., p. 424.

25. Ibid., p. 309.

26. Thackeray, *English Humorists*, vol. 13, pp. 133–49.

27. Ibid., p. 113; italics mine.

28. See Lester, "Thackeray's Narrative Technique," in Preyer, ed., *Victorian Literature*, pp. 159–81, for a fine discussion of Thackeray's narrator.

29. For illuminating insights on this subject, see Jean Sudrann, "The Philosopher's Property: Thackeray and the Use of Time," *Victorian Studies* 10 (1967): 359–88.

30. Joyce, *Ulysses*, p. 34.

31. T. S. Eliot, "*Ulysses*, Order and Myth," *Dial* 75 (November, 1923): 483.

32. George Eliot, *Middlemarch*, Finale, book 8, p. 607.

33. Frederick Engels, *The Condition of the Working Class in England*, W. O. Henderson and W. H. Chaloner, trans. and ed. (New York, 1958), p. 313.

6. TROLLOPE'S *BARCHESTER TOWERS*

1. Ruth apRoberts, *The Moral Trollope* (Athens, Ohio, 1971), p. 123.

2. There is still comparatively little criticism of Trollope's individual novels, including *Barchester Towers*. This chapter relies on many of the ideas and implications of the discussion of *Barchester Towers* in my

book *The Changing World of Anthony Trollope* (Berkeley and Los Angeles, 1968). In writing it, I found especially illuminating the recent insights of Ruth apRoberts's *The Moral Trollope;* David Skilton's *Anthony Trollope and His Contemporaries* (London, 1972); U. C. Knoepflmacher's *Laughter and Despair,* chaps. 1 and 2, pp. 3–49; C. P. Snow's *Trollope: His Life and Art* (New York, 1975); and Lowry Pei's "Anthony Trollope's Palliser Novels: The Conquest of Separateness" (Ph.D. dissertation, Stanford University, 1975). Other interesting and provocative criticism of *Barchester Towers* appears in James R. Kincaid's *The Novels of Anthony Trollope* (Oxford, 1977); in William Cadbury's "Character and the Mock Heroic in *Barchester Towers,*" *Texas Studies in Literature and Language* 5 (1963–64): 509–19; in W. David Shaw's "Moral Drama in *Barchester Towers,*" *Nineteenth-Century Fiction* 19 (1964–65): 45–54; and in Donald Smalley's edition *Trollope: The Critical Heritage* (London and New York, 1969).

3. apRoberts, *The Moral Trollope,* p. 114.

4. Anthony Trollope, *An Autobiography* (London, 1953), World's Classics edition, chap. 12, p. 190.

5. Peter Berger, *The Social Reality of Religion,* cited by Owen Chadwick, *The Secularization of the European Mind in the Nineteenth Century* (Cambridge, 1975), p. 138.

6. America, of course, had its Fenimore Cooper; France, its Balzac.

7. John Fowles, *The French Lieutenant's Woman* (Boston, 1969), p. 105.

8. " . . . and sweetened by pathos," he continues (*An Autobiography,* chap. 7, p. 109). The pathos, however, does not apply to *Barchester Towers.*

9. Anthony Trollope, *Barchester Towers* (London, 1925), World's Classics edition, chap. 1, pp. 3–4. All subsequent citations, by chapter and page numbers, are to this edition.

10. Anthony Trollope, *Doctor Thorne* (London, 1926), chap. 11, p. 140.

11. In *The Warden,* Grantly's three sons are obvious caricatures of prominent clerical figures of the age: C. J. Blomfield, bishop of London; Henry Phillpots, bishop of Exeter; and Samuel Wilberforce, bishop of Oxford. See Owen Chadwick, *The Victorian Church* (New York, 1966), pt. 1, p. 214, 217–20, 501–3.

12. For documentation of this material, see Chadwick, *The Victorian Church,* pt. 1, esp. pp. 1–5 and 101–226.

13. William James, *The Varieties of Religious Experience* (New York, 1929), pp. 347–49.

14. Ibid., p. 36.

15. George Meredith, "Essay on Comedy," in Sypher, ed., *Comedy,* pp. 47–48.

16. The genesis of this contradiction and the reason why it recurs obsessively in Trollope's fiction may lie in an unresolved and unresolvable conflict in him between resentment and admiration for his mother—resentment for abandoning him in boyhood, admiration for her achievement and bravery. It is easy to speculate about how the fantasies of a boy left with a demented father, missing his absent and adventurous mother, and wanting to make her over into a "typical" loving mother might figure in his art (e.g., in his title *Can You Forgive Her?*). She was clever, competent, blessed with literary ability, full of joy, and the only source of hope in the family, but she neglected him. His father's futile life-project was to compile an *Encyclopedia Ecclesiastica,* which was to be a tribute to religion. How could that worthless, unfinished piece of outdated piety by a broken man compete for his emotional respect with the worldly book of success that his mother composed with humor, courage, and intellect—with almost every virtue, in fact, but tender motherliness?

17. Henry James, "Anthony Trollope," in Leon Edel, ed., *The Future of the Novel* (New York, 1956), p. 236.

18. See Trollope, *An Autobiography,* chap. 6, pp. 90–91.

19. Anthony Trollope, *The Three Clerks* (London, 1959), chap. 22, p. 241.

20. Barbara Tuchman, *The Guns of August* (New York, 1962), p. 4.

21. Trollope, *An Autobiography,* chap. 15, p. 238.

22. Ibid., chap. 12, p. 205.

23. U. C. Knoepflmacher, *Laughter and Despair,* p. 21.

24. See David Skilton, *Anthony Trollope and His Contemporaries,* for evidence of how dangerous it was for a novelist to offend normative convention and religious sensibility.

25. See Knoepflmacher, pp. 31–35, for an informative discussion of this scene.

26. Trollope, *An Autobiography,* chap. 8, p. 132.

27. Nathaniel Hawthorne, quoted by Trollope, ibid., p. 125.

28. Ibid.

29. Elizabeth Bowen, *Anthony Trollope: A New Judgement* (New York and London, 1946).

7. MEREDITH'S *THE EGOIST*

1. Sigmund Freud, *The Future of an Illusion,* James Strachey, ed. (New York, 1961), p. 6.

2. Meredith, "An Essay on Comedy," in Sypher, ed., *Comedy,* p. 49.

3. Much good and stimulating discussion of *The Egoist* has been collected recently by Robert M. Adams in his Norton Critical Edition: *George Meredith, "The Egoist": An Annotated Text, Backgrounds, Criti-*

cism (New York and London, 1979). Two other collections provide important criticism: Ian Fletcher, ed., *Meredith Now* (London, 1971), and Ioan M. Williams, ed., *George Meredith: The Critical Heritage* (London and New York, 1971). My own reading of *The Egoist* has benefited most from Judith Wilt's *The Readable People of George Meredith* (Princeton, 1975), pp. 147–79; Gillian Beer's *Meredith: A Change of Masks* (London, 1970), pp. 114–39; V. S. Pritchett's *George Meredith and English Comedy* (New York, 1969); and Margaret Comstock's discussion of *The Egoist* in "George Meredith, Virginia Woolf, and Their Feminist Comedy" (Ph.D. dissertation, Stanford University, 1975). Even though I do not always agree completely with them, I owe much to each of them for many of the ideas and insights of this chapter.

4. George Meredith, "To the Comic Spirit," in *The Works of George Meredith,* vol. 12: *Poetical Works* (London, 1919), p. 394.

5. George Meredith, *The Works of George Meredith,* vol. 6: *The Egoist* (London, 1915), "Prelude," p. 3. All subsequent citations by chapter and page numbers are to this edition.

6. Meredith, "To the Comic Spirit," p. 402.

7. Ibid., p. 399.

8. John Milton, "Paradise Lost," book 4, line 299.

9. Joseph Warren Beach, *The Comic Spirit in George Meredith* (New York, 1911), p. 130.

10. See R. D. Mayo, "*The Egoist* and the Willow Pattern," *ELH: A Journal of English Literary History* 9 (1947): 71–78, and Gillian Beer, *Meredith: A Change of Masks,* p. 131.

Gillian Beer, in her illuminating study, describes the legend: "This story, constructed from the figures on the popular blue willow pattern plate, runs thus: a widower mandarin intends to marry his daughter to a wealthy suitor but the maiden chooses a poor but honourable man serving as her father's secretary. She and the secretary escape, hotly pursued by father and betrothed and are turned into birds for their fidelity. The story had been used as the basis of a successful pantomime in 1875 by Francis Burnand, editor of *Punch* and a close friend of Meredith. . . . The parallels are clear though not insistent. The willow-pattern analogue gives a meaningful edge to the persistent references to porcelain throughout the story."

11. Margaret Comstock also points out the phallic nature of this "I," though we arrived at our conclusions independently. See pp. 144 and 174 of her dissertation, cited in n. 3, above.

12. George Eliot, *Middlemarch,* p. 156.

13. Françoise Basch, *Relative Creatures* (New York, 1974), p. 105.

14. For an excellent insight into the brilliance of this passage and its important stylistic and rhetorical implications, see Donald Stone, *Novelists in a Changing World* (Cambridge, Mass., 1972), pp. 126–27.

15. After finishing my chapter on Meredith, I read Kate Millett's provocative and excellent discussion of *The Egoist* in *Sexual Politics* (New York, 1971), pp. 185–91. She has anticipated my conclusion about the origins of *The Egoist*'s comedy and my sense of Meredith's generosity: "What is astonishing is that the book is not the revenge one would inevitably expect" (p. 186); "[it is] a feat of astounding empathy." (p. 187).

16. See, for example, Lionel Stevenson, *The Ordeal of George Meredith* (London, 1954), p. 61, and Jack Lindsay, *George Meredith: His Life and Work* (London, 1956), p. 239.

17. A. H. Able's study, *George Meredith and Thomas Love Peacock: A Study in Literary Influence* (Philadelphia, 1933), shows the literary debt that Meredith owed his father-in-law and the close literary kinship between the two.

18. For an excellent discussion of the chapter, consult Comstock, pp. 175–79.

19. Meredith, "An Essay on Comedy," in Sypher, ed., *Comedy*, p. 15.

20. For Willoughby, love is a mania of projection and self-division. The egoist in love behaves like a grotesque hermaphrodite trying to inseminate itself before an imaginary audience of applauding selves. Egoistic love is a self-feeding process, osmosis rather than intercourse. Hence the pain of love—to pursue a Meredithian idiom—often comes like the kicks of an unmasticated Jonah of otherness, alive in our whale-belly of egoism and unwilling to be digested by us. This heartburn of the Egoist-behemoth is the stuff, for Meredith, of high comedy. Women, in his fiction, resent being swallowed and so make the sexist beast cavort with diverting spasms.

21. Much of this discussion relies on the insightful reading and ideas of Rebecca Reynolds.

22. William Blake, *The Complete Writings of William Blake*, Geoffrey Keynes, ed. (London, 1957), p. 793, letter 5.

23. Of course, nature worship can become a tool of egoism and a form of sentimentality. Willoughby, for example, pays ludicrous homage to English "green" (4:30) as a pretty background to himself; Meredith can prick, in a single line, the bombast and insecure inanity of stock responses to the "sublime" of nature: "big mountains . . . tire [people] of their everlasting big Ohs" (22:255).

24. Lindsay, *George Meredith: His Life and Work*, pp. 238–44.

25. E. M. Forster, *Aspects of the Novel* (New York, 1927), p. 90.

26. For a discussion and comparison of Meredith's style with Joyce's, see Donald S. Fanger, "Joyce and Meredith: A Question of Influence and Tradition," *Modern Fiction Studies* 6 (Summer, 1960): 125–30.

8. CARROLL'S *THROUGH THE LOOKING-GLASS*

1. Wallace Stevens, "Notes toward a Supreme Fiction," *The Collected Poems* (New York, 1968), p. 383.

2. Elizabeth Sewell, *The Field of Nonsense* (London, 1952), p. 181.

3. Sewell calls attention to this Joycean phrase in discussing Carroll (ibid., p. 180).

4. The normative psychoanalytic critics, those thinly disguised, authoritarian neoidealists, have a carnival telling us that this man who gave pleasure to millions, who lived a quiet but richly creative life, who supported numerous relatives, who became one of the fine photographers of the century, who harmed almost no one and stayed out of jails and asylums, was abnormal, maladjusted, schizoid, and sick—which tempts me to repeat the Cheshire Cat's observation, "We're all mad here." See James Joyce, *Finnegans Wake* (New York, 1958), p. 115: "we grisly old Sykos who have done our unsmiling bit on 'alices, when they were yung and easily freudened."

5. Lewis Carroll, *Through the Looking-Glass*, in *The Annotated Alice*, with introduction and notes by Martin Gardner (New York, 1960), p. 174. All subsequent citations are to this edition.

6. Nearly all the outstanding criticism on Carroll has been collected in anthologies and editions published within the past twenty years. The texts I have found indispensable are Martin Gardner's *The Annotated Alice*; Robert Phillip's collection *Aspects of Alice: Lewis Carroll's Dreamchild as Seen through the Critic's Looking-Glass* (New York, 1971); Donald J. Gray's edition *Alice in Wonderland: Authoritative Texts of "Alice's Adventures in Wonderland," "Through the Looking-Glass," "The Hunting of the Snark": Backgrounds, Essays in Criticism* (New York, 1971); Edward Guiliano's anthology *Lewis Carroll Observed: A Collection of Unpublished Photographs, Drawings, Poetry, and New Essays* (New York, 1976); Henri Parisot's edition of critical writings from France, *Lewis Carroll* (Paris: Editions de l'Herne, 1971); and Donald Rackin's edition *Alice's Adventures in Wonderland: A Critical Handbook* (Belmont, Calif., 1969). Also useful to me has been Kathleen Blake's *Play, Games, and Sport: The Literary Works of Lewis Carroll* (Ithaca and London, 1974).

7. Lewis Carroll, "Stolen Waters," *The Complete Works of Lewis Carroll* (New York, 1936), p. 965.

8. The picture of the White Knight is the frontispiece to the book.

9. I am aware that "Carroll" derives from the latinized Charles, which he first used at school, and that, along with "Carroll," Dodgson submitted two other *noms de plume*, Edgar Cuthwellis and Edgar U. C. Westhill, to Edmund Yates, who made the choice. But why didn't he call himself "Lewis Charles" instead of the name of his sister, Carol?

Looking at the alternatives, does anyone think Yates really had a choice?

10. Ernst Kris, *Psychoanalytic Explorations in Art* (New York, 1964), p. 177.

11. Thomas Huxley, "A Liberal Education and Where to Find It," an address delivered at the South London Workingman's College, January 4, 1868, and published later the same year in *Macmillan's Magazine* and ultimately in Huxley's *Collected Essays* (London and New York, 1893–94), vol. 3.

12. See *Annotated Alice,* p. 206, n. 5.

13. Sigmund Freud, "Humour," in *The Complete Works of Sigmund Freud,* Standard Edition, vol. 21 (London, 1953), p. 166.

14. See *Annotated Alice,* p. 238, n. 7.

15. Harry Levin, "*Wonderland* Revisited," in Phillips, ed., *Aspects of Alice,* p. 179.

16. See Bruno Bettelheim, *The Uses of Enchantment: The Meaning of Fairy Tales* (New York, 1976), p. 205.

17. Judith Bloomingdale, "Alice as *Anima,*" in Phillips, ed., *Aspects of Alice,* p. 389.

18. W. H. Auden, "Today's 'Wonder-World' Needs Alice," ibid., p. 12.

19. Peter Coveney, *The Image of Childhood* (Baltimore, 1967), p. 245.

20. Stuart M. Tave, *Some Words of Jane Austen,* p. 208.

21. Nancy Dawson Mann, "George MacDonald: The Tradition of Victorian Fantasy" (Ph.D. dissertation, Stanford University, 1973), p. 33.

22. For an enlightening discussion of the historical use of fairytales, see Gillian Avery, "Fairy Tales with a Purpose" and "Fairy Tales for Pleasure," in Donald J. Gray's edition of *Alice,* pp. 321–30.

23. Levin, in Phillips, ed., *Aspects of Alice,* p. 187.

24. Edmund Wilson, "C. L. Dodgson: The Poet Logician," ibid., p. 201.

25. Patricia M. Spacks, "Logic and Language in *Through the Looking-Glass,*" ibid., p. 273.

26. Sigmund Freud, *Wit and Its Relation to the Unconscious* in *Selected Writings,* A. H. Brill, trans. (New York, 1938), p. 667. Brill's words give the exact meaning that I want to stress.

27. Freudian theories of comic regression help to explain how Carroll's comedy of language works, just as they help to illuminate Dickens's comedy of expression (see chapter 4, note 10). Ernst Kris, following Freud (see *Jokes and Their Relation to the Unconscious,* pp. 125–29), writes: "Under the influence of the comic, we return to the happiness of childhood. We can throw off the fetters of logical thought and revel in a long-forgotten freedom. The perfect example

of this type of behavior is talking nonsense; here we handle words as we did when children. . . . Pleasure over words . . . develops out of a complicated process. . . . The child tries to understand words and their meaning, and it is an arduous process. Children are not at home in the world of words, yet words are indispensable for they serve to establish contact . . . ; we can follow . . . the child's delight when using newly acquired words, its repetition of them in a sort of rhythmical chant, its happy experiments with sound and meaning before the difference between them is finally grasped" (*Psychoanalytic Explorations in Art,* pp. 205–7). The child's joy at playing with language it has just mastered lives on in the pleasure that adults find in words.

28. Kathleen Blake, *Play, Games, and Sport,* p. 19.

29. See Sewell, *The Field of Nonsense,* for a provocative discussion of nonsense.

30. Blake, *Play, Games, and Sport,* p. 93.

31. See *Annotated Alice,* p. 238, n. 7.

32. Sewell, *The Field of Nonsense,* p. 180.

9. JOYCE'S *FINNEGANS WAKE*

1. James Joyce, *Finnegans Wake* (New York, 1958). All subsequent citations are to page and line of this edition, which includes the author's corrections, incorporated into the text.

2. James Atherton, *The Books at the Wake* (London and New York, 1959), p. 14.

3. Quoted by Stanislaus Joyce, *My Brother's Keeper: James Joyce's Early Years* (New York, 1958), pp. 103–4.

4. Vivian Mercier, *The Irish Comic Tradition* (Oxford, 1962), pp. 208–39.

5. James Joyce, *A Portrait of the Artist as a Young Man* (New York, 1964), p. 221.

6. Richard Ellmann, *Ulysses on the Liffey* (New York, 1972), p. xi.

7. James Joyce, *Ulysses* (New York, 1961), p. 432. All subsequent references are to this edition.

8. No full-length study of "Shem" exists, but there is much annotation and discussion of its pages. Every reader of *Finnegans Wake* must depend on a vast assortment of scholarly and critical paraphernalia, as I indicate in the "Audience" section of this chapter. See the bibliography for a full account of the works I have consulted and used in writing on "Shem."

9. I am indebted to Susan Lowell Humphreys for this accurate Wakean coinage.

10. *The Critical Writings,* Ellsworth Mason and Richard Ellmann, eds. (New York, 1959), p. 144.

11. Richard Ellmann, *James Joyce* (New York, 1959), p. 559.

12. George Meredith, *The Egoist,* 43:547.

13. See Stuart Gilbert, *James Joyce's Ulysses* (New York, 1955), p. 118.

14. Joyce was drawn to the philosopher Giambattista Vico and his theories because Vico's system, without denying continual change, comprehended it. Joyce's understanding of Vico's thesis, as Samuel Beckett summarizes it, is as follows: "In the beginning was the thunder: the thunder set free Religion, in its most objective and unphilosophical form—idolatrous animism: Religion produced Society, and the first social men were the cave-dwellers, taking refuge from a passionate Nature: this primitive family life receives its first impulse towards development from the arrival of terrified vagabonds: admitted, they are the first slaves: growing stronger, they exact agrarian concessions, and a despotism has evolved into a primitive feudalism: the cave becomes a city, and the feudal system a democracy: then an anarchy: this is corrected by a return to monarchy: the last stage is a tendency towards interdestruction: the nations are dispersed, and the Phoenix of Society arises out of their ashes. To this six-termed social progression corresponds a six-termed progression of human motives: necessity, utility, convenience, pleasure, luxury, abuse of luxury" (Samuel Beckett et al., *Our Exagmination Round His Factification for Incamination of Work in Progress* [New York, 1962], p. 5).

15. The following excerpt on genealogy from the first page of *Martin Chuzzlewit* reads like a gloss on this passage: "It is remarkable that as there was, in the oldest family of which we have any record, a murderer and a vagabond, so we never fail to meet, in the records of all old families, with innumerable repetitions of the same phase of character."

16. Cf. "Shem," 169.24–170.7 and 170.20–21, respectively, with Carroll's *Alice* and *Looking-Glass,* p. 121, 254, and 235 in the *Annotated Alice.*

17. Isa Bowman, *Lewis Carroll As I Knew Him,* Morton N. Cohen, ed. (New York, 1972), pp. 23–24.

18. *The New Science of Giambattista Vico,* translated, from the third edition (1744), by Thomas Goddard Bergin and Max Harold Fisch (Ithaca, N.Y., 1948), p. 116. I am grateful to John Bishop for stressing the importance of this passage.

19. See John 1:27.

20. Cf. Wallace Stevens's line from "Sunday Morning": "Death is the mother of beauty."

21. "The Turning Point, Book I, Chapter VI," in Michael Begnal and Fritz Senn, eds., *A Conceptual Guide to "Finnegans Wake"* (University Park, Pa., 1974), pp. 67–68.

22. Beckett, *Our Exagmination,* p. 22.

23. S. L. Goldberg, *Joyce* (Edinburgh and London, 1962), p. 110.

24. See Sigmund Freud, *Jokes and Their Relation to the Unconscious,* p. 32 n. and p. 237, for a possible source for Shem's gibberish.

25. Joyce, *Portrait,* p. 215.

26. Beckett, p. 22.

27. James Joyce, in Mason and Ellmann, eds., *The Critical Writings,* p. 134.

28. James Joyce, *A First-Draft Version of "Finnegans Wake,"* David Hayman, ed. (Austin, Tex., 1963), p. 121.

29. "Because," in Joycean hieroglyphics, stands for *breasts:* "the female breasts . . . expressed by the word . . . *because*" (*Letters of James Joyce,* Stuart Gilbert, ed., vol. 1, p. 170). Syntactically, "because" here introduces a dependent clause and a generating cause of the subject; metaphorically, "breasts" connote the dependency of nurture and the generation of life. Elsewhere in the *Wake,* Joyce has a wonderful footnote making a joke of human biology that comments on this passage and the metaphorical identification of mothering and the gush of mercy: "Mater Mary Mercerycordial of the Dripping Nipples, milk's a queer arrangement" (260, n. 2).

30. Trevor Griffiths, *Comedians* (London, 1976), p. 20.

31. J. Mitchell Morse, *The Sympathetic Alien* (New York, 1959), p. 138.

32. "James Joyce," in Robert H. Deming, ed., *James Joyce: The Critical Heritage* (New York, 1970), vol. 2, p. 675.

33. Alfred Noyes, "Rottenness in Literature," ibid., vol. 1, p. 275.

34. John Bishop, "On Joyce" (Ph.D. dissertation, Stanford University, 1980). I am indebted to Mr. Bishop's brilliant discussion of *Finnegans Wake.* His work has been indispensable to me in understanding Joyce's intentions in the *Wake.* His insights inform this whole chapter and much of my thinking about Joyce.

35. Ellmann, *James Joyce,* p. 410. Bishop calls attention to this wish.

36. James Joyce, *Stephen Hero* (New York, 1963), p. 211.

37. Ibid., p. 213.

38. "Astroglodynamonologos," in Fritz Senn, ed., *New Light on Joyce* (Bloomington and London, 1972), p. 139.

39. Beckett, *Exagmination,* p. 14.

SELECT BIBLIOGRAPHY

I list here only the writings that have been of use in the making of this book. This bibliography is by no means a complete record of all the works and sources I have consulted. It indicates the substance and range of reading upon which I have formed my ideas, and I intend it to serve as a convenience for those who wish to pursue the study of humor, comic literature, the history of comic processes, the British novel, and the particular writers and fictions that are the subjects of this inquiry (Unless there is a standard edition or only one widely available edition of the complete works of the novelists I study, I have not listed their complete works.)

1. THE THEORY, PSYCHOLOGY, AND HISTORY OF THE COMIC

Auden, W. H. "Notes on the Comic." In *Comedy: Meaning and Form,* edited by Robert Corrigan, pp. 61–72. San Francisco: Chandler, 1965.

Bakhtin, Mikhail. *Rabelais and His World.* Translated from the Russian by Helene Iswolsky. Cambridge, Mass.: M.I.T. Press, 1968.

Barber, C. L. *Shakespeare's Festive Comedy: A Study of Dramatic Form and Its Relation to Social Custom.* Princeton: Princeton University Press, 1959.

Baudelaire, Charles. "On the Essence of Laughter." Translated by Jonathan Mayne. In *Comedy: Meaning and Form,* edited by Robert Corrigan, pp. 448–65. San Francisco: Chandler, 1965.

Beattie, James. "Essay on Laughter and Ludicrous Composition." In *Essays.* Edinburgh: William Creech, 1776. Reprint. New York: Garland, 1971.

Berger, Peter L. "Christian Faith and the Social Comedy." In *Holy Laughter: Essays on Religion in the Comic Perspective,* edited by M. Conrad Hyers, pp. 123–33. New York: Seabury Press, 1969.

Bergler, E. *Laughter and the Sense of Humor.* New York: Intercontinental Medical Book Co., 1956.

Bergson, Henri. "Laughter." In *Comedy,* edited by Wylie Sypher, pp. 61–190. Garden City, N.Y.: Doubleday, 1956.

Blistein, Elmer. *Comedy in Action.* Durham, N.C.: Duke University Press, 1964.

Boston, Richard. *An Anatomy of Laughter.* London: Collins, 1974.

Bradbrook, Muriel. *The Growth and Structure of Elizabethan Comedy.* London: Chatto & Windus, 1973.

Burke, Kenneth. *Language as Symbolic Action.* Berkeley and Los Angeles: University of California Press, 1966.

Capp, Al. "The Comedy of Charlie Chaplin." In *Comedy: Meaning and Form,* edited by Robert Corrigan, pp. 219–29. San Francisco: Chandler, 1965.

Carlyle, Thomas. "Jean Paul Friedrich Richter." 1827. In *Critical and Miscellaneous Essays,* vol. 1, pp. 3–22. London: Chapman & Hall, 1887.

———. "Jean Paul Friedrich Richter Again." 1830. In *Critical and Miscellaneous Essays,* vol. 1, pp. 509–64. London: Chapman & Hall, 1887.

Cazamian, Louis. *The Development of English Humor.* New York: AMS Press, 1965.

Coleridge, Samuel Taylor. "On the Distinctions of the Witty, the Droll, the Odd, and the Humorous; The Nature and Constituents of Humor; Rabelais, Swift, Sterne." In *The Complete Works of Samuel Taylor Coleridge,* edited by W. G. T. Shedd, vol. 4, pp. 275–85. New York: Harper & Bros., 1884.

Cook, Albert Spaulding. *The Dark Voyage and the Golden Mean: A Philosophy of Comedy.* Cambridge, Mass.: Harvard University Press, 1949.

Cornford, Francis M. *The Origin of Attic Comedy.* 1914. Reprint, edited by Theodore Gaster. Gloucester, Mass.: Peter Smith, 1968.

Corrigan, Robert, ed. *Comedy: Meaning and Form.* San Francisco: Chandler, 1965.

Cox, Harvey. *The Feast of Fools.* New York: Harper & Row, 1969.

Darwin, Charles. *The Expression of the Emotions in Man and Animals.* Chicago: University of Chicago Press, 1965.

Eastman, Max. *Enjoyment of Laughter.* New York: Simon & Schuster, 1936.

————. *The Sense of Humor.* New York: Scribner's, 1921.

Eliot, George. "German Wit: Heinrich Heine." In *Essays.* Philadelphia: University Library Association, 1883.

Elliott, Robert C. *The Power of Satire: Magic, Ritual, Art.* Princeton: Princeton University Press, 1960.

Emerson, Ralph Waldo. "The Comic." In *The Works of Ralph Waldo Emerson.* Vol. 8, pp. 151–66. Boston: Houghton Mifflin, 1883.

Enck, John; Porter, Elizabeth; Whitler, Alvin, eds. *The Comic in Theory and Practice.* New York: Appleton-Century-Crofts, 1960.

Feibleman, James. *In Praise of Comedy.* New York: Horizon Press, 1970.

Fielding, Henry. *Joseph Andrews.* Edited by W. K. Wimsatt. New York: Holt, Rinehart & Winston, 1955.

Freud, Sigmund. "Humour." In *The Complete Psychological Works of Sigmund Freud,* vol. 21, pp. 160–66. Translated by James Strachey. Standard Edition. 24 vols. London: Hogarth Press, 1953–74.

————. *Jokes and Their Relation to the Unconscious.* Translated by James Strachey. New York: W. W. Norton, 1960.

Fry, Christopher. "Comedy." In *Comedy: Meaning and Form,* edited by Robert Corrigan, pp. 15–17. San Francisco: Chandler, 1965.

Fry, William. *Sweet Madness.* Palo Alto: Pacific Books, 1963.

Frye, Northrop. *Anatomy of Criticism.* Princeton: Princeton University Press, 1957.

Goldstein, Jeffrey H., and McGhee, Paul E., eds. *The Psychology of Humor.* New York and London: Academic Press, 1972.

Gray, Donald J. "The Uses of Victorian Laughter." *Victorian Studies* 10 (1966): 147–76.

Gregory, J. C. *The Nature of Laughter.* New York: Harcourt, Brace, 1924.

Greig, J. Y. T. *The Psychology of Laughter and Comedy.* London: George Allen, 1923.

Grotjahn, Martin. *Beyond Laughter: Humor and the Subconscious.* New York: McGraw-Hill, 1966.

Gurewitch, Morton. *Comedy: The Irrational Vision.* Ithaca, N.Y.: Cornell University Press, 1975.

Hazlitt, William. *Lectures on the English Comic Writers.* London: Taylor & Hessey, 1819.

Huizinga, Johan. *Homo Ludens.* Boston: Beacon Press, 1955.

Hunt, Leigh. "On the Combination of the Grave and Gay." In *Leigh Hunt's Literary Criticism,* edited by Lawrence Houtchens and Carolyn Houtchens, pp. 559–66. New York: Columbia University Press, 1956.

——. *Wit and Humor Selected from the English Poets.* New York: Wiley & Putnam, 1846.

Hyers, M. Conrad. "The Comic Profanation of the Sacred." In *Holy Laughter: Essays on Religion in the Comic Perspective,* edited by M. Conrad Hyers, pp. 208–40. New York: Seabury Press, 1969.

——, ed. *Holy Laughter: Essays on Religion in the Comic Perspective.* New York: Seabury Press, 1969.

Johnson, Samuel. "The Difficulty of Defining Comedy." 1751. In *The Rambler.* 4 vols. London: Dodgley, Owen, 1794. Reprinted in *The Comic in Theory and Practice,* edited by John Enck et al., pp. 10–11. New York: Appleton-Century-Crofts, 1960.

Jonson, Ben. "Prologue to *Every Man in His Humour*" and "Induction to *Every Man Out of His Humour.*" In *The Idea of Comedy,* edited by W. K. Wimsatt, pp. 24–37. Englewood Cliffs, N.J.: Prentice-Hall, 1969.

Kallen, Horace. *Liberty, Laughter, and Tears.* DeKalb, Ill.: Northern Illinois University Press, 1968.

Kayser, Wolfgang. *The Grotesque in Art and Literature.* Translated by Ulrich Weisstein. Bloomington, Ind.: Indiana University Press, 1963.

Kierkegaard, Søren. *Concluding Unscientific Postscript.* Translated by David Swenson and Walter Lowrie. Princeton: Princeton University Press, 1941.

——. *Either/Or.* 2 vols. Vol. 1 translated by David F. Swenson and Lillian M. Swenson; vol. 2 translated by Walter Lowrie. Garden City, N.Y.: Doubleday, 1959.

——. *Fear and Trembling and The Sickness Unto Death.* Translated by Walter Lowrie. Garden City, N.Y.: Doubleday, 1954.

Knoepflmacher, U. C. *Laughter and Despair: Readings in Ten Novels of the Victorian Era.* Berkeley and Los Angeles: University of California Press, 1971.

Koestler, Arthur. *The Act of Creation.* London: Hutchinson, 1964.

Kris, Ernst. *Psychoanalytic Explorations in Art.* New York: Schocken, 1964.

Lamb, Charles. "On the Artificial Comedy of the Last Century." In *The Works of Charles Lamb.* Library Edition, vol. 2, pp. 275–87. Troy, N.Y.: Pafraets Book Co., n.d.

Langer, Susanne. *Feeling and Form.* New York: Scribner's, 1953.

Lauter, Paul. *Theories of Comedy.* Garden City, N.Y.: Doubleday, 1964.

Levin, Harry, ed. *Veins of Humor.* Cambridge, Mass.: Harvard University Press, 1972.

Loftis, John. *Comedy and Society from Congreve to Fielding.* Stanford, Calif.: Stanford University Press, 1959.

Ludovici, Anthony. *The Secret of Laughter.* London: Constable, 1932.

Mack, Maynard. "Introduction to Joseph Andrews." In *The Comic in Theory and Practice,* edited by John Enck et al., pp. 100–101. New York: Appleton-Century-Crofts, 1960.

Martin, Robert. *The Triumph of Wit: A Study of Victorian Comic Theory.* London: Oxford University Press, 1974.

McWhinney, Norman N. *Sex, Time, and Laughter: A New Theory of the Comic.* Pittsburgh: University of Pittsburgh Press, 1968.

Meeker, Joseph. *The Comedy of Survival: Studies in Literary Ecology.* New York: Scribner's, 1974.

Merchant, W. Moelwyn. *Comedy.* London: Methuen, 1972.

Mercier, Vivian. *The Irish Comic Tradition.* Oxford: Clarendon Press, 1962.

Meredith, George. "An Essay on Comedy." In *Comedy,* edited by Wylie Sypher, pp. 31–57. Garden City, N.Y.: Doubleday, 1956.

Mikes, George. *Laughing Matter: Towards a Personal Philosophy of Wit and Humor.* New York: Library Press, 1971.

Monro, D. H. *Argument of Laughter.* Melbourne: Melbourne University Press, 1951.

Nathan, David. *The Laughtermakers: A Quest for Comedy.* London: Peter Owen, 1971.

Niebuhr, Reinhold. "Humour and Faith." In *Holy Laughter,* edited by M. Conrad Hyers, pp. 134–49. New York: Seabury Press, 1969.

Olson, Elder. *The Theory of Comedy.* Bloomington: Indiana University Press, 1968.

Orel, Harold, ed. *The World of Victorian Humor.* New York: Appleton-Century-Crofts, 1961.

Pirandello, Luigi. *On Humor [L'Umorismo].* Introduced, translated, and annotated by Antonio Illiano and Daniel P. Testa. Chapel Hill: University of North Carolina Press, 1974.

Plessner, Helmuth. *Laughing and Crying.* Translated by James S. Churchill and Marjorie Grene. Evanston, Ill.: Northwestern University Press, 1974.

Potts, L. J. *Comedy.* London: Hutchinson's University Library, 1948.

Priestley, J. B. *English Humour.* London: Longmans, Green, 1929.

Pritchett, V. S. *George Meredith and English Comedy.* New York: Random House, 1969.

Reich, H. *Der Mimus: Ein litterar-entwickelungsgeschictlicher Versuch.* Berlin: Weidmann, 1903.

Santayana, George. "The Comic Mask and Carnival." In *Comedy: Meaning and Form,* edited by Robert Corrigan, pp. 73–80. San Francisco: Chandler, 1965.

Schlegel, Friedrich von. *Dialogue on Poetry and Literary Aphorisms.* Translated by Ernst Behler and Roman Struc. University Park, Pa.: Pennsylvania State University Press, 1968.

Schopenhauer, Arthur. *The World as Will and Representation.* Translated by E. F. J. Payne. Indian Hills, Colo: Falcon's Wing Press, 1958.

Scott, Nathan A., Jr. "The Bias of Comedy and the Narrow Escape into Faith." In *Comedy: Meaning and Form,* edited by Robert Corrigan, pp. 81–115. San Francisco: Chandler, 1965.

Sewell, Elizabeth. *The Field of Nonsense.* London: Chatto & Windus, 1952.

Shaftesbury, Anthony Ashley Cooper, third Earl of. "An Essay on the Freedom of Wit and Humour." In *Characteristics of Men, Manners, Opinions, Times,* edited by John Robertson, vol. 1, pp. 43–102. London: Grant Richards, 1902.

Simon, Richard. "Comedy, Suffering, and Human Existence." Ph.D. dissertation, Stanford University, 1977.

Sorell, Walter. *Facets of Comedy.* New York: Grosset & Dunlap, 1973.

Spencer, Herbert. "The Physiology of Laughter." *Macmillan's Magazine* 1 (1860): 395–402. Reprinted in H. Spencer, *Illustrations of Universal Progress.* New York: D. Appleton, 1889.

Stephen, Leslie. "Humour." *Cornhill Magazine* 33 (March, 1876): 318–26.

Sully, James. *An Essay on Laughter: Its Form, Its Causes, Its Development, and Its Value.* London: Longmans, Green, 1902.

Swabey, Marie. *Comic Laughter: A Philosophical Essay.* New Haven: Yale University Press, 1961.

Sypher, Wylie. "The Meanings of Comedy." In *Comedy,* edited by Wylie Sypher, pp. 193–258. Garden City, N.Y.: Doubleday, 1956.

Tave, Stuart M. *The Amiable Humorist: A Study in the Comic Theory and Criticism of the Eighteenth and Early Nineteenth Centuries.* Chicago: University of Chicago Press, 1960.

Thackeray, William Makepeace. "The English Humorists of the Eighteenth Century." In vol. 13 of *The Complete Works of William Makepeace Thackeray.* 22 vols. Boston: Houghton Mifflin, 1889.

Trueblood, Elton. "The Humor of Christ." In *Holy Laughter,* edited by M. Conrad Hyers, pp. 166–84. New York: Seabury, 1969.

Walsh, Chad. "On Being with It: An Afterword." In *Holy Laughter,* edited by M. Conrad Hyers, pp. 241–51. New York: Seabury Press, 1969.

Walsh, James. *Laughter and Health.* New York: D. Appleton, 1928.

Welsford, Enid. *The Fool: His Social and Literary History.* London: Faber & Faber, 1935.

Wimsatt, W. K. *The Idea of Comedy: Essays in Prose and Verse:*

Ben Jonson to George Meredith. Englewood Cliffs, N.J.: Prentice-Hall, 1969.

Zuver, Dudley. *Salvation by Laughter: A Study of Religion and the Sense of Humor.* New York: Harper & Bros., 1933.

2. JANE AUSTEN AND *EMMA*

Austen, Jane. *The Novels of Jane Austen.* Edited by R. W. Chapman. 5 vols. 3d ed. London: Oxford University Press, 1932–34.

————. *Minor Works.* Edited by R. W. Chapman. Vol. 6 of *The Novels of Jane Austen.* London: Oxford University Press, 1954.

————. *Jane Austen's Letters to Her Sister Cassandra and Others.* Edited by R. W. Chapman. 2d ed. London: Oxford University Press, 1952.

————. *"Emma": An Authoritative Text, Backgrounds, Reviews, and Criticism.* Edited by Stephen M. Parrish. Includes commentary and criticism by Sir Walter Scott, George Henry Lewes, Richard Simpson, Henry James, A. C. Bradley, Reginald Ferrar, Virginia Woolf, E. M. Forster, Mary Lascelles, Arnold Kettle, Wayne Booth, G. Armour Craig, A. Walton Litz, W. A. Craik, and W. J. Harvey. New York: W. W. Norton, 1972.

Austen-Leigh, James E. *Memoir of Jane Austen.* 1871. Reprint, edited by R. W. Chapman. 2d ed. Oxford: Clarendon Press, 1967.

Babb, Howard S. *Jane Austen's Novels: The Fabric of Dialogue.* Columbus: Ohio State University Press, 1962.

Bowen, Elizabeth. "Jane Austen." In *The English Novelists: A Survey of the Novel by Twenty Contemporary Novelists,* edited by Derek Verschoyle. London: Chatto & Windus, 1936.

Bradbrook, Frank W. *Jane Austen and Her Predecessors.* Cambridge, Eng.: At the University Press, 1966.

Bradbury, Malcolm. "Jane Austen's *Emma.*" *Critical Quarterly* 4 (Winter, 1962): 335–46.

Brown, Julia Prewitt. *Jane Austen's Novels: Social Change and Literary Form.* Cambridge, Mass.: Harvard University Press, 1979.

Burrows, J. F. *Jane Austen's "Emma."* Sydney: Sydney University Press, 1968.

Butler, Marilyn. *Jane Austen and the War of Ideas.* Oxford: Clarendon Press, 1975.

Cecil, Lord David. *Jane Austen.* Cambridge, Eng.: At the University Press, 1935.

Chapman, R. W. *Jane Austen: Facts and Problems.* Oxford: Oxford University Press, 1948.

Duckworth, Alistair M. *The Improvement of the Estate.* Baltimore: Johns Hopkins University Press, 1972.

Duffy, Joseph M., Jr. "*Emma:* The Awakening from Innocence." *ELH: A Journal of English Literary History* 21 (March, 1954): 39–53.

Halperin, John, ed. *Jane Austen: Bicentenary Essays.* Cambridge and New York: Cambridge University Press, 1975.

Harding, D. W. "Regulated Hatred: An Aspect of the Work of Jane Austen." *Scrutiny* 8 (March 1940): 346–62.

Hardy, Barbara. *A Reading of Jane Austen.* New York: New York University Press, 1976.

Hughes, R.E. "The Education of Emma Woodhouse." *Nineteenth-Century Fiction* 16 (1961): 69–74.

Jones, Evan. "Characteristics and Values: *Emma* and *Mansfield Park.*" *Quadrant* 12 (July–August, 1968): 35–45.

Knoepflmacher, U. C. "The Importance of Being Frank: Character and Letter-Writing in *Emma.*" *Studies in English Literature* 7 (Autumn, 1967): 639–58.

Kroeber, Karl. *Styles in Fictional Structure: The Art of Jane Austen, Charlotte Brontë, George Eliot.* Princeton: Princeton University Press, 1971.

Lascelles, Mary. *Jane Austen and Her Art.* Oxford: Oxford University Press, 1961.

Lawry, J. S. "'Decided and Open': Structure in *Emma.*" *Nineteenth-Century Fiction* 24 (June 1969): 1–15.

Leavis, Q. D. "A Critical Theory of Jane Austen's Writings." *Scrutiny* 10 (1942): 61–75.

Lerner, Lawrence. *The Truthtellers: Jane Austen, George Eliot, D. H. Lawrence.* New York: Schocken, 1967.

Liddell, Robert. *The Novels of Jane Austen.* London: Longmans, Green, 1963.

Litz, A. Walton. *Jane Austen: A Study of Her Artistic Development.* London: Chatto & Windus, 1965.

Lodge, David, ed. *Jane Austen: "Emma": A Casebook.* London: Macmillan, 1968.

Minter, David Lee. "Aesthetic Vision and the World of *Emma.*" *Nineteenth-Century Fiction* 21 (June 1966): 49–59.

Morgan, Susan. *In the Meantime: Character and Perception in Jane Austen's Fiction.* Chicago: University of Chicago Press, 1980.

Mudrick, Marvin. *Jane Austen: Irony as Defense and Discovery.* Princeton: Princeton University Press, 1952.

Paris, Bernard J. *Character and Conflict in Jane Austen's Novels: A Psychological Approach.* Detroit: Wayne State University Press, 1977.

Schorer, Mark. "The Humiliation of Emma Woodhouse." *Farleigh-Dickinson Literary Review* 2 (Summer, 1959): 547–63. Reprinted in David Lodge, ed., *Jane Austen: "Emma": A Casebook.*

Shannon, Edgar F., Jr. "*Emma:* Character and Construction." *PMLA* 71 (September, 1956): 637–50.

Southam, B. C. *Critical Essays on Jane Austen.* London: Routledge & Kegan Paul, 1968.

———. *Jane Austen: The Critical Heritage.* London: Routledge & Kegan Paul; New York: Barnes & Noble, 1968.

———. *Jane Austen's Literary Manuscripts.* London: Oxford University Press, 1964.

Tave, Stuart M. *Some Words of Jane Austen.* Chicago: University of Chicago Press, 1973.

Trilling, Lionel. "*Emma* and the Legend of Jane Austen." In *Beyond Culture: Essays on Literature and Learning,* pp. 31–55. London: Secker & Warburg, 1966.

Watt, Ian. *Jane Austen: A Collection of Critical Essays.* Englewood Cliffs, N.J.: Prentice-Hall, 1963.

Wiesenfarth, Joseph. *The Errand of Form: An Assay of Jane Austen's Art.* New York: Fordham University Press, 1967.

Wilson, Edmund. "A Long Talk about Jane Austen." In *Classics and Commercials,* pp. 196–203. New York: Farrar, Straus, 1950.

Wright, Andrew. *Jane Austen's Novels: A Study in Structure.* London: Chatto & Windus, 1953.

3. THOMAS LOVE PEACOCK AND *NIGHTMARE ABBEY*

Able, A. H. *George Meredith and Thomas Love Peacock: A Study in Literary Influence.* Philadelphia: University of Pennsylvania, 1933.

Butler, Marilyn. *Peacock Displayed: A Satirist in His Context.* London: Boston & Henley, Routledge & Kegan Paul, 1979.

Campbell, Olwen W. *Thomas Love Peacock.* London: Arthur Barker, 1953.

Dawson, Carl. *His Fine Wit: A Study of Thomas Love Peacock.* Berkeley and Los Angeles: University of California Press, 1970.

Dyson, A. E. *The Crazy Fabric: Essays in Irony,* pp. 61–71. London: Macmillan; New York: St. Martin's Press, 1965.

Hoff, Peter. "Comedy and Satire in the Novels of Thomas Love Peacock." Ph.D. dissertation, Stanford University, 1970.

House, Humphry. "The Novels of Thomas Love Peacock." *The Listener* 62 (December 8, 1949): 997–98.

Jack, Ian. *English Literature 1815–32.* Oxford: Oxford University Press, 1963.

Klingopulos, G. D. "The Spirit of the Age in Prose." In *From Blake to Byron,* pp. 130–51. Vol. 5 of *A Guide to English Literature,* edited by Boris Ford. Baltimore: Penguin, 1957.

Mayoux, Jean-Jacques. *Un Epicurien anglais: Thomas Love Peacock.* Paris: Presses Modernes, 1932.

Mills, Howard. *Peacock: His Circle and His Age.* London: Cambridge University Press, 1969.

Peacock, Thomas Love. *The Novels of Thomas Love Peacock.* Edited by David Garnett. London: Rupert, Hart-Davis, 1948.

Priestley, J. B. *Thomas Love Peacock.* London: Macmillan, 1927.

Sage, Lorna, ed. *Peacock: The Satirical Novels: A Casebook.* London: Macmillan, 1976.

Salz, P. J. "Peacock's Use of Music in His Novels." *Journal of English and German Philology* 54 (1955): 370–79.

Stewart, J. I. M. *Thomas Love Peacock.* Writers and Their Work, no. 156. London: Longmans, Green, 1963.

Van Doren, Carl. *The Life of Thomas Love Peacock.* London, 1911. Reprint. New York: Russell & Russell, 1966.

Wilson, Edmund. *Classics and Commercials.* New York: Farrar, Straus & Giroux, 1950.

4. CHARLES DICKENS AND *MARTIN CHUZZLEWIT*

Axton, William. *Circle of Fire.* Lexington, Ky.: University of Kentucky Press, 1966.

Benjamin, Edwin B. "The Structure of *Martin Chuzzlewit.*"

Philological Quarterly 34 (1955): 39–47.

Brogunier, Joseph. "The Dreams of Montague Tigg and Jonas Chuzzlewit." *The Dickensian* 55 (1959): 165.

Burke, Alan R. "The House of Chuzzlewit and the Architectural City." *Dickens Studies Annual* 3 (1973): 14–40.

Butt, John, and Tillotson, Kathleen. *Dickens at Work*. London: Methuen, 1957.

Carey, John. *The Violent Effigy: A Study of Dickens' Imagination*. London: Faber & Faber, 1973.

Chesterton, G. K. *Appreciations and Criticisms in the Works of Charles Dickens*. New York: Haskell House, 1966. First published 1911.

Churchill, R. C. "Charles Dickens." In *From Dickens to Hardy*, pp. 119–43. Vol. 6 of *A Guide to English Literature*, edited by Boris Ford. Baltimore: Penguin, 1958.

Cockshut, A. O. J. *The Imagination of Charles Dickens*. London: William Collins, 1961.

Collins, Philip. *Dickens and Crime*. New York: St. Martin's Press, 1962.

——, ed. *Dickens: The Critical Heritage*. London: Routledge & Kegan Paul; New York: Barnes & Noble, 1971.

——. *Dickens and Education*. New York: St. Martin's Press, 1963.

Dabney, Ross H. *Love and Property in the Novels of Dickens*. Berkeley and Los Angeles: University of California Press, 1967.

Daleski, H. M. *Dickens and the Art of Analogy*. New York: Schocken, 1970.

Davis, Earle. *The Flint and the Flame: The Artistry of Charles Dickens*. Columbia, Mo.: University of Missouri Press, 1963.

Dickens, Charles. *The Life and Adventures of Martin Chuzzlewit*. London: Oxford University Press, 1951.

——. *The Letters of Charles Dickens*. Vol. 1, *1820–1839*, and Vol. 2, *1840–1841*, edited by Madeline House and Graham Storey. Vol. 3, *1842–1843*, edited by Madeline House, Graham Storey, and Kathleen Tillotson. Vol. 4, *1844–1846*, edited by Kathleen Tillotson. The Pilgrim Edition. Oxford: Clarendon Press, 1965, 1969, 1974, 1977.

Dyson, A. E. *The Inimitable Dickens*. London: Macmillan, 1970.

Fanger, Donald S. *Dostoevsky and Romantic Realism*. Cambridge, Mass.: Harvard University Press, 1965.

Fielding, K. J. *Charles Dickens: A Critical Introduction.* Boston: Houghton Miffllin, 1964.

Ford, George H. *Dickens and His Readers: Aspects of Novel Criticism since 1836.* Princeton: Princeton University Press for the University of Cincinnati, 1955.

—— and Lane, Lauriat Jr., eds. *The Dickens Critics.* Ithaca, N.Y.: Cornell University Press, 1961.

Forster, John. *The Life of Charles Dickens.* New edition, with notes and index by A. J. Hoppé and additional authors' footnotes. 2 vols. London: Dent, 1966.

Frye, Northrop. "Dickens and the Comedy of Humors." In *Experience in the Novel,* edited by Roy Harvey Pearce. New York and London: Columbia University Press, 1968.

Furbank, P. N. Introduction and notes to the Penguin edition of *Martin Chuzzlewit.* Harmondsworth, Eng.: Penguin, 1968.

Garis, Robert. *The Dickens Theatre: A Reassessment of the Novels.* Oxford: Clarendon Press, 1965.

Gold, Joseph, comp. *The Stature of Dickens: A Centenary Bibliography.* Manitoba and Toronto: Published for the University of Manitoba Press by the University of Toronto Press, 1971.

Gross, John, and Pearson, Gabriel, eds. *Dickens and the Twentieth Century.* Toronto: University of Toronto Press, 1962.

Guerard, Albert J. *The Triumph of the Novel,* pp. 235–60. New York: Oxford University Press, 1976.

Hardy, Barbara. *The Moral Art of Charles Dickens.* New York: Oxford University Press, 1970.

Heilman, Robert B. "The New World in Dickens's Writings." *The Trollopian* 1 (1947): 11.

House, Humphry. *The Dickens World.* London: Oxford University Press, 1941.

Johnson, Edgar. *Charles Dickens: His Tragedy and Triumph.* 2 vols. New York: Simon & Schuster, 1952.

Kincaid, James R. *Dickens and the Rhetoric of Laughter.* Oxford: Clarendon Press, 1971.

Leavis, F. R., and Leavis, Q. D. *Dickens the Novelist.* Baltimore: Penguin, 1972.

Lindsay, Jack. *Charles Dickens.* London: A. Dakers, 1950.

Manning, Sylvia. *Dickens as Satirist.* New Haven: Yale University Press, 1971.

Marcus, Steven. *Dickens: From Pickwick to Dombey.* New York: Basic Books, 1965.

Miller, J. Hillis. *Charles Dickens: The World of His Novels.* Cambridge, Mass.: Harvard University Press, 1959.

———. "The Sources of Dickens's Comic Art: From *American Notes* to *Martin Chuzzlewit.*" *Nineteenth-Century Fiction* 24 (March, 1970): 467–76.

Monod, Sylvère. *Dickens the Novelist.* Norman: University of Oklahoma Press, 1968.

Mudrick, Marvin. "Afterword." In *Martin Chuzzlewit,* edited by Marvin Mudrick. New York: New American Library, 1965.

Nisbet, Ada. "The Mystery of *Martin Chuzzlewit.*" In *Essays Critical and Historical Dedicated to Lily B. Campbell by Members of the Department of English, University of California,* pp. 201–16. English Studies, vol. 1. Berkeley and Los Angeles: University of California Press, 1950.

Orwell, George. "Charles Dickens." In *Dickens: A Collection of Critical Essays,* edited by Martin Price. Englewood Cliffs, N.J.: Prentice-Hall, 1967.

Pratt, Branwen. "Dickens and Freedom: Young Bailey in *Martin Chuzzlewit.*" *Nineteenth-Century Fiction* 30 (September, 1975): 185–99.

Pritchett, V. S. "The Comic World of Dickens." In *The Dickens Critics,* edited by George H. Ford and Lauriat Lane, Jr., pp. 309–24. Ithaca, N.Y.: Cornell University Press, 1961.

Scott, P. J. M. *Reality and Comic Confidence in Charles Dickens.* London: Macmillan, 1979.

Slater, Michael, ed. *Centenary Essays by William Allen and Others.* London: Chapman & Hall, 1970.

———, ed. *Dickens on America and the Americans.* Austin: University of Texas Press, 1979.

Smith, Graham. *Dickens, Money, and Society.* Berkeley and Los Angeles: University of California Press, 1968.

Spilka, Mark. *Dickens and Kafka: A Mutual Interpretation.* Bloomington: Indiana University Press, 1963.

Stewart, Garret. *Dickens and the Trials of Imagination.* Cambridge, Mass.: Harvard University Press, 1974.

Stoehr, Taylor. *Dickens: The Dreamer's Stance.* Ithaca, N.Y.: Cornell University Press, 1965.

Stone, Harry. "Dickens's Use of His American Experiences in *Martin Chuzzlewit.*" *PMLA* 72 (1957): 464.

———. *Dickens and the Invisible World.* Bloomington: Indiana University Press, 1979.

Sucksmith, Harvey Peter. *The Narrative Art of Charles Dickens: The Rhetoric of Irony and Sympathy in His Novels.* Oxford: Clarendon Press, 1970.

Van Ghent, Dorothy. "The Dickens World: A View from Todgers's." In *The Dickens Critics,* edited by George H. Ford and Lauriat Lane, Jr., pp. 213–32. Ithaca, N.Y.: Cornell University Press, 1961.

Watt, Ian. "Oral Dickens." *Dickens Studies Annual* 3 (1974): 165–81.

Welsh, Alexander. *The City of Dickens.* Oxford: Clarendon Press, 1971.

Westburg, Barry. *The Confessional Fictions of Charles Dickens.* De Kalb, Ill.: Northern Illinois University Press, 1977.

Wilson, Angus. *The World of Charles Dickens.* New York: Viking Press, 1970.

Wilson, Edmund. "The Two Scrooges." In *The Wound and the Bow.* New York: Oxford University Press, 1965.

5. WILLIAM MAKEPEACE THACKERAY AND *VANITY FAIR*

Auchincloss, Louis. "The Two Ages of Thackeray." In *Reflections of a Jacobite.* Boston: Houghton Mifflin, 1961.

Betsky, Seymour. "Society in Thackeray and Trollope." In *From Dickens to Hardy,* pp. 158–68. Vol. 6 of *A Guide To English Literature,* edited by Boris Ford. Baltimore: Penguin, 1958.

Craig, G. Armour. "On the Style of *Vanity Fair.*" In *Style in Prose Fiction,* edited by Harold C. Martin, pp. 87–113. English Institute Essays. New York: Columbia University Press, 1958. Reprinted in *Thackeray: A Collection of Critical Essays,* edited by Alexander Welsh, pp. 87–103, and in *Twentieth-Century Interpretations of Vanity Fair,* edited by M. G. Sundell, pp. 55–72 (see below).

Dodds, John W. *Thackeray: A Critical Portrait.* London and New York: Oxford University Press, 1941.

Dyson, A. E. "*Vanity Fair: An Irony against Heroes.*" In *The Crazy Fabric: Essays in Irony,* pp. 72–95. London: Macmillan; New York: St. Martin's Press, 1965.

Ennis, Lambert. *Thackeray: The Sentimental Cynic.* Evanston, Ill.: Northwestern University Press, 1950.

Greig, J. Y. T. *Thackeray: A Reconsideration.* London: Oxford University Press, 1950.

Hardy, Barbara. *The Exposure of Luxury: Radical Themes in*

Thackeray. London: Peter Owen, 1972.

Iser, Wolfgang. "The Reader as a Component Part of the Realistic Novel: Esthetic Effects of Thackeray's *Vanity Fair.*" In *The Implied Reader: Patterns of Communication in Prose Fiction from Bunyan to Beckett,* pp. 101–20. Baltimore: Johns Hopkins University Press, 1974.

Kettle, Arnold. "Thackeray's *Vanity Fair.*" In *An Introduction to the English Novel,* vol. 1, pp. 156–70. 2 vols. New York: Harper Torchbooks, 1960.

Kiely, Robert. "Victorian Harlequin: The Function of Humor in Thackeray's Critical and Miscellaneous Prose." In *Veins of Humor,* edited by Harry Levin, pp. 147–66. Cambridge, Mass.: Harvard University Press, 1972.

Knoepflmacher, U. C. "*Vanity Fair:* The Bitterness of Retrospection." In *Laughter and Despair: Readings in Ten Novels of the Victorian Era,* pp. 50–83. Berkeley and Los Angeles: University of California Press, 1971.

Lester, John A., Jr. "Thackeray's Narrative Technique." In *Victorian Literature: Selected Essays,* edited by Robert O. Preyer, pp. 159–81. New York: Harper Torchbooks, 1966.

Loofbourow, John. *Thackeray and the Form of Fiction.* Princeton: Princeton University Press, 1964.

Marshall, William. *The World of the Victorian Novel,* pp. 245–60. New York: A. S. Barnes; London: Thomas Yoseloff, 1967.

McMaster, Juliet. *Thackeray: The Major Novels.* Toronto: University of Toronto Press, 1971.

———. "Thackeray's Things: Time's Local Habitation." In *The Victorian Experience: The Novelists,* edited by Richard Levine, pp. 49–86. Athens, Ohio: Ohio University Press, 1976.

Olmsted, John Charles. *Thackeray and His Twentieth-Century Critics: An Annotated Bibliography, 1900–1975.* New York: Garland, 1977.

Phillips, Kenneth C. *The Language of Thackeray.* London: Deutsch, 1978.

Rawlins, Jack P. *Thackeray's Novels: A Fiction That Is True* Berkeley and Los Angeles: University of California Press, 1974.

Ray, Gordon N. *The Buried Life: A Study of the Relation between Thackeray's Fiction and His Personal History.* Cambridge, Mass.: Harvard University Press, 1952.

———. *Thackeray.* Vol. 1, *The Uses of Adversity, 1811–1846.* Vol. 2, *The Age of Wisdom, 1847–1863.* New York: McGraw-Hill, 1955, 1958.

Rogers, Winslow. "Thackeray's Self-Consciousness." In *The World of Victorian Fiction*, edited by Jerome Buckley, pp. 149–63. Cambridge, Mass.: Harvard University Press, 1975.

Saintsbury, George. *A Consideration of Thackeray*. New York: Russell & Russell, 1968. Reprinted from 1931 edition.

Stevenson, Lionel. *The Showman of Vanity Fair*. New York: Scribner's, 1947.

Sudrann, Jean. "The Philosopher's Property: Thackeray and the Use of Time." *Victorian Studies* 10 (1967): 359–88.

Sundell, M. G., ed. *Twentieth-Century Interpretations of "Vanity Fair."* Englewood Cliffs, N.J.: Prentice-Hall, 1969.

Sutherland, John. *Thackeray at Work*. London: Athlone Press, 1974.

Taube, Myron. "Contrast as a Principle of Structure in *Vanity Fair*." *Nineteenth-Century Fiction* 18 (1963): 119–35.

Thackeray, William Makepeace. *Vanity Fair*. Edited, with an introduction and notes, by Geoffrey Tillotson and Kathleen Tillotson. Boston: Houghton Mifflin, 1963.

——. *The Letters and Private Papers of William Makepeace Thackeray*. Edited by Gordon N. Ray. 4 vols. Cambridge, Mass.: Harvard University Press, 1945–46.

Tillotson, Geoffrey. *Thackeray the Novelist*. Cambridge, Eng.: At the University Press, 1954.

——, and Hawes, Donald, eds. *Thackeray: The Critical Heritage*. London: Routledge & Kegan Paul; New York: Barnes & Noble, 1968.

Welsh, Alexander, ed. *Thackeray: A Collection of Critical Essays*. Englewood Cliffs, N.J.: Prentice-Hall, 1968.

Wheatley, James H. *Patterns in Thackeray's Fiction*. Cambridge, Mass.: M.I.T. Press, 1969.

Williams, Ioan M. *Thackeray*. London: Evans, 1968.

Van Ghent, Dorothy. "On *Vanity Fair*." In *The English Novel: Form and Function*, pp. 139–52. New York: Holt, Rinehart & Winston, 1953.

6. ANTHONY TROLLOPE AND *BARCHESTER TOWERS*

Aitken, David. "A Kind of Felicity: Some Notes about Trollope's Style." *Nineteenth-Century Fiction* 20 (1965–66): 337–53.

apRoberts, Ruth. *The Moral Trollope*. Athens, Ohio: Ohio University Press, 1971.

Betsky, Seymour. "Society in Thackeray and Trollope." In *From Dickens to Hardy,* pp. 158–68. Vol. 6 of *A Guide to English Literature,* edited by Boris Ford. Baltimore: Penguin, 1958.

Booth, Bradford A. *Anthony Trollope: Aspects of His Life and Art.* Bloomington: Indiana University Press, 1958.

Bowen, Elizabeth. *Anthony Trollope: A New Judgement.* New York and London: Oxford University Press, 1946.

Brown, Beatrice Curtis. *Anthony Trollope.* 2d ed. London: Arthur Barker, 1967.

Cadbury, William. "Character and the Mock Heroic in *Barchester Towers." Texas Studies in Literature and Language* 5 (1963–64): 509–19.

———. "Shape and Theme: Determinants of Trollope's Forms." *PMLA* 78 (1963): 326–32.

Chadwick, Owen. *The Secularization of the European Mind in the Nineteenth Century.* Cambridge, Eng.: At the University Press, 1975.

———. *The Victorian Church,* part 1. New York: Oxford University Press, 1966.

Davies, Hugh Sykes. *Trollope.* London: Longmans, Green, 1960.

Escott, T. H. S. *Anthony Trollope: His Work, Associates, and Literary Originals.* London: John Lane, 1913.

Gerould, Winifred, and Gerould, James Thayer. *A Guide to Trollope.* Princeton: Princeton University Press, 1948.

Halperin, John. *Trollope and Politics: A Study of the Pallisers and Others.* New York: Barnes & Noble, 1977.

Hennedy, Hugh L. *Unity in Barsetshire.* The Hague: Mouton, 1971.

James, Henry. "Anthony Trollope." In *The Future of the Novel,* edited by Leon Edel, pp. 233–60. New York: Random House, Vintage Books, 1956.

Johnson, Pamela Hansford. "Trollope's Young Women." In *On the Novel: A Present for Walter Allen on His Sixtieth Birthday from His Friends and Colleagues,* edited by B. S. Benedikz, pp. 17–33. London: J. M. Dent, 1971.

Kincaid, James R. "*Barchester Towers* and the Nature of Conservative Comedy." *ELH: A Journal of English Literary History* 37 (1970): 595–612.

———. *The Novels of Anthony Trollope.* London: Oxford University Press, 1977.

Knoepflmacher, U. C. "Introduction: Entering a Victorian Novel—*Barchester Towers*" and "*Barchester Towers:* The Comedy of Change." In *Laughter and Despair,* pp. 3–24 and 25–49. Berkeley and Los Angeles: University of California Press, 1971.

McMaster, Juliet. *Trollope's Palliser Novels.* New York: Oxford University Press, 1978.

Olmsted, John Charles, and Welch, Jeffrey Egan. *The Reputation of Trollope: An Annotated Bibliography, 1925–1975.* New York and London: Garland, 1978.

Pei, Lowry. "Anthony Trollope's Palliser Novels: The Conquest of Separateness." Ph.D. dissertation, Stanford University, 1975.

Polhemus, Robert M. *The Changing World of Anthony Trollope.* Berkeley and Los Angeles: University of California Press, 1968.

Pollard, Arthur. *Anthony Trollope.* London: Routledge & Kegan Paul, 1978.

Pope-Hennessy, James. *Anthony Trollope.* Boston: Little, Brown, 1971.

Ray, Gordon N. "Trollope at Full Length." *Huntington Library Quarterly* 31 (1967–68): 313–40.

Sadleir, Michael. *Trollope: A Commentary.* 3d ed. London: Oxford University Press, 1961.

Shaw, W. David. "Moral Drama in *Barchester Towers.*" *Nineteenth-Century Fiction* 19 (1964–65): 45–54.

Skilton, David. *Anthony Trollope and His Contemporaries.* London: Longman Group, 1972.

Smalley, Donald, ed. *Anthony Trollope: The Critical Heritage.* London: Routledge & Kegan Paul; New York: Barnes & Noble, 1969.

Snow, C. P. *Trollope: His Life and Art.* New York: Scribner's, 1975.

Stebbins, Lucy, and Stebbins, Richard Poate *The Trollopes: The Chronicle of a Writing Family.* New York: Columbia University Press, 1945.

Terry, R. C. *Anthony Trollope: The Artist in Hiding.* Totowa, N.J.: Rowman & Littlefield, 1977.

Tracy, Robert. *Trollope's Later Novels.* Berkeley and Los

Angeles: University of California Press, 1978.

Trollope, Anthony. *An Autobiography.* World's Classic edition. London: Oxford University Press, 1953.

——. *Barchester Towers.* World's Classics edition. London: Oxford University Press, 1925.

——. *The Letters of Anthony Trollope.* Edited by Bradford A. Booth. London: Oxford University Press, 1951.

Walpole, Hugh. *Anthony Trollope.* New York: Macmillan, 1928.

7. GEORGE MEREDITH AND *THE EGOIST*

Able, A. H. *George Meredith and Thomas Love Peacock: A Study in Literary Influence.* Philadelphia: University of Pennsylvania, 1933.

Adams, Robert M., ed. *"The Egoist": An Annotated Text, Backgrounds, Criticism.* Includes notes, Meredith's "An Essay on Comedy and the Uses of the Comic Spirit," and critical discussions by Robert D. Mayo, Richard B. Hudson, Jenni Calder, Gillian Beer, John Goode, Charles J. Hill, Michael Sundell, Virginia Woolf, John Lucas, and Robert M. Adams. New York: W. W. Norton, 1979.

Beach, Joseph Warren. *The Comic Spirit in George Meredith.* New York: Longmans, Green, 1911.

Beer, Gillian. *Meredith: A Change of Masks.* London: Athlone Press, 1970.

Comstock, Margaret. "George Meredith, Virginia Woolf, and Their Feminist Comedy." Ph.D. dissertation, Stanford University, 1975.

Fanger, Donald S. "Joyce and Meredith: A Question of Influence and Tradition." *Modern Fiction Studies* 6 (Summer, 1960): 125–30.

Fletcher, Ian, ed. *Meredith Now: Some Critical Essays.* London: Routledge & Kegan Paul, 1971.

Goode, John. *"The Egoist:* Anatomy or Striptease?" In *Meredith Now: Some Critical Essays,* edited by Ian Fletcher, pp. 205–30. London: Routledge & Kegan Paul, 1971.

Halperin, John. *Egoism and Self-Discovery in the Victorian Novel: Studies in the Ordeal of Knowledge in the Nineteenth Century.* New York: Burt Franklin, 1974.

Hill, Charles J. "Theme and Image in *The Egoist." University of Kansas Review* 20 (Summer, 1954): 281–85.

Hudson, Richard B. "The Meaning of Egoism in George Meredith's *The Egoist.*" *The Trollopian* [*Nineteenth-Century Fiction*] 3 (1948–49): 163–76.

Kelvin, Norman. *A Troubled Eden.* Stanford, Calif.: Stanford University Press, 1961.

Lindsay, Jack. *George Meredith: His Life and Work.* London: Bodley Head, 1956.

Meredith, George. *The Letters of George Meredith.* Edited by C. L. Cline. 3 vols. Oxford: Clarendon Press, 1970.

——. *The Works of George Meredith.* Standard Edition. 18 vols. London: Constable, 1910–20.

Millett, Kate. *Sexual Politics.* New York: Avon, 1971.

Olmsted, John Charles. *George Meredith: An Annotated Bibliography of Criticism.* New York and London: Garland, 1978.

Priestley, J. B. *George Meredith.* London: Macmillan, 1926.

Pritchett, V. S. *George Meredith and English Comedy.* New York: Random House, 1969.

Stevenson, Lionel. *The Ordeal of George Meredith.* London: Peter Owen, 1954.

Stevenson, Richard C. "Laetitia Dale and the Comic Spirit in *The Egoist.*" *Nineteenth-Century Fiction* 26 (1972): 406–18.

Stone, Donald David. *Novelists in a Changing World: Meredith, James, and the Transformation of English Fiction in the 1880's.* Cambridge, Mass.: Harvard University Press, 1972.

Van Ghent, Dorothy. "On *The Egoist.*" In *The English Novel: Form and Function,* pp. 183–94. New York: Holt, Rinehart & Winston, 1953.

Vicinus, Martha. *Suffer and Be Still: Women in the Victorian Age.* Bloomington: Indiana University Press, 1972.

Williams, Ioan, ed. *George Meredith: The Critical Heritage.* London: Routledge & Kegan Paul; New York: Barnes & Noble, 1971.

Wilt, Judith. *The Readable People of George Meredith.* Princeton, N.J.: Princeton University Press, 1975.

Wright, Walter F. *Art and Substance in George Meredith.* Lincoln, Neb.: University of Nebraska Press, 1953.

8. LEWIS CARROLL AND *THROUGH THE LOOKING-GLASS*

Alexander, Peter. "Logic and the Humor of Lewis Carroll." *Proceedings of the Leeds Philosophical and Literary Society* 6

(1951): 551–66.

Atherton, James S. "Lewis Carroll and *Finnegans Wake.*" *English Studies* 33 (1952): 1–15.

Auden, W. H. "Today's 'Wonder-World' Needs Alice." In *Aspects of Alice,* edited by Robert Phillips, pp. 3–12. New York: Vanguard, 1971.

Avery, Gillian. *Nineteenth-Century Children: Heroes and Heroines in English Children's Stories, 1780–1900.* London: Hodder & Stoughton, 1971.

Ayres, Harry Morgan. *Carroll's Alice.* New York: Columbia University Press, 1936.

Bettelheim, Bruno. *The Uses of Enchantment: The Meaning of Fairy Tales.* New York: Alfred A. Knopf, 1976.

Blake, Kathleen. *Play, Games, and Sport: The Literary Works of Lewis Carroll.* Ithaca, N.Y.: Cornell University Press, 1974.

Bloomingdale, Judith. "Alice as *Anima:* The Image of a Woman in Carroll's Classic." In *Aspects of Alice,* edited by Robert Phillips, pp. 378–90. New York: Vanguard, 1971.

Bowman, Isa. *Lewis Carroll As I Knew Him.* Edited by Morton N. Cohen. New York: Dover, 1972. Originally published in 1899 as *The Story of Lewis Carroll.*

Burke, Kenneth. "The Thinking of the Body." In *Language as Symbolic Action,* pp. 308–44. Berkeley and Los Angeles: University of California Press, 1966.

Carroll, Lewis. *See* Dodgson, Charles Lutwidge.

Cohen, Morton N. *Lewis Carroll's Photographs of Children: Four Nude Studies.* New York: Clarkson N. Potter, 1979.

Collingwood, Stuart Dodgson. *The Life and Letters of Lewis Carroll.* London, Unwin, 1898.

Coveney, Peter. *The Image of Childhood,* pp. 242–49. Baltimore: Penguin, 1967.

de la Mare, Walter. *Lewis Carroll.* London: Faber & Faber, 1932.

Dinnage, Rosemary. "Dodgson's Passion." *New York Review of Books* 26 (August 16, 1979): 10–14.

Dodgson, Charles Lutwidge. *The Diaries of Lewis Carroll.* Edited by Roger Lancelyn Green. 2 vols. London: Cassell, 1953.

——. *The Complete Works of Lewis Carroll.* Modern Library edition. New York: Random House, 1936.

——. *The Letters of Lewis Carroll.* Vol. 1, *1837–1885;* vol. 2, *1886–1898.* Edited by Morton N. Cohen, with the assistance of Roger Lancelyn Green. New York: Oxford University Press, 1979.

Empson, William. "Alice in Wonderland: The Child as Swain." In *Some Versions of the Pastoral,* pp. 241–82. New York: New Directions, 1960.

Gardner, Martin, ed. *The Annotated Alice: "Adventures in Wonderland" and "Through the Looking-Glass."* New York: Clarkson N. Potter, 1960.

Gattegno, Jean. *Lewis Carroll.* Paris: Librairie Jose Corti, 1970.

Gernsheim, Helmut. *Lewis Carroll, Photographer.* New York: Chanticleer Press, 1949.

Gordon, Jan B. "The Alice Books and the Metaphors of Victorian Childhood." In *Aspects of Alice,* edited by Robert Phillips, pp. 93–113. New York: Vanguard, 1971.

Gray, Donald J., ed. *Alice in Wonderland: Authoritative Texts of "Alice's Adventures in Wonderland," "Through the Looking-Glass," "The Hunting of the Snark": Backgrounds, Essays in Criticism.* Norton Critical Edition. New York: W. W. Norton, 1971.

Green, Roger Lancelyn. *Lewis Carroll.* London: Bodley Head, 1960.

Greenacre, Phyllis. *Swift and Carroll: A Psychoanalytic Study of Two Lives.* New York: International Universities Press, 1955.

Guiliano, Edward, ed. *Lewis Carroll Observed: A Collection of Unpublished Photographs, Drawings, Poetry, and New Essays.* New York: Clarkson N. Potter, 1976.

Hinz, John. "Alice Meets the Don." In *Aspects of Alice,* edited by Robert Phillips, pp. 143–55. New York: Vanguard, 1971.

Holmes, Roger W. "The Philosopher's *Alice in Wonderland.*" *Antioch Review* 19 (1959): 133–49.

Holquist, Michael. "What Is a Boojum? Nonsense and Modernism." *Yale French Studies* 43 (1969): 145–64.

Hudson, Derek. *Lewis Carroll.* London: Constable, 1954.

Huxley, Francis. *The Raven and the Writing Desk.* New York: Harper & Row, 1976.

Kelly, Richard. *Lewis Carroll.* Boston: Twayne, 1977.

Kenner, Hugh. "Alice in Chapelizod." In *Dublin's Joyce,* pp. 276–300. Boston: Beacon Press, 1956.

Lennon, Florence Becker. *The Life of Lewis Carroll.* New York: Collier, 1962.

Levin, Harry. "*Wonderland* Revisited." In *Aspects of Alice,* edited by Robert Phillips, pp. 175–97. New York: Vanguard, 1971.

Mann, Nancy Dawson. "George MacDonald and the Tradition of Victorian Fantasy." Ph.D. dissertation, Stanford University, 1973.

Parisot, Henri, ed. *Lewis Carroll.* An important collection of French criticism and discussion on Carroll, including, among others, pieces by Hélène Cixous, Ernest Coumet, Luc Etienne, Jean Gattegno, Jean Paul Martin, Jean-Jacques Mayoux, and Raymond Queneau. Paris: Editions de l'Herne, 1971.

Phillips, Robert, ed. *Aspects of Alice: Lewis Carroll's Dreamchild as Seen through the Critics' Looking-Glass.* New York: Vanguard, 1971.

Pitcher, George. "Wittgenstein, Nonsense, and Lewis Carroll." *Massachusetts Review* 6 (Spring–Summer, 1965): 591–611.

Prickett, Stephen. *Victorian Fantasy.* Bloomington: Indiana University Press, 1979.

Rackin, Donald. "Alice's Journey to the End of Night." *PMLA* 81 (1966): 313–26.

——, ed. "*Alice's Adventures in Wonderland*": *A Critical Handbook.* Belmont, Calif.: Wadsworth, 1969.

Sewell, Elizabeth. *The Field of Nonsense.* London: Chatto & Windus, 1952.

Spacks, Patricia Meyer. "Logic and Language in *Through the Looking-Glass.*" In *Aspects of Alice,* edited by Robert Phillips, pp. 267–75. New York: Vanguard, 1971.

Taylor, Alexander L. *The White Knight: A Study of C. L. Dodgson.* Edinburgh: Oliver & Boyd, 1952.

Wilson, Edmund. "C. L. Dodgson: The Poet Logician." In *Aspects of Alice,* edited by Robert Phillips, pp. 198–206. New York: Vanguard, 1971.

9. JAMES JOYCE AND *FINNEGANS WAKE*

A Wake Newslitter. Edited by Clive Hart and Fritz Senn. Periodical. 1962——.

Atherton, James. *The Books at the Wake.* London and New York: Viking Press, 1959.

Beckett, Samuel, et al. *Our Exagmination Round His Factification for Incamination of Work in Progress. James Joyce/Finnegans Wake: A Symposium.* New York: New Directions, 1962.

Begnal, Michael H., and Senn, Fritz, eds. *A Conceptual Guide to "Finnegans Wake."* University Park, Pa.: Pennsylvania State University Press, 1974.

——, and Eckley, Grace. *Narrator and Character in "Finnegans Wake."* Lewisburg, Pa.: Bucknell University Press,; Cranbury, N.J.: Associated Universities Press, Inc., 1975.

Benstock, Bernard. *Joyce-Again's Wake: An Analysis of "Finnegans Wake."* Seattle: University of Washington Press, 1965.

Bishop, John. "On Joyce." Ph.D. dissertation, Stanford University, 1980.

Bonheim, Helmut. *A Lexicon of the German in "Finnegans Wake."* Berkeley and Los Angeles: University of California Press, 1967.

Boyle, Robert. "Astroglodynamonologos." In *New Light on Joyce,* edited by Fritz Senn, pp. 131–40. Bloomington and London: Indiana University Press, 1972.

Budgen, Frank. *James Joyce and the Making of "Ulysses."* Bloomington: Indiana University Press, 1960.

Burgess, Anthony. *Joysprick: An Introduction to the Language of James Joyce.* New York: Harcourt Brace Jovanovich, 1973.

——. *Rejoyce.* New York: W. W. Norton, 1965.

Campbell, Joseph, and Robinson, Henry Morton. *A Skeleton Key to "Finnegans Wake."* New York: Viking Press, 1944.

Chace, William M., ed. *Joyce: A Collection of Critical Essays.* Englewood Cliffs, N.J.: Prentice-Hall, 1974.

Cheng, Vincent. "Shakespeare in *Finnegans Wake.*" Ph.D. dissertation, Stanford University, 1979.

Christiani, Dounia Bunis. *Scandinavian Elements of "Finnegans Wake."* Evanston, Ill.: Northwestern University Press, 1965.

Cixous, Hélène. *The Exile of James Joyce.* New York: David Lewis, 1972.

Dalton, Jack P., and Hart, Clive, eds. *Twelve and a Tilly.* Evanston, Ill.: Northwestern University Press, 1965.

Deming, Robert H., ed. *James Joyce: The Critical Heritage.* 2 vols. New York: Barnes & Noble, 1970.

Ellmann, Richard. *James Joyce.* New York: Oxford University Press, 1959.

Garvin, John. *James Joyce's Disunited Kingdom and the Irish Di-*

mension. New York: Barnes & Noble, 1977.

Givens, Seon, ed. *James Joyce: Two Decades of Criticism.* New York: Vanguard Press, 1963.

Glasheen, Adaline. *A Third Census of "Finnegans Wake": An Index of Characters and Their Roles.* Berkeley and Los Angeles: University of California Press, 1977.

Goldberg, S. L. *The Classical Temper: A Study of James Joyce's "Ulysses."* New York: Barnes & Noble, 1961.

——. *Joyce.* Edinburgh: Oliver & Boyd, 1962.

Hart, Clive. *A Concordance to "Finnegans Wake."* Minneapolis: University of Minnesota Press, 1963.

——. *Structure and Motif in "Finnegan's Wake."* Evanston, Ill.: Northwestern University Press, 1962.

Hayman, David. *A First-Draft Version of "Finnegans Wake."* Austin: University of Texas Press, 1962.

Hodgart, Matthew J. C., and Worthington, Mabel P. *Song in the Works of James Joyce.* New York: Columbia University Press, 1959.

Joyce, James. *Dubliners.* New York: Viking Press, 1961.

——. *Finnegans Wake.* New York: Viking Press, 1958.

——. *The Letters of James Joyce.* Edited by Stuart Gilbert and Richard Ellmann. 3 vols. New York: Viking Press, 1957, 1966.

——. *A Portrait of the Artist as a Young Man.* New York: Viking Press, 1964.

——. *Selected Letters.* Edited by Richard Ellmann. New York: Viking Press, 1957.

——. *Stephen Hero.* New York: New Directions, 1963.

——. *Ulysses.* New York: Random House, 1961.

Joyce, Stanislaus. *The Complete Dublin Diary of Stanislaus Joyce.* Edited by George H. Healey. Ithaca, N.Y.: Cornell University Press, 1971.

——. *My Brother's Keeper: James Joyce's Early Years.* New York: Viking Press, 1958.

Kenner, Hugh. *Dublin's Joyce.* Boston: Beacon Press, 1956.

——. *Flaubert, Joyce, and Beckett: The Stoic Comedians.* Boston: Beacon Press, 1961.

——. *Joyce's Voices.* Berkeley and Los Angeles: University of California Press, 1978.

Levine, Jennifer S. "Originality and Repetition in *Finnegans Wake* amd *Ulysses.*" *PMLA* 94 (January, 1979): 106–20.

384

Litz, A. Walton. *The Art of James Joyce.* New York: Oxford University Press, 1968.

Mason, Ellsworth, and Ellmann, Richard, eds. *The Critical Writings of James Joyce.* New York: Viking Press, 1959.

Mercier, Vivian. *The Irish Comic Tradition.* Oxford: Clarendon Press, 1962.

Mink, Louis O. *A "Finnegans Wake" Gazetteer.* Bloomington: Indiana University Press, 1979.

Morse, J. Mitchell. *The Sympathetic Alien: James Joyce and Catholicism.* New York: New York University Press, 1959.

Murillo, L. A. *The Cyclical Night: Irony in James Joyce and Jorge Luis Borges.* Cambridge, Mass.: Harvard University Press, 1968.

Noon, William. *Joyce and Aquinas.* New Haven: Yale University Press, 1957.

Norris, Margot. *The Decentered Universe of "Finnegans Wake."* Baltimore: Johns Hopkins University Press, 1976.

O'Hehir, Brendan. *A Gaelic Lexicon for "Finnegans Wake."* Berkeley and Los Angeles: University of California Press, 1967.

——, and Dillon, John M. *A Classical Lexicon for "Finnegans Wake."* Berkeley and Los Angeles: University of California Press, 1977.

Ryan, John, ed. *A Bash in the Tunnel: James Joyce by the Irish.* Brighton, Eng.: Clifton Books, 1970.

Senn, Fritz, ed. *New Light on Joyce from the Dublin Symposium.* Bloomington: Indiana University Press, 1972.

Solomon, Margaret C. *Eternal Geomater: The Sexual Universe of "Finnegans Wake."* Carbondale, Ill.: Southern Illinois University Press, 1969.

Staley, Thomas F., ed. *James Joyce Today: Essays on the Major Works.* Bloomington: Indiana University Press, 1966.

Tindall, William York. *A Reader's Guide to "Finnegans Wake."* New York: Farrar, Straus & Giroux, 1969.

Vico, Giambattista. *The New Science of Giambattista Vico.* Edited by Thomas Goddard Bergin and Max Harold Fisch. Ithaca, N.Y.: Cornell University Press, 1948.

10. THE NOVEL; LITERARY THEORY; NINETEENTH-CENTURY BRITISH LITERARY AND HISTORICAL BACKGROUND: GENERAL HISTORICAL AND INTELLECTUAL BACKGROUND

Abrams, M. H. *Natural Supernaturalism: Tradition and Revolution in Romantic Literature.* New York: W. W. Norton, 1971.

Allen, Walter. *The English Novel: A Short Critical History.* New York: E. P. Dutton, 1955.

Altick, Richard. *The English Common Reader, 1800–1900.* Chicago: University of Chicago Press, 1957.

——. *Victorian People and Ideas.* New York: W. W. Norton, 1973.

Ariès, Philippe. *Centuries of Childhood: A Social History of Family Life.* Translated by Robert Baldick. New York: Random House, Vintage Books, 1962.

Auerbach, Erich. *Mimesis: The Representation of Reality in Western Literature.* Translated by William Trask. Princeton: Princeton University Press, 1953.

Barthes, Roland. *Critical Essays.* Translated by Richard Howard. Evanston, Ill.: Northwestern University Press, 1972.

——. *On Racine.* Translated by Richard Howard. New York: Hill & Wang, 1964.

Bloom, Harold. *The Anxiety of Influence: A Theory of Poetry.* New York: Oxford University Press, 1973.

——. *Kabbalah and Criticism.* New York: Seabury Press, 1975.

Booth, Wayne. *The Rhetoric of Fiction.* Chicago: University of Chicago Press, 1961.

Briggs, Asa. *Victorian People: A Reassessment of Persons and Themes, 1851–1867.* Chicago: University of Chicago Press, 1972.

Brown, Norman O. *Life Against Death.* Middletown, Conn.: Wesleyan University Press, 1959.

——. *Love's Body.* New York: Random House, 1966.

Buckley, Jerome H. *Season of Youth: The Bildungsroman from Dickens to Golding.* Cambridge, Mass.: Harvard University Press, 1974.

——. *The Triumph of Time: A Study of the Victorian Concepts of Time, History, Progress, and Decadence.* Cambridge, Mass.: Harvard University Press, 1966.

——. *The Victorian Temper: A Study in Literary Culture.* London: Allen & Unwin, 1952.

Chadwick, Owen. *The Secularization of the European Mind in the Nineteenth Century.* Cambridge, Eng.: At the University Press, 1975.

——. *The Victorian Church.* Part 1. New York: Oxford University Press, 1966.

Chapman, Raymond. *The Victorian Debate: English Literature and Society, 1832–1900.* New York: Basic Books, 1972.

Collingwood, R. C. *Faith and Reason: Essays in the Philosophy of Religion.* Edited, with an introduction, by Lionel Rubinoff. Chicago: Quadrangle Books, 1968.

Crews, Frederick C. *Out of My System: Psychoanalysis, Ideology, and Critical Method.* New York: Oxford University Press, 1975.

Culler, Jonathan. *Structuralist Poetics: Structuralism, Linguistics, and the Study of Literature.* Ithaca, N.Y.: Cornell University Press, 1975.

Derrida, Jacques. *Of Grammatology.* Translated by G. C. Spivak. Baltimore: Johns Hopkins University Press, 1976.

Engels, Frederick. *The Condition of the Working Class in England.* Translated and edited by W. H. Chaloner and W. O. Henderson. New York: Macmillan, 1958.

Erikson, Erik H. *Childhood and Society.* New York: W. W. Norton, 1963.

——. *Young Man Luther: A Study in Psychoanalysis and History.* London: Faber & Faber, 1959.

Faber, Richard. *Proper Stations: Class in Victorian Fiction.* London: Faber & Faber, 1971.

Fleishman, Avrom. *The English Historical Novel: Walter Scott to Virginia Woolf.* Baltimore: Johns Hopkins University Press, 1971.

Ford, George H., ed. *Victorian Fiction: A Second Guide to Research.* New York: Modern Language Association, 1978.

Forster, E. M. *Aspects of the Novel.* New York: Harcourt, Brace, & World, 1954.

Foucault, Michel. *The Archaeology of Knowledge.* Translated by A. M. Sheridan Smith. New York: Pantheon, 1972.

——. *The Order of Things.* New York: Pantheon, 1970.

Freud, Sigmund. *The Complete Psychological Works of Sigmund*

Freud. Translated by James Strachey. Standard Edition. 24 vols. London: Hogarth Press, 1953–74.

Friedman, Alan. *The Turn of the Novel.* New York: Oxford University Press, 1966.

Frye, Northrop. *Anatomy of Criticism: Four Essays.* Princeton: Princeton University Press, 1957.

Fussell, Paul. *The Great War and Modern Memory.* New York: Oxford University Press, 1977.

Girard, René. *Deceit, Desire, and the Novel: Self and Other in Literary Structure.* Translated by Yvonne Freccero. Baltimore: Johns Hopkins University Press, 1965.

Goldknopf, David. *The Life of the Novel.* Chicago: University of Chicago Press, 1972.

Gombrich, E. H. *Art and Illusion.* Princeton: Princeton University Press, 1961.

Graff, Gerald. *Literature against Itself: Literary Ideas in Modern Society.* Chicago: University of Chicago Press, 1979.

Griest, Guinevere L. *Mudie's Circulating Library and the Victorian Novel.* Bloomington: Indiana University Press, 1970.

Halperin, John, ed. *The Theory of the Novel: New Essays.* New York: Oxford University Press, 1974.

Hardy, Barbara. *Tellers and Listeners: The Narrative Imagination.* London: Athlone Press, 1975.

Harvey, W. J. *Character and the Novel.* Ithaca, N.Y.: Cornell University Press, 1965.

Heidegger, Martin. *Being and Time.* Translated by John MacQuarrie and Edward Robinson. New York: Harper & Row, 1962.

Himmelfarb, Gertrude. *Victorian Minds.* New York: Harper & Row, 1970.

Holland, Norman. *The Dynamics of Literary Response.* New York: Oxford University Press, 1968.

Houghton, Walter E. *The Victorian Frame of Mind: 1830–1870.* New Haven: Yale University Press, 1957.

James, William. *The Varieties of Religious Experience.* New York: New American Library, 1948.

Jameson, Frederick. *The Prison-House of Language: A Critical Account of Structuralism and Russian Formalism.* Princeton: Princeton University Press, 1972.

Keating, P. J. *The Working Classes in Victorian Fiction.* New York: Barnes & Noble, 1971.

Kermode, Frank. *The Classic: Literary Images of Permanence and Change.* New York: Viking Press, 1975.

——. *The Genesis of Secrecy: On the Interpretation of Narrative.* Cambridge, Mass.: Harvard University Press, 1979.

——. *The Romantic Image.* London: Routledge & Kegan Paul, 1957.

——. *The Sense of an Ending.* New York: Oxford University Press, 1967.

Kettle, Arnold. *An Introduction to the English Novel.* 2 vols. New York: Harper & Row, 1960.

Knoepflmacher, U. C. *Religious Humanism and the Victorian Novel.* Princeton: Princeton University Press, 1965.

Lacan, Jacques. *The Language of the Self: The Function of Language in Psychoanalysis.* Translated by Anthony Wilden. Baltimore: Johns Hopkins University Press, 1968.

Leavis, F. R. *The Great Tradition.* London: Chatto & Windus, 1948.

Levine, George. *The Boundaries of Fiction.* Princeton: Princeton University Press, 1968.

Lévi-Strauss, Claude. *The Savage Mind.* Chicago: University of Chicago Press, 1966.

——. *Structural Anthropology.* Translated by Claire Jacobson and Brooke Grundfest Schoepf. Garden City, N.Y.: Doubleday, Anchor Books, 1967.

——. *Tristes Tropiques.* Translated by John Russell. New York: Atheneum, 1969.

Lodge, David. *The Novelist at the Crossroads and Other Essays on Fiction and Criticism.* Ithaca, N.Y.: Cornell University Press, 1971.

Lubbock, Percy. *The Craft of Fiction.* New York: Scribner's, 1921.

Lukács, G. *The Historical Novel.* Translated by Hannah Mitchell and Stanley Mitchell. London: Merlin Press, 1962.

Marcus, Steven. *The Other Victorians.* New York: Basic Books, 1964.

Marx, Karl. *Economic and Philosophic Manuscripts of 1844.* Edited by Dirk J. Struik. New York: International Publishers, 1964.

——, and Engels, Frederick. *Selected Works.* New York: International Publishers, 1968.

Meyerhoff, Hans. *Time in Literature.* Berkeley and Los

Angeles: University of California Press, 1960.

Miller, J. Hillis. *The Form of Victorian Fiction: Thackeray, Dickens, Trollope, George Eliot, Meredith, and Hardy.* Notre Dame, Ind.: University of Notre Dame Press.

Miyoshi, M. *The Divided Self.* New York: New York University Press, 1969.

Ortega y Gasset, José. *The Dehumanization of Art and Other Writings on Art and Culture.* Translated by W. R. Trask. Garden City, N.Y.: Doubleday, Anchor Books, 1956.

Page, Norman. *Speech in the English Novel.* London: Longmans, Green, 1973.

Poulet, George. *The Interior Distance.* Translated by Elliott Coleman. Ann Arbor: University of Michigan Press, 1964.

Praz, Mario. *The Hero in Eclipse in Victorian Fiction.* Translated from the Italian by Angus Davidson. New York: Oxford University Press, 1956.

Pritchett, V. S. *The Living Novel and Later Appreciations.* New York: Random House, 1964.

———. *The Myth Makers: Literary Essays.* New York: Random House, 1979.

Raleigh, John Henry. *Time, Place, and Idea: Essays in the Novel.* Carbondale, Ill.: Southern Illinois University Press, 1968.

Said, Edward. *Beginnings: Intention and Method.* New York: Basic Books, 1975.

———. *Orientalism.* New York: Pantheon, 1978.

Sartre, Jean-Paul. *Search for a Method.* Translated by Hazel E. Barnes. New York: Random House, Vintage Books, 1968.

Scholes, Robert. *Structuralism in Literature: An Introduction.* New Haven: Yale University Press, 1974.

———, and Kellogg, Robert. *The Nature of Narrative.* New York: Oxford University Press, 1966.

Stang, Richard. *The Theory of the Novel in England, 1850–1870.* New York: Columbia University Press, 1959.

Steiner, George. *Language and Silence: Essays on Language, Literature, and the Inhuman.* New York: Atheneum, 1967.

———. *On Difficulty and Other Essays.* New York: Oxford University Press, 1978.

———. *Tolstoy or Dostoevsky: An Essay in the Old Criticism.* New York: Knopf, 1959.

Stevick, Philip, ed. *The Theory of the Novel.* New York: Free Press, 1967.

Stone, Donald David. *Novelists in a Changing World: Meredith, James, and the Transformation of English Fiction in the 1880's.* Cambridge, Mass.: Harvard University Press, 1972.

Sussman, Herbert. *Victorians and the Machine: The Literary Response to Technology.* Cambridge, Mass.: Harvard University Press, 1968.

Swinden, Patrick. *Unofficial Selves: Character in the Novel from Dickens to the Present Day.* London: Macmillan, 1973.

Thomson, David. *England in the Nineteenth Century.* London: Penguin, 1953.

Tillotson, Kathleen. *Novels of the Eighteen-Forties.* Oxford: Clarendon Press, 1954.

Van Ghent, Dorothy. *The English Novel: Form and Function.* New York: Holt, Rinehart & Winston, 1953.

Watt, Ian. *The Rise of the Novel.* Berkeley and Los Angeles: University of California Press, 1957.

———. *The Victorian Novel: Modern Essays in Criticism.* New York: Oxford University Press, 1971.

Williams, Raymond. *The Country and the City.* New York: Oxford University Press, 1973.

———. *Culture and Society, 1780–1950.* New York: Harper & Row, 1966.

———. *The English Novel from Dickens to Lawrence.* New York: Oxford University Press, 1970.

———. *Marxism and Literature.* New York: Oxford University Press, 1977.

Wilson, Edmund. *Axel's Castle: A Study of Imaginative Literature, 1870–1930.* New York: Scribner's, 1969.

Winters, Yvor. *In Defense of Reason.* Chicago: Swallow Press, 1947.

———. *The Function of Criticism: Problems and Exercises.* Denver: Alan Swallow, 1957.

Wittgenstein, Ludwig. *Philosophical Investigations.* Translated by G. E. Anscombe. Oxford: Basil Blackwell & Mott, 1958.

Woolf, Virginia. *The Common Reader.* First and Second Series. New York: Harcourt Brace, 1948.

Young, G. M. *Victorian England: Portrait of an Age.* Garden City, N.Y.: Doubleday, 1954.

INDEX

393